D0793582

The Letters of Vita Sackville-West to Virginia Woolf

The Letters of Vita Sackville-West to Virginia Woolf

Edited by Louise DeSalvo
and Mitchell A. Leaska

With an Introduction
by Mitchell A. Leaska

William Morrow and Company, Inc. • New York

Grateful acknowledgment is given for permission to reprint the following:

Excerpts from *The Letters of Virginia Woolf,* Volumes 3, 4, 5, 6, edited by Nigel Nicolson and Joanne Trautmann, are reprinted by permission of Harcourt Brace Jovanovich, Inc.; copyright © 1977, 1978, 1979, 1980 by Quentin Bell and Angelica Garnett.

Library of Congress Catalog Card Number: 84-60758

ISBN: 0-688-03963-4

Printed in the United States of America

First Edition

1 2 3 4 5 6 7 8 9 10

BOOK DESIGN BY LINEY LI

CONTENTS

EDITORIAL NOTE

All the letters of Vita Sackville-West to Virginia Woolf, with the exception of eighteen, are preserved in the Henry W. and Albert A. Berg Collection in the New York Public Library. The remaining letters are at the University of Sussex Library in England. At the foot of each letter, either *Berg* or *Sussex* has been inscribed to indicate the present location of the original. With one or two exceptions, they are all handwritten and, for the most part, legible. Vita was an accurate speller and she followed the rules of traditional grammar, syntax, punctuation, and paragraphing.

Establishing the chronological order of the letters, however, was quite another matter. Vita did not especially bother herself with dates. Often only the day of the week is given. Sometimes she added the numerical date, and sometimes the month as well. But rarely did she enter the day, the number, the month, *and* the year. In almost every instance, however, after a good deal of searching, we were able to deduce the letter's exact placement in the sequence either from its internal evidence or from the date given in Virginia's corresponding letter—or both. All other dating information, added editorially, has been set within square brackets.

Most of Vita's letters were written on printed stationery headed "Long Barn, Weald, Sevenoaks" or, after 1932, "Sissinghurst Castle, Kent." These addresses have been reproduced exactly as they appear in the original letters. When she wrote on blank sheets, she occasionally wrote only part of the address: "Long Barn," for example. In these cases all information added for fuller place identification has also been set within brackets.

Annotations have been provided to identify minor characters and to clarify otherwise obscure allusions. And brief summary narratives have been entered at intervals to provide a context for the people and events about to follow, as well as to supply the reader with a little background material to which the letters themselves make no direct reference.

All of Virginia Woolf's letters were published in six volumes both in the United States and in England between 1975 and 1980. As the editing of Vita's letters to Virginia proceeded, it became clear that their friendship was an extremely complex affair, and Vita's letters contained numerous and often mysterious allusions and barely detectable innuendos that could not be accounted for satisfactorily in a footnote alone. It became clear, too, that Virginia herself must be given a fair hearing—however minimal the space allotted—if we were to convey authentically something of the changing emotional tone of their relations during their nineteen years together. To these ends, we have included some 175 extracts from the nearly 400 surviving letters Virginia wrote to Vita. As with Vita's letters, here too, at the foot of each extract, we have printed in italics the present location of the letter from which the extract was taken.

There are several references in these letters which are explained in one or another of Virginia's letters, all of which, fortunately, have been chronologically numbered by their editors. So that when the reader comes across, let's say, "See *VW 1733*" in one of our annotations, we mean simply that the reader should turn to *The Letters of Virginia Woolf*, and specifically to the letter numbered 1733.

One other small matter needs a word of explanation. There were several periods of two or three months' duration when Vita went to Teheran or to Berlin to stay with her husband. During these times, the sequence of dates in Vita's and Virginia's letters may appear to be out of order. They are really not out of order at all. Because of the irregularity of international mail delivery, it was necessary to sequence the letters not by the dates on which they were written but rather by the dates on which either Vita or Virginia received a letter and subsequently replied to it.

A number of volumes, already published, have been extremely helpful in the editing of this collection of letters. To the authors and editors responsible for those volumes we acknowledge a debt of gratitude. They are, specifically: Nigel Nicolson and Joanne Trautmann, editors of *The Letters of Virginia Woolf* (6 vols.); Vita's biographer Victoria Glendinning for her *Vita: The Life of V. Sackville-West*; Anne Olivier Bell, editor of *The Diaries of Virginia Woolf* (5 vols.); Quentin Bell for *Virginia Woolf: A Biography*; Nigel Nicolson for *Portrait of a Marriage;* and James Lees-Milne for *Harold Nicolson: A Biography* (2 vols.).

For permission to quote from *The Letters of Virginia Woolf* and *The Diaries of Virginia Woolf*, we thank Harcourt Brace Jovanovich in America, and in England the Hogarth Press. We express our gratitude to Lola L.

Szladits, curator of the Berg Collection, the New York Public Library, and A. N. Peasgood of the University of Sussex Library. Dr. Szladits and her staff offered generous assistance in making the originals of Vita's letters available to us for transcription. Mr. Peasgood kindly located, photocopied, and sent us from England Vita's eighteen letters presently housed in the Sussex Collection.

To Maria Guarnaschelli, our editor at William Morrow in New York, we tender thanks for her good faith, wise counsel, and unfailing confidence in the publication of these letters; and to Betsy B. Cenedella, also from William Morrow, under whose watchful eye this volume gained appreciably in editorial consistency.

Our final and deepest thanks are offered to Nigel Nicolson, Vita Sackville-West's son and literary executor. The editing of this collection was at his invitation, and throughout its course he answered questions and provided us with information he alone possessed. His generosity and judgment have been extraordinary. And we are grateful for being the privileged beneficiaries of his trust.

—L.D. and M.A.L.

INTRODUCTION

BY MITCHELL A. LEASKA

The letters in this volume chronicle the story of two extraordinary women: Vita Sackville-West, who quested for glory, and Virginia Woolf, who sought her love and affection. Rarely can a collection of correspondence have cast into more dramatic relief two personalities more individual or more complex; and rarely can an enterprise of the heart have been carried out so near the verge of archetypal feeling. Their adventure was filled with love and with expectation, and many of these pages effervesce with excitement and hope and verbal caress. In their fertility and abundance, these documents belong as much to literature as they do to life. In letter after letter we come across little dramas of daily affairs; cameos of friends caught in folly; snatches of gossip, sometimes serious, more often profane; multicolor snapshots of exotic travelogue; and little shared confidences of literary craft. Sometimes there are muffled warnings of wounded affection or injured pride, and as often the small benedictions of loving appeasement. But below the surface tremor of words, we sense occasionally the strange alchemy of love mixed with uncertainty and of compulsion mingled with constraint. Such are the hieroglyphs of emotion imprinted across these pages.

The chronicle covers almost two decades. These were years filled for each of them with as many large public successes as there were personal failures and private sorrows. But in their art as in their lives, however great the differences that separated them, they were, alike, women of formidable resilience and determination. In their writing, Virginia, the innovator, tunneled her way into the future, and Vita, the traditionalist, sorted out the past. And during these years of alternating confidence and doubt, in their private lives Virginia learned all the adverbs of manner and motive, and Vita mastered all the verbs of love and passion.

In the early months Virginia saw Vita as supple, savage, and patrician. To Vita, Virginia was the "gentle genius"—lovely, idolized, and remote. Even through the calculated medium of letters, where verbal risks are minimized, it is evident that in the first days of their friendship Vita's attention settled on Virginia with obstinate concentration and Virginia responded with a blend of apprehensive mockery and guarded acquiescence. Each clearly had something the other wanted. Vita was the superior woman in Virginia's eyes, and Virginia was the superior writer in Vita's. It would soon become apparent to both of them that just as one quested for glory, the other was in search of affection. In those dual pursuits, large loyalties and high proprietorial claims would soon emerge, and with them four distinct personalities as well. Vita would become for Virginia the voluptuous aristocrat some of the time, and some of the time she would be the protective maternal figure, crooning affectionate reassurance. Virginia would represent to Vita the mistress of English letters at one moment, and at the next, the helpless, affectionate child soliciting Vita's custodial embraces. The rapport between them was by no means simple, and both women would eventually be reminded, more often perhaps than they liked, that every human being needs something and that neither of them would ever love the other for herself alone. So that just as there was passion and promise in the beginning, in the end there would be compassion and compromise.

Virginia, the writer, was a woman of swift perception and incisive analytical power—an intellectual who weighed and probed and tested for the exact motives of human action and utterance. She was by all standards a brilliant "experimentalist in humanity"; but she appeared unattainable, unpredictable, sometimes even unapproachable. With so much of her emotional side kept under cover, she was reserved and at the same time mysterious. More than that, Virginia was a woman at once curious and independent—her curiosity frequently misconstrued as affection and her independence often interpreted as absentminded detachment—so that she sometimes gave the impression of being a part of everyone yet belonging to no one. To the small Dionysian figure hidden in Vita, this Apollonian frieze of intellect and intuition was an irresistible challenge.

There was another part of Virginia, however, that Vita found easier to warm up to, and that was the childlike, affectionate side of her. The self-absorbed, impatient, and demonstrative girl who forever needed practical reassurance and confidence-bolstering. The vulnerable creature who was prone to emotional bruising, who hated criticism, demanded directness, craved affection—the brave "Potto" who over and over got knocked down but refused to admit defeat. This was the Virginia that Vita loved and protected and mothered.

Vita, on her side, was a catalogue of contradiction. She was rebellious and she was reticent. She was fearless and she was frightened; she was sociable and reclusive; bold as well as shy. She was a woman who concealed an essentially timid nature under a carapace of managerial competence and extravagant courage. Then she was a woman who saw only what she wanted to see, who was lavish with those whose love and obedience she was sure of, but who neglected those whose wishes failed to coincide with her own; and she was someone who had taught herself from a very early age to spot the weaknesses of others.

What Virginia saw in Vita, however, was a sensuous person who could be just noticeably elusive and often puzzling. This was "the real woman," as Virginia often said, and a passionate one she was too. But, as with all highly contradictory personalities, there was something slightly deceptive about her. Not far from the surface, one could touch the stargazer, the lonely Vita who sought privacy and shunned messy emotional embroilments. Yet it was this same woman who lived often enough on false promise and counterfeit hope, who seemed forever fanning the embers of love and was forever stepping back from its blaze.

There were other sides to Vita that Virginia seems to have detected almost from the beginning. One of them was the indomitable woman who took charge of one's life and charted one's destiny, whose arrogance flattened obstacles and whose vanity refused to acknowledge shabbiness, poverty, or familiarity. This was the exalted woman who strode her own private acres and lived in castles and who spoke her mind with devastating simplicity. Then there was the compassionate woman who understood life's miseries and dispensed her bounty on the world's downtrodden—the gentle Vita whose strong hands cupped the fragile moth and nursed the injured nightingale. And there was also the heroic Vita who worked like a slave and played like a prince and saw the whole world as her personal challenge. All of these Vitas, wrapped into one, held Virginia magnetized in a bright circle of high romance and adventure.

Vita's emotional terrain, however, contained a dark sadistic province that few people saw and still fewer acknowledged. Virginia seems to have felt it from the very start, and there is enough in these letters to suggest that in recognizing it she assumed a role sufficiently submissive to indicate to the woman she would soon love that she was prepared to accept—indeed she would encourage—their relations to develop along the lines of dominance and compliance. In Virginia's mind this stratum of friendship was perhaps the closest she felt she would ever get to playing the part of the submissive child to the dominant, affectionate, and protective mother.

Little phrases scattered throughout the letters and cushioned in often deceptive contexts support the notion that Virginia placed a sufficiently low value on herself in relation to Vita to permit her to feel both helpless and needy and at the same time to feel a certain strange contentment with whatever small abuses Vita might inadvertently cause her to suffer. Virginia was too sensitive an observer of human behavior not to recognize the role she was creating for herself. "Is it true you love giving pain?" she asked Vita once in mock seriousness. In one of the earliest pieces of the correspondence, Virginia wrote: "I enjoyed your intimate letter. . . . It gave me a great deal of pain—which is I've no doubt the first stage of intimacy. . . . Never mind: I enjoyed your abuse very much." Later she would beg Vita not to "snuff the stinking tallow out of your heart—poor Virginia to wit. . . ." Later still: "Chuck me as often as you like, and dont give it a moments thought." One year before her death Virginia would still write: ". . . you'll never shake me off—"

Running parallel to this line of submission or self-depreciation or whatever we choose to call it were two accompanying strands of Virginia's feeling for Vita. One was her "childlike dazzled affection" and the other was the extraordinary serenity and comfort Vita's presence brought her during her frequent periods of illness. It is true that these scattered citations are mere scraps of evidence, little more than fragments broken off at odd, unpremeditated moments. Yet for all their scrappiness and seeming irrelevance, these odds and ends of feeling do indicate the thrust of Virginia's emotional alignment to Vita. For they illuminate the otherwise unexplained roles of dominance and compliance that both women acted out in their lives in the guise of parent and child, healer and patient, and, metaphorically, perhaps even victor and victim. Virginia could only have been more explicit if she had said to Vita: Your maternal protection strengthens the lost and wandering child in me; your healing hand soothes me in illness; and your abuses assure me that I matter to you. There is no question that she sensed in Vita the fearless competence and mastery she needed to demonstrate, together with the aggression she tried to conceal. So that by the time she came to write the first sentence of *Orlando*, there wasn't the slightest doubt in Virginia's mind that Orlando should make his entrance committing an act of violence—"slicing at the head of a Moor."

Vita's perception of herself is more difficult to ascertain, for contradictory as she was, self-deception came easily to her and she saw only what she wanted to see. But she did say something in a letter to Virginia that seems to sum up the way she approached life. She would rather "fail gloriously than dingily succeed," she wrote. Those five words appear to hold the key to much of Vita's inner domain of feeling, for they define the nature of her quest for glory—a quest rooted in the assumption that the world is a potential battlefield, that people are safe only when they are in captivity, that one's resources should be mobilized not in the interest of survival but in the continuing struggle to triumph. No risk was too perilous, no sacrifice too great for that necessary achievement. Even her intimacy with Virginia she saw as a "catch," as a conquest: Vita was "rather proud, really, of having caught such a big silver fish," she said to her husband, Harold Nicolson. Nor is it an accident of phrasing that she called the novel describing her turbulent love affair with Violet Trefusis *Challenge.* Everyone in her life, it seems, began as a potential challenge, and everything she came up against was, to her mind, susceptible to conquest. Virginia summed her up accurately when she said that Orlando "liked to think that she was riding the back of the world."

"Is it better to be extremely ambitious, or rather modest?" Vita asked, regarding the novel she was about to write. "Probably the latter is safer; but I hate safety. . . . Anyhow I don't care about what is 'better,' for however many resolutions one makes, one's pen . . . always finds its own level." To this Virginia replied: "Why need you be so timid and prideblown, both at once . . . ? Please write your novel, and then you will enter into the unreal world, where Virginia lives—and poor woman, can't now live anywhere else."

Virginia knew perfectly well what Vita's question meant, but she knew, too, that living in the "unreal world" of fantasy was also living with a sense of freedom and power—something she had discovered on her own during the pains and uncertainties of adolescence. For Virginia's artistic roots stretched back to the unsettled world of a childhood dominated by an often absent mother. If one could move back in time to January 25, 1882, the day of Virginia's birth, one would catch a glimpse of Julia Stephen, the beautiful and mysterious mother whose chief concern in life, for some equally mysterious reason, was nursing the sick and the dying; a woman who was convinced that the "ordinary relations between the sick and the well are far easier and pleasanter than between the well and the well." This was the woman Virginia would one day capture in the person of Mrs. Ramsay in *To the Lighthouse*—the mother whose mysteries haunted the novelist for so much of her life.

Whatever her motives, Julia Stephen's unceasing benevolence killed her at the age of forty-nine, leaving Virginia, aged thirteen, motherless, numb with terror, and about to descend into her first black period of insanity. When she recovered two years later—that is, in 1897—she learned that private feeling and public fact were fearfully discrepant, and until she could correct that discrepancy her world was in danger and herself at everyone's mercy. With a mother who had been away so much of the time, Virginia's childhood had lacked plan, continuity, and coherence. With her mother now dead, there was no telling what might happen. But it didn't take long for this precocious girl to discover that although feeling and fact were out of synchrony, feeling and fantasy were not; and with that discovery the world of the future novelist opened up to her. If she could teach herself to fuse feeling *with* fantasy, she could create her own world: a spacious republic populated only by those she chose to put there, a place where fact could not disturb, an invented realm entirely under her control, where sorrow and doubt had no place. But however sovereign and almighty the storyteller might be, there still remained the stark fact of having no mother. Until that emptiness could be filled (which was impossible) or some reasonably satisfying substitute presented itself (which was highly improbable), the safest place to live was in the "unreal world" of imagination. So that Virginia knew the power of fantasy perhaps better than did Vita. Her way of dealing with it, however, would always be different from Vita's.

Thus, when the women met for the first time on December 14, 1922, two highly organized personalities faced each other. They had a great deal in common, but an even greater deal differentiated them. What mattered, however, and would continue to matter in the years ahead was that each was in possession of something the other felt she had been denied. Vita envied Virginia the writer, and Virginia stood in awe of Vita the woman. In the woman Virginia would find a strong mother, and in the writer Vita would discover a dependent child. It was an auspicious beginning.

Vita's earliest history also tells us much about the woman who speaks in the pages ahead, and although countless little details complicate her portrait, it is safe to say that when Vita was born at Knole in the small hours of March 9, 1892, she already had two strikes against her. The first was having been born female. According to the family entail, as a woman she would never inherit Knole, the great ancestral house granted to Thomas Sackville by Queen Elizabeth in 1566. The second was being the daughter of Victoria Sackville-West. Victoria, later Lady Sackville, was an essentially destructive woman. She was rapacious; she was ruthless; she was self-centered; she was beautiful. She was also overwhelmed with self-doubt. Without much thought to the consequences, she bribed her little daughter for endless validation by showering her with every kind of material reward if she would make her mother feel adored and indispensable. No matter how much the child tried, however, the effort was never enough. Vita was simply inadequate to the task. Lady Sackville moreover believed it her privilege, indeed her right, to indulge in great pendulum swings of mood and temper whenever it took her fancy, with Vita always the innocent and confused recipient of her mother's flamboyant emotionalism. Day after day, as a child, Vita was treated as though she were a plaything—smothered with love one moment, hated the next; called beautiful and cherished in the morning, condemned as ugly and unwanted in the afternoon. Throughout much of her adult life, and even after her marriage, Vita lived in the shade of this egotistical and power-hungry woman who "wounded and dazzled and fascinated" her. More important, Vita grew up with a sense of personal impotence. Never was she allowed to feel herself a separate person with rights of her own.

Before and even during her marriage Lady Sackville's beauty had attracted countless suitors—among them, John Murray Scott, Pierpont Morgan, William Waldorf Astor—all men of fabulous wealth and influence. It's not hard to see how Vita, when she was old enough to acknowledge her sex, became fearful that it might put her in deadly combat with her mother for male favor. And so she subconsciously did what must somehow have seemed to her the most logical thing to do: She suppressed her feminine side and, when it was safe enough to do so, granted ascendancy to masculine behavior, male pursuits, and boyish mannerisms. What better way was there of avoiding confrontation with her mother in the arena of male contestants? And what more effective way was there than this not only to imagine herself male, but to fantasize herself successor to Knole as well?

Somewhere in the confusion of these early years, Vita assimilated her mother's conviction that "the world was a hard place where one must fight one's own battle for one's own best advantage." In addition to the fighting spirit, Vita appears also to have learned some conjuring tricks from Lady Sackville, who "possessed more than anybody I have ever known the faculty of delusion. . . . She entered the only world she knew, the world of unreality which she made real to herself, and into which she persuaded other people by the sheer strength of her own personality and conviction to enter." As long as one was in her presence, one was almost "tempted to believe in all the fables she told one."

Thus raised in the shadow of a mother whose life was disordered, whose habits were erratic, and whose affections were unreliable, it was perfectly natural for Vita to realize at some early period of her life that if she genuinely needed stability, order, and permanence, she would have to invent them for herself. And this she did. How easy it is to imagine her as a child roaming the hundreds of rooms of Knole—rooms that had survived these hundreds of years—acknowledging their durability, imagining their history, inventing little fables of beauty, valor, and bloodshed. Those ancient paintings and tapestries—each of them must contain some magnificent tale hidden somewhere. Each of them must hoard some mystery of forsaken honor and defeated love. One sees her in the guarded secrecy of an impressionable youth, stepping timidly down the silent corridors of the past, searching the farthest corners of antiquity, where all had once been solid and unchanging.

Vita's retreat into the past was her defense against the present. Knole was the only place she knew, and it grew to symbolize for her all the permanence and security her present life was denied. Knole also carried with it all the ceremony of history and the poetry of romance, and in these Vita sought refuge. In history and in romance she could put aside her confusion and fear, and imagine herself to be anyone she chose.

This step backward into antiquity was only one short move from freedom. If Vita could shed her bondage to the present altogether, she might be free to invent a new persona to bear the weight of heroism and reflect the burnish of glory. There was one obstacle, however. She was a female. But there was nothing in the world to prevent her from stretching her fantasy to the extent of changing her sex. Of that she was certain. And so, step by step, with trial and caution, Vita moved toward the ground customarily trod by men; and as she did so, a substantial part of the female persona receded; made room for the new male figure she was constructing, a figure of power and courage and a certain lusty recklessness.

This might all have begun as a child's game, as a fantasy of adolescence to ward off the unhappiness of growing up under Lady Sackville's dictatorship. But for Vita the feeling of dominance was magnificent, and the male self she had created would become the personal myth that would govern the way she lived for the remainder of her life. As a male, moreover, there was nothing to discourage her from courting her mother with the same ceremonious rituals her other suitors observed. This was something she could never have done as Vita the daughter. And there was a certain high drama in Vita's adoration for her beautiful, wicked mother, something lusty and primitive. Lady Sackville might abuse or humiliate her in any way she chose, and still "I would have died for her," wrote Vita. "I would have murdered anyone that breathed a word against her. I would have suffered any injustice at her hands."

But as with all attempts to establish harmony, however artificial, out of the chaos of one's life, this attempt, too, would produce a conflict with unhappy results. Vita had learned from childhood that she needed autonomy as well as affection, privacy as well as intimacy, but she had also learned under her mother's disobliging hand just how unlovable she was. She must have realized, too, that being loved and being free somehow didn't go together. Independence required emotional distance from others, just as affection called for submission and acquiescence. This was the awful tug-of-war that Vita had no way of resolving, but she learned with the passage of time that negotiation and compromise might go a long way toward bridging the rift. In her future love affairs with women, the compromise she settled on to reconcile these opposing urges took the form of deep maternal compassion accompanied by extravagant gestures of passion—a combination these women interpreted as love. But passion and pity neither singly nor in sum ever equal love. It was in fact this very combination that caused her so much heartache. Yet however much turmoil her amorous embroilments caused her, Vita couldn't live without love—or, more accurately, without the *idea* of love in her life, another conviction she seems to have inherited from her mother. "*Mais enfin, ma chérie,*" Lady Sackville insisted in her characteristic mix of languages, ". . . you know love is the most beautiful thing on earth? *Et c'est ce qui le plus* to most people." One of the little ironies in this story was that Lady Sackville herself became the principal beneficiary of Vita's love.

It was thus through many conflicting shades and tangled paths of childhood that Vita grew to the woman who would one day write these letters. She carried with her, in fantasy at least, the banner of conquest, the emblem of history, and the shield of manhood. These were her defenses for fighting her own battles for her own best advantage, as Lady Sackville had taught her, and to Vita, her best advantage meant personal franchise and self-jurisdiction. These she must have if she was eventually to gain fame and prestige, the only really enduring safeguards in what she felt to be a potentially hostile world. The sadistic streak in her which so few people knew of was rooted not in the desire to inflict pain, but rather in the urgency to feel in possession of sufficient power to direct the course of her life as a separate and autonomous woman with her own locus of rights. Only in her fiction do we find scenes of physical violence. The women in her factual life dramatize a different story.

In this distant light, Vita's preferring to "fail gloriously than dingily succeed" assumes a larger significance. It speaks of her attitude toward life, and it lays bare the range of her striving for domination, for authority, and for control. It was an attitude of aggressiveness reflected even in her letters to Virginia. How often we come across phrasing like "I don't want to drag you down here"; "I shall pin you down"; "let me come and carry you off"; "the wish to steal Virginia overcomes me"; "I shall have to make you come by main force," and so much more. These citations are indeed so slight that they might pass unnoticed, and some of us might even insist upon seeing them as negligible. They are nevertheless from the lexicon of abduction and they belong to the language of aggression.

With the same pen she used to write her letters to Virginia, Vita would in a few years write a novel in which her sadistic hero would say to his lover: "I should like to chain you up . . . naked and beat you and beat you till you screamed." This is of course very strong fantasy, but we don't need psychoanalytic assistance to interpret the underlying message, which stated simply runs something like this: "Only when I've relieved my inferior sense of myself by putting you in bondage can I feel comfortable with you emotionally—and sexually." This was a language Vita understood perfectly.

The same tough strand of muscle runs through these letters, though certainly no violence was ever directed toward Virginia. It is important only to notice the spontaneous word choices, for they bespeak Vita's buried conviction that life, in all its diversity, was something that needed to be fought and conquered; something that required competence and force. This was clearly the emotional atmosphere in which she lived. Her smallest acts of affection were colored and often twisted with the romance of power and ravishment. Such was the cast of her mind. Vita's dream world was a world fraught with danger—and the prospect of conquest. We need to remind ourselves, however, that the Vita who fantasized muscular force and sadistic torture was the woman who, first of all, had her entire life been overwhelmed and diminished by a grasping mother, and secondly, in losing Knole, was daily reminded of the inferior status of her sex. Little wonder that she should learn to see the vulnerable spots in others. Less wonder still that she should emotionally brutalize anyone who threatened her precarious sense of sovereignty. "Social relations," said Vita, "are just the descendants of the primitive tribal need to get together for the purposes of defence." In her interior world, only the "fittest" survived. Weakness was devoured by strength.

In a letter to Virginia—Vita was tending the Woolfs' spaniel, Pinker, at the time—she wrote:

Pinker and I try to console one another. She sleeps on my bed, and clings to me as the one comparatively familiar thing in a strange and probably hostile world. . . . I had to explain that Mrs Woolf lived in London, a separate life, a fact which was as unpleasant to me as it could be to any spaniel puppy. . . . I explained that everybody always betrayed one sooner or later, and usually gave one away to somebody else, and that the only thing to do was to make the best of it.

People were not kind, and nature was indifferent to human wishes. This was an atavistic world ruled by laws that inevitably destroyed what one loved. "Something always does, when one wants a thing too passionately," she had written just a little earlier.

Just how savage or indifferent people could be, to Vita's way of thinking, emerges in a letter written during her first voyage to Persia. En route she fell ill, and "all last night I had a fever and a sore throat, and was quite certain through my nightmares that I should be put ashore at Karachi with diphtheria and left there alone. . . . I am all alone, and there is no one on this ship who cares whether I live or die." Of course a great many people cared very much whether she lived or died, but the subjective world she experienced was under the primal powers of the jungle, and it was from its dense and perilous growth that her emotional life drew its characteristic mood. If she didn't master life she would forever be its slave, at its mercy. So that what looked like overpowering aggressiveness on Vita's part was fundamentally a determination to survive through the exercise of personal might. She had to deal competently with the techniques of life in order to master it—or else be mastered by it. It is unlikely that Vita herself would have articulated her feelings in quite this way, but it is clear from hundreds of accumulated details scattered throughout these letters that the atmosphere of combat was the one she genuinely felt herself to be in much of the time.

Her superior sense of efficiency often led her into misunderstanding and difficulty. In a letter to Virginia in the earliest months of their friendship, for example, Vita suggested an expedition to the Basque provinces. Thinking that Virginia might need some powerful incentive for going, Vita suggested that she look on the trip "as copy,—as I believe you look upon everything, human relationships included. Oh yes, you like people, through the brain better than through the heart,—forgive me if I am wrong."

Virginia was justifiably hurt by that remark and said so. What is so astonishing, however, is that Vita didn't have the slightest notion of what she'd said to hurt Virginia. This was the truth. What someone else might consider a heartless remark—not understanding her hidden motives—Vita regarded simply as a suggestion of efficiency. Four years later, when Vita's father lay dying at Knole, she said again and with the same disconcerting directness, "What good copy it would all be for Virginia's book [*Orlando*]. The whole thing," she added with her characteristic penchant for high romance, was a "mixture of the tragic, the grotesque, and the magnificent."

By the time she met Vita Sackville-West in 1922, Virginia Woolf had survived three major periods of insanity and had published three novels. She was forty years old and already a writer of acknowledged importance, but she had yet to become a commercial success. And by 1922, Vita had already published several volumes of poetry and fiction, and was also an established author. She was thirty years old, ten years Virginia's junior.

The day after that first encounter on December 14, Virginia recorded in her diary meeting "the lovely aristocratic Sackville-West last night at Clive's. Not much to my severer taste . . . with all the supple ease of the aristocracy, but not the wit of the artist. She writes 15 pages a day—has finished another book—publishes with Heinemanns—knows everyone—But could I ever know her?"

Up to this time Virginia had had only two infatuations in her life, one in her teens with Madge Vaughan (after whom Clarissa Dalloway was modeled), and one in her early twenties with Violet Dickinson, a woman many years her elder. So that her willing surrender to Vita Sackville-West's magnetism would be the first in Virginia's adult life, and Vita would be the first woman to appear on the domestic scene of Virginia's married life with Leonard Woolf. But Vita was something special, and Virginia appears to have been willing to search out the possibilities. "Mrs Nicolson thinks me the best woman writer—" Virginia wrote in her journal, "& I have almost got used to Mrs Nicolson's having heard of me. But it gives me some pleasure." If Mrs. Nicolson liked Mrs. Woolf's writing, well . . . at least she had that much in her favor. More important than that, however, Vita had aroused something childlike in Virginia: "The aristocratic manner is something like the actresses—no false shyness or modesty: a bead dropped into her plate at dinner—given to Clive—asks for liqueur—has her hand on all the ropes—makes me feel virgin, shy, & schoolgirlish. . . . She is a grenadier; hard; handsome, manly. . . ."

Following their first meeting, there was a quick exchange of dinners and books. Virginia read Vita's novel and poems with approval, and confided again to her diary: "She is a pronounced Sapphist, & may . . . have an eye on me, old though I am. Nature might have sharpened her faculties. Snob as I am, I trace her passions 500 years back, & they become romantic to me, like old yellow wine." It's pretty clear that Virginia wouldn't at all mind if Vita had an eye on her, for she was fascinated by this "pronounced Sapphist."

The fascination was reciprocal. Vita's letter to her husband, Harold Nicolson, just after their meeting fills in her page of the story:

I simply adore Virginia Woolf, and so would you. You would fall quite flat before her charm and personality. . . . Mrs. Woolf is so simple: she does give the impression of something big. She is utterly unaffected. . . . At first you think she is plain, then a sort of spiritual beauty imposes itself on you, and you find a fascination in watching her. . . . She is both detached and human, silent till she wants to say something, and then says it supremely well. She is quite old. I've rarely taken such a fancy to anyone, and I think she likes me. At least she's asked me to Richmond where she lives. Darling, I have quite lost my heart.

Such was Vita's letter of December 19, 1922.

Virginia was indeed "both detached and human," as Vita had observed, and in the next nineteen years she would learn in full measure exactly how detached Virginia Woolf could be—as well as how human. The detachment held a certain magical pull for Vita, and she saw it as a challenge. Didn't winning the friendship of this genius of letters mean a kind of triumph? Virginia Woolf was, after all, a "big silver fish."

But here a long pause interrupted the proceedings of Love. Whether their first steps had been taken too quickly, or whether Virginia became apprehensive, or whether Vita simply grew impatient is not clear, but for many months an almost complete silence separated them. In March 1924, however, when the Woolfs moved from Richmond to Tavistock Square, Bloomsbury, it was Virginia who broke the silence: Would Vita come and have lunch in the new flat? "But prepare for a complete picnic, among the ruins of books and legs of tables, dirt and dust and only fragments of food." This was the first time they had ever been alone together, and Vita went away with her "head swimming with Virginia."

Something of greater importance was in the offing, however—an opportunity that would serve Vita's ambitions as a novelist. Would she write a book for the Hogarth Press to publish? Virginia asked her in May. "If so, what and when? Could it be this autumn?" This was rather a challenge, being asked to produce a book on three months' notice. But Vita thrived on challenges—the bigger, the better. Of course she would give them a book. Better still, she would write it during her holiday on the peaks of the Italian Alps! But *that* was really no challenge. How could Virginia so underestimate her? Writing a book was a mere "commercial proposition." The real challenge was Virginia's charging her with writing "letters of impersonal frigidity." Well, now, that was quite a different proposition. First, however, the book must get written, as indeed it was; and it turned out to be perhaps Vita's most imaginatively conceived novel. Its title was *Seducers in Ecuador.* She dedicated it to Virginia, and with that dedication the first real step was taken toward a deeper intimacy.

When the manuscript arrived, Virginia wrote again for her own eyes:

Vita was here for Sunday, gliding down the village in her large new blue Austin car, which she manages consummately. She was dressed in ringed yellow jersey, & large hat, & had a dressing case all full of silver & night gowns wrapped in tissue. Nelly [servant] said 'If only she weren't an honourable!' . . . But I like her being honourable & she is it; a perfect lady, with all the dash & courage of the aristocracy. . . . She left with us a story which really interests me rather. I see my own face in it, its true. But she has shed the old verbiage, & come to terms with some sort of glimmer of art; so I think; & indeed, I rather marvel at her skill, & sensibility; for is she not mother, wife, great lady, hostess, as well as scribbling? How little I do of all that: my brain would never let me milk it to the tune of 20,000 words in a fortnight. . . .

But, she went on, Vita "is like an over ripe grape in features, moustached, pouting, will be a little heavy; meanwhile, she strides on fine legs, in a well cut skirt . . . has a manly good sense & simplicity. . . . Oh yes, I like her; could tack her on to my equipage for all time; & suppose if life allowed, this might be a friendship of a sort."

The Hogarth Press published *Seducers in Ecuador* in November of that year. Virginia offered small criticisms, but it was, she said to Vita, "much more interesting (to me at least) than you've yet done. . . . I am very glad we are going to publish it, and extremely proud and indeed touched, with my childlike dazzled affection for you, that you should dedicate it to me." Thus, little by little, visit by visit, and letter by letter the friendship grew—Aphrodite was beginning to exert her influence.

In 1925, Virginia's *The Common Reader* and *Mrs Dalloway* both made their debut. Vita was in awe of their brilliance. One thing that *Mrs Dalloway* had done for her, she said to its author, was to make it unnecessary ever to go to London again, for the "whole of London in June *is* in your first score of pages. (Couldn't you do a winter London now? . . .)" She could not of course foresee that in three years' time she would be reading about herself, garbed as Orlando, skating on the Thames during the Great Frost. By late summer, while Vita was writing *The Land*—which would become her most enduring work—Virginia was forced to bed with headache and exhaustion. So that their letters alone once more carried the weight of their developing intimacy.

Harold Nicolson had been informed by the Foreign Office in September that he was being posted to the British legation in Teheran, and it was settled that Vita would join him there in January and remain until May. This news made Virginia see for the first time, and to her surprise, exactly how much Vita had come to mean to her. Vita was "doomed to go to Persia; & I minded the thought so much (thinking to lose sight of her for 5 years) that I conclude I am genuinely fond of her. There is the glamour of unfamiliarity to reckon with; of aristocracy . . . of flattery. All the same, after sifting & filing, much, I am sure, remains. Shall I stay with her?"

By December, Virginia was pronounced sufficiently recovered to brave a change of scenery, and on December 17 was efficiently "carried off" by Vita to Long Barn, where she stayed for three nights. It was during this weekend that the goddess Astarte descended upon them and advanced their friendship to the deeper level of love. Vita made a note in her diary for December 17: "A peaceful evening." For the 18th, however: "Talked to her till 3 a.m.—Not a peaceful evening."

Virginia, too, recorded the event—a little defensively: "These Sapphists *love* women: friendship is never untinged with amorosity." But, she went on:

I like her & being with her, & the splendour—she shines in the grocers shop in Sevenoaks with a candle lit radiance, stalking on legs like beech trees, pink glowing, grape clustered, pearl hung. That is the secret of her glamour, I suppose. Anyhow she found me incredibly dowdy, no woman cared less for personal appearance—no one put on things the way I did. Yet so beautiful, &c. What is the effect of all this on me? Very mixed. There is her maturity & full breastedness: her being so much in full sail on the high tides, where I am coasting down backwaters; her capacity I mean to take the floor in any company, to represent her country . . . to control silver, servants, chow dogs; her motherhood . . . her being in short (what I have never been) a real woman. Then there is some voluptuousness about her; the grapes are ripe; & not reflective. No. In brain & insight she is not as highly organised as I am. But then she is aware of this, & so lavishes on me the maternal protection which, for some reason, is what I have always most wished from everyone.

From Long Barn, Vita wrote her side of the adventure to Harold. Having suffered only a few years earlier through Vita's devastating affair with Violet Trefusis as well as through the slightly less destructive liaison with Geoffrey Scott, Harold was understandably worried. But he had no reason to be, Vita assured him on December 17, for she would not "fall in love with Virginia," nor would Virginia fall in love with her. On the 18th, Vita assured him again: "She says she depends on me. She is so vulnerable under all her brilliance. I do love her, but not b.s.ly [back-stairs-ly, i.e., homosexually]." And again on the 19th: "We have made friends by leaps and bounds in these two days. I love her, but couldn't fall 'in love' with her, so don't be nervous."

In the years ahead Virginia would return again and again to that precious image of Vita "pink with pearls" in a Sevenoaks' fishmonger's shop. In her mind, that memory marked a change in her life. But here and now, in January 1926, Virginia realized that she was almost completely in Vita's thrall, and the departure for Teheran was dreadful. "Parting," as the poet said, would "turn their hearts into clocks." They were both dedicated literary women, however, and in the months that followed they created an *epistolarium* of love that was large, complicated, and obsessive.

So the weeks passed—and the months. Vita returned to England in May, and Harold, who had remained in Teheran, needed once more to be reassured: "Oh my dear, I do hope that Virginia is not going to be a muddle! It is like smoking over a petrol tank." But there was no muddle, Vita insisted.

I love Virginia—as who wouldn't? But really, my sweet, one's love for Virginia is a very different thing: a mental thing; a spiritual thing, if you like, an intellectual thing, and she inspires a feeling of tenderness, which is, I suppose, owing to her funny mixture of hardness and softness—the hardness of her mind, and her terror of going mad again. She makes me feel protective. Also she loves me, which flatters and pleases me. . . . I am scared to death of arousing physical feelings in her, because of the madness. I don't know what effect it would have, you see: it is a fire with which I have no wish to play. I have too much real affection and respect for her. . . . Besides, Virginia is not the sort of person one thinks of in that way. There is something incongruous and almost indecent in the idea. I have *gone to bed with her (twice), but that's all. Now you know all about it, and I hope I haven't shocked you.*

Vita was an impresario of passion and there were times when her life rang with a chorus of lovers; but she showed great wisdom in having "too much real affection and respect" for Virginia to play with her emotionally. Virginia possessed artistic genius, something Vita greatly valued and would have liked to have had herself. It is true that the few sexual episodes between them flattered Virginia's vanity, but their real emotional center lay elsewhere. Vita idolized the mistress of letters and felt compassionate love for the vulnerable child who resided within; and with Vita's extraordinary competence so much on display, it was easy for Virginia to forget that underneath, here was a woman who also needed understanding and love. As usual, however, the old conflict reared its uncompromising head: So long as Vita's need for affection vied with her need for independence, and so long as both these opposing urges claimed equal ascendancy, she would never be on open and equal terms with anyone, Virginia included. Nor, it seems, did Virginia realize how often she threatened Vita's loyalty with her inquisitorial cross-examinations and sometimes exasperating demands for attention. It's no wonder that below her patrician surface Vita felt unsatisfied and solitary. Even less wonder that she was promiscuous and sometimes ruthless with her lovers. They didn't understand her, and she simply couldn't help them to. That would have amounted to confessing how much she needed their affection, and that would have betrayed her own weakness. It was easier to see herself in command in a world of strife. Maintaining that magisterial posture at least justified her craving for autonomy. And so she continued to force the people in her universe to conform to her own limitations. What Vita did not perhaps realize was that at the loneliest of times, when she managed to laugh, she should have permitted herself to weep. For with the laughter, the real woman went deeper into hiding and the sovereign Vita climbed a step higher, hardening even further the already brittle architecture of conflict.

The nicknames Virginia and Vita used with one another identify the alternating roles they assumed. When Virginia addressed "dearest Vita," she was appealing to the loving, protective maternal figure. When "Donkey West" was summoned, she sought the haughty and glamorous woman who wrote novels and poetry. On Vita's side, when a letter began with "My dearest Virginia," she was talking to her "lovely and remote" mistress of prose. When "Potto" was called upon, it was the child in Virginia who was being invited out for a romp.

Thus at least two Vitas were in constant negotiation with at least two Virginias. Their ten-year difference in birth dates really mattered very little in the organization of their relations, although Virginia did occasionally resort to her seniority when it suited her plan or when she needed to scheme for sympathy. And there was plenty of room for confusion in the intense, and sometimes untidy, game of love they so beautifully dramatized. How often Virginia, with one breath, shouted at "Donkey West" for muddling up human relations and, with the next breath, implored her "Dearest Vita" to repeat to her on which "rung of the ladder" Potto stood in Vita's affections. That is, at any given moment, the elegant writer of prose called upon the aristocratic woman and wheedled her into repeating how much the dominating mother loved the anxious child. This could be very confusing indeed.

There is something "obscure" in you, Virginia unexpectedly wrote to Vita one day. It was a flaw in Vita's makeup that affected everything she did and everything she wrote. "There's something that doesn't vibrate in you: It may be purposely—you dont let it: but I see it with other people, as well as with me: something reserved, muted—God knows what. . . . It's in your writing too, by the bye. The thing I call central transparency—sometimes fails you there too."

Who can say from what depths of perception Virginia came to identify the very conflict that Vita worked so hard to conceal. It was, nevertheless, a conflict that Virginia thought responsible for blocking her expression of feeling with people as well as in her books.

"Damn the woman," Vita wrote to Harold, "she has put her finger on it. There is something muted. . . . Something that doesn't vibrate, something that doesn't come alive. . . . It makes everything I do (i.e. write) a little unreal; gives the effect of having been done from the outside. It is the thing which spoils me as a writer; destroys me as a poet. But how did Virginia discover it? I have never owned it to anybody, scarcely even to myself. It is what spoils my human relationships too. . . ."

Virginia saw it, Vita should have realized, because Virginia suffered from the same affliction: the need of affection in combat with the need for independence. There was one large difference between the women, however. Virginia, we know, like many another writer, shielded herself from life's insults with pen and ink. But her particular sense of intellectual superiority, pressed directly beside a pronounced emotional submissiveness, permitted her as a novelist to surrender herself completely and willingly to the mental atmospheres of her characters. With astonishing ease she could crawl in and out of her characters' minds, however different from one another they might be, and record for each of them feelings so deeply wrought as to bear the stamp of lifelike authenticity. That is, she was sure enough of herself intellectually and compliant enough emotionally to abdicate her deepest Self in order to imagine the emotions of others during the act of creation. And this was something Vita simply could not do.

Vita's orientation to the world was one of competition and conquest, and hers was an aggressive stance. The very notion of submission was foreign to her nature and menacing to her deepest and most vulnerable sensibilities. In consequence, she often wrote lavish descriptions *about* her characters' feelings, but rarely permitted herself—and hence the reader—a taste of what the experience itself felt like. The basic timidity hidden under her aggression, and in combination with it, didn't allow her to enter the minds of her fictional people and surrender herself to the experience of *their* feelings. This is why she wrote "from the outside."

But Virginia had somehow ferreted out her secret, and the discovery seemed to make a difference to their relations in the months ahead. Vita would have given anything to be able to write from "the inside," and so she began to look at Virginia's art with greater concentration. Virginia may have found Vita's attention intellectually flattering, but certainly not emotionally satisfying. For now the affectionate Potto—the thirteen-year-old Virginia—would have to move over and make room for Virginia the "gentle genius" of fiction. She would now assume the part of literary mentor, and Vita would follow her like "a puppy on a string" and wag an appreciative tail for whatever morsels she might sniff out. In this vaguely defined office, the gentle genius had now become "essential" to Vita.

"I don't know how I shall get on without you," Vita wrote at her second departure for Teheran. "Darling, please go on loving me—I am so miserable—Don't forget me—" On the next day: "I shall work so hard, partly to please you, partly to please myself. . . . It is quite true that you have had infinitely more influence on me intellectually than anyone, and for that alone I love you. . . . You do like me to write well, don't you? And I do hate writing badly—and having written so badly in the past."

Again what seems not to have crossed Vita's mind was not that her writing was bad—for she was indeed a proficient novelist—but that her writing was so different from Virginia's; and that difference had its provenance in the structure of her personality, not in scriptural performance. What she could not have known at the time, however, was that eventually she would hit upon a subject for a novel for which her exterior mode of writing would be not only appropriate but necessary to its success. That novel would be *The Edwardians.*

Vita returned from Teheran in 1927 at about the same time Virginia's *To the Lighthouse* was published, and she was "dazzled and bewitched" by it. "Darling, it makes me afraid of you," she wrote. "Afraid of your penetration and loveliness and genius." In this novel, Virginia had performed one of her most brilliant analyses of the minds and motives of her characters. "Only if I had read it without knowing you, I should be frightened of you," Vita added.

Virginia's "penetration" was indeed frightening, for in Vita's mind it translated to domination over people; it was an advantage that Vita as an exterior writer didn't have. Hadn't Virginia's penetration already discovered Vita's weak spot? Wasn't it possible that she might unearth others and render Vita even more vulnerable than secretly she already was? There was something terrifying about being under Virginia's intellectual and moral scrutiny.

There were other matters, too, troubling Vita. She was frustrated. She needed an adventure, not minute cerebral dissections. Her months away from England had lowered what little immunity she had to Cupid's darts—Virginia or no Virginia. And the adventure she hankered for now appeared in the person of Mary Campbell, wife of the poet Roy Campbell. (Vita, one might add parenthetically, had a tendency, perhaps even a talent, for coming between husbands and wives. Danger may have been part of the attraction, and of course the challenge too. Earlier she had been in part responsible for the marital warfare between Violet and Denys Trefusis; she had been the cause of Geoffrey Scott's divorce; and there was even some suspicion that she had been instrumental in separating Dorothy Wellesley from her husband.)

At any rate, Vita met Roy and Mary Campbell on May 22. On May 23 the Campbells dined with her at Long Barn. On October 1 they moved into Long Barn cottage, by which time Vita had become Mary's lover—and her mother as well. Soon there would trail behind Mary a small procession of new love affairs and passionate encounters of which Margaret Voigt, Hilda Matheson, and Evelyn Irons would be the first in line. Yet Vita's love letters to Virginia continued without interruption as though no one else in the world existed.

Fear sharpens one's perception, and Virginia sensed immediately that something was amiss. She had warned Vita only a few months earlier to be careful in her "gambollings, or you'll find Virginia's soft crevices lined with hooks. You'll admit I'm mysterious—you don't fathom me yet—" She was right. Virginia kept a good deal of herself "up her sleeve," as Vita phrased it, and there were still large unknown areas to be explored. Little did Vita know that when Virginia felt threatened by her lapses in fidelity, she would seize whatever Opportunity chose to offer; and as it happened, Opportunity put pen and ink within easy reach. The result was to become one of the most personal footnotes in English literary history: a fictional biography of Vita Sackville-West.

The Campbells had moved into Long Barn cottage on October 1, 1927. On October 5, Virginia noted in her diary the idea for "a biography beginning in the year 1500 & continuing to the present day, called Orlando: Vita; only with a change about from one sex to another." She began immediately to write the biography. On October 9, she wrote to let Vita know that she was indeed aware of the beautiful Mary Campbell's existence, as well as to tell her about the birth of *Orlando*. "But listen," she urged, "suppose Orlando turns out to be Vita; and its all about you and the lusts of your flesh and the lure of your mind (heart you have none, who go gallivanting down the lanes with Campbell). . . . Shall you mind? Say yes, or No." Five days later, in a more tranquil mood: "Never do I leave you without thinking, its for the last time." (Vita confessed to gallivanting because Virginia left her "unguarded.") "If you've given yourself to Campbell," Virginia went on, "I'll have no more to do with you, and so it shall be written, plainly, for all the world to read in Orlando."

There was more truth in that statement than Virginia herself knew at the time. She was aware of Vita's past love affairs. She must also have sensed from the start that women younger than Virginia herself caught Vita's attention; and certainly she recognized the truth that even if Vita had found her sexually desirable, Virginia was psychologically and temperamentally unsuited to satisfy Vita's physical appetite. There was little she could do. But there was nothing in the world of fiction or fantasy to prevent her from inscribing for posterity Vita's lusty delinquencies, fierce ambitions, and yearnings for fame. With all the elegance at her command, Virginia would show the world a Vita in full plumage—and in all her magnificent contradiction.

Thus, in much the same proprietorial spirit as Browning's jealous Duke, preserving for himself his "Last Duchess" in a portrait, Virginia preserved for herself the Vita she loved in the spectacular world of *Orlando*. No matter how many slips in fidelity or how much gamboling there might be in the months and even years ahead, Orlando—the seductive aristocrat of Virginia's imagination—would remain inviolate, safely beyond the menacing lure of other women, and permanently beyond the threat of loss. The Orlando of Virginia's book had stepped outside the irrelevancies of life and into the purer chambers of art, where she would remain forever. Others might seduce Vita in the flesh, but no one could sully the Vita of Virginia's creation.

While *Orlando* was in the making, Virginia became a little philosophical about Vita, even a little withdrawn. So much of what Vita had done was *not* an affirmation of love, in any of its ambiguous senses; and that knowledge was too alive and too submerged in Virginia to be ignored. But art, not life, now consumed her attention. "I'm not afraid of your not wanting me," she wrote in October, "only of what one calls circumstances. . . . My questions about your past can wait till you're in London." By November, however, Roy Campbell, having discovered the affair between his wife and Vita, first threatened Mary's life and then threatened divorce. Vita turned to her biographer for help. Virginia listened carefully. She weighed the pros, considered the cons, and then reproached Vita roundly for disrupting the lives of others—her own included. Vita left in tears. She "was a failure all round."

"You made me feel such a brute," Virginia wrote the next day, "and I didn't mean to be. . . . And I'm half, or 10th, part, jealous, when I see you with the Valeries and Marys: so you can discount that. . . . I'm happy to think you *do* care." Yet however open-minded or generous Virginia wanted to be, the little girl inside would inevitably erupt in molten jealousy. "Promiscuous you are," she would soon write, "and that's all there is to be said of you. Look in the Index to Orlando—after Pippin [Vita's dog] and see what comes next—Promiscuity *passim.*"

Vita's affair with Mary Campbell meanwhile grew stronger as the months passed. By early December, Vita had written fourteen sonnets to her, while Virginia continued assiduously to weave the fantastic world of *Orlando*.

Following a visit to Long Barn in the summer of 1928, Virginia, in a contemplative mood, pondered her changing relations with Vita:

I'm interested by the gnawing down of strata in friendship; how one passes unconsciously to different terms; takes things easier; dont mind hardly at all about dress or anything. . . . Lay by the black currant bushes lecturing Vita on her floundering habits with the Campbells for instance. Mrs C. beat by her husband, all because V. will come triumphing, with her silver & her coronets & her footmen into the life of a herring-cooker. She cooks herrings on her gas stove, I said, always remembering my own phrases [in Orlando*].*

Virginia's detachment at this time probably puzzled Vita, for Virginia now looked analytically on Vita's affair with Mary and saw it as some grim charade of love gone wrong; yet there could be something in it that she might sift out and weave into the gauzy web of biographical prose. But the ground on which she and Vita now stood was shifting perceptibly, and Virginia found herself often comparing the Vita she was in the process of creating to the living model who stood before her. She wondered at the differences, pondered the similarities, and tried to imagine new variations.

In September 1928 the two women finally made the trip to France they had planned for so long. It was the first and only expedition they would make together, and the first trial of what the close company of day-to-day living might produce. "This is written on the verge of my alarming holiday in Burgundy," Virginia confided to her diary. "I am alarmed of 7 days alone with Vita: interested; excited, but afraid—she may find me out, I her out." Virginia's fear notwithstanding, the expedition turned out to be a success. The French countryside was beautiful, the food delicious, and the days full of adventure. From Burgundy, Virginia wrote to Leonard: "Vita is a perfect old hen, always running about with hot water bottles, and an amazingly competent traveller, as she talks apparently perfect French. . . . The truth is she is an extremely nice, kind nature; but what I like, as a companion, is her memories of the past."

To Harold, Vita wrote: "Virginia is very sweet, and I feel extraordinarily protective towards her. The combination of that brilliant brain and fragile body is very lovable. She has a sweet and childlike nature, from which her intellect is completely separate." To her diary: "In the middle of the night I was woken up by a thunderstorm. Went along to Virginia's room thinking she might be frightened. We talked . . . and then as the storm had gone over I left her to go to sleep again."

It is not by chance that both the letters and the diary entry call attention to Virginia's need for protection and Vita's need to protect her. Virginia's childlike helplessness stimulated Vita's sense of domination. Virginia's fragility aroused her sense of power. It fed and simultaneously appeased the deep vein of aggression that ran through Vita's nature. Strong, self-sufficient women, however brilliant or beautiful, would never have great appeal for her. But to need her protection, to be dependent upon her, was always a deep though temporary satisfaction, and the closest Vita would ever get to achieving simultaneously the privacy she coveted and the intimacy she craved. Her bounty, her protection, her passion—these were not love, exactly, but they were the only generous expedients she could offer in its place. Virginia came close to describing the dominant-compliant character of their relations when she said to Vita just after their expedition: "I have seen a little ball kept bubbling up and down on the spray of a fountain: the fountain is you; the ball me. It is a sensation I get only from you."

They returned to London and to the publication of *Orlando*. Vita had up to this time been kept entirely in the dark about the book. She had not been allowed to read even a single line. But now it was here, finished, indeed for all the world to see. And it was a great success. Reviewers couldn't find words enough in praise. As Nigel Nicolson said, *Orlando* was "the longest and most charming love letter in literature." More than that, the fact that Lord Sackville had died when the book was half written made *Orlando*, in one sense, a kind of "memorial mass"; and Vita was "enchanted, under a spell."

Harold Nicolson wrote to Virginia from Berlin: "It really *is* Vita—her puzzled concentration, her absent-minded tenderness. . . . She strides magnificent and clumsy through 350 years." One black cloud hovered over the book's publication, however, and that cloud was Lady Sackville. "You have written some beautiful phrases in Orlando," wrote Vita's mother to Virginia, "but probably you do not realise how *cruel* you have been. And the person who inspired the Book has been crueller still." (Beside Virginia's photograph, which she pasted into her copy, Lady Sackville wrote: "The awful face of a mad woman whose successful mad desire is to separate people who care for each other. I loathe this woman for having changed my Vita and taken her away from me.")

Orlando, however, affected Vita in a very private way. With Lord Sackville's death in January of this year—1928, the year of the book's publication—Vita was made to face the one reality she dreaded most: the permanent loss of Knole. She no longer had any legitimate claim to her ancestral home. Knole now passed to Vita's uncle Charles and would in turn eventually fall to her cousin Edward Sackville-West. That monumental loss and all it represented to Vita was monstrous. With the birth of Orlando, however, its edge had been dulled. For in the deepest symbolic sense, Knole had been restored to her. Their pasts had been reunited. "You made me cry with your passages about Knole, you wretch," Vita wrote to its maker.

But there was something else Virginia had done in *Orlando* which was harder to talk about, and that was her uncovering of the hidden side of her subject. Virginia had indeed "found her out." There for all the civilized world to read was Orlando's violence; his lust for glory and his swings of temper; his rages, his dreams, his wish for solitude; and there was that terrible flaw in his nature of substituting "a phantom for reality." Virginia came nearest to touching the very soul of her subject when she said that Orlando would surrender everything he owned in the world "to write one little book and become famous." "Desire for fame"—that was the vital force in Orlando's life. And in Vita's too. "There was a glory about a man who had written a book."

So much of Vita's life—past, present, and future—could be understood if one knew how much fame meant to her. With it, she had approval, power, recognition. It was the achievement of glory that excited her most extravagant passions. If she could not be remembered in the histories of England as the successor to Knole, surely she could take her place forever as one of England's poets. Fame was the hidden key. And Virginia had unearthed it. Vita saw that at once. If Virginia's penetration into the human heart in *To the Lighthouse* had made Vita "afraid" of her, we must try to imagine how unshielded she felt now, with *Orlando* staring at the world from the windows of bookshops. Virginia had been relentless in her search and brilliant in her exposition. Indeed the entire creation had about it a kind of ruthless virtuosity.

Now there was nothing, Vita realized, either too private or too personal that she could withhold from Virginia, and with that realization, her feeling for her began once more to change. Toward Virginia the artist, Vita's adoration increased, but so did the distance that would now further separate them. "Darling, you're my anchor," Vita said, following the debut of *Orlando*. "An anchor entangled in gold nuggets at the bottom of the sea." And she began to drift more openly from her adored Virginia. The anchor would remain forever steadfast. Of that she was certain, and with that certainty the restless Vita bobbed and plunged and dipped on the sea above. Just as she had had her adventures in the past, so she would have them in the months ahead. Virginia would continue to love her, perhaps with greater ease now that she was captured in the permanent edifice of words. So that while the jealous child remained cradled in Vita's affection, the author of *Orlando* stood poised, watchful, and just a little out of reach.

In the often bewildering interplay of these multiple roles, there was always a danger: The more openly Virginia tried to monopolize Vita, the greater the strain she put on their relations. Vita was generous with everything she had except her personal freedom, the emotional franchise her biographer repeatedly put to the test. Virginia, however, was reasonably assured of Vita's yielding to her whenever her maternal susceptibilities were touched, and she frequently took advantage of that weakness. How often she waved good-bye to Vita feeling like "a baby having drunk sweet milk." Even in her chronic illnesses Virginia knew that she could arouse Vita's protective instincts more effectively by pretending she was well when she wasn't—and Vita knew she wasn't—than by acting the simpering, propitiatory invalid. Vita never failed to come to her side. The lover posed all kinds of difficulties. But Vita, the mother, was as steady as the Rock of Gibraltar.

Much of this maternal benevolence, which Vita carried into all her intimacies, made her strangely and even paradoxically inaccessible to the women she attracted. For in secretly guarding her privacy Vita made it impossible for them ever to know her well enough to meet her securely on an open and emotionally equal footing. Her generosity and protective affection tended to deny her love-partners the privilege of behaving maturely and responsibly toward her. They became something like dependent and loving children. For this reason, in none of these intimacies could Vita experience herself as a fully valued human being. That is, she wasn't able to feel loved and validated by an adult woman, because her loving beneficiary, in submitting to Vita's protective embraces, simultaneously forfeited her status of equality.

As if still under the feudal system of old, the lord dispensed her bounty and guardianship, and her vassals pledged in return their fealty. Vita gave. They took. Vita requisitioned. They supplied. The intimacies were skewed, unbalanced, unsymmetrical. But there seemed no other way for her to assuage her deep and abiding sense of isolation. When these women asked for genuine love, Vita would be made to realize once more that love wasn't hers to give. She wrote somewhere that her mother, for all her amorous extravagance, "was a dictator: not a colleague." In a much subtler way, this applied to Vita as well.

Leonard Woolf, assessing her from a different angle, once observed that being driven by Vita through London traffic and hearing her put an "aggressive taxi driver in his place, even when she was in the wrong, made one recognise a note in her voice that Sackvilles . . . were using to serfs in Kent 600 years ago, or even Normandy 300 years before that."

I . . . would rather fail gloriously than dingily succeed. It is easy to imagine those words coming from Orlando, so charged are they with heroism. Vita wrote them when the idea came to her for *The Edwardians*—six weeks before the publication of *Orlando*. Virginia, in the early months of her work on the book, had recruited Vita's help in collecting facts about Knole: tracing its history, taking photographs, wandering through its great halls. It appears that in the process of Virginia's creation, Vita's own imagination began to kindle. What was there to prevent her from making up her own story of Knole?

In early February 1929, Vita wrote from Germany, with a Tauchnitz Edition of *Orlando* before her, that she couldn't read it without shedding tears. "Whether it is the mere beauty of the book, or whether it is because of you, or because it is Knole," she didn't know; but in late June she began writing at top speed about her magnificent ancestral home in *The Edwardians*, which would mark a major change in her literary life.

From Savoy, where she continued to work on the book, she wrote to Virginia one of her most private statements as a writer; it is the letter of one novelist to another:

This is perhaps not what you call an intimate letter? But I disagree. The book that one is writing at the moment is really the most intimate part of one, and the part about which one preserves the strictest secrecy. What is love or sex, compared with the intensity of the life one leads in *one's book? A trifle; a thing to be shouted from the hilltops. Therefore if I write to you about my book, I am writing really intimately, though it may not be very interestingly. . . . But you would rather I told you I missed Potto and Virginia, those silky creatures . . . and so I do. . . .*

At the beginning of their friendship, Virginia had written a little unfairly to Jacques Raverat that Vita wrote "with complete competency, and with a pen of brass." The truth is that Vita was a very skilled writer, and as for the "pen of brass"—well, that was rather a matter of taste. Vita's novels almost always sold well and she had considerable popular success—more, in fact, than Virginia herself. But Vita Sackville-West could not write like Virginia Woolf any more than Virginia Woolf could write like Vita Sackville-West. One does not criticize a pianist for failing to play like a harpsichordist.

"Novels by serious writers of genius," wrote Leonard Woolf, "often eventually become best-sellers, but most contemporary best-sellers are written by second-class writers whose psychological brew contains a touch of naïvety, a touch of sentimentality, the story-telling gift, and a mysterious sympathy with the day-dreams of ordinary people. Vita was very nearly a best-seller of this kind. She only just missed being one because she did not have quite enough of the third and fourth element in the best-selling brew." What Virginia or Leonard thought of Vita's writing is ultimately beside the point. What does matter is that the Woolfs, from the very start, saw in her a highly marketable author, and (fame aside for the moment) with the publication of *The Edwardians* in 1930, Vita made a great deal of money for the Hogarth Press, as well as a great deal of money for herself—money that would soon be put to use in realizing one of her most persistent dreams.

In early March 1930, as it happened, the view from the terrace of

Long Barn was being threatened by poultry farmers who were negotiating the purchase of a neighboring farm. The thought of having in the future to look out on chicken houses appalled Vita. It was time to move on. And so she began looking for another house. On a rainy April day she discovered Sissinghurst Castle, a monumental ruin set gloriously in acres of mud and rubble. "Fell flat in love with it," Vita wrote in her diary. Her offer of £12,375 was accepted and Sissinghurst was hers.

With the money she would earn from *The Edwardians* in the months ahead, Sissinghurst was to become something like her own private version of Knole. The castle's traceable history went back at least as far as Orlando's. Was it not right, then, that Sissinghurst should eventually come into Vita's hands? Orlando had sought fame and glory through writing a book. Now Vita's book had earned her that fame, and Sissinghurst would concretize her glory. Thus the dream and the quest of a lifetime converged in *The Edwardians*, materially and metaphorically. There was an additional prize. Sissinghurst had a rose-brick tower which would soon become Vita's most guarded sanctuary and most bastioned citadel. If she wanted solitude and safety she would have them—but now with a certain lofty splendor.

All Passion Spent, another success, followed in 1931, and in 1932 the Nicolsons left Long Barn to take up full-time residence at Sissinghurst. During this interval, although Vita and Virginia saw each other from time to time and exchanged letters, the rift widened, on Vita's part primarily. She had a castle to restore, a garden to create, and a great deal more money to earn; and Harold, who had resigned from diplomatic life, was now living permanently in London and about to turn his talents to literature and politics.

The space left by Vita in Virginia's life in the early 1930s was taken, to some degree, by Ethel Smyth, composer, autobiographer, and incurable egotist. Now well into her seventies, she became Virginia's most frequent visitor and correspondent, and her insatiable curiosity about Virginia's personal history was undoubtedly flattering. This new friendship, however, did not usurp or even disturb Vita's place in Virginia's heart. Her love for Vita simply folded its wings and waited in silence.

Virginia spoke of Vita in her diary from time to time, as though to keep the image sharp: "Vita last night," she wrote in January 1931: ". . . she says she gets more pain than pleasure from praise of her books, which I believe to be true. Never was there a more modest writer. And yet she makes £74 in a morning—I mean a cheque drops in for a story." In March 1932: "We went to Sissinghurst. . . . Vita in breeches & pink shirt.

We went over the grounds . . . ate cold salmon & raspberries & cream & little variegated chocolates given by Lady Sackville . . . & drank oh lots of drinks; & then climbed Vita's tower; lovely pink brick; but like Knole, not much view, save of stables that are to be guest rooms. So home."

Like many another rejected lover, out of sheer self-protection Virginia shut her eyes to a good many changes in Vita which were obvious to others; but she continued to see the essential portrait, and her own deep sense of honesty forbade her to falsify that portrait, as the following letter to Ottoline Morrell testifies:

I remain always very fond of her—this I say because on the surface, she's rather red and black and gaudy, I know: and very slow; and very, compared to us, primitive: but she is incapable of insincerity or pose, and digs and digs, and waters, and walks her dogs, and reads her poets, and falls in love with every pretty woman, just like a man, and is to my mind genuinely aristocratic; but I cant swear that she wont bore you. . . . But do let her come from her rose-red tower where she sits with thousands of pigeons cooing over her head.

But Virginia persisted. In a letter of April 1934 she began: "Yes, I must really write to you, because I want to know what is happening. But that said, I've nothing to say. Thats because you're in love with another, damn you! . . . The week after next we go to Ireland. . . . And there I may be windswept in to the sea. But what would Vita care. 'No', she'd say, we had Petulaneum Ridentis in that bed last year: we'll try Scrofulotum Penneum there this.' So she'd bury me under, wouldn't she Vita?"

In her diary she wrote a few months later: "Vita to lunch, after many weeks, yesterday. . . . She has grown opulent & bold & red—tomato coloured, & paints her fingers & lips which need no paint . . . underneath much the same; only without the porpoise radiance, & the pearls lost lustre." So Virginia ended, thinking back once more to December 1925, a scene touched with the loving brushstrokes of nostalgia.

Then, finally, the diary entry of March 11, 1935: "My friendship with Vita is over. Not with a quarrel, not with a bang, but as ripe fruit falls. . . . But her voice saying 'Virginia?' outside the tower room was as enchanting as ever. . . . & thats an end of it. And there is no bitterness, & no disillusion, only a certain emptiness."

The friendship did not come to an end. It was Virginia's depression that spoke. The deaths of Lytton Strachey and Roger Fry had cut her off from two of her closest friends. *The Years* had got out of control and was causing her months of tortured writing. She was in her fifty-third year and feeling old, unendorsed, and irrelevant. All of these troubles coalesced in her mind and pressed her into a state of vulnerability not far from despair. Her rapport with Vita had now reached, for Virginia at least, a less fanciful, more realistic footing that would endure for the remaining years of her life, but the diminished privilege in their relations appeared to Virginia as a separation: The voluptuous aristocrat she loved so much was drifting beyond her reach; the passionate woman with Gypsy blood coursing her English veins was moving away from her anchorage, and there was nothing Virginia could do to stop it.

Sissinghurst Castle, with all its symbolic meaning, was becoming the center of Vita's world, a safe, reclusive world of continuity and pattern. She strode her own grounds now attired almost exclusively in whipcord breeches and high boots, pearls and earrings. Her earliest fantasies of manhood were swelling to life, and her craving for self-governance was now taking the shape of solitude in the guarded privacy of her tower room. There Vita sat, alone for long periods, writing her books and scanning her poems with "thousands of pigeons cooing over her head." Within the next year or two she would be ready to write *Solitude*, the poem that had for so long been accumulating in some sequestered corner of her mind.

Lady Sackville died in 1936, and Vita discovered among her papers the testimonies from Spanish witnesses she had collected in 1910 in preparation for the Knole succession case. Vita's father had inherited Knole, soon after Vita's birth, from his uncle, old Lionel Sackville-West, on the assumption that old Lionel had no legitimate male heir. There followed a long and costly legal dispute involving certain family members who began making monetary claims and insisting upon certain "rights." Vita's mother was not about to accede to family claims or to family greed. So she went about collecting disclamatory evidence from people who had known Lady Sackville as a child, as well as Pepita, Vita's Spanish Gypsy grandmother. The discovery of these papers made Vita's "mouth water." Here was a book she must write. The materials were made to order, and at once her imagination went to work. *Pepita* was begun in August 1936 and was published in October 1937 by the Hogarth Press. Ten thousand copies were sold within the first eight weeks of publication. She had scored another success.

The second half of the book is devoted to "Pepita's Daughter, 1862–1936"—that is, to Vita's mother; and of course the years from 1892 to 1936 include Vita herself. As we read through those pages today, we cannot fail to notice that Vita was not writing about her mother alone. As principal observer of and participant in the drama of Lady Sackville's life, Vita, without realizing it, was also writing a kind of oblique memoir of her own youth and young womanhood. Her values, her attitudes, her preoccupations permeate every page. So that in her effort to get her mother into perspective, Vita, now in her rose-brick tower at Sissinghurst, was forced to take a long, unflinching look at her earlier self. And she didn't like all of what she saw. With the passage of years, she began to realize how much terrible waste there had been in her many adventures into passion. Now she saw them as

> *Those cheap and easy loves! . . .*
> *Those rash intruders into darkest lairs? . . .*
> *That lure the flesh and leave it slightly smutched. . . .*

Such were the lines Vita would write into *Solitude*. To have abandoned so much of her life to the rituals of passion had been destructive and wasteful. Worse than that, she had repeatedly dramatized a scalding rapture without feeling the salve of love. It had been so much caressing without much caring.

Virginia was the one exception. But then she understood Vita as the others had not. She knew that there was something blocked, hidden, permanently frozen. That knowledge by no means diminished the intensity of her feeling. In understanding the source of Vita's "floundering habits," however, the "gentle genius" of letters saw the "cheap and easy loves" and did her best to wait in patience, while the possessive child, the demanding Potto, continued to squirm in pain and fear and anger.

With the approach of the Second World War in 1938, international tension was mounting. The tension in Virginia's workroom mounted too. She had just gone through five years of "sweat and tears" with her longest and most troublesome book, *The Years*. Her nephew Julian Bell had just been killed in the Spanish Civil War. Her world was becoming a madhouse of brutality and slaughter. And it was in this strange atmosphere of noisy emptiness and in a state of increasing exhaustion that she wrote *Three Guineas*, a passionate denunciation of wars and the men who fought them. The book was published in 1938, and it provoked one of her very few notable quarrels with Vita. *Three Guineas*, Virginia said, was meant to stir up popular feeling; she had meant to "say irritating things," to "rouse objections." But Vita's charge that the book advanced "misleading arguments" amounting to dishonesty made her wince. The pain turned quickly to anger, and the anger brought Virginia's professional integrity surging to the surface. What, she wanted to know, did Vita mean by "misleading arguments"? Did she mean that Virginia had arranged the facts in a dishonest way so as to produce a desired effect? If so, then they would have to have the matter out—"whether with swords or fisticuffs. And I dont think *whichever we use*, you will, as you say, knock me down. It may be a silly book, and I dont agree with you that its a well-written book: but its certainly an honest book. . . ."

Vita's letter had stung, but Virginia stood firm, even refusing to read Vita's manuscript until the matter was settled. In July another letter to Sissinghurst was fired off: ". . . I feel I cant read your poem impartially while your charges against me . . . remain unsubstantiated. . . . You said something about its [*Three Guineas*] being 'misleading' and suggested that if only you weren't incurably clumsy honest and slow witted yourself you could demolish my specious humbug. You could knock me down with your honest old English fists and so on. And then you sicklied me over with praise of charm and wit."

"Horrified by your letter," Vita wired her. More letters shot back and forth before Virginia was certain that she had not been accused of dishonesty—"and thats the only thing I mind. So forgive and forget," said Virginia a little submissively, just as so much else, whether rightly or wrongly, had been forgiven and forgotten. Where Vita was concerned, the stakes were too high, the potential loss too great. Virginia would continue to remain compliant.

Far more serious trouble lay ahead, however. *The Years* had been an enormous drain, not only on Virginia's energy but on her confidence as a writer, and the hostility *Three Guineas* aroused in some quarters did little to bolster her flagging self-assurance. So that when she began the life of Roger Fry as well as *Pointz Hall* (which became *Between the Acts*) in April of 1938, it was rather in the spirit of defeat. The Fry biography, because it was so personal, caused her endless trouble and doubt, and the more she struggled with it, the less sure of herself she became. She had convinced herself that it wasn't going to be a good book. Leonard Woolf, always Virginia's most reliable critic, found it inadequate and told her so.

Over all this private hardship loomed the dark shadow of Hitler, threatening the fate of the civilized world. An approaching war, and all its companion horrors, added considerably to an already heavily charged atmosphere. To both novelists this meant a shift to herd conformity. It meant relinquishing private satisfactions for the benefit of the greater good. To Virginia this was intolerable. To Vita it was necessary. In fact, the very differences that separated them in their private lives differentiated them in their response to the war as well. When the bombs began to fall on England, Vita's intrinsic mood for combat was quickened to life. She might write pastoral verse and reflective poetry in the solitude of her pink tower, but in a crisis of war she rolled up her sleeves and took over civic duties. The urge to literary creation yielded to the spirit of patriotism. War to Vita was one thing. Writing was another. She could take it up. She could put it down. Her writing was not inextricably woven into her sense of self, and the two never got confused.

For Virginia, war held a different meaning. She was always actively a part of the world in ordinary life; but when she came to write she invariably drew apart from it. On one level, war of course meant loss and privation. At a deeper level, however, it meant having no reader; and to Virginia's way of thinking, without a reader there was no writer. Numerous other circumstances in her life during this period of trial conspired to exaggerate her situation, to get things out of all proportion. And it took no great stretch of imagination for her to begin to feel herself a piece of excess baggage. More than that, war meant the end of personal independence, the end of public recognition. Everything she had worked for now hung in the balance. Without readers, without the public echo, there was nothing.

It is not clear whether Virginia herself understood the struggle within during these last years. If she did, it is unlikely that she would have mentioned it to Vita, for the struggle was too close to death, and death was "the one experience I shall never describe," she had once said. Perhaps there was no need to.

There is no effective way to document loneliness at times like this. One can only try to approximate the sense and the intensity of emptiness a human being is capable of feeling. As often happens, however, when one's world is threatened with annihilation and death lurks just around the corner, people who at some earlier time have loved deeply tend to want to relive those earlier feelings and recall once more the happiest of those times past. And in this crisis Vita seemed to realize more than ever before just how much Virginia meant to her. For they lived through these dark days with the full knowledge that every visit might be their last. Bombs were falling near Sissinghurst, just as they fell in the garden at Monk's House.

"I did like your letter," wrote Virginia in the fall of 1939. "And if I'm dumb and chill it doesn't mean I dont always keep thinking of you—

one of the constant presences is your's, and so—well, no more." In March of 1940: ". . . how I long to hear from your own lips whats been worrying you—for you'll never shake me off—no, not for a moment do I feel ever less attached." A few days later, with enemy aircraft closer than ever: "What can I say—except that I love you. . . . You have given me such happiness."

By October 1940, the Woolfs' two London houses had been either destroyed or made uninhabitable by German air attacks. Whatever remaining possessions they could salvage they moved to Rodmell, where Virginia was trying desperately to finish *Between the Acts*. And it was during this time and in the early months of 1941 that she began to drift into a strange kind of serenity, something like a state of exhausted euphoria. The strain of war, the fatigue of compulsive writing, the terror of failing as a novelist, the horror of old age and dependency, her fear of madness—all converged, finally, and reversed the spurious euphoria into the blackest of depressions. But Vita knew nothing of this.

In her letter to Sissinghurst dated Saturday, March 22, Virginia inquired about Vita's dying birds—her budgerigars. The Woolfs' housekeeper kept budgerigars too, but "Louie's survive: and she feeds them on scraps—I suppose they're lower class, humble, birds. If we come over, may I bring her a pair if any survive? Do they die all in an instant? When shall we come? Lord knows—"

Those were her last words to Vita. Virginia ended her life on Friday, March 28, 1941.

There is a curious little detail connected with Virginia's last reference to dying birds. In the closing scenes of *Between the Acts,* posthumously published in July 1941, there is a line about "birds syllabling discordantly life, life, life." When Vita read this passage some months after Virginia's death, she could not have failed to recognize its origin in *Orlando*, which runs:

Let us go, then, exploring, this summer morning, when all are adoring the plum blossom and the bee. And humming and hawing, let us ask of the starling (who is a more sociable bird than the lark) what he may think on the brink of the dust bin, whence he picks among the sticks combings of scullion's hair. What's life, we ask, leaning on the farmyard gate; Life, Life, Life! cries the bird, as if he had heard. . . .

In 1945, four years after Virginia's death, Vita, together with Harold Nicolson, compiled an anthology of poetry called *Another World Than This . . .* In that volume we find a "poem" by Virginia Woolf which Vita lineated from this *Orlando* passage:

Let us go, then, exploring
This summer morning,
When all are adoring
The plum-blossom and the bee.
And humming and hawing
Let us ask of the starling
What he may think
On the brink
Of the dust-bin whence he picks
Among the sticks
Combings of scullion's hair.
What's life, we ask;
Life, Life, Life! cries the bird
As if he had heard. . . .

That Vita should have chosen this very passage from *Orlando*, Virginia's longest love letter to her, has by itself a certain commemorative importance. But its valedictory significance to Vita becomes clear only when we remember that in her teens Virginia had lessons in Latin and Greek. For in this posthumous novel, "Life, Life, Life!" translates into Latin as "Vita, Vita, Vita!" And nothing could have been more fitting for Virginia's last farewell to Vita, who had given her so much life—with all its happiness and sorrow—in almost twenty years of love and friendship.

March 1923–Early 1924

Vita Sackville-West and Virginia Woolf first met at a dinner party given by Clive Bell in London on December 14, 1922. Soon afterward Virginia dined with Vita at her house in Ebury Street, and on January 11, 1923, Vita paid her first visit to Hogarth House, Richmond, where the Woolfs had begun to print short books, including T. S. Eliot's The Waste Land. *Their friendship at first seemed to develop rapidly. After the Hogarth visit, Vita wrote to her husband, Harold Nicolson, "I love Mrs Woolf with a sick passion," but it was more instant admiration than instant infatuation. Then, for the remainder of 1923 and early 1924, there was a hiatus in their relationship. They seldom met or corresponded, Vita having felt snubbed by Virginia's refusal to join P.E.N., as the first of these letters records. Besides, Vita had fallen temporarily in love with Geoffrey Scott, wrecking his marriage in the process. She lived mostly in the country, writing novels, while Virginia was working on* Mrs Dalloway *and* The Common Reader.

182 Ebury Street
London S.W.1
26th March [1923]

Dear Mrs Woolf

I write this tonight, because I think you said you were going to Spain on the 27th, and I want it to catch you before you go. The P.E.N. club committee are very anxious for you to join the club, and at their request I proposed you,—now will you be nice and let them make you a member?[1] for my sake if for no other reason. It is only a guinea a year, and they would be so pleased. They dine once a month; it is quite amusing. Do, please, and come to the May dinner when they are entertaining distinguished foreign writers. There was a little shout of excitement from the committee about you, and Galsworthy (so to speak) got up and made a curtsey.

I hope you will have fun in Spain. It is the best country I know. Please let me know when you come back, as I do want you both to come and stay at Long Barn,[2] and come up to Knole with me. And I shan't know when you are back unless you tell me.

Yours very sincerely
Vita Nicolson

Berg

1. Vita was a member of the committee of P.E.N., the international authors' society of which John Galsworthy was chairman. Virginia had received a previous invitation from P.E.N. in the autumn of 1921 and had refused it.
2. Vita's home in Kent, two miles from Knole, the great house of the Sackvilles where she was born in 1892.

Good Friday [30 March 1923] *Hotel Ingles, Madrid*

Dear Mrs Nicolson,

(But I wish you could be induced to call me Virginia). I got your letter as we left Richmond. I am much flattered that the P.E.N. should ask me to become a member.

I would do so with pleasure, except that I don't know what being a member means. Does it commit one to make speeches, or to come regularly, or to read papers or what? Living so far out, dinners are apt to be difficult, and I cant speak. . . .

Berg

Long Barn, Weald,
Sevenoaks.
8th April [1923]

My dear Virginia

(You see I don't take much inducing. Could you be induced likewise, do you think?)

It is nice of you to say you will join the P.E.N. club provided you don't have to make speeches. I can guarantee that, as by one of the club rules they are forbidden. The most you ever get is a statement from the chairman. Nor need you go to any dinners unless you want to. Nor does anyone read papers. You just go to a dinner when the spirit moves you, and take your chance of sitting next to Mr. H. G. Wells or an obscure and spotty young journalist.

I don't suppose this letter will ever reach you. It always seems to me quite incredible anyway that any letter should ever reach its destination. But I seem to remember that you have already said—or, rather, written—all that there is to be said about letters. So I won't compete.

I am envying you Spain more than I can say. I wish I were with you—But the lady's smocks are very nice, along the hedges, and my tulips are coming out.

Yours very sincerely
Vita Nicolson

[Written in pencil:] This paper is like blotting paper to write on in ink.

Berg

❧ *April 15th 1923* *Murcia, Spain*

Dear Mrs Nicolson

The secretary of the P.E.N. club has written to me to say that I have been elected a member. Very regretfully I have had to decline—since I see from the club papers that it is wholly a dining club, and my experience is that I can't, living at Richmond, belong to dining clubs. I've tried two dining clubs, with complete disaster. But I'm very sorry, as I should like to know the members, and see you also.

But this last I hope can be managed in other ways. . . .

Berg

March–December 1924

In March 1924 the Woolfs moved from Richmond to Tavistock Square, Bloomsbury, taking the Hogarth Press with them, and Vita was among their first visitors. Virginia invited her to contribute a book to the Press, and she responded by writing Seducers in Ecuador *while on a walking tour through the Dolomites with Harold Nicolson. Virginia was impressed by it and began to regard her with new respect and admiration. In July, Virginia paid her first visit to Long Barn, Vita's house, and to Knole, the ancestral home of Vita's father, Lord Sackville, who had been separated from his wife since 1919. Lady Sackville, who figures frequently in this correspondence, lived alone in a huge house at Brighton. In September, Vita paid a return visit to Monk's House, Rodmell, in Sussex, where the Woolfs spent the summer and many weekends. Their friendship was still not intimate.*

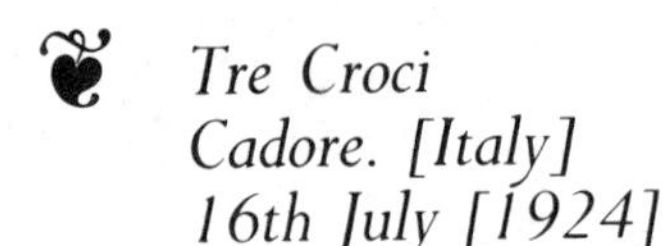

Tre Croci
Cadore. [Italy]
16th July [1924]

My dear Virginia

I hope that no one has ever yet, or ever will, throw down a glove I was not ready to pick up. You asked me to write a story for you. On the peaks of mountains, and beside green lakes, I am writing it for you. I shut my eyes to the blue of gentians, to the coral of androsace; I shut my ears to the brawling of rivers; I shut my nose to the scent of pines; I concentrate on my story [*Seducers in Ecuador*].[1] Perhaps you will be the Polite Publisher, and I shall get my story back,—"The Hogarth Press regrets that the accompanying manuscript," etc,—or whatever your formula may be. Still, I shall remain without resentment. The peaks and the green lakes and the challenge will have made it worth while, and to you alone shall it be dedicated. But of course the real challenge wasn't the story, (which was after all merely a 'commercial proposition,') but the letter. You said I wrote letters of impersonal frigidity. Well, it is difficult, perhaps, to do otherwise, in a country where two rocky peaks of uncompromising majesty soar into the sky immediately outside one's window, and where an amphitheatre of mountains encloses one's horizons and one's footsteps. Today I climbed up to the eternal snows, and there found bright yellow poppies braving alike the glacier and the storm; and was ashamed before their courage. Besides, it is said that insects made these peaks, deposit on deposit; though if you could see the peaks in question you would find it hard to believe that any insect, however industrious, had found time to climb so far towards the sky. Consequently, you see, one is made to feel extremely impersonal and extremely insignificant. I can't tell you how many Dolomitic miles and altitudes I have by now in my legs. I feel as though all intellect had been swallowed up into sheer physical energy and well-being. This is how one ought to feel, I am convinced. I contemplate young mountaineers hung with ropes and ice-axes, and think that they alone have understood how to live life—Will you ever play truant to Bloomsbury and culture, I wonder, and come travelling with me? No, of course you won't. I told you once I would rather go to Spain with you than with anyone, and you looked confused, and I felt I had made a gaffe,—been too personal, in fact,—but still the statement remains a true one, and I shan't be really satisfied till I have enticed you away. Will you come next year to the place where the gipsies of all nations make an annual pilgrimage to some Madonna or other?[2] I forget its name. But it is a place somewhere near the Basque provinces, that I have always wanted to go to, and next year I AM GOING. I think you had much better come too. Look on it, if you like, as copy,—as I believe you look upon everything, human relationships included. Oh yes, you like people through the brain better than through the heart,—forgive me if I am wrong. Of course there must be exceptions; there always are. But generally speaking . . . . .

And then, I don't believe one ever knows people in their own surroundings; one only knows them away, divorced from all the little strings and cobwebs of habit. Long Barn, Knole, Richmond, and Bloomsbury. All too familiar and entrapping. Either *I* am at home, and you are strange; or *you* are at home, and I am strange; so neither is the real essential person, and confusion results.

But in the Basque provinces, among a horde of zingaros [Gypsies], we should both be equally strange and equally real.

On the whole, I think you had much better make up your mind to take a holiday and come.

Vita

Sussex

1. Vita wrote the larger part of her long story *Seducers in Ecuador*, which she dedicated to Virginia, while she and Harold were walking in the Dolomites from July 8 to July 21, 1924.
2. Santiago de Compostela

❧ *19th August [1924]* *Monk's House, Rodmell, Lewes, Sussex*

My dear Vita,

Have you come back, and have you finished your book [Seducers in Ecuador]*—when will you let us have it? Here I am, being a nuisance, with all these questions.*

I enjoyed your intimate letter from the Dolomites. It gave me a great deal of pain—which is I've no doubt the first stage of intimacy—no friends, no heart, only an indifferent head. Never mind: I enjoyed your abuse very much. . . .

But I will not go on else I should write you a really intimate letter, and then you would dislike me, more, even more, than you do.

But please let me know about the book.

Berg

Long Barn, Weald, Sevenoaks. 22nd August [1924]

My dear Virginia

Aren't you a pig, to make me feel one? I have searched my brain to remember what on earth in my letter could have given you "a great deal of pain." Or was it just one of your phrases, poked at me? Anyhow, that wasn't my intention, as you probably know. Do you ever mean what you say, or say what you mean? or do you just enjoy baffling the people who try to creep a little nearer?

My story I fear is but a crazy affair. If you gave me a severe date by which it must reach you, typed and tidy, I should obey, being very tractable. If you say you must have it next week I will sit up all night and finish it. If you say "any time will do" I shall continue to glance at it disgustedly once a day and shove it back into its drawer with no word added. Three quarters of it exist at present, and your letter gave it a fillip. Please issue an irrevocable command.

"Dislike you more, even more." Dear Virginia, (said she putting her cards on the table,) you know very well that I like you a fabulous lot; and any of my friends could tell you *that*. But I expect you are blasée about people liking you,—no, you aren't, though,—I take that back.

I nearly came to see you last Sunday, as I was coming back from my mother [Lady Sackville] at Brighton, but I thought you mightn't like it. And it was such a horrible day of gale and rain.

Now I had better go on with that story.

Vita

Sussex

❧ *Aug. 26th [1924]*

Monk's House, Rodmell,
Lewes [Sussex]

My dear Vita

The position about your story is this: if you could let us have it by Sept. 14th, we should make an effort to bring it out this autumn; if later, it is highly improbable that we could bring it out before early next year. . . .

But really and truly you did say—I cant remember exactly what, but to the effect that I made copy out of all my friends, and cared with the head, not with the heart. As I say, I forget; and so we'll consider it cancelled. . . .

Berg

❧ *Sunday [31 August 1924]*

Monks House, Rodmell,
Lewes, Sussex

My dear Vita,

. . . could you come on Saturday 13th, not Sunday 14th, as Leonard has to disappear [to Yorkshire] on Monday at dawn, and therefore wouldn't see you at all.

I ought to warn you of the inconveniences and discomforts of this house, especially when it rains, but they are too many to begin on. Anyhow, we shall enjoy seeing you.

Berg

❦ *Long Barn, Weald,*
Sevenoaks.
[15 September 1924]

My dear Virginia,

In the first place this must be a Collins[1] to thank you for the great enjoyment of my hours with you,[2] and in the second place it must be an explanation, for I find I have cut a paragraph out of my story, meaning to insert it in another place; so if you came on any passage which failed to make sense, that is the reason.

It is quite a short paragraph, and I can put it into the proof.

(I like the way I go on the assumption that the story has found sufficient favour in the eyes of the Press, when all the time it may be in the post on its way back to me.)

I have not forgotten the Flying Terrapin,[3] but can't find it. Someone must have taken it. I will send it when it turns up.

I have ordered a dozen lilium croceum for your garden, just to convert you to Dutch bulbs.

Will you ask Mr Leonard if I may review [for *The Nation*] a book of poems by Claude Colleer Abbott, which is to appear shortly? I don't like the man, but they are country poems lamentably like my own, and I thought some of them rather good. So if he is sending them to anyone, may it be to me?

I did love being with you both; I was so happy there. I look forward to coaxing you to Knole in December!

Yours affect'ly
Vita

Sussex

1. A thank-you letter named after Mr. Collins in *Pride and Prejudice*

2. Vita spent her first night with Virginia and Leonard Woolf at Monk's House, Rodmell, on Saturday, September 13, 1924. In her diary of September 15, Virginia wrote about her: "A perfect lady, with all the dash and courage of the aristocracy, and less of its childishness than I expected." They also visited Vanessa Bell at Charleston.

3. *The Flaming* (not Flying) *Terrapin*, a book of poems by Roy Campbell

Monday [15 September 1924] *Monk's House, Rodmell, Lewes [Sussex]*

My dear Vita,

*I like the story [*Seducers in Ecuador*] very very much—in fact, I began reading it after you left, . . . went out for a walk, thinking of it all the time, and came back and finished it, being full of a particular kind of interest which I daresay has something to do with its being the sort of thing I should like to write myself. I don't know whether this fact should make you discount my praises, but I'm certain that you have done something much more interesting (to me at least) than you've yet done. . . .*

I am very glad we are going to publish it, and extremely proud and indeed touched, with my childlike dazzled affection for you, that you should dedicate it to me. We sent it to the printers this morning.

. . . By the way, you must let me have a list of people to send circulars to—as many as you can. And to do this you must come and see me in London for you should have heard Leonard and me sitting over our wood fire last night and saying what we don't generally say when our guests leave us, about the extreme niceness etc etc and (I'm now shy—and so will cease.)

Berg

 *Long Barn, Weald, Sevenoaks. 17th September [1924]*

My dear Virginia

I have walked on air all day since getting your letter. I am more pleased than I can tell you at your approval, and if I *can* tighten I will,—I felt myself that it needed this. Any suggestion would be welcomed?

I will make out a list for circulars.

I send the Terrapin—also the typist's address, which I forgot to give you: Mrs Candy
Hi Amore
Richmond Park Avenue
Bournemouth

How charming of you to sit on the millstones and say nice things.

Altogether after reading your letter I felt like a stroked cat. You see, I appreciate the fact that you are neither of you easy-going critics . . . . whether of work or persons.

The small stout key which I have lost unlocks a cupboard in which reposes not only my reputation but my stationery,[1] so as I can't get at my envelopes I must use an old one to fit the Terrapin. Forgive it. The Terrapin is a wild uneven thing, almost ridiculous in parts, almost magnificent in others. I wonder what you will think of it.

Yours ever
Vita

Sussex

1. The key to the cabinet where Vita kept all her private letters, and her "confession" about her love affair with Violet Trefusis, later (1973) published by her son Nigel Nicolson in *Portrait of a Marriage*

❧ *[4 October 1924]* *52 Tavistock Sqre, W.C.1*

We are just back; what did I find on the drawing room table, but a letter from which (to justify myself and utterly shame you) I make this quotation:

"Look on it, if you like, as copy,—as I believe you look upon everything, human relationships included. Oh yes, you like people through the brain, rather than through the heart" etc: So there. Come and be forgiven. Seducers in Ecuador looks very pretty, rather like a lady bird. The title however slightly alarms the old gentlemen in Bumpuses [booksellers].

Berg

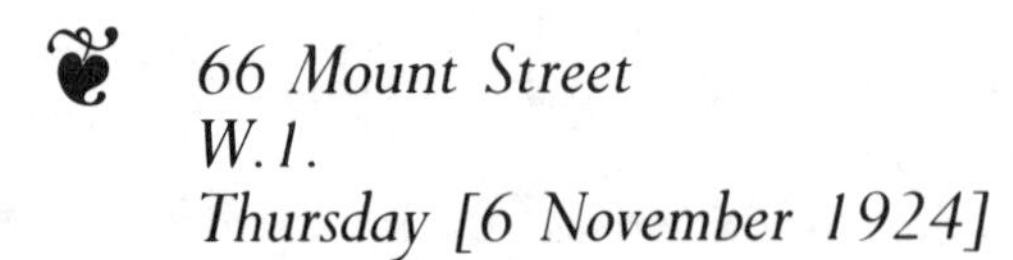

66 Mount Street
W.1.
Thursday [6 November 1924]

My dear Virginia

I came to Tavistock Square today. I went upstairs and rang your bell—I went downstairs and rang your bell. Nothing but dark inhospitable stairs confronted me. So I went away disconsolate. I wanted

(a) to see you.
(b) to ask you whether any copies of our joint progeny had been sold, and if so how many.[1]
(c) to ask for some more circulars.
(d) to ask you to sign two of your books which my mother had just been out to buy.
(e) to be forgiven.

I came away with all these wants unappeased.

Now I am going back to my mud till December 1st when I remove to Knole.

I await reviews in some trepidation.

I got a nice letter from Raymond Mortimer.

Yours ever
Vita

Sussex

1. *Seducers in Ecuador*

❧ *Sunday [9 November 1924]* *52 Tavistock Sqre, W.C.1*

My dear Vita,

You have added to your sins by coming here without telephoning—I was only rambling the streets to get a breath of air—could easily have stayed in, wanted very much to see you. . . .

. . . I will sign as many books as Lady Sackville [Vita's mother] wants. No: I will not forgive you. Wont you be coming up for a day later, and won't you let me know beforehand?

Berg

❦ *Long Barn, Weald,*
Sevenoaks.
13th November [1924]

My dear Virginia

I have just received from your press a surprise packet of which the enclosed is the invoice. As I didn't ask for any of these books, I imagine they were meant for some one else, so let you know at once. I am however keeping the books, as I shall easily use up 7 seducers for Xmas—and I am glad to have the other two.

This in haste.

I shan't be up till December now, but will then take the precaution of telephoning! Only I hate bothering people on the telephone.

I was grateful for the little bulletin—I hope the 430 copies [of *Seducers*] will increase in splendour.

SINS:

1. Saying V.W. looked on friends as copy.
2. Coming without telephoning [to 52 Tavistock Square].

What else?

I will try to make up by passing on some remarks I got in a letter today, "I am reading Jacob's Room again. I think it is one of the first books of the day. It terrifies me. It is a book that leaves every other book both commonplace and common. One's own stuff seems horrible and vulgar."

There now: incense to your censer.

Vita

I suppose a review copy went to the Observer? as Garvin wrote to me to say he hoped to get one.[1]

Sussex

1. J. L. Garvin was editor of *The Observer*.

January–November 1925

At the beginning of 1925, Vita and Virginia met infrequently in London. Vita was occupied with gently shaking herself free of her lover Geoffrey Scott and beginning to write her long poem The Land. *But during the summer she turned increasingly to Virginia, and Virginia to her, both finding a common bond in literature, specially each other's books, and in their growing mutual sympathy. Although Virginia was suffering from periodic bouts of headaches and exhaustion, she had started to write* To the Lighthouse. *Then, in early November, Harold Nicolson was posted by the Foreign Office to the British Legation in Teheran, and the friendship of the two women blossomed suddenly in December.*

 *Long Barn, Weald,*
Sevenoaks.
26th May [1925]

My dear Virginia,

I have been horribly remiss in writing to thank you for "Mrs Dalloway," but as I didn't want to write you the "How-charming-of-you-to-send-me-your-book-I-am-looking-forward-to-reading-it-so-much" sort of letter, I thought I would wait until I had read both it and The Common Reader,[1] which I am sorry to say I have now done. Sorry, because although I may and shall read them again, the first excitement of following you along an unknown road is over, and nothing gives way so quickly as surprise to familiarity. I feel however that there are passages of the Common Reader that I should like to know by heart; it is superb; there is no more to be said. I can't think of any book I like better or will read more often. Mrs. Dalloway is different; it is a novel; its beauty is in its brilliance chiefly; it bewilders, illuminates, and reveals; The Common Reader grows into a guide, philosopher, and friend, while Mrs. Dalloway remains a will-of-the-wisp, a dazzling and lovely acquaintance. One thing she has done for me for ever: made it unnecessary ever to go to London again, for the whole of London in June *is* in your first score of pages. (Couldn't you do a winter

London now? with fogs and flares at the street corners, blue twilights, lamps, and polished streets?)

How I envy you your English—How do you manage to make it as limpid as French, and yet preserve all the depth of its own peculiar genius?

When will you come here? for a weekend or in the week? and who am I to ask to meet you? You did promise to come in the summer, you know,—if a promise given on your area steps can bind you. I am going away for Whitsun, but apart from that I propose to be here immoveably for several months. I cannot write, so am keeping chickens instead.

Please come. I shan't think you "nice" any longer if you don't.

Yours ever
Vita

Berg

1. *Mrs Dalloway* was published by the Hogarth Press on May 14. *The Common Reader* had appeared on April 23.

❧ *Wednesday [27 May 1925]* *52 Tavistock Square, London, W.C.1*

My dear Vita,

Hah ha! I thought you wouldn't like Mrs Dalloway.

On the other hand, I thought you might like The Common Reader, and I'm very glad that you do—all the more that its just been conveyed to me that Logan P. Smith thinks it very disappointing. But oh, how one's friends bewilder one!—partly, I suppose, the result of bringing out two books at the same time. I'm trying to bury my head in the sand, or play a game of racing my novel against my criticism according to the opinions of my friends. Sometimes Mrs D. gets ahead, sometimes the C. R.—

Berg

❦ *Long Barn, Weald,*
Sevenoaks.
25th August [1925]

My dear Virginia,

Last Friday at midnight I stood on the top of your Downs, and, looking down over various lumps of blackness, tried to guess which valley contained Rodmell and you asleep therein. And now comes your letter, making me think that on the contrary you were probably awake and in pain.[1] But knowing nothing of that at the time, I reluctantly recovered my dogs who had been galloping madly across the Downs, climbed into the motor, and drove on along deserted roads and through the sleeping villages of Sussex and Kent, with the secret knowledge in my own mind that I had paid you a visit of which you knew nothing,—more romantic, if less satisfying, than the cup of tea to which Leonard had bidden me on Saturday.

I like extremely your corybantic picture of me and Eddy dancing in the vats.[2] Please preserve it. I will not tell you the truth, of stained fingers and the East End [hop-pickers] let loose. Yet a page later you contradict yourself in your magnificent manner, and call loudly for exactitudes of the most prosaic description. Oddly enough, you have hit on the very things with which my poem (which is not at all beautiful) does deal;[3] you could run a small-holding on the information supplied. I tell you exactly how and when to cut hay, cereals, and beans; how to stack, thatch, and thresh; how to spray orchards against the Woolly aphis, the blossom weevil, and the apple saw-fly. It is crabbèd enough even for your avowed taste. Which reminds me, our argument at the Morrells[4] took Crabbe as a spring-board, and the third person concerned was your lovely young god, Rylands.[5] We have not met since, which is a pity. But to revert to my poem, (you see what an egoist I am,) I have come to the conclusion that there is no longer any room for merely purple poetry; only for the prosaic, (which has its own beauty,) or for the intellectual. A bad definition, but no doubt you will get my meaning. Purple occurs incidentally, but only with its roots ground stalworth in heavily manured soil—My interest in my own poem was dying down like an old fire, but you've fanned the embers and today there is quite a little blaze.

Why do you give so much of your energies to the manuscripts of other people? You told me in London that you had at least six novels in your head but were being severe with yourself until you should get to Rodmell. Now you are at Rodmell, and what of the six novels? Between Ottoline, Gertrude Stein, and bridal parties which make you faint, what time is left for Virginia? Also you go whoring after Vogue and such-like,—though you *did* make the Common Reader up out of these things, and though I did quite particularly like your observations on Genji. But I'm becoming a bit of a Logan about Vogue, especially for you. Why should Todd batten at your expense?[6] I should like to see all literary papers suppressed, always excepting, of course, The Nation.

If ever you feel inclined, let me come and carry you off from Rodmell. I know that road so well, from going to see my mother at Brighton, that I can bundle along it with my eyes shut. I could devise many places to take you to,—Amberley, Bodiam, Romney Marsh.

I am enclosing a cheque for the 100 Seducers; I sent a wire about them today. I will recover it from the misguided enthusiast [Lady Sackville] who wanted them. And will you tell Leonard that I will try to concoct an article on hop-picking for him? in about a fortnight's time—if that will do. Sciatica has abandoned me. I hope he can say the same.

Do take care of yourself

Vita

Berg

1. Virginia had collapsed in the middle of an August 19 celebration for her nephew Quentin Bell's birthday and the marriage of Maynard Keynes and Lydia Lopokova.

2. Virginia had written: "I have a perfectly romantic and no doubt untrue vision of you in my mind—stamping out the hops in a great vat in Kent—stark naked, brown as a satyr, and very beautiful." Eddy Sackville-West was Vita's cousin.

3. *The Land*, a long pastoral poem, mainly about the different functions of the farming year.

4. Lady Ottoline and Philip Morrell

5. George ("Dadie") Rylands had written a poem, "Russet and Taffeta," which he dedicated to Virginia. The Hogarth Press published it in December 1925.

6. Dorothy Todd, editor of *Vogue*. Logan Pearsall Smith had abused Virginia for writing articles for it.

❧ *Tuesday [1 September 1925]* *Monks House, Rodmell [Sussex]*

My dear Vita,

How nice it would be to get another letter from you—still better, to see you. I haven't suggested it since the headache has been an awful nuisance this time, and I have had another week in bed. Now, however, even Leonard admits that I'm better.

My notion is that you may be motoring past and drop in and have tea, dinner, whatever you will, and a little conversation. One day next week? I'm going to be awfully quiet, and don't dare suggest what I long for—a drive to Amberley [West Sussex]. But when I'm in robust health, as I shall be, could it really be achieved? . . .

*In bed I have been fuming over your assumption that my liking for the poet Crabbe is avowed. I assure you I bought a copy out of my own pocket money before you were weaned. What's more, I have read Peter Grimes I daresay 6 times in 10 years; "But he has no compassion in his grave"—That is where that comes from. There is also a magnificent description of wind among bulrushes which I will show you if you will come here. But I find to my surprise that Crabbe is almost wholly about people. One test of poetry—do you agree?—is that without saying things, indeed saying the opposite, it conveys things: thus I always think of fens, marshes, shingle, the East Coast, rivers with a few ships, coarse smelling weeds, men in blue jerseys catching crabs, a whole landscape in short, as if I had read it all there: but open Crabbe and there is nothing of the sort. One word of description here and there—that is all. . . . So if your poem [*The Land*] is as you say all about the woolly aphis, I may come away from it dreaming of the stars and the South Seas. But hurry up, and write it.*

I must stop: or I would now explain why its all right for me to have visions but you must be exact. I write prose; you poetry. Now poetry being the simpler, cruder, more elementary of the two, furnished also with an adventitious charm, in rhyme and metre, can't carry beauty as prose can. Very little goes to its head. You will say, define beauty—

But no: I am going to sleep.

Berg

❦ *Long Barn, Weald,*
Sevenoaks.
[2 September 1925]

My dear Virginia

How much I like getting letters from you.

With what zest do they send me to meet the day.

So much do I like getting them, that I keep them as the last letter to open of my morning post, like a child keeps the bit of chocolate for the end—

But I like it less when I read that you have been ill for a week. It makes me feel guilty for every moment that I have spent, hearty and well, in such gross pursuits as gardening and playing tennis—

I shall be going to see my mother next week, one day. May I stop at Rodmell for dinner on my way back? (But not if it is a bore.) I would let you know *which* day. This depends on my mother. Early in the week, I expect. I shall suggest, to her, Monday or Tuesday. And Amberley *any* time you like—you may see in my underlining, a readiness to throw over any other engagement in order to fall in with your plans—

What nonsense you talk, though. There is 100% more poetry in one page of Mrs. Dalloway (which you thought I didn't like) than in a whole section of my damned poem. And as for Mr Palmer! [1] yes I daresay you did give *him* pleasure, but only to him. Not to his readers. I can't forgive Desmond [MacCarthy] for Mr Palmer,—his ewe-lamb, his dove.

There are two people in the room, now, talking; and such fragments of their talk as reach me, make me write frenziedly and-in-italics to you—out of a furnace of indignation—If my letter seems disjointed and hysterical, you must forgive it on that account.

I am puzzled by your resentment over my saying that your liking for Crabbe was avowed, that I am driven for explanation to the very improbable theory that you had forgotten what "avowed" means! Or did you simply mean that I thought you had concealed it up till now, and were at last coming out into the light? For the rest, if one could at will convey one thing by saying another, one would indeed have mastered half the secret of poetry—But how is it done? By what formula of allusion, sounds of vowel or consonant? by what sheer noise suggesting a complementary noise, as blue suggests red, or whatever it is? Why should "bare ruined choirs"[2] sound so very twiggy?

And along with this power, goes the faculty of kindling the desire to write in others—at least I find it so. I know just what to pick out of the shelf in order to strike sparks off myself, don't you? Or are you tinder-and-flint in one? I suspect so.

Will you give Leonard a very tiresome message from me? with apologies? It is this: I can't possibly review John Drinkwater,[3] I know him too well, and there is nothing I could say which wouldn't offend him horribly. If Leonard will say what he wants done, I will send the books to anyone he wants. I feel this must be one of the typical trials which beset an editor.

I have been making a tiny garden of Alpines in an old stone trough—A real joy. It makes me long for the spring. My botanical taste tends more and more towards flowers that can hardly be seen with the naked eye—Shall I make an even tinier one for you? in a seed pan, with Lilliputian rocks? I'll bring it next week. But you must be kind to it, and not neglectful. (This all fits in with the theory that people who live in the country and like flowers are good.)

Yours ever
Vita

Berg

1. Herbert E. Palmer, *Songs of Salvation, Sin & Satire*, printed by the Press and published in October 1925
2. Shakespeare's Sonnet 73
3. The poet, playwright, and actor (1882–1937). Leonard had sent Vita his *New Poems* (1925).

Monday [7 September 1925] *Monk's House, Rodmell [Sussex]*

My dear Vita,

Well, I dont see why you don't write to me, but perhaps it is my turn, only you are better situated for writing letters than I am. There are two people in your room, whom you can hear talking. There is one dog in my room, and nothing else but books, papers and pillows and glasses of milk and quilts that have fallen off my bed and so on. This has bred in me such a longing to hear what your two people are saying that I must implore you to tell me. . . . Tell me who you've been seeing; even if I have never heard of them—that will be all the better. I try to invent you for myself, but find I really have only 2 twigs and 3 straws to do it with. I can get the sensation of seeing you—hair, lips, colour, height, even, now and then, the eyes and hands, but I find you going off, to walk in the garden, to play tennis, to dig, to sit smoking and talking, and then I cant invent a thing you say—This proves, what I could write reams about—how little we know anyone, only movements and gestures, nothing connected, continuous, profound. But give me a hint I implore.

. . . "Avowed" should be simple; but has now taken the meaning "protested insincerity"; for me at least, who am, I suppose, grown hoary in sin, and impute meanings to good English words which, I agree, they dont bear. But write to your affectionate villain all the same.

Berg

Long Barn, Weald,
Sevenoaks.
Tuesday [8 September 1925]

My dear Virginia

I *am* so sorry. . . .

Your tale of fallen quilts really wrings my heart. And I am going to Brighton today, over your Downs, and shall leave this letter on your door step together with your garden-in-a-saucer. It looks dull at present, but in the spring it will give you flowers. You must keep it well watered.

The two people in my room were really Bulldog Drummond and Benjamin Constant.[1] They didn't know it, and elected to go about their business under quite other names, but that's who they were. You may imagine that there were many points on which they didn't see eye to eye; and what irritated me was that I kept finding myself in agreement with both of them at the same time. My contrariness was aroused both ways at once. I disliked Drummond for his bulldoggery, and Constant for his inconstance, yet wanted to inoculate each with a dash of the faults of the other. This however appears to be an impossibility to the English character.

I went hop-picking, and have written half an article for Leonard.[2]

I'll try to finish it today or tomorrow, or all the hops will have turned into beer by the time it reaches the Nation.

My spaniel has seven puppies. My cat has five kittens. The spaniel steals the kittens, and, carrying them very carefully in her mouth, puts them into the puppies' basket. She then goes out for a stroll, and the cat in search of her progeny curls up in the basket and suckles the puppies. The spaniel returns, chases out the cat, curls up in the basket, and suckles the kittens. I find myself quite unable to cope with this situation. The kittens will bark and the puppies will mew,—That's what will happen. But at present it makes a charming family party,—such a warm soft young heap.

I wish you were well and that I could see you. This is not really as selfish as it sounds, because most of all I wish that you were well, even if I were not to benefit. Is there anything you would like and that I could get you? Books,—but like the housemaid's mother, "She's got a book." I feel quite helpless, yet would like to please you. So you have only to say.

It will be very tantalising, stopping at your house. I shan't even ring the bell, but trust to luck that Leonard will fall over the saucer as he goes out.

Vita

Berg

1. Bulldog Drummond was the main character in H. C. McNeile's ("Sapper") series of adventure novels. Benjamin Constant, the French politician and writer (1767–1830), was in Vita's mind because she was reading Geoffrey Scott's *Portrait of Zélide*, where he figures prominently.
2. *The Garden and the Oast* (*The Nation*, October 10, 1925)

❧ *Tuesday [15 September 1925]* *Monks House, Rodmell [Sussex]*

Oh you scandalous ruffian! To come as far as this house and make off! When the Cook came up to me with your letter, and your flowers and your garden, with the story that a lady had stopped a little boy in the village and given him them I was so furious I almost sprang after you in my nightgown. . . .

Berg

❦ *Long Barn, Weald,*
Sevenoaks.
18th September [1925]

My dear Virginia

You are a very, very remarkable person. Of course I always knew that,—it is an easy thing to know,—the Daily Xpress knows it,—the Dial [New York] knows it,—organs so diverse,—the Daily Herald quotes you as an authority on the vexed question as to whether one should cross the road to dine with Wordsworth,—but I feel strongly that I have only to-night thoroughly and completely realised how remarkable you really are. You see, you accomplish so much. You are one perpetual Achievement; yet you give the impression of having infinite leisure. One comes to see you: you are prepared to spend two hours of Time in talk. One may not, for reasons of health, come to see you: you write divine letters, four pages long. You read bulky manuscripts. You advise grocers. You support mothers, vicariously. You produce books which occupy a permanent place on one's bedside shelf next to Gerald [*sic*] MANLY Hopkins and the Bible. You cast a beam across the dingy landscape of the Times Literary Supplement. You change people's lives. You set up type. You offer to read and criticise one's poems,—criticise, (in the sense which you have given to the word,) meaning illumination, not the complete disheartenment which is the legacy of other critics. How is it done? I can only suppose that you don't fritter. Now here am I, alone at midnight, and I survey my day, (the first that I have spent in peace for some weeks,) and I ask myself what I have done with it. I finished the hops for Leonard, found an envelope and a stamp, and sent it off. I planted perhaps a hundred bulbs. I played tennis with my son. I endeavoured to amuse my other son, who has whooping-cough, and tries to crack jokes between the bouts. I read a detective story in my bath. I talked to a carpenter. I wrote five lines of poetry. Now what does all that amount to? Nothing. Just fritter. And yet it represents a better day than I have spent for a long time.

Do you do it by concentration? Do you do it by organisation? I want a recipe so badly.

I assure you, it was misery to stop your anonymous little village boy and turn him into the Mercury who would ultimately reach your cook, who would ultimately reach you [with the saucer-garden]. It was unselfish, wasn't it? also, to be honest, I was frightened of Leonard. I knew he would look disapproving if I appeared at the house. He would look the more disapproving because he wouldn't know how much *I* approved,—of his care of you, I mean. After leaving Rodmell I took a road that wasn't a road at all; that is to say, it started by being a road and then melted away into grass, so that the last five miles of my journey were accomplished over pure Down,—very bumpy, but full of larks. A shepherd whom I met stared incredulously at the appearance of a blue motor in the middle of miles of rolling turf.

Yes I will send you my georgics [*The Land*] when they are more consecutive; at present there is a spider here and a farrowing sow there,—not tied together by any intelligible link. I will take advantage, quite unscrupulously, of your offer; but I shall continue to wonder how you fit it all in.

I like the sense of one lighted room in the house while all the rest of the house, and the world outside, is in darkness. Just one lamp falling on my paper; it gives a concentration, an intimacy. What bad mediums letters are; you will read this in daylight, and everything will look different. I think I feel night as poignantly as you feel the separateness of human beings; one of those convictions which are so personal, so sharp, that they *hurt*. It seems to me that I only begin to live after the sun has gone down and the stars have come out.

Vita

Berg

❧ *Wednesday [23 September 1925]* *Monks House [Rodmell, Sussex]*

My dear Vita,

Do keep it up—your belief that I achieve things. I assure you, I have need of all your illusions after 6 weeks of lying in bed, drinking milk, now and then turning over and answering a letter. We go back on Friday; what have I achieved? Nothing. Hardly a word written, masses of complete trash read, you not seen, but what was the good of asking you to come for half an hour, and then being furious to see you go? The blessed headache goes—I catch a cold or argue violently and it comes back. But now it has gone longer than ever before, so if I can resist the delights of chatter, I shall be robust for ever. But what I was going to say was to beg for more illusions. I can assure you, if you'll make me up, I'll make you. . . .

This is miserable scribbling, the effervescence of idleness. (I'm waiting for luncheon) but I shall rouse up in London. However, I'm going to live the life of a badger, nocturnal, secretive, no dinings out, or gallivantings, but alone in my burrow at the back. And you will come and see me there—please say you will: if you're in London, let me know. A little quiet talk in the basement—what fun! And then I'm going this winter to have one great gala night a month: The studio will be candle lit. . . .

Berg

Long Barn, Weald,
Sevenoaks.
Sunday [11 October 1925]

My dear Virginia

I wrote to you to Rodmell before I had got your letter telling me that you were going back to London. A simple calculation leads me to the conclusion that you will receive these two letters simultaneously,—or possibly even this one before the other. It all depends on the Rodmellian posts. I will therefore conceal from you the destination of my journeying, so that the other letter should not be deprived of its little bit of news. (Although news is the last thing one wants or expects to find in letters.) I will only tell you that it is *not* the Riviera or Italy, or even Egypt, but some country wild, beautiful, and unsophisticated; further away in time, though not in space, than China.[1] The ideal travel letter should be without address, I think; it should arrive like the Dove at the Ark, with no hint of where it has come from, so that it may evoke a landscape romantically beautiful but geographically vague. How I shall enjoy writing to you; how poignant it will be to feel that ink is one's only means of communication; how ruthlessly I shall lay upon you the burden of writing to the absent friend.

You might think from all this that I was taking some interest in my travels. I am not. I am taking interest only in the toothache which is boring its little hot gimlet into my head. The world centres there, and nothing else really matters. Did you feel like this about your headache? How cruel of your headache to destroy a six weeks which would otherwise have been crowded with achievement. It is not a fair argument against yourself, to say that you *don't* achieve, when an entirely outside thing happens to prevent you. I shall continue to think of you as a monument. Besides, you manage to be a lamp surrounded by bumping moths. All this takes a lot of time. I still don't see how you do it. You seem to combine in yourself at least 6 whole-time jobs: novelist, journalist, printer, publisher's reader, friend, relation. Each of these an occupation in itself; and none of them scamped. And now you are going to be a Lady Colefax[2] once a month and give parties! I shall come to one, (if you will ask me, that is,) like the opposite of a ghost,—what is that? Not one returning, but one about to depart.

Vita

Berg

1. Harold Nicolson was told by the Foreign Office that he had been posted to the British legation in Teheran.
2. Sibyl Colefax, the famous London hostess. Vita and Virginia spelled her first name alternatively Sibyl or Sybil. The correct spelling is Sibyl. In this volume the spelling has been corrected throughout without further comment.

Tuesday [13 October 1925] *52 Tavistock Square, W.C.1*

My dear Vita,

But for how long?

For ever?

I am filled with envy and despair. Think of seeing Persia—think of never seeing you again.

The Dr has sent me to bed: all writing forbidden. So this is my swan song. But come and see me.

Berg

❦ *Long Barn, Weald,*
Sevenoaks.
13th October [1925]

My dear Virginia

No, not for ever. And not even immediately. Harold goes [to Teheran] next month, and I follow in January, to return in May, and then go again next October. So you see there will be a good deal of coming and going. In the meantime what concerns me much more is you and your evident un-wellbeing; I can't tell you how sorry I am. Of course I will come and see you if you are really allowed to see people. Leonard wrote me a letter which moved me almost to tears; please tell him this from me, and thank him, and tell him I wrote forty lines of georgics on the strength of it. It is nice to be told one will be missed. Tell him too that I will turn myself into a Mrs. Eliza Fay [an eighteenth-century traveler and letter writer] for his benefit, and make the desert flower.

I don't expect any answer to this, you know, because I know you are not allowed to write.

I wish you could see Harold's luggage,—half tropical and half arctic. Fur coats and sun-helmets; skates and khaki shorts. I dress him up to look like a game of Consequences. You soar from the desert to mountain-passes, putting on an extra garment with every thousand feet. I wish you would both come to Teheran. But it seems improbable that this wish will ever be fulfilled. And indeed it is a devil of a way.

Please, please get better—and be careful of yourself. You have been ill such a long time, and it must be so wearying. If I may come to see you, I shall observe the 4.30 to 5.30 to the minute. and feel guilty even then.

Vita

Berg

 *Long Barn, Weald,*
Sevenoaks.
23rd October [1925]

My dear Virginia

When I got home the other day I found that the puppet show of memory had disappeared, so I ordered it to be sent to you; I hope that it has turned up.[1]

You let fall some words to the effect that they "wanted you to go away" presently; if you want a refuge, will you come here? I shall be all alone after Harold has gone, and I can promise you that you should be neither worried, excited, nor disturbed—also it would be easily accessible for Leonard. You could stay in bed all day if you wished; write if you wished, and talk if you wished.

I've evolved some theories about friendship, but as I've got a cold in the head I will leave their exposition for another day. I feel like a roll of cotton-wool,—not even medicated. I think, among other things, that a set hour is full of peril; what one wants is the sudden desultory talk,—the look-up from the book one is reading, the burst of argument between two regions of silence. The set hour is first-cousin to being presented with an ear-trumpet into which one has to improvise a remark.

All this is to invite your attention to the advantages of Long Barn as a convalescent home.

I enclose a poem in case Leonard would like it.[2]

I do hope I didn't tire you—I was afraid I had.[3] If you came here I should leave you alone to the point of neglect. I should realise my responsibility fully—

Vita

Sussex

1. *The Puppet Show of Memory* (1922) was Maurice Baring's autobiography.
2. *On the Lake* (*Nation & Atheneum*, December 26, 1925)
3. Vita had had tea with Virginia on October 19.

❧ *[26? October 1925]* *52 Tavistock Square, W.C.1*

My dear Vita—only it ought to be all execration—

I asked you to LEND *me M.B—Now you* GIVE *him. Very well—I'll never ask you for so much as the loan of a boot button again.*

Nevertheless, your present was perfectly timed—All Friday I was sick without stopping (my own fault—I refused to believe the doctor who said it would stop if I ate a mutton chop—when I did I was cured instantly) but by 6 p.m. I was almost extinct with the horror and then your present came: I ate my chop, revived, and read till I fell asleep. Nothing could have suited better. . . .

L. likes your poem, and is printing it. I like it—I'll tell you why, if you can face another hours torture. You did not tire me: it was enchanting: and next time I would arrange for some silence for you—

Berg

 *Long Barn, Weald,*
Sevenoaks.
Saturday, 31st October [1925]

My dear Virginia

Yes, I thought I should get into a row. My intentions however were quite honourable, until I arrived home to discover that someone had made away with my puppet-show, so I ordered one hoping that you wouldn't notice it came from a shop. I hope that this explanation may earn forgiveness for me, and restore you to that frame of mind in which you might regard my boot-buttons as yours if you stood in need of them.

I was distressed to hear from Sibyl [Colefax] that you were ill again; I had meditated a descent upon you, but that news caused me to change my mind. If you are truly better, and no longer require chops, shall I pay you a *brief* visit on Tuesday next between 5. and 6.? I shall be driving Harold about, while he makes his little round of farewells, and while he is in your romantic neighbourhood I could come in for a minute. A postcard to 182

Ebury Street, where I go on Monday, will find me. But not if you are not well.

Leave it as open as you like about coming here. I shall be here till December 20th. I would love you to come, as you know; I can't say more—

Yours ever
Vita

Sussex

December 1925–January 1926

On December 17, Virginia went to stay for three days with Vita at Long Barn (Harold being in Teheran), and their love affair began—without alarm, it seems, on Virginia's side, nor guilt on Vita's. Vita hinted at it in letters to Harold but lied when challenged by friends like Clive Bell. Leonard, who soon became aware of what was happening, did not interfere, and joined them at Long Barn on December 19. During the next few weeks Vita and Virginia met often, first at Charleston, Vanessa Bell's house near Rodmell, and thereafter in London until Vita's departure for her first visit to Persia.

Long Barn.
Tuesday 8th December [1925]

My dear Virginia

I have been doing something so odd, so queer,—or rather, something which though perhaps neither odd nor queer in itself, has filled me with such odd and queer sensations,—that I must write to you; (The thing, by the way, was entirely connected with you, and wild horses won't drag from me what it was.) And high time, too, that I did write.[1] I meant to come and see you last Friday, but the fog and a variety of complaints prevented me. I was furious. Next morning I had to come home early. I motored down. Everything was white; and the hedges looked as though they had grown old in the night. Everything glistened and was still; the whole country was like Sleeping Beauty's park. Now it has all gone, and there is only slush.

May I come and see you on Monday 21st? which is my nearest London date.

I *never* said you were cruel. You must have been answering someone else's letter when you wrote to me. (I suspect you of dozens of correspondents.) I did say "esteem." But I meant "love." Only I was afraid of getting snubbed. You see you have only to be a little testy with me to get the truth.

I contrast my illiterate writing with your scholarly one, and am ashamed.

So dull, I am; dull outwardly, at least; all oafish and muddy; but not dull inside. A week's solitude restores me to the sense that I am a person and not a rag-heap for other people to pick over.

I got an advertisement addressed in your handwriting this morning, which gave me a shock. I thought it was a letter, till I turned it over and saw it was only a postcard,—and printed at that—Why do you address advertisements? Has it a hypnotic effect on you? I can think of no other reason why you should do it.

A mine seems to have exploded under all my friends, blowing them first sky-high, and then peppering them down neatly in various distant places: one in Sumatra, another in Mexico, a third in India, myself in Persia. All this quite suddenly. Can you see me and Raymond [Mortimer] in the Syrian hills together?[2] No, of course not. Yet so it will be. I have become a planet-snob—drunk with journeying.

This makes me savour my last days here all the more keenly.

May I, too, like the school girls, be told how to read a book?[3] I am in such a temper with Proust.

Yours,
Vita

Berg

1. On December 7, Virginia had written in her diary that she was feeling depressed. "It is partly that devil Vita. No letter. No visit. No invitation to Long Barn. She was up last week and never came."
2. Raymond Mortimer joined Harold and Vita in Teheran in April 1926.
3. Virginia's lecture, given to a girls' school at Hayes Common on January 30, 1926, was published as *How Should One Read a Book?* (*Yale Review*, October 1926).

❧ *Wednesday [9 December 1925]* *[52 Tavistock Square, W.C.1]*

My dear Vita,

The dr. says I may go away. Would you like me to come to you for a day or two, if you are alone, before the 20th? I expect this is too late and too difficult; I only suggest it on the off chance. . . .

Berg

❧ *Thursday [10 December 1925]* *52 Tavistock Sqre, WC[1]*

My dear Vita,

Would Tuesday afternoon suit you?
Should I stay till Friday or Saturday?
Should Leonard come and fetch me back?
Should you mind if I only brought one dressing gown?
Should I be a nuisance if I had breakfast in bed?

Berg

Long Barn, Weald,
Sevenoaks.
15th December [1925]

My dear Virginia

I am so sorry to have put you off till Wednesday, but I had a sick servant. It will be all right tomorrow. Will you come by the train you mentioned? 4.18 at Sevenoaks, I think.

Yes you can have breakfast lunch and dinner in bed if you feel like it.

Yes bring a dressing gown.

Yes let Leonard come whenever he likes.

What a pity you can't stay till Sunday—as I am going up on Sunday morning and it would have been nice to have taken you up—

It will be a great joy to have you. I will look after you very well, and you shan't be bothered by anybody.

Yours ever
Vita.

Berg

❧ *Tuesday, Dec. 22nd [1925]* *52 Tavistock Square, W.C.1*

I am dashing off to buy, a pair of gloves. I am sitting up in bed: I am very very charming; and Vita is a dear old rough coated sheep dog: or alternatively, hung with grapes, pink with pearls, lustrous, candle lit, in the door of a Sevenoaks draper. I'll ask Nessa whether Saturday or Sunday [at Charleston] and write to Knole. But do not snuff the stinking tallow out of your heart—poor Virginia to wit, and Dog Grizzle (who is scratching under my bed) Now for a Bus down Southampton Row.

Ah, but I like being with Vita.

Berg

Knole,
Sevenoaks,
Kent.
Christmas-eve [1925]

Virginia, dear and lovely,

Saturday be it,[1] with this sole reservation: that IF by any evil chance my mother should have asked people to lunch that day, I must come to you after lunch only; but this is as unlikely as it would be unfortunate. I wrote to ask her, but thanks no doubt to Xmas I've had no reply. I will appear at about 1. and *please* remember that your household will alarm me exceedingly—except Clive—who is a refuge—

I shall be oh so glad to see you again. So glad, that it makes me incapable of writing to you now. I must write you either a long letter, or else a note to say I will come to lunch. ("Damn you then, Vita, why not let it be the long letter?")

V.

Berg

1. Virginia had invited Vita to lunch at Charleston (Vanessa's house) on December 26. The others present were Clive Bell, Duncan Grant, and Vanessa's three children, Julian, Quentin, and Angelica.

Sherfield Court,
Sherfield Upon Loddon,
Basingstoke.
1st January 1926

My darling Virginia

I write to you in a state of extreme perturbation—I'll tell you why, when I see you.[1]

I was taken off my guard.

It's early morning in the new year.

I'll write you a proper letter—but I am upset now—It is Clive who is responsible.

The house is full of children[2] and noise.

Your bewildered
Vita

Berg

1. Sherfield Court was Dorothy [Dottie] Wellesley's country house in Hampshire where Vita was spending the New Year. Clive Bell, another guest, asked Vita whether she and Virginia had slept together. Vita firmly denied it.
2. Valerian and Elizabeth Wellesley, Benedict and Nigel Nicolson

Sherfield Court,
Sherfield Upon Loddon,
Basingstoke.
[3 January 1926]

It might seem strange, at first sight, that I should have talked of you so little, having thought of you so much. I had, after all, Clive at my elbow,—not merely your brother-in-law, but an authority who had loved you in his day,—yet I chose not to profit by his presence. Something kept me back; and now of course I regret the missed opportunity. No, that's not true: I don't. If I had the last three days over again, I should do the same.

I think I prefer making my own explorations. Also I don't fancy the idea of taking a false advantage.

I was rather indiscreet, all the same.

The conversation last night was free. I don't know what you would have thought, or what contributed. I wondered several times. I wondered also what report Clive would give you, if any. Can I see you on Wednesday? afternoon? I have asked for an appointment to be inoculated (damn it) at 5. I put it off as late as possible, because I suppose I must go home directly afterwards, mustn't I? This inoculation nonsense makes me furious.

Such a lot of noisy children here, banging about the house. My head whirls with them.

Keep some more circulars for me to put into envelopes. I was very happy doing this on your floor. Or if it is fine we might go to the aquarium and look at the fish who are, after all, so like one's friends.

And it's on Wednesday fortnight that I go [to Persia]. Melancholy descends on me; but perhaps it's a good thing. What effect does absence have on you? Does it work like the decreasing charm of Dog Grizzle, which endears her to you the more?

I hope so, otherwise . . .

V

Berg

Tuesday [5 January 1926] *[52 Tavistock Square, W.C.1]*

Yes, my dear Creature, do come tomorrow, as early as possible . . . and we'll stick stamps or see fish—But I want to know why *you were perturbed, and wrote in such a whirl, and* what *your fire talk was about—oh and crowds of things.*

But I'm in a rush—have just taken Grizzle to a vet. in the Grays Inn Rd. and now must dash off—Ah, if you want my love for ever and ever you must break out into spots on your back. . . .

Berg

❧ *Thursday [7 January 1926]* *[52 Tavistock Square, W.C.1]*

This is simply to ask how you are. . . . Feeling very miserable, half asleep, taking a little tea and toast, and then, I daresay, towards evening becoming rather luminous and remote, and irresponsible. All this takes place in a room in the middle of Knole—What takes place in all those galleries and ballrooms, I wonder? And then, what goes on in Vita's head, lying under her arras somewhere, like a tiny kernel in a vast nut?

. . . But tell me what you are feeling? Are you aching? And if you were asked, do you like Canute [Vita's elkhound], Canute's wife, or Virginia best, what would you say?

I left a rain coat, a crystal ruler, a diary for the year 1905, a brooch, and a hot water bottle somewhere—Either Long Barn or Charleston—and so contemplate complete nudity by the end of the year.

Berg

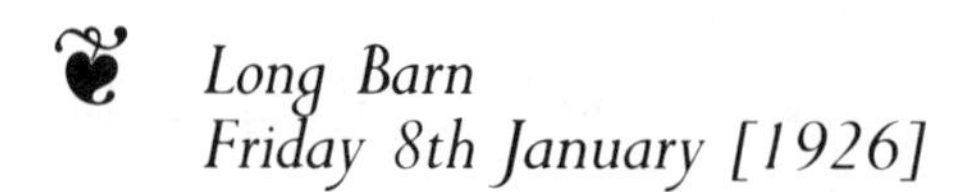

You angel, to have written. And I like your attitude towards illness: "luminous and remote," where most people would have said "hot and sticky." I had (and have) a damned sore arm, but otherwise I didn't disenjoy the Asiatic plagues [inoculations]. I lay in an immense bed, with firelight flickering on the ceiling, and read a book by a theosophist. He had it revealed to him, by psychometry that the Pyramids and Stonehenge, far from having been built by a mere Cheops and mere Druids, were really the work of occult survivors from the Atlantean continent, after the final disappearance of their country in 11,500 B.C. And did they employ anything so gross as mechanical resources? no! Not for them were the cranes and levers of the barbarous Egyptians. Standing beside the Nile, or in the middle of Salisbury Plain, they moved granite blocks or trilithons by the simple expedient of mesmerically depriving them of weight; in other words, they levitated. So next time you go to Stonehenge you may picture this little group of Atlantean "adepts" standing by, while tons of stone slowly rose of their own accord, floated feather-wise in the air, and finally settled themselves across the uprights already raised for their reception.

Eddy [Sackville-West] limped into my room, wasted away to a

ghost, and limped out again, back to bed. He had had a visit from the devastating Tomlin[1]—Will Tomlin devastate Virginia? and precisely how susceptible is Virginia? this is a thing I should very much like to know. Oh what a lot of *little* things there are in life: Xmas boxes for the postman, wages for the gardener; and tonight Boy Scouts, good God. The black baby is still here. I was right when I foresaw that I had him for ever. And in all these little things, where's the place for poetry? And I have cut my finger, and my handkerchief is all bloody, and I can't blow my nose.

Please, in all this muddle of life, continue to be a bright and constant star. Just a few things remain as beacons: poetry, and you, and solitude. You see that I am extremely sentimental. Had you suspected that?

Christ, how vaccination tickles. What I would give for a good scratch.

I must go back to Knole. I get the illusion of living here; my sitting-room unaltered, and no one but my old Louise [Genoux, maid] bundling about. It is difficult to remember that one is a straw whirling down a drain.

Why does one ever read anybody but Shakespeare? He is coming to Persia with me,—complete works.

Hot-water bottle: not here.

Diary: not here.

Brooch: I must ask my maid [Louise] who is at Knole.

Rain-coat: not here.

Crystal ruler: not here—

Italian note book: here, and rescued, and shall be brought on Tuesday.[2]

Somebody sent Ben an unexpurgated edition of Gulliver for Xmas. He had read most of it before I discovered. It was disguised as a child's book. What is to be done?

Oh dear, I must go. Bother.

V.

Poor Canute, his feelings would be so terribly hurt if I answered your question truthfully, that loyalty forbids me. Are you coming to Clive's farewell party on the 18th?

Berg

1. Garrow Tomlin, who was killed flying in 1931, aged thirty-three, was the elder brother of Stephen Tomlin the sculptor, who did a bust of Virginia in 1931.
2. The 1905 "diary" was found elsewhere and is now in the Berg Collection.

Saturday [9 January 1926] *[52 Tavistock Square, W.C.1]*

Isn't it damned? Here I am in bed with the flu, caught the moment I'd written to you about the delights of fever. Hot and sticky describes it. . . .

But it is a great comfort to think of you when I'm not well—I wonder why. Still nicer—better to see you. So I hope for Tuesday. . . .

A very nice dumb letter from you this morning. Tell me about the Boy Scouts?

Berg

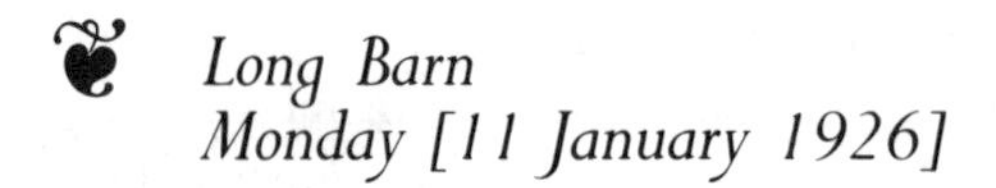

Long Barn
Monday [11 January 1926]

Oh my poor dear, ill again, and the novel [1] thwarted—How maddening for you. I have a great deal to say. Firstly that I don't care a damn, not a little row of pins, whether I catch it [influenza] or not; I'd travel all the way to Egypt with the fever heavy upon me sooner than not see you—so rule that out please. Secondly that not for all the world would I tire you; so if you want to lie in a miserable heap, alone, just say so. I'll ring up at luncheon time tomorrow, and you can say "Come" or "Go to Hell" as you feel inclined. Thirdly, I am glad you are not susceptible to the mind, for otherwise you would find mine but a dingy thing. (I have just lunched, off a veal cutlet and cabbage, divinely cooked by Louise, with Mrs. Dalloway open on my knee, and am consequently in a mood of intellectual humility.) Fourthly, the Tomlin who went to see Eddy was not the right one [Stephen], but his brother. Fifthly, my letters are not dumb, but vociferous: it is you who do not know how to read. And you presume to lecture to schoolgirls on this subject! Sixthly, that letters are the devil, disregarding Einstein and being subservient to so fallacious a thing as time, e.g. if you write to me in Persia and say you have got the ague it is no use my writing back to say I'm so sorry, because by the time you get it you'll have recovered, whereas if I write from the Weald you'll still be wretched when you get it and my condolence will be of some slight grain of use, but *my* feelings will be the same, whether in Persia or the Weald. Seventhly that I have got to give a lecture in Sevenoaks tonight and have LOST IT. Eighthly that I find life altogether intoxicating,—its pain no less than its pleasure,—in which Virginia plays no mean part.

The Boy Scouts were adorable, with their little pink bare knees and eager eyes. And Knives stuck into their belts.[2]

And I have such a lot to do—and I know perfectly well that I shall slip away without doing it, and in May I shall come back to find Ossa piled upon Pelion, and the salmon-like fecundity of neglected duty busily at work.

I know I had lots more to say, but I forget.

How do you manage to keep your head at all, in the exciting life you lead?

Now I must go and talk to the gardener [Barnes]. He has a moustache like a walrus.

Eddy and I talked emotionally till one o'clock last night.

I am glad you are not bad (if that is true.) You will be truthful on the telephone tomorrow?

V.

Berg

1. Virginia's *To the Lighthouse*
2. A Scout Jamboree in the park at Knole

 *66 Mount Street*
W.1.
[13 January 1926]

How are you today? I am all right—No

Are you all right, my dear? I don't like your being ill.

I am just off to acquire a fresh dose of the plagues [inoculations].

I made a mistake: Clive's party is the night before I have to take my children to the play. So, so far as I am concerned, there is no reason why he shouldn't have his party at 10.30. Will you tell him, if you feel you are able to come?

There is a packet of Zoo tickets lying on this writing table—I have amused myself by altering "adult" to "adulterer" on each.

I'll write from Brighton. This is just to ask how you are,—oh yes, and I had a letter from you this morning, which you had sent to Ebury Street—

Your faithful Towser doesn't like your being ill—

It was nice yesterday,—wasn't it?

I'll see you on Monday? and Tuesday? And then no more for months. . . .

V.

Sussex

❧ *Friday [15 January 1926]* *[52 Tavistock Square, W.C.1]*

Dearest Creature,

I saw Clive yesterday, who says will you and Leonard and I dine with him on Monday at the Ivy? If you cant, (as I fear) come to his rooms as soon as you can—We will come at 10.30, but I suppose I shan't be allowed to stay late.

Berg

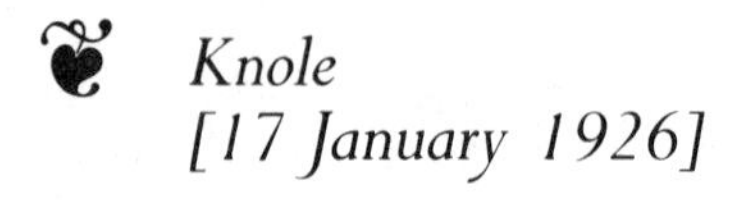

Snow means such special things to me. It means a fat soft plop, plop, as it is shovelled off the roofs and falls into the courtyard below. It means the strange melancholy halloo by which the deer are called to be fed, and which brings them bounding from all corners of the park. It means these things in an intimate way, like the ticking of the clock in one's own room means something; and is part of one.

I *was* dining out tomorrow, but have quite cynically chucked, so I can dine with you (with Clive I mean) at the Ivy. So you see that if my letters are dumb, my actions aren't. They are a practical demonstration of my wish to be with you. Will you tell Clive? Eddy is very anxious to come to Clive's party. He will be staying with Raymond [Mortimer]. May he? I said I would ask.

I hope Clive's version didn't differ materially from mine, otherwise it is clear that one or the other is breaking the ninth commandment. And did your answer differ from mine? alas no.

Such a fuss here. The luggage all plastered with labels. Things scattered all over the room. And Eddy chattering while I try to remember what I have to pack. "Do you know Tom Eliot?" "No, I don't.—Kodak films, aspirin, fur gloves, tooth powder." "Aren't the woodcuts in the Anatomy of Melancholy *too* lovely!" "No, Eddy, I think they're quite awful.—Don't put my riding boots in my suit-case, one doesn't ride on board ship." "Shall I have my sitting room pink or yellow?" And so on. So is my packing conducted. Where is Virginia's quiet room, with the scaffolding outside?

I will come there tomorrow and hide for a bit, say 4.30? but Tuesday too, please, for longer. A message to Vic. 5194 will stop or alter me tomorrow, if you are busy. I shall be at Ebury St. (i.e. Vic 5194) at 10.45 for a minute.

Oh curse, here are people and I must stop as the post goes early. I'm *longing* to see you. Someday I'll write and tell you all the things you mean to me in my mind. Shall I?

V.

Berg

January–February 1926

Vita left London on January 20, bidding good-bye to a disconsolate Virginia on the doorstep at Tavistock Square, and writing her first "Persian" letter in the train to Dover. She was accompanied as far as India by Dorothy Wellesley, but Dorothy is mentioned only three times in the long letters Vita wrote to Virginia from Italy, the Mediterranean, Egypt, Aden, and India itself (which she hated). Then she went on alone by sea through the Persian Gulf (where she fell ill) to Basra, and thence to Baghdad, where she stayed with Gertrude Bell. The onward journey was by car through the snowbound mountains on the Persian frontier, to Kermanshah, where Harold met her and escorted her to Teheran. The whole roundabout journey, described in her book Passenger to Teheran, *had taken six weeks.*

21 Acacia Road
Balham [joke address]
[20 January 1926]

No, it's no good: the train is too shaky to allow me to pretend. I *am* in the train, and there are sensational labels on my luggage—so there it is—and I did leave Virginia standing on her doorstep in the misty London evening—and God knows when I shall see her again. You said one thing which pleased me so much: namely, that you would try not to be in France when I came back. This gave me a real sense of counting in your life. Bless you.

I have got your little Pope in my pocket—and have already presented it instead of my passport. This will happen all along the line—

Oh dear it has all been so bloody—and as for mixed emotions I think I've lived through them all.

Gone, the quiet room with the crane.

Goodbye, my darling; and bless you.[1]

Your
Vita

Berg

1. In her diary of January 19, Virginia wrote: "She is not clever, but abundant and fruitful, truthful too. She taps so many sources of life: repose and variety, was her own expression."

 *Milan [mailed in Trieste]*
Thursday 21st [January 1926]

I am reduced to a thing that wants Virginia. I composed a beautiful letter to you in the sleepless nightmare hours of the night, and it has all gone: I just miss you, in a quite simple desperate human way. You, with all your un-dumb letters, would never write so elementary a phrase as that; perhaps you wouldn't even feel it. And yet I believe you'll be sensible of a little gap. But you'd clothe it in so exquisite a phrase that it would lose a little of its reality. Whereas with me it is quite stark: I miss you even more than I could have believed; and I was prepared to miss you a good deal. So this letter is just really a squeal of pain. It is incredible how essential to me you have become. I suppose you are accustomed to people saying these things. Damn you, spoilt creature; I shan't make you love me any the more by giving myself away like this—But oh my dear, I *can't* be clever and stand-offish with you: I love you too much for that. Too truly. You have no idea how stand-offish I can be with people I don't love. I have brought it to a a fine art. But you have broken down my defences. And I don't really resent it.

However I won't bore you with any more.

We have re-started, and the train is shaky again. I shall have to write at the stations—which are fortunately many across the Lombard plain.

Venice.

The stations were many, but I didn't bargain for the Orient Express not stopping at them. And here we are at Venice for ten minutes only,—a wretched time in which to try and write. No time to buy an Italian stamp even, so this will have to go from Trieste.

The waterfalls in Switzerland were frozen into solid iridescent curtains of ice, hanging over the rock; so lovely. And Italy all blanketed in snow.

We're going to start again. I shall have to wait till Trieste tomorrow morning. Please forgive me for writing such a miserable letter.

V.

Berg

❧ *Tuesday, January 26th, 1926* *52 Tavistock Sqre [W.C.1]*

Your letter from Trieste came this morning—But why do you think I don't feel, or that I make phrases? "Lovely phrases" you say which rob things of reality. Just the opposite. Always, always, always I try to say what I feel. Will you then believe that after you went last Tuesday—exactly a week ago—out I went into the slums of Bloomsbury, to find a barrel organ. But it did not make me cheerful. . . . And ever since, nothing important has happened—Somehow its dull and damp. I have been dull; I have missed you. I do miss you. I shall miss you. And if you don't believe it, your a longeared owl and ass. Lovely phrases? . . .

But of course (to return to your letter) I always knew about your stand-offishness. Only I said to myself, I insist upon kindness. With this aim in view, I came to Long Barn. Open the top button of your jersey and you will see, nestling inside, a lively squirrel, with the most inquisitive habits, but a dear creature all the same—

Berg

❧ *Sunday, Jan. 31st 1926* *The Hogarth Press, 52 Tavistock Square, W.C.1*

Look, I have stolen a piece of the press notepaper to write on, and it is Sunday morning about half past eleven, and I have written all I am going to write this morning. . . . Shall I write the letter I made up in bed this morning? It was all about myself. I was wondering if I could explain how miserable I have been the past 4 days, and why I have been miserable. Thought about, one can gloss things over, bridge them, explain, excuse. Writing them down, they become more separate and disproportioned and so a little unreal—Only I found I had to write the lecture for the girl's school, and so had to stop writing To the Lighthouse. That began my misery; all my life seemed to be thwarted instantly: It was all sand and gravel; and yet I said, this is the truth, this guilty misery, and the other an illusion. . . .

. . . Yes, I miss you, I miss you. I dare not expatiate, because you will say I am not stark, and cannot feel the things dumb people feel. You know that is rather rotten rot, my dear Vita. After all, what is a lovely phrase? One that has mopped up as much Truth as it can hold.

Berg

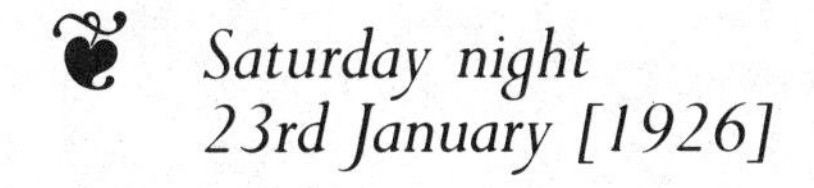

Saturday night
23rd January [1926]

We are somewhere off the coast of Greece, and pretty beastly it is too: very rough, and the boat rolling about like an old tub. She has a deck too many, and consequently is top-heavy. There were a lot of things I wanted to ask you: whether you couldn't invent a new form of type for emphatic passages; a new system of punctuation; whether you shared my preference for the upper berth in a wagon-lit (which I believe to be atavistic,) and my dislike of scraping past the stomachs of Frenchmen on the way to the wagon restaurant; and whether you would one day come on a journey with me? (Dottie says she will give me a good character.) But the elements have put all these things out of my head. You must imagine me please, as sitting up in a small bunk, at an angle of 45°, with my suit-case tobogganing up and down the floor, and all my possessions disappearing under my bed; the ship filled with the clatter of crockery at every lurch; and me trying to write to you. But you see one's whole system of values changes, and the important thing is merely to keep one's balance—

Sunday night. I had to stop writing, it was impossible; and now my eyes are filled with the beauty of Crete struck by a sudden rainbow. But it's still pretty rough, and at one moment today I thought the boat was going to turn turtle, as her sister-ship did on her last voyage. (This encouraging piece of information was given me by a fellow passenger.) I have picked up a young Italian who is more Boccaccio than you can conceive, with golden hair and the figure of a greyhound; he is going to ride through Persia from Bushire through Shiraz and Isfahan, to Teheran, like Marco Polo. A most romantic young man, but very sea-sick poor dear. I shall look forward to seeing him ride into Teheran on a fine April morning.

Have you ever seen Crete? If not, you should.

My dear, I'll write you from Cairo. This is hopeless, and I must go to dinner.

V.

I wrote you a frantic letter from Trieste.

Berg

❧ *Feb. 3rd 1926* *52 Tavistock Square, W.C.1*

Heres a letter from Cairo, I mean from the shores of Greece [Crete], come this morning, a dumb letter; but I'm getting good at reading them. I did like it. And I wrote to you yesterday, to Baghdad, and see that I must write now to catch the mail, to Teheran; so theres no news—Also, you'll be so excited, happy, and all that. You'll have forgotten me, the room, the crane. We cut a very poor show against Teheran. . . .

On Friday (but this will have happened weeks ago) we go to Rodmell. Dearest, how nice to have you there, in a month or two. I made £20 unexpectedly yesterday, and vowed to spend it perfecting the water closet on your bahalf. But Teheran is exciting me too much. I believe, at this moment, more in Teheran than in Tavistock Square. I see you, somehow in long coat and trousers, like an Abyssinian Empress, stalking over those barren hills. But really what I want to know is how the journey went, the 4 days through the snow, the caravan. Shall you write and tell me? And the affectionate letter—whens that coming?

Berg

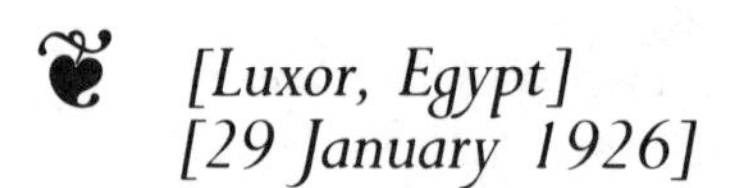

[Picture postcard]

This is the entrance to the tomb of Tut-ankh-amen—or rather to the tomb of Rameses, and that of Tut etc. is below it.

Isn't the scenery superb? They are lion-coloured rocks. Desolation like the mountains of the moon.

V.

2 days ago they found 2 more chambers full of things.

Berg

❦ *Luxor*
29th January [1926]

The only way I can deal with Egypt is as Molly MacCarthy did with Christmas: alphabetically. Amon, Americans, alabaster, Arabs; bromides, buffaloes, beggars, Bronx; camels, crocodiles, colossi, Cook's; donkeys, dust, dahabeeahs, dragomen, dervishes, desert; Egyptians, Evian; fezzes, fellaheen, feluccas, flies, fleas; Germans, goats, granite; hotels, hieroglyphics, hoopoes, Horus, hawks; Isis, imshi, irrigation, ignorance; jibbahs; kites, Kinemas, Kodaks; lavatories, lotus, Levantines; mummies, mud, millionaires; Nubia, Nile; ophthalmia, Osiris, obsidian, obelisks; palms, pyramids, parrakeets; quarries; Ramses, ruins; sunsets, sarcophagi, steamers, soux, sand, shadoofs, stinks, Sphinx; temples, tourists, trams, Tut-ankh-amen; Uganda; vultures, Virginia; water-bullocks, warts; Xerxes, Xenophon; yaout; zest, (my own.) Having said this, there doesn't seem to be anything else to say, except that Mr. Robert Hichens is living in this hotel and that I met him today riding a fiery Arab stallion.[1] But indeed, and there is much more to say, only I can't say it: there is the great untidy desolation of Karnak, and the mountains-of-the-moon landscape of the Theban hills, where I am going to build myself a brown mud house and end my days. And I dined with some super-millionaire Americans, and found The Common Reader in their sitting room. It gave me a shock. There was your name sprawling on the table. They had just arrived from Thibet, where they had dragged forty-seven Innovation trunks and twenty-five pieces of smaller luggage over the spurs of the Himalaya on yaks, an animal which hitherto I believed to exist only in Belloc [Hilaire Belloc, *The Bad Child's Book of Beasts*, 1896]. The Common Reader had been to Thibet with them, and was about to engender copies of all your other works. As they didn't, and still don't, know that I knew you, this was a perfectly unsolicited testimonial.

What else? I miss you horribly, and apart from that am permanently infuriated by the thought of what you could make of this country if only you could be got here. You see, you ought to. However, that sounds too much like your own parody of my probable letters, so I'll refrain from saying it.

What fills me with dismay is the idea that I cannot hear from you till

I get to Bombay, another fortnight at least. I wish I had given you an address at Cairo. You may be ill or anything. It is an odd sensation being so cut-off. And even the clock different. We kept dropping half-hours at sea. What becomes of those poor waifs of one's existence over which one has skipped? Mine are flotsam and jetsam now somewhere on the Adriatic.

Do thin silk clothes and sunburn make you envious? No, you wretch, you prefer your old misty Gloomsbury and your London squares. The wish to steal Virginia overcomes me,—steal her, take her away, and put her in the sun among the objects mentioned alphabetically above. You know you liked Greece. You know you liked Spain. Well, then? If I can get myself to Africa and Asia, why can't you? (But with *me*, please.) I sent you a picture postcard today, just as an insult. I went down into the bowels of the earth and looked at Tut-ankh-amen. At his sarcophagus and outer mummy-case, I mean. This is merely of gilded wood. The inner one is at Cairo, (I saw it,) and is of solid gold. You know, the Valley of the Kings is really the most astonishing place. Tawny, austere hills with a track cut between them; no life at all, not a bird, not a lizard, only a scavenger Kite hanging miles high; and undiscovered Kings lying lapped in gold. And English spinsters in sun-helmets and black glasses. But then I got away from the spinsters and climbed where no one was, and looked down into the Valley on one side, and on to the Nile on the other, a fine contrast in barrenness and fertility; and got into a state of rapture.

You see, I have really got a very cheap mind. (You say you like to know what goes on inside, so I tell you.) If human beings are one-half as exciting to you as natural objects are to me, then indeed I see why you like living in London. I cannot explain why they should have this intoxicating quality. I can quite see why human beings should have. But why the yellow mountains, and the yellower pariah dog with whom I shared my lunch? But there it is. And,—mark you,—I do care so satisfactorily for the few people that matter to me. (For Virginia? oh dear me YES, for Virginia.) Please solve this riddle for me.

I am now going to Karnak.[2] It is full moon, and it quite frightens me to think what it will be like. *Damn* that you're not here.

Your
V.

Berg

1. Robert Hichens (1864–1950), the writer of popular novels, of which the best-known was *Garden of Allah* (1904), spent much of his life traveling in Egypt.
2. The Karnak temple of Amen, just north of Luxor, on the east bank of the Nile

❧ *Feb. 17th 1926* *52 Tavistock Sqre. [W.C.1]*

You are a crafty fox to write an alphabet letter, and so think you have solved the problem of dumbness. . . .

. . . I've been awfully worried by elderly relations. Three old gentlemen, round about 60, have discovered that Vanessa is living in sin with Duncan Grant, and that I have written Mrs Dalloway—which equals living in sin. Their method of showing their loathing is to come to call, to ask Vanessa if she ever sells a picture, me if I've been in a lunatic asylum lately. Then they intimate how they live in Berkley Sqre or the Athenaeum and dine with—I don't know whom: and so take themselves off. Would this make you angry?

. . . Do you know it was 4 weeks yesterday that you went? Yes, I often think of you, instead of my novel; I want to take you over the water meadows in the summer on foot, I have thought of many million things to tell you. Devil that you are, to vanish to Persia and leave me here! . . . And, dearest Vita, we are having two *waterclosets made, one paid for by Mrs Dalloway, the other by The Common Reader: both dedicated to you.*

Berg

S.S. Rajputana
In the Red Sea
4th February [1926]

My darling Virginia

I feel as though I should like to write you a long letter. An endless letter. Pages and pages. But there is too much to say. Too many emotions, and too much Egypt, and too much excitement. And really it all reduces itself to the perfectly simple thing that I wish you were here.

You see it is so easy for you sitting in Tavistock Square to look inward; but I find it very difficult to look inward when I am also looking at the coast of Sinai; and very difficult to look at the coast of Sinai when I am also looking inward and finding the image of Virginia everywhere.

So this combination makes my letter more dumb than usual.

You manage things better. You have a more tidily sorted mind. You have a little compartment for the Press, and another little compartment for Mary Hutchinson,[1] and another for Vita, and another for Dog Grizzle, and another for the Downs, and another for London fogs, and another for the Prince of Wales, and another for the lighthouse [*To the Lighthouse*],—no, I'm wrong, the lighthouse is allowed to play its beam over the whole lot,—and their only Common Denominator is your own excitability over whichever compartment you choose to look into at the moment. But with me they all run together into a sort of soup.

Ever since I left England I've been like a person in an advanced stage of intoxication. Cocktails made not of gin and vermouth, but of thrill and misery, adventure and homesickness. So I can't write you a tidy letter.

And so many people, too. The young man who wants one to play deck tennis. The young woman who wants one to take a ticket in a sweepstake. The Captain who wants one to sit at his table. (Avoided, this, so far. But only by dint of starving and remaining absent from meals. And now, like a beleaguered city, we're on the point of capitulation.) There is all one's luggage, too: the extra bits one has brought because one couldn't re-pack one's belongings into their original boxes; and then the American millionaires gave me a gramophone, and a refrigerator. And then pictures in the mind of things seen, like photographs pushed higgledy-piggledy into a drawer, waiting to be stuck into an album, in that pathetically optimistic way old photographs have. And pictures of things not yet seen,—India, Agra, Baghdad, snow mountains,—negatives not yet developed. All this is very confusing. And the solid, known life of England, which is at one and the same time a fact that one can bang about, and a vision as fantastic as the actual distant shores of Arabia.

We returned from Luxor to Cairo with the train on fire; the dining car blazing merrily behind us like the tail of a comet. Nobody seemed to mind, except my beautiful Bedouin, who lingered for comfort round the door of my compartment until in self-defence I went to bed. It was a nice scene for Virginia: the long slim white train pulled up in the night, and flames licking out from under the carriage, and a crowd of dark men throwing buckets of water. I talked to the engine driver; a tiny black man in a scarlet turban. He said it was a single line, and that as there was another train due we should probably run into it. He said also that robbers were in the habit of putting boulders on the line, but that he never took any notice of these, but drove full speed at them, lest by pulling up he should be accused of complicity with the robbers. I had a lingering regret for the South-Eastern.[2]

Feb. 6th. I have no brain left. It has melted. I am sticky from head to foot. And I have made friends with a Parsee who specialises in Persian, and has determined that I should become proficient in the language before I reach Bombay. So I'm having a wretched time,—kept at work as hard as a schoolboy, and no brain to do it with. I like the night-sky, though, with the stars getting bigger and bigger, and odder and odder, and the phosphorus in the water.

The rest of the time I read Proust. As no one on board has ever heard of Proust, but has enough French to translate the title, I am looked at rather askance for the numerous volumes of Sodome et Gomorrhe which litter the decks.

But why did he take 10 pages to say what could be said in 10 words?

Near Aden. Your faithful Towser is extremely sticky. A vile climate: very hot, very relaxing, with a strong hot wind.

It transpires that my Parsee is High Priest Designate of all the Parsees in India, and is on his way home to take up the duties of his high office. He is taking me ashore at Aden, where I'll post this. I greatly prefer his sister, who has an olive skin and gazelle eyes; but there it is: the High Priest is bent on making the most of his last secular days, and dogs my footsteps.

Oh my dear Virginia. Is there really a London? and are you in it? or am I thinking of, and writing to, a wraith? Don't get ill. Be severe with *les importuns*. How is the novel? Blown by this hot gale, I can't write a word. But I hope my little granary is filling up, under the Southern Cross. If I don't get a letter from you at Bombay, I shall die of disappointment—

My love to Leonard.

V.

Berg

1. With whom Clive Bell was having a love affair
2. The railway that served Kent and Sussex from London

❧ *March 1st, 1926* — *52 Tavistock Sqre [W.C.1]*

Yes, dearest Towzer, it is all very well about Bloomsbury being a rotten biscuit, and me a weevil, and Persia being a rose and you an Emperor moth—I quite agree: but you are missing the loveliest spring there has ever been in England. We were motored all through Oxfordshire two days ago. . . .

The people who took us were Leonards brother and his wife. I promptly fell in love, not with him or her, but with being stock brokers, with never having read a book (except Robert Hitchens [sic]*) with not having heard of Roger, or Clive, or Duncan, or Lytton. Oh this is life, I kept saying to myself; and what is Bloomsbury, or Long Barn either, but a contortion, a temporary knot; and why do I pity and deride the human race, when its lot is profoundly peaceful and happy? . . .*

I've arranged our French motoring so that we shall be back by May 10th. So please see to it that you land that day. A lovely dumb letter from you came on Saturday, written on board ship. I extract by degrees a great deal from your letters. They might be longer; They might be more loving. But I see your point—life is too exciting. . . .

Berg

S. S. Rajputana
In the Indian Ocean
8th February [1926]

Such an absurd day at Aden yesterday: tearing across salt-marshes in a small open motor, in a hot gale; cyclones of dust; hundreds of tiny windmills madly spinning; salt-heaps in rows like the tents of a regiment; tunnels under hills; empty tanks of a hundred-million-gallon capacity, (there are no springs, and it hasn't rained there for 10 years;) small black boys at the bottom of the tanks, like bears at the Zoo at the bottom of the Mappin Terraces, beating their stomachs and crying reverberatingly "No father, no mother, thank you"; Scotch soldiers in kilts; then Aden again, and [caged] lions suddenly in the middle of a Ford lorry garage; and tea with an old Parsee in cool rooms over an apothecary's shop. Pure Conrad, this: the merchant-prince of Aden in a shiny black cap, and shrewd eyes twinkling behind owlish glasses. A photograph of the King on the table. Bunches of herbs strung up to keep illness and misfortune from the house. Photograph groups of Parsee generations. Ledgers; a globe; models of ships. A dark young secretary in a suit of white duck. Sweet biscuits. Talk of cargoes for Somaliland. And Aden lying outside, swept by its hot wind, the most god-forsaken spot on earth. And then a motor-launch, and the ship again, with gulls and hawks wheeling together above the refuse, and sellers of shells bobbing round in tiny canoes, and the Resident coming on board.[1] And then the steaming out into the night, and no more land ahead for two thousand miles, and the self-contained life of the ship closing round one once more.

The Indian ocean is grey, not blue; a thick, opaque grey. Cigarettes are almost too damp to light. At night the deck is lit by arc-lights, and people dance; it must look very strange seen from another ship out at sea,—all these peple twirling in an unreal glare, and the music inaudible. One's bath, of sea-water, is full of phosphorus: blue sparks that one can catch in one's hand. The water pours from the tap in a sheet of blue flame. The parties of Proust gain in fantasy from being read in such circumstances, (I don't mean in the bath, but on deck;) they recede, achieve a perspective; they become historical almost, like Veronese banquets through which flit a few masked Longhi figures, and ruffled by the uneasy impish breeze of French Freud. I re-enter their company after struggling with the Persian irregular verbs. My own poem [*The Land*] on the other hand has ceased to have any existence for me at all: it seems just silly. I thought I should be able to stand back and look at it; but no: it is crammed right-up against my nose, and I can't see it at all. Mme de Guermantes [Proust] and Khwastanrasi alone have reality.

But by the time I come home I shall have written a book, which I hope will purge me of my travel-congestion, even if it serves no other purpose.[2] The moment it is released, it will pour from me as the ocean from the bath-tap,—but will the blue sparks come with it, or only the blanket-grey of the daytime sea? (By the way, I have discovered since beginning this letter that one can draw pictures on oneself with the phosphorus; it's like having a bath in glow-worms; one draws pictures with one's fingers in trails of blue fire, slowly fading.)

For the rest, it is a perpetual evading of one's fellow-beings. Really what odd things grown-up, civilised human beings are, with their dancing and their fancy-dress, (Charles I stalking the deck with his head under his arm like an umbrella,) and their sports, and their blind man's buff, and an indignant [Dorothy] Wellesley being forced to give away prizes. ("Really I do think it's a little hard that because I happened to marry Gerry[3] I should have to make a fool of myself on a P. & O.") But I come up on deck at dawn when there is no one about but a stray Lascar cleaning brasses, and watch the sun rising straight ahead, out of the east, and the sky and sea are like the first morning of Genesis. This is all before the hearty clergymen are awake, or the people who approach and say they think they know one's aunt. (Why have aunts so many friends?)

I expect you think this is a dumb letter. It is rather. But of such things life is made at present. Everything else has been stripped away, and one remains a sponge, just drinking things up. What will happen when it's all over, do you think? What would happen to *you*, I wonder chiefly, if you could be so thoroughly disturbed out of Bloomsbury? my greatest desire at present is to try that experiment. Also I want nine lives at least,—another desire. And nine planets to explore. You have no idea how silly the tiny refinements of introspection can become.

If all this happens on a mere passage to India, what oh what is going to happen to poor Vita when she reaches the heart of Asia?

Perhaps some sense of selection will blessedly return, to order the traffic, like an archangel, or a policeman.

We have crept onward a few hundred miles since I began this letter, and the sun has come tropically out, and the clergymen have put on their sun-helmets. Tomorrow I shall be bouncing across India in a dusty train.

Have you quite forgotten this poor pilgrim? I haven't forgotten that I am to tell you I think of you, but I think that will be a nice occupation for the Persian Gulf. In the meantime I think of you a terrible great deal. You make a wonderful cynical kindly smiling background to the turbulence of my brain. Shall I find a letter from you at Bombay I wonder?

I don't mind if you do laugh at me—

Your
V.

Berg

1. Aden was a British protectorate, under the control of the viceroy of India.
2. Vita's travel book, *Passenger to Teheran,* was published by the Hogarth Press in November 1926.
3. Lord Gerald Wellesley (afterward seventh duke of Wellington). They separated in the mid 1920s.

Delhi
14th February [1926]

We arrived at Bombay at four in the morning; it was the silence that woke me, acclimatised as I was to noise. After four days of blank ocean, there was suddenly a harbour, ringed with lights, and pale colours beginning behind the hills. We were still moving when I looked out, though the engines were shut off; we were gliding quite silently across a black mirror of water. At first I couldn't think where we were. After four days of ocean one forgets about the land. And Aden, two thousand miles away, was the last land I had seen. Since then there had seemed no particular reason to believe we were making for one place rather than for another, or indeed for any place at all. Still more miraculous did it seem,—when one came to think of it,—that out of the immensity of ocean one should hit off one small particular spot of land. Then I got a stab: India!

Well, I had India to myself for a couple of hours, while the stars paled and the dawn spread over it; and then the usual row began, and I met the Parsee in the customs house looking very foolish with a garland of white waxen flowers round his neck, over his *petit complet gris-perle*, like a sacrificial heifer. And I went for my letters, but there was none from you, which blackened India until I remembered that I had told you to write to Rocky Hill Flats—We drove there for breakfast, and although the rooms were cool and creamy, with the windows open on the sea, and punkahs stirring the air, and great jars of oleander everywhere, still there were no letters. And as I had been counting on that letter for at least three weeks, the delicious fruits that I was given for breakfast might have been handfuls of dust for all I cared. But then suddenly a black servant (whose name appeared to be Vita,) entered with armfuls of correspondence. And of course there was quite a simple explanation, that your letter had travelled with me on the Rajputana. So I sat in the window above the bay and read it, and below me was a Hindu burning-ground with a cremation in full progress, and beyond that the sea, and behind me Irene Forbes Adam[1] nursing her fortnight-old baby,—a sight that you would have appreciated.

You will agree that it was a pretty setting for your letter to be read in, that had been written in the dark north—and frightened out of its life in a mail-bag down in the hold of a ship? Poor little thing, if I had known that it lay cowering there, I would have rescued it. But no; the seals of the G.P.O. are inviolable, (like Virginia.) It is nevertheless an odd sensation to peer down into the hold, to see the brown mail-bags lying there higgledy-piggledy, with bits of names appearing: NDIA, or YLON, or PER, as I saw those in the Rajputana, and to reflect that therein hides a letter which will someday come into one's own hands. It is a sensation of the same family as that which you experienced when you wrote to me knowing that I had but five minutes earlier left your doorstep, or as one experiences when one writes a letter, designed to be found on arrival, to a person who is still in the house, or the very room, with one.

But to return to your letter—I cannot believe that any absurdity of mine blossoms in your mind,—except that you are truly a picture-maker,—I wish I could believe it more, for I might then translate to you a few of the seeds which have fallen on my own mind and promise to grow into a banyan-tree—(observe the local colour of the horticultural image.) Only, if I do so, you must not be pained and disappointed at meeting those seeds again later on in a more finely developed form! Because I *must* write about all these things, and naturally my stock is not infinite, though rich. In fact I must write a traveller's tale, when I get to Persia and have a writing table instead of a knee to write on. I was never at my best on my knees. And some chapters will make articles for Leonard,—if he still wishes to have them—

I hope that you have not outgrown the 50 pages of fertility,[2] or else that that intoxicating feeling has accompanied you beyond its usual limit; what I mean is, that, I hope you are still happy about your book, and that birds as varied, as decorative, and as stimulating as the birds of India continue to beat in flocks against the windows of your lighthouse, so that you have to drive them away rather than entice them in. I was terribly pleased when I read that you had been excited, writing. Also terribly envious. And yet I feel, you know, that if I could get really embarked on something I should become excited about it too. But of course there is nothing like a novel for that peculiar thing: as good as conducting an orchestra, or modelling in clay. A sense of really giving shape. Very illusive, too, for I suppose that of all works of art the novel is about the most shapeless—But it is the *life* of fictitious people that gives their author the illusion of shaping; making it out of nothing, like those slates that children rub with a magic pencil, and out of nothingness a picture appears.

Well, I must go to sleep, for I am spending 4 out of 6 nights in the train, and had another 3. a.m. arrival last night,—this time at Agra, where at the sleeping hotel we were greeted by two men with spears. Why spears? But then why anything, indeed? One very quickly ceases to think anything out-of-the-way.[3] Dottie, who is a romantic and has romantic ideas about India (which I'm glad to say are rapidly dissolving under the beams of experience,) is trying to shake snakes out of her shoes. But the only snake I've seen so far was a poor dear drugged old python, wound in comfortable somnolence round the neck of a charmer. He blew into a little gourd which made a noise like a punctured bag-pipe. The python took no notice at all.

The tree-rats are very sweet. Like tiny green squirrels. I tried to catch one, and it bit me. Not like Virginia, who has inquisitive habits, but is a dear creature, and for whom I have a terrible and chronic homesickness. It is a persistent complaint,—sortes virginiana.

Your
V.

Sussex

1. She was the wife of Colin Forbes-Adam, an employee of the Indian Civil Service, and in 1926 secretary to the governor of Bombay. She was then thirty-six. Vita had known her since childhood, when she was Irene Lawley. Her son Desmond was born on January 27, 1926.
2. Virginia had written to Vita: "I have been very excited writing. I have never written so fast" (*To the Lighthouse*).
3. See Dorothy Wellesley's account of this journey in *Far Have I Travelled* (1952).

S.S. Varela
At sea.
[In the Persian Gulf]
20th February [1926]

So many strange faces have floated up at me since I last wrote to you, faces of animals and of men; buffaloes and Hindus, horned or turbaned; faces of Eurasians, oddly wrong; faces of young soldiers. Faces of monkeys in the trees; of a dead but still sacred cow lying in the road; of an all-but dead Babu flung almost into our cab from his bicycle. Then stations,—little noisy jabbering stations which I shall never see again, and flashed through once, or perhaps snatched an orange at. Jungle on either side of the train; rocks looking like mediaeval castles; peacocks paddling in the village pond. Roads tracked in the dust, seen from train windows, leading where? A jackal staring in the scrub. An English general. The Taj Mahal like a pure and sudden lyric. And everywhere squalor, squalor, squalor. Children's eyes black with flies. Men with sores. Mangy dogs. Filthy hovels not fit for pigs. And a bridge that was a concourse of men and animals and carts, all shoving, huddling, shouting, as our motor clove its way through like a snow-plough. Noise and squalor, squalor and noise everywhere.

Then there was a deserted city, which was a pool of miraculous silence; the abandoned capital of the Moghul emperors, inhabited only by monkeys, goats, parrots, and tree-rats.[1] On the height is the vast red palace of Akbar, and, in a courtyard, the tiny red house of his Poet! And views over miles of country,—India, apparently uninhabited too, in spite of its 320 millions. But they are the same colour as the earth, so they don't show up. It was very quiet at the deserted city, and aromatic herbs grew in the ruins. It was very hot, and a naked man dived eighty feet from a rampart into a well.

Now I am on a ship again, limping about with two sticks on a sprained ankle; and all last night I had fever and a sore throat, and was quite certain through my nightmares that I should be put ashore at Karachi with diphtheria and left there alone. But today the fever is gone, and the throat better, and I am limping about again as saucily as a jackdaw with a broken leg. There are whales about; they have been spouting. I am all alone, and there is no one on this ship who cares whether I live or die.[2] This is very wholesome, I suppose, and quite all right at 3. o'clock on a sunny afternoon when one feels well, but not so pleasant at 3. in the morning with a temperature of 102, and crippled into the bargain.

There is a Hindu temple appeared now, on a promontory, and the steerage passengers are casting coconuts into the sea towards it; not so much for the sake of using it as a coconut-shy, but as a mark of respect. Just see what funny and charming things drift in and out of life when one travels. You cannot imagine coming round the corner from the Coliseum, and seeing Lady Colefax throwing coconuts at St Martin-in-the-Fields.

But India is a loathesome place, without one shred of any quality, and I never want to go there again. A fortune teller at Luxor, however, told me that Harold would be Viceroy, so perhaps I may yet return. But I fear I should not, in that case, be tolerated by Virginia any longer, so Harold's career will have to be wrecked before it reaches that stage.

I meant to have written such a lot, but somehow I haven't; there is always a whale or a murder to look at, (a tortoise or a theorbo!) so I have written a few letters,—precious few,—and read a lot of Proust, and that's all. But I shall begin now to try and collect myself, and write some articles. I don't know whether to be dejected or encouraged when I read the works of Virginia Woolf. Dejected because I shall never be able to write like that, or encouraged because somebody else can? (I sound rather like the young ladies of Hayes' Common, who wished to model their style upon yours.)

My next letter will be posted at Baghdad and written in the Persian Gulf. It will be all about Virginia. Indeed it may arrive before this one, as it will go part of the way by air.

V.

Sussex

1. Fatehpur Sikri. Vita added a few lines to *The Land* after her visit there: "I have known bees within the ruined arch/Of Akbar's crimson city hang their comb . . ." and used the same scene in her novel *All Passion Spent* (1931).
2. After Agra, Vita and Dorothy Wellesley went to New Delhi, where they met the architect Sir Edwin Lutyens, and saw his half-finished Government House. Dorothy then returned home while Vita continued her journey to Persia alone.

British India Steam Navigation Co., Ltd.
S.S. "Varela"
23rd February [1926]

In how fastidious and amused a grin (like Grizzle's) would your lips curl if you could see me at the present moment. Somewhere off the coast of Baluchistan, lame, and newly risen from three days of fever, I have literally pushed the other passengers (five in number) into each other's arms to dance to my gramophone. They were really too dreary for words; something had to be done about it; so I hauled the gramophone out from under my bunk, and now they are all as merry as crickets. They consist of the chief of police in Karachi, (C.I.E.,[1] and don't you forget it,) a MAJOR from Mosul, the wife of a railway engineer in Baghdad, and a pair of young lovers, avocation unknown. You see, I am so pleased to find that I am *not*, after all, going to die and be buried at sea, swathed in a Union Jack and decently weighted, that I am full of the milk of human kindness towards my fellows. If anyone had told me, quite simply, that new-comers were liable to fever in these parts, I should not have lain envisaging (1) diphtheria (2) dysentery (3) plague (4) scarlet fever alone in my cabin for three days, but according to my all-too insular ideas one does not suddenly shoot up to 103 without good reason. Here, however, apparently one does. I said to myself "Perhaps Virginia will be a little sorry." I wrote to you, in fact, I think, just when it was beginning. I composed telegrams so moving that when I realised I should not have to send them, I was quite disappointed. I thought it was *almost* as good as Rupert Brooke [buried on Skyros in 1915] to be thrown overboard in the Gulf of Oman.* I wondered whether it would make my books sell any better. I feared not.

And now I am quite spry again, and have even written six pages of my new book [*Passenger to Teheran*]. It is a rambling, discursive sort of affair. And I think of your lovely books, and despair.

Why is it that critics pay so little attention to style and surface-texture? It is the last thing you ever see mentioned, whether for good or evil. Either you go in for style or else you don't; the Russians apparently don't, judging by the translation which I somehow feel reproduces pretty exactly the manner of the original; but if you do, then I think you ought to get credit for it. Now you (oh yes, I know I said I would write about Virginia going up the Persian Gulf,) have the mot juste more than any modern writer I know. The only rival I could advance in that particular line would be Max [Beerbohm]. I wonder whether it costs you a lot of thought or trouble, or springs ready-armed like Athene from the brow of Zeus? I don't believe it does cost you trouble (confound you!) because you have it in your letters too, where you certainly haven't made a draught (draft?), and where there is never anything but an impatient scratching or two.

("If yee-ou knee-ou See-ousie,
as I know See-ousie . . ." oh God, why did I ever bring that gramophone on deck?)

But to go back to Virginia and leave Susie. To Virginia herself, and not her God-given style. (Le style c'est la femme?) The funny thing is, that you are the only person I have ever known properly who was aloof from the more vulgarly jolly sides of life. And I wonder whether you lose or gain? I fancy that you gain,—*you*, Virginia,—because you are so constituted and have a sufficient fund of excitement within yourself, though I don't fancy it would be to the advantage of anybody else. I feel with Proust, "Il faut avoir passé par là." You will say you have. But not in precisely the way I mean. (You'll think I'm perpetually trying to pull you down from your pedestal, but really I like you best up there. Only it would be fun to transplant you, pedestal and all, just once . . .)

No, I don't really mean that. What I should really like to do would be to take you to some absurdly romantic place,—vain dream, alas! what with Leonard and the Press—Besides, by romantic I mean Persia or China, not Tintagel or Kergarnec. Oh what fun it would be, and Virginia's eyes would grow rounder and rounder, and presently it would all flow like water from a Sparklets siphon, turned into beautiful bubbles.

But I am writing nonsense, and anyway this letter cannot be posted till Baghdad. So that you will get two together, and that will be a bore.

Goodnight, darling and remote Virginia.

V.

*Oman, not Onan, the person in the Bible who (like the old lady's canary, named after him,) spilled his seed upon the ground.

Berg

1. Companion of the Order of the Indian Empire, a high award for British civil servants in India

❧ *16th March 1926* *52 Tavistock Square, London, W.C.1*

. . . As for the mot juste, *you are quite wrong. Style is a very simple matter; it is all rhythm. Once you get that, you can't use the wrong words. But on the other hand here am I sitting after half the morning, crammed with ideas, and visions, and so on, and can't dislodge them, for lack of the right rhythm. Now this is very profound, what rhythm is, and goes far deeper than words. A sight, an emotion, creates this wave in the mind, long before it makes words to fit it; and in writing (such is my present belief) one has to recapture this, and set this working (which has nothing apparently to do*

with words) and then, as it breaks and tumbles in the mind, it makes words to fit it: But no doubt I shall think differently next year. Then there's my character (you see how egotistic I am, for I answer only questions that are about myself) I agree about the lack of jolly vulgarity. But then think how I was brought up! No school; mooning about alone among my father's books; never any chance to pick up all that goes on in schools—throwing balls; ragging: slang; vulgarity; scenes; jealousies—only rages with my half brothers, and being walked off my legs round the Serpentine by my father. This is an excuse: I am often conscious of the lack of jolly vulgarity but did Proust pass that way? Did you? Can you chaff a table of officers? . . .

Yes, dearest Vita: I do miss you; I think of you: I have a million things, not so much to say, as to sink into you.

Berg

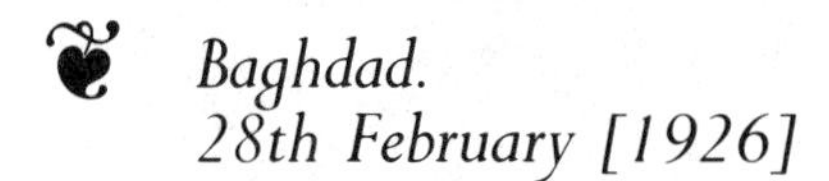

Still limping across Asia you see, I have reached this city of fabulous romance, which is not, believe me, as we saw it in Hassan,[1] but just a merry muddle of donkeys, motors, Arabs, dogs, mud, cabs, and camels. Whips crack, boys shout, pistols go off, cars remain stuck in the mud, enormous bales fall off the back of tiny donkeys and burst in the road,—nothing seems to matter. The mud is such that you would hesitate to drive an ordinary English farm-cart through it—Yet motors career gaily, sliding sideways like crabs; if you stick, everybody pushes, and there you are,—what a pleasant happy-go-lucky life.

Ah, let me see, what have I seen, done, or felt since I last wrote? I was very miserable in the Gulf with incessant fever; then I landed at Basrah, and was carried off by the Consul, and plunged for twenty-four hours into his family life. Kind people, Scotch, living in a big shadowy house; of Mrs Berry it is related that once when the tribes rebelled and the consulate was stormed by wild Arabs bent on murder, her only concern was that she had not had time to bring in the washing. That sums up her whole attitude towards life. Then I learnt all the local gossip, and what I now don't know about the goings-on of Molly Brown and Mirabelle Kernander isn't worth knowing. But one isn't a pilgrim for nothing, and next day I had to leave this kind new home, with its dogs and all, ("We were rather intellectual just then, so we called the dogs after books we had been reading: Tarzan and Bindle,") and start off again across Iraq, which, if it is really the Garden of Eden, then I agree with the Tommy who said it wouldn't need a flaming sword to drive *him* out of it. A yellow plain, strewn with skeletons of animals; a lump on the horizon,—Ur of the Chaldees;[2] another lump,—Babylon, under the moon. And then Baghdad in the early morning, with a little pastoral life charmingly going on in the station yard; a flock of goats browsing off bits of paper between the lines, a couple of tents pitched, a tethered horse; then the Tigris, and a drive through the streets, lurching and pitching; a door in a wall, a garden, pigeons, dogs asleep, a verandah, a cool room, hot water, coffee, Gertrude Bell.[3]

Very kind she is; we went to tea with the King, too, and Lady Colefax came to dinner—or so like as makes no difference. And during the day the overland mail came in, and brought me an evil-looking typed envelope, which I thought could be only a solicitor's dun, but it poured two generous sheets from Virginia into my lap. But you musn't abuse me if by Feb. 2nd you hadn't heard from me from Egypt; remember I only landed there on the 26th. I go into this question, because it alarms me to think that you are one of those who makes no allowance for the poor letter having to travel too, nor for the ever-widening distances.

My heart goes out to you over the hat, and the mattresses, and the impossibility of privacy; I live permanently in that state; but beware: it becomes a mania. It has poisoned my life. I have quarrelled with at least three people because of it. I feel very strongly about it. I go down into precisely those troughs of desperation which you describe. Not so much through shops, which I like, as through the privacy problem. It cuts one's life up into little dice like lumps of sugar,—no, not even that, for they haven't the dignity of a cube; it's just slices, snippets,—and then one is expected to write. One is told that one has had two days undisturbed, when one is feeling like a rag-bag, a waste-paper basket, a dust-heap.

It exhausts the nerves so much less to travel from London to Teheran, than from London to Sevenoaks, or from Tavistock Square to Heal's in the Tottenham Court Road.

I am ordering the Common Reader for my hostess—She already has Jacob's Room. Its yellow face greeted me friendlily at breakfast.

I've bought a dog. The garden here has been filled with dogs that were potentially mine,—all come in from the desert, led on leash by Arabs.

This one is a marvel of elegance,—long tapering paws, and a neck no thicker than your wrist. So off we set together tonight, the sloughi [Saluki] puppy and I, to face the snows in the high passes.

Like a little warm coal in my heart burns your saying that you miss me. I miss you oh so much. How much, you'll never believe or know. At every moment of the day. It is painful but also rather pleasant, if you know what I mean. I mean, that it is good to have so keen and persistent a feeling about somebody. It is a sign of vitality. (No pun intended.)

V.

Sussex

1. A play by James Elroy Flecker (1884–1915), posthumously published, which had been seen by Vita and Virginia in January 1923

2. The Sumerian city, c. 2500 B.C., which was then being excavated by Sir Leonard Woolley. Vita went by train from Basra to Baghdad.

3. The traveler and writer. She was then director of antiquities of Iraq and political adviser to the Iraqi government. Vita stayed with her for four nights. She died four months later, aged fifty-eight, probably by suicide.

March–May 1926

Vita loved Persia, but not the diplomatic life. She did her duty as Harold's wife in the social world of the legations, and helped to organize the coronation of the Shah, which she enjoyed more. She escaped as often as she could to the bazaars and the hills that surrounded Teheran, and paid one extended visit to Isfahan. She made many last additions to The Land, *and wrote a large part of* Passenger to Teheran *in Persia itself. Virginia, who was less adventurous as a traveler, missed her dreadfully but did not envy her. Her loving replies to Vita's letters reached her at long intervals. After four months' absence, Vita returned home by the shorter route through the Caspian, Moscow, Poland, and Germany, and arrived in London on May 16.*

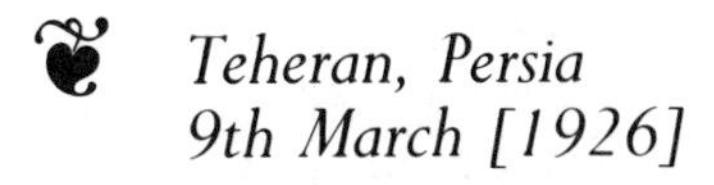

Teheran, Persia
9th March [1926]

You can't think how much I enjoy writing the above address. I have discovered my true function in life: I am a snob. A geographical snob. Every morning when I wake up, with the sun flooding into my white conventual room, I lie bewildered for a minute; then very slowly, like a child rolling toffee round in its mouth, I tell myself "You are in Central Asia." And on the way here, crossing the brown plains, whenever the car stopped I got out, and taking a clod of earth in my hand looked at it and gave it its name: It satisfies my soul as the dissection of the human insect satisfies yours; and so, being satisfied, my soul is not prominent; a great mercy.

Now I shall not tell you about Persia, and nothing of its space, colour, and beauty, which you must take for granted—but please *do* take it for granted, because it has become a part of me,—grafted on to me, leaving me permanently enriched. You smile? Well, I have been stuck in a river, crawled between ramparts of snow, been attacked by a bandit, been baked and frozen alternately, travelled alone with ten men, (all strangers,)[1] slept in odd places, eaten wayside meals, crossed high passes, seen Kurds and Medes in caravans, and running streams, and black lambs skipping under blossom, seen hills of porphyry stained with copper sulphate, snow-mountains in a great circle, endless plains, with flocks on the slopes. Dead camels pecked by vultures, a dying donkey, a dying man. Come to mud towns at nightfall, stayed with odd gruff Scotchmen, drunk Persian wine. Worn a silk dress one day, and a sheepskin and fur cap the next. Met Harold, with letters in his pocket,—two letters from Virginia, which I read first. Been taken to a party, and introduced to about 500 English people, 500 foreign diplomats, and 1000 Persians. Dined with the Prime Minister [Mirza Ferughi], who has a black beard. Began to stammer in Persian. And today's my birthday. [She was thirty-four.]

But all this, as you say, gives no idea at all. How is it that one can *never* communicate? Only imaginary things can be communicated, like ideas, or the world of a novel; but not real experience. I see you very clearly, though, going to Rodmell, and lunching with Eddy; but that's because I know Rodmell and I know Eddy. I should like to see you faced with the task of communicating Persia. How I wish I could bring you here; *couldn't* you and Leonard come next spring? No, of course you won't: what, leave the press? I don't believe Isfahan and Persepolis are any temptation to you. I wish life was three times as long, and every day of it 48 hours instead of 24.

I have got to go to tea with Bridges' daughter;[2] she has married a Persian, and has square red hair and a square white face. I have also met Mrs. Arfa, (Hilda something,—can't remember her name,—Berwick? Bewick?) but she is going to England in 10 days time. Shall you see her? I believe you know her, or anyway she knows all your friends. She is the only attractive person here, but the country makes up for the people; and as you know, I am not good at people. I have to be rushed . . . Oh, and Raymond [Mortimer] is coming. But you must know that.

I'm coming back through the Caucasus. They say it is possible.

I have got England in wonderful focus from here. One sees the people who go out like candles, and those who remain as fixed stars. Such unexpected people float suddenly into one's mind, too, apart from the permanencies. I wish I had a photograph of you. (Has mine ever turned up?) It is a torment not being able to visualise when one wants to. I can visualise you as a matter of fact surprisingly well,—but always as you stood on your door-step that last evening, when the lamps were lit and the trees misty, and I drove away.

There will be a vast gap between the letters I sent from Baghdad and this one, and you will think I have forgotten; but I haven't. The post-bag goes only once a fortnight from here. That in itself makes life different. One had come to take the ordinary conveniences of civilisation so much as a matter of course; but here one hears otherwise ordinary people talking in the mediaeval way of "So-and-so was three weeks on the road," or "Snow has fallen and So-and-so won't get through," or "So-and-so is going to Baghdad and can take letters." All values are altered. Consequently you can imagine the scramble that takes place when the mail-car drives in between saluting soldiers through the Legation gates, caked in mud, with bent mudguards, and the words "TRANS-DESERT MAIL" barely legible on the bonnet.

This is how you must imagine your letters arriving, and me carrying them off to read in peace, and saying "oh *darling* Virginia," and smiling to myself, and reading them all over again. Whereas mine just come with the postman.

The mid-day gun, and the bag shuts at half past! I will try writing through Russia, but it's very uncertain. Think kindly of your exile, distant but very very loving. And very constant. I must write you a letter about constancy. Now that I have come to the end, I think of all sorts of things I wanted to write about. Bother.

V.

Berg

1. From Baghdad, Vita went by train to the Persian frontier and then joined a convoy of cars over the mountains to Kermanshah, where Harold Nicolson met her. They reached Teheran on March 5.
2. Elizabeth Dayrush, the daughter of Robert Bridges, the Poet Laureate, and herself a poet. Harold called her "a shy, defensive, little blue-stocking with a pudding face."

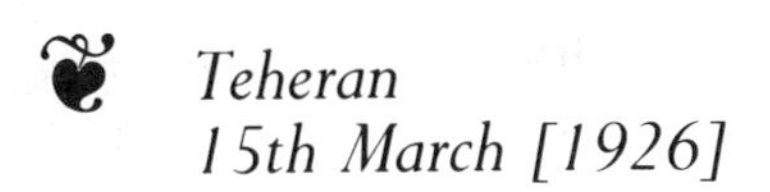

Teheran
15th March [1926]

Today being the birthday of the Shah, (though common report has it that he knows neither his birthday nor his age, being of low extraction,)[1] last night a dinner was given in his honour at the Foreign Office. So at 8.15, an immense yellow motor draws up at the door: Harold in uniform and gold lace, little sword getting between his legs; Vita derisive, but decked in emeralds; escort in scarlet and white, (the Minister is all for swank,—thinks it impresses the Persians;) the yellow motor proceeds down the street. Pulls up at the Foreign Office. Sentries present arms. The scarlet *escort escorts*. The sentries' boots are muddy; everything is very shoddy here. Seventy people to dinner; the china doesn't match,—not enough to go round,—the Persian ministers wear their robes of honour: grubby old cashmere dressing-gowns, with no collars to their evening shirts; dinner cold; I escape the awful fate of sitting between two Persians who talk nothing but their own language, and get Sir Percy,[2] who is nice, and the Belgian minister, who tells me about the Emperor of Korea. (I never knew there was such a person; he sounds incredibly romantic; Halkuyt's voyages, and all that.) Suddenly, an awful pause, and we stand up to drink the health of the eleven states represented. But first their national anthems must be played; and, glass in hand, we endure God Save the King, the Brabançonne, (I feel the Belgian minister at my side stiffen to attention,) the International Soviet Hymn, the Marseillaise, the Wacht am Rhein, and six unidentifiable minor powers. An unfortunate incident ushers in the ceremony: all the dirty plates have been stacked under Sir Percy's chair, all the dirty knives and forks under mine, so as we rise to our feet shoving back our chairs there is a clatter . . . Having drunk to our respective sovereigns and presidents, we drink to the Shah. We adjourn. There are fireworks. Now the Persians are really good at fireworks. The garden, from the balconies, corruscates with wrestling babies of Herculean promise, taxi-cabs with revolving wheels, aeroplanes with revolving propellers, catherine wheels, and VIVE SA MAJESTÉ IMPERIALE PAHLEVI in letters of gold reflecting in the central tank,—all very lovely, really, and fantastic, seen through clouds of smoke from above; while Tamur Tasch, officially minister of works, but really the Power behind the Throne, enquires in my ear as to the merits of Thos. Goode and Son, South Audley Street, and the Army & Navy Stores.

This is diplomatic life.

This morning, the yellow motor again; and Sir Percy and Harold, both in uniform again, with fluttering plumes in their hats, (Sir Percy loving it, and Harold wretched,) going off to the Shah's reception, the scarlet-and-white servants and the Indian lancers trotting before and behind the car.

Do not imagine, however, that life is all like that. There are days of going into the mountains, and eating sandwiches beside a stream, and picking wild almond, and of coming home by incredible sunsets across the plain. And every morning at 7. we ride, and the freshness and beauty of the morning are inconceivable.

Then once a fortnight the muddy car comes in, and there are letters: the only rift opening on the outside world. Otherwise it is all very self-contained,—what with the old white horse who goes his rounds every morning, bringing two barrels of water to every house in the compound, and the Sanitary Cart, which drawn by a donkey performs a sordid emptying function henceforward unknown at Rodmell . . . .[3] There is a great deal of compound life. (The compound is really the Legation garden, surrounded by a mud wall; and, dumped down among the plane-trees, are the various houses: the Military Attaché's house, the Secretaries' house, the Counsellor's house, the Consul's house, and houses E.-and-F.-on-the-office-plan, from which on Sunday mornings proceed the plaintive sounds of an harmonium.) Compound life means that at 8. a.m. the Consul's son aged ten starts an imitation of a motor horn; that at 9 a.m. somebody comes and says have I been letting all the water out of the tank; that at 10. a.m. the Military Attaché's wife strolls across and says how are your delphiniums doing; that at 11. a.m. Lady Loraine appears and says wasn't it monstrous the way the Russian Ambassador's wife cut the Polish Chargé d'Affaires' wife last night at the Palace; that at 12. noon a gun goes off and all the muezzins of Teheran set up a wail for prayer; that at 1. p.m. it is time for luncheon, and Vita hasn't done any work.

Then in the evening the white stems of the plane-trees turn pink, and the stars come out, and the little owls begin to hoot, and Vita says to the servant in very careful Persian, thought-out in advance, "If any body calls say I'm not at home." And then gets out Roget's Thesaurus of the English language, a rhyming dictionary, and the proofs of her poem (alas alas alas that they don't bear the superscription of the Hogarth Press.)

This brings me to what I really wanted to say: that you upset me dreadfully about the central transparency.[4] Because it is what I have always felt myself. Only how to do it? If only you had put down those unexpressed thoughts instead of letting them fall on the carpet! How invaluable they would have been.

You see from this that the muddy car has come in, and that I have had a letter from you (with a picture enclosed, which was an insult,—an insult to you, I mean.) You had fallen in love with being a stock-broker.[5] Well . . . . And I had galvanised you into asking Leonard to come to the South Seas; but, darling Virginia, that wasn't the point *at all*. The point was that you should come to Persia with *me*; that *I* should waft you to these brown plains; not that you should matrimonially disappear for a year out of my ken. Or were you teasing me? You see, it becomes clearer and more clear that I shall spend the next two years in tearing backwards and forwards across Europe and Asia, and it is my dream to take you with me.

Leonard would like it too; he can fish and shoot here, if he likes that; and there are at least 12 horses to ride. Believe me, Burmah is not a patch on Persia;[6] it has no classical traditions, and the architecture is abominable. As for the South Seas, I am sure they are over-rated; vulgar to a degree; and you wouldn't like hibiscus. Whereas this ancient country . . . This is the place for you. Indeed, if you won't come by kindness, I shall have to make you come by main force. But it would make me *so* happy, that I am sure no one as kind-hearted as you could refuse me that pleasure? We would come by the desert, and go back through Russia, which with your Soviet connections you would appreciate. Certainly it must be done.

March 25th. Do you know what nice little job I have on hand now? Arranging the palace for the coronation.[7] I go down there and put on an apron, and mix paint in pots in a vast hall, and wonder what the Persian is for "stipple." At one end of the hall is the Peacock Throne, and all round the walls are ranged glass cases containing every conceivable sort of object from Sèvres vases to the late Shah's toothbrush. This is known as the Museum. Lady Loraine is away, so I'm responsible. I've got to re-organise the Museum next week, and shall make Raymond help. He will trot about, under giant scaffolding, carrying alabaster bowls, while the paint drips on him from the brushes of the men skied up against the ceiling. I am sure the Shah will come to the coronation in tennis-shoes, with the twin-diamond of the Koh-i-Nur blazing in his hat. This is the principle upon which everything is conducted here.

Why do grammars only teach one such phrases as "Simply through the courage of the champion's sword," when what one wants to say is Bring another lamp?

Now this letter is long if apparently un-loving, but a lot of love gets spilt over them, like sand to dry the ink, of which no trace remains when the letter arrives, but which nevertheless was there, an important ingredient. And I send you a picture, much nicer than the one you sent me. I perceive there are a lot of questions I wanted to ask you, such as Who is Clive's new hand?[8] (said by him to be more like the knave than the queen of spades,—but girls will be boys,) also how is dear Grizzle? no longer like a rainbow trout, I trust; and why were you tired for two days? and is the Press overworking you? I suppose you will be motoring about France when this arrives; be careful, I pray; though I'm sure the dangers of motoring in France are nothing to the re-adjustment of standards which I have had to undergo here, with precipices and what-not. (I daren't however spin you too much of a traveller's tale, since Raymond is coming; he has squared my pitch badly.)

The little owls are hooting, and the bag leaves tomorrow on its long journey. You can write me only one more letter after you get this, for I shall be starting home. Or, if you are in France, address it to me here, and put it in a covering envelope addressed to Charles Hartopp Esq, The Residency, Cairo, and mark the inside envelope *By air-mail via Baghdad*. It will reach me quicker so. Your letters are always a shock to me, for you typewrite the envelope, and they look like a bill, and then I see your writing. A system I rather like, for the various stabs it affords me.

Now this letter is really getting disproportionately long, and you will be bored. It leaves such chasms of non-information, too; regular continents of unmapped territory. I have added bits to my poem, but they are nothing without the context. As you may suppose, they are almost entirely Asiatic in character. I mind about that poem, never having minded about any other book. I hope you will think I have improved it. My interest in it is however almost completely cancelled by the fact that I couldn't give it to you.[9] I do see that it would have been impossible, but nevertheless am full of resentment.

What fun it will be to sit on your floor again and stick on stamps. And to carry you off in the little blue motor. If you knew what you meant to me, you might be pleased.

Your
V.

Berg

1. Riza Khan Pahlevi, a soldier who rose from the ranks and in 1925 seized the Persian throne from the Qajar dynasty, which had held it for 150 years. In 1926 he was about forty-nine.
2. Sir Percy Loraine, British Minister in Teheran, 1921–1926. He was known to his staff as "Ponderous Percy." Harold satirized him as "Lord Bognor" in *Some People*.
3. Virginia and Leonard had just replaced the earth closets in their Sussex house with flush toilets.
4. Virginia had written to Vita about *The Land*: "I imagine it wants a little central transparency. Some sudden intensity."
5. Virginia had been staying with Leonard's brother Herbert, a stockbroker, and envied him and his wife their unintellectual, unadventurous lives.
6. Virginia had written to Vita: "I worried Leonard for an hour about taking a year off and seeing the world. We will go to Burma, I said: the South Seas."
7. The Shah was to be crowned on April 25.
8. Virginia had written: "Clive would parade a new affair of his. 'I've been dealt a new hand,' he kept saying. 'It takes me, I'm glad to say, into the lower walks of society.'"
9. *The Land* was published by Heinemann, to whom Vita was committed by contract, and not by the Hogarth Press.

❦ *Teheran*
8th April [1926]

Persia has turned magenta and purple: avenues of judas-trees, groves of lilac, torrents of wisteria, acres of peach-blossom. The plane-trees and the poplars have burst into green. I know you had a lovely Easter in England,—Reuter chronicled it. (Reuter is a great joy to us, because it always arrives all wrong, e.g. "Lady Fisher has just completed her 27 days fast, undertaken to cure her of an illness caused by General de Bility.") But I suppose you are in France now, tearing about,—well I, too, am about to tear, for we are going down to Isfahan. And, dear me, I can write you only one more letter after this, for the next fortnightly bag will bring me to the eve of my starting for home. I have been studying Mme. Dieulafoy, a ravishing character, in fact I wrote an article about her, which you may see in Vogue.[1] (Vogue is illustrated, and Mme. Dieulafoy is incomplete without a portrait, or I would have sent it to Leonard.) Raymond and I have agreed to divide the world; rather like the Versailles peace conference we are: he is to have Palestine, Syria, and the desert, and I am to have Persia, for journalistic purposes. (We are both rather resentful of Aldous Huxley.)[2] Raymond has arrived, you see; he fell over a precipice and was fired on, but survived. It seems odd to see him here. He is very happy, and as good as gold: scribbles away, and gives no trouble. But we both find it difficult to write about travel. My drawer is full of loose sheets, that refuse to connect up. I daresay you are right about rhythm; all I can say is, that rhythm and I are out of gear. I have finished my poem though, and it goes off by this bag. There are large patches of Asia in it now. Will you approve, I wonder?

But indeed my bringing-up wasn't so very different from yours: I mooned about too, at Knole mostly, and hadn't even a brother or a sister to knock the corners off me. And I never went to school.[3] If I am jolly and vulgar, you can cry quits on another count, for you have that interest in humanity which I can never manage,—at least, I have the interest, but not the diabolical skill in its practice which is yours. And as I get older (I had a birthday only the other day,) I find I get more and more disagreeably solitary, in fact I foresee the day when I shall have gone so far into myself that there will no longer be anything to be seen of me at all. Will you, please, remember to pull away the coverings from time to time? or I shall get quite lost. It is, I think, a pity to allow oneself to come to that stage when one only wants to be with people with whom one is intimate or perhaps in love. One ought to have a larger repertoire. But there, you see, am I saying "one ought to,"—and that gives away the whole trouble: that I live by theories, or rather they revolve and jostle in my head, and then I neglect to put them into practice, or perhaps am incapable of so doing. And that perhaps is one of the reasons why I like women better than men, (even platonically,) that they take more trouble and are more skilled in the art of making friendship into a shape; it is their business; men are too spoilt and lazy.

There now is a long egoistic passage; but from time to time I get seriously worried, and have a longing to be gregarious, and pour it out on poor Virginia.

I met a young American poet called [Archibald] MacLeish who has a passionate admiration for you. He is a serious young man, who has come here on an opium commission. You and Eliot are the only two writers in England today, etc etc. By the way I would like to read Middleton Murry's invectives, but you didn't say what they were in.[4] Will you keep them for me?

Darling Virginia, you mustn't write me any more, because I shall be coming home. On the 25th is the coronation; then we are going to climb a mountain, then I am going to start. I can't find anything about my journey; tourist agencies are unknown here, and the continental time-tables ignore Russia altogether. So I shall just launch off into the blue and trust to luck, and ought to reach England on the 14th, laden with rugs for old [Robert] Bridges. If you aren't very careful I shall really bring you a tortoise, as the place is alive with them. (Have you read Lawrence, D.H., on tortoises?)

Have you read "Comment débuta Marcel Proust"?[5] I cried over it. (By the way, that might be a good book to publish in translation; it's quite short.)

How pleased I shall be to sit on your floor again.

I have got to go and see the Crown jewels, which is unexpectedly cutting my letter short, and I daren't risk the bag not being closed when I get back—I'm also going to see that they've painted the room the right colour for the coronation, and am to be rewarded for my trouble by being allowed to pour bowls of emeralds through my fingers! So, at least, says the high functionary who is gracious enough to accord me this favour. I am taking Raymond. I must fly—

Your
V.

Postscript.
Just back from the palace, with ½ an hour before the bag shuts.

I am blind. Blinded by diamonds.

I have been in Aladdin's cave.

Sacks of emeralds were emptied out before our eyes. Sacks of pearls. *Literally.*

We came away shaking the pearls out of our shoes. Ropes of uncut emeralds. Scabbards encrusted with precious stones. Great hieratic crowns.

All this in a squalid room, with grubby Persians drinking little cups of tea.

I can't write about it now. It was simply the Arabian Nights, with décor by the Sitwells. Pure fantasy. Oh, *why* weren't you there?

Berg

1. "Mme. Dieulafoy," *Vogue* (June 1926), pp. 77, 112. Jane Dieulafoy traveled overland to Persia with her husband, Marcel, in the 1890s, and together they excavated the palace of Darius at Susa. She wrote an account of her adventures which attracted great acclaim. Vita reprinted much of her article in *Passenger to Teheran*.
2. Huxley was traveling around the world, and described his journey in *Jesting Pilot* (October 1926).
3. She did. She regularly attended the school run by Miss Woolff in Mayfair, London, and won most of the prizes there. (See Victoria Glendinning, *Vita* (1983), pp. 22–26.)
4. In the *Adelphi* of February 1926, where Murry abused *Jacob's Room* and *The Waste Land*
5. By Louis de Robert, 1925

29th March 1926

The Hogarth Press,
52 Tavistock Square,
London, W.C.1

. . . Now you must pretend to be interested in your friend's fortunes: but it will all seem so remote and silly to you: you have forgotten a paper called The Nation; Leonard was literary editor once: and since Wednesday he is no longer. We have resigned. Thank God. What a mercy—no more going to the office and reading proofs

and racking ones brains to think who to get to write. We shall have to make £500 a year . . . but this is the first step to being free, and foreign travel and dawdling about England in a motor car; and we feel 10 years younger, utterly irresponsible, and please, dearest Vita, do make Harold do the same thing. . . .

I cannot think what it will interest you to be told of, now you are embedded in Persia. . . .

[There was] a ghastly party at Rose Macaulays, where in the whirl of meaningless words I thought Mr O'donovan said Holy Ghost, whereas he said "The Whole Coast" and I asking "Where is the Holy Ghost?" got the reply "Where ever the sea is" "Am I mad, I thought, or is this wit?" "The Holy Ghost?" I repeated. "The Whole Coast" he shouted, and so we went on, in an atmosphere so repellent that it became like the smell of bad cheese, repulsively fascinating . . . until Leonard shook all over, picked up what he took to be Mrs Gould's napkin, discovered it to be her sanitary towel and the foundations of this tenth rate literary respectability (all gentlemen in white waistcoats, ladies shingled, unsuccessfully) shook to its foundations. I kept saying "Vita would love this" Now would you?

Berg

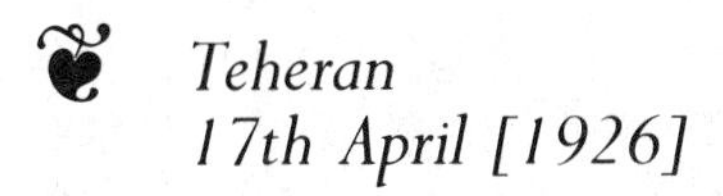

Teheran
17th April [1926]

I left you blinded with pearls, and now ten days have gone by, and meanwhile Teheran has been slowly filling up with barbarians who have ridden in from the mountains for the coronation, and who parade the streets on their wild ponies, dressed to emulate the plumage of peacocks,—huge turbans of silk and fur, wide sashes like Joseph's coat, stuck with silver-mounted weapons of every description; all 15th century, not a day later. And now comes your letter, late, because of floods, (Baghdad was saved only by the skin of its teeth,) positively bursting with news: The Nation gone, the Press perhaps to go.[1] *Please* not the latter. I didn't know what an affection I had for the Press till I heard it was threatened. Besides, it keeps you in London; and if it disappeared, you might disappear too, and be off to—oh, anywhere but Persia. It is all very exciting, and I congratulate

Leonard upon his rashness. You might exert your influence over Harold next year to do likewise.

We are going to Isfahan tomorrow, but heaven knows if we shall get there, as the floods are said to be all over the road; brown torrents, and bridges swept away. And this will be my last letter. The next thing you'll know of me, will be that I walk in and fondle Grizzle. Unless, indeed, I fall into a Russian prison on the way.

What have I been doing? I went to a Persian tea-party. *Ravishing* women; almond eyes, red lips, babbling like little birds, pulling their veils about them whenever they heard a noise. Completely silly, but oh so lovely! Much better than your stockbrokers. And one old monster of a mother-in-law, hanging over them, like a hawk over a flock of doves.

Have you seen Harold's Swinburne?[2] it is out. It appears that you told him you wanted to review it, which he hasn't forgotten, even if you have. We haven't got it; very tantalising. I've written a good deal [*Passenger to Teheran*], but all pretty bad, (I send a chunk to Leonard by this post,) and envy your thousands of words. Is it all west coast of Scotland?[3] I think I had better take you there, in the blue motor.

I had a long, obscene letter from Eddy, but for some dim psychological reason cannot bring myself to answer it. He says he "never enjoyed himself so much in his life" as the evening when he induced *you* to dine with him. He says he "paid you compliments, without being vulgar, which is more than a mere womaniser could have done." What with my correspondence, and Raymond's, and Harold's, we get most of your London happenings as seen from three different angles, and spend some happy evenings piecing the different accounts together. It is much more amusing than seeing the actual thing,—an exercise of the imagination. But none of us, alas, have heard from Sibyl.

A curious fact: nearly all letters seem to contain at least *one* irritating phrase, but yours never. They leave one feeling more intelligent, charming, and desirable than one really is.

I wish you would do your 150 pages which shall sum up the whole of literature.[4] It would tidy up the rubbish-heap of many people's minds, not least my own. And please don't give up the Press.

My mind *is* such a rubbish-heap; it distresses me.

This is a silly letter, but I shall arrive a week after it. In the meantime I am (as we say here) your sacrifice. I will recite Hafiz to you, bring you silks and scents, and make myself generally agreeable. I'll do Viola's index for you if you like.[5] Or anything else, and try to corrupt you in every possible way. I've ordered a barrel of the Spanish wine you liked, so you will have to come and drink it. Like Belloc, who says he has just bought 2000 bottles of Burgundy at 2d½ a bottle. You will be very nice to me please? because you know what a miserable letter I wrote from Trieste, and I shall be exactly correspondingly glad to see you again.

V.

Berg

1. Leonard had resigned as literary editor of *The Nation* but was persuaded to remain until 1930. The Woolfs were also thinking of selling the Hogarth Press, but never in fact did so.
2. Harold Nicolson's *Swinburne* was receiving generally favorable reviews, but a few were condemnatory of his unfairness to his subject.
3. *To the Lighthouse* was ostensibly about the Hebrides but in fact was set in Cornwall.
4. Virginia started this book in the last year of her life (1940–1941) but did not complete it. Her draft was entitled *Anon*. See Brenda Silver, ed., "'Anon' and 'The Reader': Virginia Woolf's Last Essays," *Twentieth Century Literature*, Virginia Woolf Issue (Fall–Winter 1979), 25:3/4.
5. Viola Tree, *Castles in the Air: The Story of My Singing Days*, published by Hogarth in April 1926.

❧ *13th April 1926* — *52 Tavistock Sqre. [W.C.1]*

. . . *How odd it is—the effect geography has in the mind! I write to you differently now you're coming back. The pathos is melting. I felt it pathetic when you were going away; as if you were sinking below the verge. Now that you are rising, I'm jolly again.*

Berg

May–September 1926

The hot summer of 1926 was spent by both women in the country, Vita at Long Barn, Virginia at Monk's House, and they frequently exchanged visits. There were a few expeditions: to Oxford (separately) to visit Robert Bridges, the Poet Laureate, and by Virginia to see Thomas Hardy in Dorset. Vita took her two sons on holiday to the Loire valley. She finished her Persian travel book; and The Land *was published, to great acclaim, in September. The Vita-Virginia affair continued intermittently, but with less intensity than before. Vita wrote to Harold (August 17): "I am sagacious, though probably I would be less sagacious if I were more tempted, which is at least frank." She was seeing more of Dorothy Wellesley (to whom she dedicated* The Land*) than of Virginia.*

❧ *Wednesday [19 May 1926]* *52 Tavistock Square, W.C.1*

. . . Everybody is longing to see you. Grizzle in paroxysms. Lunch here *at 1. Friday. Better still come to the basement at 12.30 and have a preliminary talk . . . with me in my studio——then 6 or 7 hours upstairs. (unless you'll dine with me on* Thursday*, when I happen to be alone)*

Berg

❧ *Saturday [22 May 1926]* *52 Tavistock Square, W.C.1*

. . . You said you were going to finish a book in Persia. Would you let us have it? The point is I dont want to press you, if you feel, as you may, that Heinemann's has a right, and is, as maybe too, more profitable. At the same time I dont want these refinements of feeling to lose us a chance which would give a great fillip to our autumn season. So consider.

Berg

 *Long Barn, Weald,*
Sevenoaks.
29th May [1926]

My darling Virginia,

This intoxication of solitude . . . . All day I weed,—a fine crop of potatoes coming up in the new flower beds,—take the puppies for a walk through the buttercups, hear the cuckoo, see him even,—flying in a festooned flight from spinney to spinney,—come in to dinner, a lonely dinner: cold lamb and the Spanish wine you liked; then the old problem: what shall I read at dinner, propped open by a fork? decide finally on Virginia, grab the common reader, a pair of spectacles, a pencil, go in to dinner, get into conversation with the highly respectable old butler [George Horne, nicknamed Moody] through saying we must look over Harold's clothes that they be not mildewed; "Are there Court clothes, madam? gold braid needs black tissue paper;" "No, he's got his uniform with him," (visions of Harold in a vile temper, tumbling over his sword;) "Ah yes, so he would have, madam; and a very long time it must seem, if I may say so, madam, for Mr. Nicolson not to see the young gentlemen." "Have you ever been abroad?" I ask, embarrassed. "To the Argentine, madam, with two gentlemen; at least, not reeel [*sic*] gentlemen they weren't, if I may so express myself, madam; but very *interesting* all the same, but Egypt now, that's the country that always took my fancy, if only I could get there, perhaps with Mr. Nicolson if he was Viceroy, that's been my dream always." (Dear me, how romantic the English are, I think to myself; and aloud:) "Why Egypt particularly?" "Well, madam, I understand as how the Sanitary Arrangements are greatly improved there from what as they used to be."

This baffles me; I can't follow the train of thought at all. I wish to pursue the conversation, but am interrupted by Pippin starting to have puppies under my chair. Hasty exile of Pippin to the shed. Louise, who indulges Pippin's every whim, obviously thinks me a brute. The atmosphere becomes suddenly and horribly obstetrical. The butler, feeling this is a Woman's Job, retires to the pantry. And here I am now, feeling curiously paternal, while Pippin yelps in travail in the shed,—all my fault, for having caused her to be sent to the champion red spaniel of England while I was safely in Asia two months ago. (63 days; to be exact.)

My travel book: I see that I must quarrel with Heinemann for your sake; so be it. You shall have it. But I warn you that it is not worth having. And oh, dear, idolised Virginia that you are, how *could* you publish Viola [Tree]? it makes me vomit. I don't like you to sell your soul.

How is Leonard's cold? and your headache? Tell Leonard my cold was a fiend; and thank him for nothing.

My mother is not coming here; she has got to stay in London and have her food weighed for a month. I saw her on Thursday, more lovely and charming than words can say. So I am at liberty to have parties. So will you both be my first and probably only party, and come here for next weekend, (5th–7th, I think.)

Signed:
Sibyl Colefax

Anyone you like I'll ask, or no one else at all; just as you like. Or *you* come on Friday and Leonard on Sat.—just what suits you—only tell me. I have a village maiden to cook for me, and no coal, but am felling an oak to show my rustic independence of the coal strike.[1]

How happy you must have been among your water-meadows these days; and pulling the plug and what-not.

My garden *was* nice, but every tulip has been finished off by the wind—There will be nothing if you come—and you will think me a bad gardener.

I have shingled my hair.

V.

Berg.

1. The General Strike, which had disrupted British transport and industry, ended on May 12, but the coal miners remained on strike for several more months.

❧ *Tuesday [1 June 1926]* *52 Tavistock Square, W.C.1*

It is all infinitely good of you—what we thought of, for your travels, was to have large, numerous photographs.

At the same time, we are a little conscience (oh damn! I've been addressing envelopes all the afternoon, and cannot write a word) I was saying we feel a little guilty about taking you from the prosperous Heinemann. Lets talk it over in cold blood

Berg

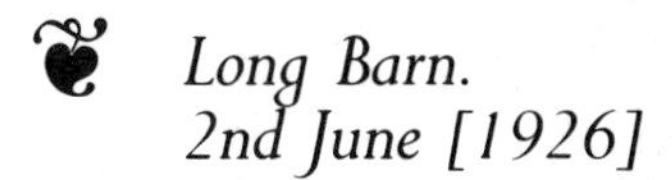

Long Barn.
2nd June [1926]

Dearest, I don't like to drag you down here just for one night,—it's tiring and unsettling for you,—besides I should like Leonard to come, so I'll be unselfish and forgo the joy of having you here on Friday, and say 'Come both of you on Sat. the 12th,' though by then all the lupins and irises will have gone, and nothing will have taken their place, and Leonard (who is a gardener) will think my garden nasty.

What a dazzling life you do lead,—Gertrude Stein and the Sitwells!—you make me feel a bumpkin.[1]

I can't interpret Sibyl's dream.[2] Are you dining with her on the 15th? I am; but I feel you would certainly have been used as a decoy if you were going.

Are you all right? and headaches gone?

Of course if you could come on Friday 11th, so much the better, but I suppose that's too much to hope for?

V.

The puppies are well, thank you, but Pippin is greatly distressed because we have cut their tails off with a carving knife.

Berg

1. Virginia had written to her sister Vanessa Bell: "We were at a party at Edith Sitwell's last night, where a good deal of misery was endured. . . . It was in honour of Miss Gertrude Stein who was throned on a broken settee. . . ."
2. Sibyl Colefax's dream was that Virginia had been twice to the theater with Dorothy Wellesley.

❧ *Monday [7 June 1926]* *52 Tavistock Square, W.C.1*

Not much news. Rather cross—Would like a letter. Would like a garden. Would like Vita. Would like 15 puppies with their tails chopped off, 3 doves, and a little conversation. The Sitwells was a ghastly frost. I put it in to make you feel a bumpkin—and it did, and thus confirmed my view that other peoples parties have a mystery and glamour one's own are without. Are you writing poetry? If so, then tell me what is the difference between that emotion and the prose emotion? What drives you to one and not the other? . . .

Berg

 *Long Barn, Weald,*
Sevenoaks.
Thursday, 17th June [1926]

Dear Mrs Woolf

I must tell you how much I enjoyed my weekend with you . . .

Darling Virginia, you don't know how happy I was.

I am sorry you should think me crafty. I don't think I am half crafty enough.

About prose and poetry, and the difference between them. I don't believe there is any, with all due respect to Coleridge. It is surely only a question of the different shape that words assume in the mind, not a question of drunkenness and sobriety. All too often the distinction leads people to think they may mumble inanities which would make them blush if written in good common English, but which they think fit to print if split up into lines. This alone shows that there isn't any real difference. None of the definitions fit. Matthew Arnold says that poetry describes the flowing, not the fixed; why should not prose?

A brilliant gathering at Sibyl's,—what you missed! The drawing room at Argyll House [Chelsea] corruscated. Sibyl was, I thought, very stuffy about you; evidently cross at being cheated of a star in her firmament. "If she could come up to London with *you*," she snapped, "she could have come here tonight." I drew a touching picture of your frailty; she sniffed. Molly McCarthy [*sic*] looked amused.

Now, having annoyed you (as I hope) by telling you what you missed and what bad odour you are in with her ladyship, I'll tell you that I disenjoyed myself extremely; would have exchanged all the champagne in the cellar for a glass of Rodmell water; would have sent everybody flying with a kick. Sibyl tried to draw me about Persia; I turned sulky, wouldn't be drawn, shan't be asked again, and let Aldous Huxley have it all his own way as the only traveller.[1] Then I came down here next day, composing on the way a very beautiful speech to be addressed to girl-guides; discovered on arrival that they were shop-girls and not girl-guides at all; had to improvise; was bunched with sweet peas; felt like Princess Mary [daughter of King George V]; had to buy a lot of things I didn't want; went to Knole and saw the Comedy of Errors played in the garden; and so home, feeling very miserable because I had lost you and because I had had a bad report about my mother. So I collected as many dogs as I could take to bed with me; and rats ate the doves during the night.

But this morning I thought of you writing away as hard as you could go, and that consoled me. I hope it was a true and right thought?

If you *should* feel inclined to write to me, send it to Sherfield Court, Sherfield on Loddon, Basingstoke where I go on Saturday after the 80 publishers. I shall expect to find that you have prepared a little store of trouble for me with Clive.

Desmond said suddenly to me, "I see that Clive is going as minister to Teheran."[2] To me there is only one Clive [Bell]: my world reeled.

I wish I were back at Rodmell. I wish you were coming here. Is it any good suggesting (you see that I am in a despondent mood,) that you should do so? It is very nice here, you know; but I expect you are busy. Only, it would be a nice refuge if you wanted to escape from London, and I would fetch you in the motor. In any case I shall see you on Friday? a damned long way off, too. Is this a dumb letter? You did spoil me so at Rodmell. I was terribly happy. *Tell me how you are.*

V.

Berg

1. See note 2, page 120.
2. Sir Robert Clive, who had been British consul general in Munich and Tangier, was now appointed Minister to Teheran, where he remained until 1931.

 *Long Barn, Weald,*
Sevenoaks.
17th June [1926]

Ha, ha! Look what I've found. Only send it back, please, because it's too precious to lose. I like my name,—I mean, Harold's name,—spelt wrong.[1]

I shall have, however, to give up reading your works at dinner, for they are too disturbing. I can't explain, I'll have to explain verbally some day. Unless you can guess. *How well you write*, though, confound you. When I read you, I feel no one has ever written English prose before,—Knocked it about, put it in its place, made it into a servant. I wonder perpetually how you do it; like one might see a conjuror do a trick over and over again, and be none the wiser. Only one knows that it will always come off. There is an odd effect peculiar to a few writers, I don't know if you will know what I mean, and if you don't it is hopeless to make you understand: they exercise some mysterious power over print, to make certain words,—perhaps quite ordinary words,—start up out of the page like partridges out of a turnip field, getting a new value, a new surprise. I suppose it is really done by context. You have it; Lawrence has (or used to have) it; de la Mare (who bores me now) has it; Max [Beerbohm] has it.—But, as I say, you won't know what I mean.

I am an awful snob about you. About your writing, I mean.

God, how it rains—A pigeon has come to live with me. I think it must be the ghost of the dove that flew out of the Ark. I do wish you were here. Tomorrow I have to dine with an old bibliophile who also collects water-colours of the most horrible description; two old brothers; the younger is the echo of the elder; they have First Editions, and a Cellar, and they tell Anecdotes.[2] I love them, and they ceremoniously flirt with me. They are the sort of people you fall in love with,—like stockbrokers.

Your
V.

Berg

1. One of Virginia's first letters to Vita had begun: "Dear Mrs. Nicholson."
2. The two bachelor brothers Johnson, solicitors of Sevenoaks, Kent, who had been Vita's friends since her childhood and remained trustees of the Knole Estate.

❧ *Friday [18 June 1926]* *[52 Tavistock Square, W.C.1]*

*. . . Yes, I do write damned well sometimes, but not these last days, when I've been slogging through a cursed article, and see my novel [*To the Lighthouse*] glowing like the Island of the Blessed far far away over dismal wastes, and cant reach land.*

Berg

Sherfield Court,
Sherfield Upon Loddon,
Basingstoke.
[20 June 1926]

Commanded to write to you about Sunday, what am I to say?

But first of all: YES, come on Thursday if any chance offers. It fits in admirably, because I must be in London that day to go to a matinée with my mother (who has a strange incongruous passion for matinées, and *always* has a row with the person behind her because she won't take off her hat,—so now has a black lace veil which becomes her admirably,) and can fetch you afterwards in the motor; moreover will bring you up on Friday—so you'll have no trouble with trains and stations. So let me know—to Long Barn.

I had a fright there yesterday: I was fetched as I was goodly gardening, "There is a long telegram for you on the telephone, from Monk's House." "My God!" I thought, "something has happened to Virginia." I rushed, I flew; arrived all out of breath. And then it was only a telegram from some people called Monk at Oakhampton who wanted to buy a puppy. I stuck on a guinea, just to pay them out.

My first glimpse of Clive was somehow suitable: I ran into him as he emerged from the rear [lavatory], doing up his buttons. But he was prim about it, ignored my grin of welcome, my outstretched hand—nay, my opened arms,—scurried back, attended to his toilet, re-appeared, not pleased to see me a bit; I was damped, crushed. During the course of the 24 hours he has recovered himself, and become friendly again; so friendly indeed that we walked round the moat after dinner, on a warm misty evening, and talked, and he made some bad breaches in my little fort of discretion.[1] You see he was skilful enough to pique me with remarks about your general indifference, lack of response etc, and I rose like a trout to the bait. Still, I don't think I've very seriously compromised you, and Clive, at any rate, was entertained. Then Sir Arthur[2] had to be rescued from Desmond [MacCarthy], or rather Desmond had to be rescued from Sir Arthur, and we got separated—which was perhaps fortunate.

Eddy tells me he is going to meet you at Garsington.[3] Now I can forgive Eddy much,—inheriting Knole instead of me, for instance,—but not this.

This letter has been written in bits.

Who made you a declaration of love? and what did Wells say?[4] You know quite well that you will tell me, so why so coy?

I shall tell Clive that he is not to open this letter and read it in the train. It will, I fear, burn a hole in his pocket. He is a pet, anyhow, and I have ever such a warm feeling for him. I meant to flirt with him, didn't I? and forgot. I was too much engaged in fencing about you. What a disturbing element you are to be sure!

Bless you.

V.

Berg

1. Vita wrote to Harold on the same day: "Clive follows me all over the place. Have I been to bed with Virginia yet? If not, am I likely to do so in the near future? If not, will I please give it my attention? As it is high time Virginia fell in love." (*Lilly Library, Indiana University*)
2. Sir Arthur Colefax (1866–1936), husband of Sibyl, an eminent lawyer, but usually regarded by her friends as tedious, loquacious, and no match for his wife
3. Home of Lady Ottoline Morrell
4. H. G. Wells had said to Leonard that Virginia was "too intelligent—a bad thing." (See Virginia's diary entry for June 9). The "declaration of love" was from Philip Morrell.

❧ *[Typewritten]* *[52] Tavistock Square [W.C.1]*
Tuesday [22 June 1926]

Darling Mrs Nicolson,

I think I won't come on Thursday for this reason; I must get on with writing; you would seduce me completely; I have to spend two nights (I suppose) at Garsington. . . .

Also will you come on after your play on Thursday and see me alone? I've put

off Sibyl in case you can. Come early on Friday. The typewriter calls you instinctively Darling Mrs Nicolson. . . .
Of course, if you want to meet Sibyl and you've only to say so. Will you dine with me off radishes alone in the kitchen?

Berg

❧ *[15 July 1926]* *52 Tavistock Square, W.C.1*

Dear Mrs Nicolson,

This is only business, not affection—I suppose you're not coming to see me; so please, as a darling send me (oh but better far come and bring me—)
(1) Tennyson by H.N [Harold Nicolson].
(2) Venetian Glass Nephew the authoress [Elinor Wylie] said severely "Really! Not read any of my books!" Oh what an evening! I expected a ravishing and diaphanous dragonfly, a woman who had spirited away 4 husbands, and wooed from buggery the most obstinate of his adherents: a siren; a green and sweetvoiced nymph—that was what I expected, and came a tiptoe in to the room to find—a solid hunk: a hatchet minded, cadaverous, acid voiced, bareboned, spavined, patriotic nasal, thick legged American. All the evening she declaimed unimpeachable truths; and discussed our sales: hers are 3 times better than mine, naturally; till thank God, she began heaving on her chair and made a move as if to go, gracefully yielded to, but not, I beg you to believe, solicited, on our parts. Figure my woe, on the stairs, when she murmured, "Its the other *thing I want. Comes of trying to have children. May I go in there?" So she retired to the W.C., emerged refreshed; sent away her cab, and stayed another hour, hacking us to pieces. But I must read her book.*

Berg

❦ *Long Barn, Weald,*
Sevenoaks.
Friday [16 July 1926]

Poor Towser is sadly distracted, and has a stary coat: can't write, and does nothing but run up and down stairs with telephone messages. My mother's visit is being prolonged; and although I adore having her, it interrupts the pursuit of literature. I can't get to London till the 28th,—will you be gone to Rodmell? Or if I came up in the evening of the 27th instead, would you dine with me? Otherwise I can see nothing for it but that you should both come here with Clive, which would be perfect,—Though not so perfect as having you alone.

1) I sent you Tennyson today.[1]

2) The Venetian Glass Nephew was borrowed by Wellesley, who has been told to send it direct to you. What did you think of her poem?

3) The coronet appears to be an English marquis' coronet; see accompanying illustration; remove the cushion, and the rest is identical.[2] But of course a French marquis' may be the same, and I have no book which will tell me.—Yes, I have, though, and it isn't.—The motto and arms do not belong to any *present* English marquis, as I have looked them all up. But it may be extinct. See also accompanying postcard, which gives you the titles of two books on English family mottos;[3] I have neither of these books, but London Library? British Museum?

4) What is the matter with Sibyl? I got a cryptic phrase in a letter from her: "*How* naughty to have given E.G.'s message to Virginia." This mystified me completely till I thought of Edmund Gosse and his remarks about your father.[4] Have I made mischief? I didn't mean to. I don't know what else she can mean, however I shall see her tomorrow as I have got to take her and some bloody American over Knole; they, (the Colefaxes) aren't coming here for the weekend after all, as I have had to put them off on account of my mother.

Last night Pippin returned home from hunting and proceeded to have convulsions. With my usual efficiency I diagnosed strychnine, and rushed her into Sevenoaks at 2 a.m. to the vet. We gave her a morphia injection, and she was immediately and magnificently sick,—really impressive it was,—and so her life is saved. But it was a dramatic dash. I felt like the person who brought the good news from Aix to Ghent.[5]

A New Zealand poet walked in, two days ago; damn bad his poems were, but he was an interesting young man, penniless, tramping England selling his poems for 6 d for a living. So you are not alone in your association with authors.

Oh dear I do so want to see you.

V.

Berg

1. By Harold Nicolson, published in 1922
2. Virginia had sent Vita a picture of a coronet which had descended to her great-aunt Julia Cameron. Vita had identified it as the coronet of an English marquis, not that of the crest of the eighteenth-century Chevalier Antoine de l'Etang, Julia Cameron's grandfather, as Virginia had hoped. Also enclosed was a Chevalier De l'Etang bookplate. The De l'Etang motto is: *SICUT FLOS INTER SPINAS.*
3. On the postcard was written: Fairbairn: Book of family crests. 1856. Wachbourne: Book of family crests. 1882. 2 vols.
4. See *VW 1726*. "Gosse still says, only two weeks ago, 'Ah Mrs Woolf! doesnt respect her father.'"
5. The reference is to Robert Browning's poem "How They Brought the Good News from Ghent to Aix."

❧ *[19? July 1926]* *52 Tavistock Square, W.C.1*

You are an angel, but I didn't mean you to take so much trouble. God knows about the Marquis. Probably the whole thing is different in France—he may have been the son or the nephew of a Marquis (I think that was the legend), and anyhow I suppose I can say, vaguely, 'aristocratic', and leave it. I want to prove her base and noble—it fits in with her oddities. I might spend a lifetime over her; but can't face going to my halfbrother who knows all about the Marquis. Tennyson has not yet come; but will, I make no doubt. I quail before the Venetian nephew. Another meeting with that arid desert [Elinor Wylie] has sickened me. . . .

. . . About coming—I'm dashing off, you'll be amused to hear, on my chronic visit to Hardy. I expect I shall be back on Saturday: I shall only stay one day and drink one cup of tea, and be so damned nervous I shall spill it on the floor, and what shall I say? Nothing, but arid nonsense. Yet I feel this is a great occasion. . . .

. . . I'm sitting in an old silk petticoat at the moment with a hole in it, and the top part of another dress with a hole in it, and the wind is blowing through me, and I'm reading de Quincey, and Richardson, and again de Quincey—again de Quincey, because I'm in the middle of writing about him ["Impassioned Prose"*], and my*

God Vita, if you happen to know do wire whats the essential difference between prose and poetry—It cracks my poor brain to consider.

Berg

Long Barn, Weald,
Sevenoaks.
Wednesday [21 July 1926]

Yes, please, I would very much like to come on Monday. I would still more like you to come on Saturday, and shine, but I see quite clearly that you don't intend to do that.

But why, instead of going up to London again on Tuesday morning and down to Rodmell that afternoon, not let me motor you over to Rodmell on Tuesday? it seems to me that it would save you trouble and fatigue. But you decide on this when you come.

I am glad you are going to Rodmell at last. I am sure all these excitements are not good for you.

And old Hardy![1] well, well. You will come back quite converted, as you always are by Public Monuments,—George Moore, Bridges,—and with no use for your contemporaries.

Raymond is back and is coming here on Saturday. You may have seen him, but he has gone dutifully to visit his aunt.

I'm glad Leonard will print Gertrude Bell.[2] I sent the proof back by return. I've written to Byard[3] to tell him you're going to have that book [*Passenger to Teheran*]—as he will be cross if he first learns it from an advertisement. He will be cross anyhow, but I have told Ozzie[4] to pacify him in Venice.

Did you know Ozzie was motoring to Italy with Sibyl? What *will* be left of all our reputations!

Berg

1. Virginia's visit to Thomas Hardy at Max Gate in Dorset on July 23 is fully described in her diary entry of July 25.

2. Vita's article "Gertrude Bell in Baghdad," *Nation and Athenaeum* (July 24, 1926)

3. Theodore Byard, director of Heinemann

4. Oswald Dickinson (1869–1954), the bachelor brother of Violet Dickinson, Virginia's intimate friend in adolescence

 *Sherfield Court,*
Sherfield upon Loddon
Basingstoke.
4th August [1926]

If I have not written *to* you, it is because I have been writing *for* you,—tyrant, slave-driver, how am I to write 20,000 words in 10 days, tell me? I turn a deaf ear to all pleadings; will I play tennis? will I come out in the punt? will I come and bathe? no, no, no, I say, you remember Mrs Woolf? Well, I have got to finish a book for her to publish, so run away darlings, and don't worry; and then back I go to Isfahan; and meanwhile Virginia sits in the water-meadows and thinks about the Hebrides. (What, exactly, is a he-bride? see Raymond Mortimer on a Defence of Homosexuality.[1] Raymond Mortimer was here for the weekend; had rather a bad time in the shape of a good many home-truths; but happy on the whole.)

Now that's all, because I have two chapters still to write, and several to finish, and am getting frantic about it. Dottie says I am a bore. I tell her that it is your fault. I *am* a bore, I know, and nobody is allowed near the writing-table except me. As for the children, their passion for Mrs Woolf is rapidly on the decline.

Mine, alas, is not.

V.

Berg

1. A pamphlet he wrote for the Hogarth Press which they were (legally) advised not to publish

❧ *Sunday [8 August 1926]* *Monks House, Rodmell*
[Sussex]

Yes, it does seem hard, that we should make you spend all the fine weather with your nose to the pen [Passenger to Teheran]*. But think of your glory; and our profit, which is becoming a necessary matter, now that your puppy has destroyed, by eating*

holes, my skirt, ate L's proofs, and done such damage as could be done to the carpet—But she is an angel of light. Leonard says seriously she makes him believe in God . . . and this after she has wetted his floor 8 times in one day.

Berg

❧ *[19 August 1926]* *Monks House, Rodmell*
[Sussex]

Will you come on Wednesday? to lunch at 1? Leonard will be in London for the day. Would you like me to ask Clive? If so, let me know. Sleep night.

You'll be even more uncomfortable than usual.

I say, please bring 2 bottles wine (not cider) which I want to BUY.

Cant get any.

Berg

Long Barn, Weald,
Sevenoaks.
Friday [20 August 1926]

What is this alarming invitation [to Charleston?] you have sent on to me? I take it that you are not going; and as for me, I should be much too frightened to go,—even under your wing, I think.

I am going to Normandy for a week, with the boys, on the 28th,[1] but am going to Brighton on Wednesday—could I see you? How could I see you? Sleep Wednesday night? or lunch Thursday? We ought to decide about these photographs, and other details. I am calling it "Passenger to Teheran," which I think covers everything, 1) not too dull, 2) not too romantic, 3) explicit. Anyhow I can't think of anything better. I will bring the thing completed on Wednesday,—a bit late, I fear, but my calculations were completely thrown out by Mother's visit. Otherwise you should have had it a fortnight ago. It is very bad. I feel ashamed; but perhaps it will sell.

I have been amusing myself by filling in the religious questionnaire,[2] and showing the result to the tutor [Charles Farrell] who is reading for the Church.

Do let me know about next week. To stay the night Wednesday would be nicest, but just as it suits you.

V.

Berg

1. And then to the Loire valley with Ben and Nigel, and Dorothy Wellesley, from August 28 till September 6.

2. In *The Nation*, starting with Question 1: "Do you believe in a personal God?" The answers, tabulated, were printed in the issue of October 16: 743 affirmative, 1,024 negative.

❧ *Sunday [22 August 1926]* *Monks House, Rodmell [Sussex]*

Yes—that will be perfect. I think I shall be alone on Wednesday—couldn't you come early and enjoy a scrambly lunch?

*The title [*Passenger to Teheran*] seems very good—far the best. I'm longing, in spite of having read 3 mss, to read yours—a great testimony to you: I'm compunctious that you should have worked so hard. Seven hours a day My God. . . .*

Damn you for going to Normandy—I have just refused to stay with Ethel Sands, in order to write

But whats one's writing worth that one should refuse to cross the Channel?—at this moment the thing I long for: Shall we go in Sept.?

Berg

❧ *Sept 15th, [1926]* *Monks House, Rodmell [Sussex]*

They've only just sent the second batch of proofs [of Passenger to Teheran*] which I have swallowed at a gulp. Yes—I think its awfully good. I kept saying 'How I should like to know this woman' and then thinking 'But I do', and then 'No, I dont—not altogether the woman who writes this' I didn't know the extent of your subtleties: Here's a brave attitude—emeralds, staircases, Raymond subjugated—thats familiar enough: but not the sly, brooding thinking evading one. The whole book is full of* *nooks and corners which I enjoy exploring Sometimes one wants a candle in one's hand though—Thats my only criticism—you've left (I daresay in haste) one or two dangling dim places. . . .*

Berg

 *Long Barn, Weald,*
Sevenoaks.
17th September [1926]

So happy tonight because I had your letter. But what have you done to your finger? and how cut your chin? Yes, I expect Grizzle is in for it; and all your fault. What would be the result if Grizzle mated with a dog twice her size? God! what a monster!

I *am* glad you like the book. I did write it in a hurry, you know, so no wonder there are dim dangling places. I'm glad too that you would like to know me: we must get some common friend to arrange a meeting, dear Mrs Woolf, when I am next in London. At present I am oppressed by the thought of having to give a lecture there in October [1]—can think of nothing else, and the horror of it. Fool that I was, rash fool, ever to accept.

Could you understand the map? [2] I can't, and feel that I am the one sane person left in a world of lunatics, for everyone else seems to fall naturally into the map-maker's distorted vision. Oh, I am very glad you like it. I had such qualms after you sent it off without even reading it. No, of course The Land is not out, or you should have had a copy. [3] It will be out next week or week after that,—I forget which. 30th Sept. I now hear. I am in a bit of a turmoil, 1) the Land coming out, 2) got to give a lecture, 3) Virginia likes my book. These three things trot round and round in my head, making a tune like the wheels of a railway train.

At this point sleep overcame me and I went to bed. It is now Saturday morning, and Leonard's letter has come about the map. I am relieved to find that I am not quite an idiot after all. Tell him from me: Scrap map, and go ahead. I only hope it has not delayed the book already. Tell L. too that I did give the man the right proportions, and can't think why he ignored them. I will retrieve the offending object when I come to retrieve the [photograph] album. I'm now longing for the book to come out. When will that be?

This to catch the early post so you ought to get it today. Must send it—

V.

Berg

1. On October 27, to the Royal Society of Literature, about modern poetry. Gosse was in the chair, Virginia in the audience.
2. Intended for *Passenger to Teheran*, but not printed
3. Vita's *The Land* was published on September 30, 1926.

❧ *[Typewritten]* *Monks House, Rodmell*
21st Sept. [1926] *Lewes [Sussex]*

Hope to bring out book in early Oct. Any names to send cards to? If so please let me have them. What is your lecture about? When? Where? May I come? Will clap. Grizzle seduced again. . . .

Berg

Long Barn, Weald,
Sevenoaks.
Tuesday [21 September 1926]

Oh darling Virginia! damn, I can't come tomorrow, got to go to Brighton—but would love to come Thursday, *if* I can get away. I'll send you a line from Brighton tomorrow when I know how long Mother wants me to stay. I'll bring lots to drink. If I looked tired it was because I had been up all night [with Lady Sackville], and went to bed at 6 a.m. that morning, with a cold dawn creeping over the sea. I'll bring the circulars, and list.

Rather harassed, thank you.

Do just as you like about Clive; yes, I'd like to see him and hear his jolly laugh.

I sent you The Land yesterday. Doesn't it look pretty in its cover?

How is the finger?

V.

Berg

October 1926–January 1927

Virginia began to introduce Vita more frequently into the Bloomsbury circle, which alarmed her (she called it Gloomsbury—"All the old vocabulary trotted out"), and she was also scared of Leonard, whom she described to Harold, unfairly, as "a funny, grim, solitary creature" in contrast to Virginia, who was "an angel of wit and intelligence." Virginia came for several weekends to Long Barn, spent Christmas in Cornwall, and for two nights in mid-January went again to Knole, where, said Vita, "We wandered all over the house, pulling up blinds. She was thrilled."

 *Long Barn, Weald,*
Sevenoaks.
Sunday [3 October 1926]

I feel I have been very tiresome, what with saying I would come and then not coming, and one thing and another. But if you knew how uncertain everything has been, and how I have been kept dangling about, and had my plans upset several times, you would perhaps forgive me. Will you?

Will you tell Leonard I received and have returned the proofs of the illustrations? I am glad he warned me, but even so I didn't think them so bad. I think it is rather a pity they did not enlarge the small one, but I suppose it is too late now that the block is made?

That aeroplane nearly fell on my head yesterday, and was still blazing on the ground when I reached it.[1] It flew right over Long Barn in flames. Such a horrible sight I shall never forget. There was nothing to be done, as they were all dead, and men were dragging out the bodies with wooden hay-rakes.

Shall you be in London on Thursday when I dine with Clive?

Oh by the way I told Tanqueray to send you a dozen of the Spanish wine. They will send you the bill,—30/- —so don't start getting angry with me. It will go to Tavistock Square.

I'm glad you thought The Land looked pretty. I await reviews in trepidation. I have never minded before, and am cross with myself for minding now. It's silly.

V.

Berg

1. It crashed in the fields near Long Barn. Five people were killed.

❧ *Sunday [10 October 1926]* *[Monk's House, Rodmell, Sussex]*

Darling Mrs Nicolson,

Could you be an entire angel and tell me (for the 50th time) the name and address of the old widow who typewrites? Lost again, and needed instantly.

Well, did you like Squire? I did: I think the better of him for it, though his manner is always that of a curate, a grocer, a churchwarden, someone sticky with jam and buns at a School treat, however, he admires you; and I'm jealous. Yes: that yellow moon is rising on the horizon—Everyone admiring Vita, talking of Vita. Now there remain the Times Literary Supt. for which I have an unreasoning respect: Nation: New Statesman. All of these are negligible compared with one word of mine or any other casual vivid outspoken human being: but one can't see it oneself—not the author. . . .

Berg

❧ *[12? October 1926]* *[Monk's House, Rodmell, Sussex]*

Mr Barrington Gates (the Nation reviewer) says may he take a whole column for The Land, as in his opinion it is 'so outstanding' that it should not be lumped in with others. . . . So there He's going to have a column.

Berg

 *182, Ebury Street,*
S.W.1.
Thursday evening [18 November 1926]

My darling Virginia,

I am really miserable that you are ill—Put me off tomorrow if you are no better.

In any case I'll escape tomorrow afternoon—and we'll go off to Kew—If you want to send a message to put me off, ask to speak to me—and don't give a message—as I shan't say where I am going or I shall be lunching here for certain.

I do hate your having a headache—my poor darling—

V.

Berg

❧ *[19 November 1926]* *52 Tavistock Sqre [W.C.1]*

You are a miracle of discretion—one letter in another. I never thought of that. I'll answer when I see you—the invitation, I mean. Oh dear, Sibyl has given me a headache. What a bore I cant write, except to you. I lie in a chair. It isn't bad: but I tell you, to get your sympathy: to make you protective: to implore you to devise some way by which I can cease this incessant nibbling away of life by people: Sibyl, Sir Arthur [Colefax], Dadie—one on top of another. Why do I put it on you? Some psychological necessity I suppose: one of those intimate things in a relationship which one does by instinct. I'm rather a coward about this pain in my back: You would be heroic: . . .

But you dont see, donkey West, that you'll be tired of me one of these days (I'm so much older) and so I have to take my little precautions. Thats why I put the emphasis on 'recording' rather than feeling. But donkey West knows she has broken down more ramparts than anyone. And isnt there something obscure in you? There's something that doesn't vibrate in you: It may be purposely—you dont let it: but I see it with other people, as well as with me: something reserved, muted—God knows what. . . . It's in your writing too, by the bye. The thing I call central transparency—sometimes fails you there too. . . .

Berg

Long Barn, Weald,
Sevenoaks.
Saturday morning [20 November 1926]

My poor darling, I am *so sorry* about the headache. I haven't time to write much of a letter as unless I catch the early post you won't get this till Monday; so only time, really, to say how sorry I am and how angry with that stuffed Ethiopian mummy [Sibyl Colefax] for giving it to you. Also this: that if it is not gone, utterly and completely by Monday morning, you must put me off. I won't have you made ill, by myself any more than by anybody else.

Look here, your sister asks me to her party,[1] but I am in a quandary: what am I to call her? She calls me Vita, quite rightly. I shall send a telegram.

I must send this, my darling, but I can't bear to think of you 'lying in a chair' with a pain in your back. I *wish* I were there, or you here, or at all events that you were recovered.

Another book from the Laureate [Robert Bridges] this morning!

Berg

1. A party given by Vanessa Bell on November 24

 *Long Barn, Weald,*
Sevenoaks.
Sunday [21 November 1926]

Enclosed you will find a miserable poem written on the strength of your letter. I think you are a witch, or a dowser in psychology. You must be. My respect for you increases.

Look here, if you would like to go to the ballet tomorrow night (and Leonard) will you ring me up before 12 and say so? I only suggest it because it is the first night of L'Oiseau de feu, and I would get tickets. I should like to go, but will only go if you will come.

I am longing to see you and have been in a state all yesterday and today. I spent most of yesterday in bed which is why I said next weekend would be better than this. I have been in a black temper (with myself, not with you,) and have travelled over a lot of country. If I were not going to see you tomorrow anyhow, I should take steps to do so. Are you recovered from Sibyl? Furious with that woman for giving you a headache. Altogether I am in a rage.

I'll come in by the basement at 2.30 or thereabouts.[1] Thank Heaven for that.

V.

Berg

1. They met in London next day. Virginia wrote in her diary afterward: "She was sitting on the floor in her velvet jacket and red striped silk shirt, I knotting her pearls into heaps of great lustrous eggs. . . . So we go on—a spirited, creditable affair, I think, innocent (spiritually) and all gain, I think; rather a bore for Leonard, but not enough to worry him." Vita wrote to Harold about the same meeting: "I am a little bothered about Virginia, but fortunately she is a busy and sensible person and doesn't luxuriate in vain repinings. She is an absolute angel to me, and the value of her friendship is not to be measured in gold." *(Lilly Library, Indiana University)*

66 Mount Street
W.1.
Saturday night [27 November 1926]

My beloved Virginia, I am worried about you—I thought you were tired and depressed. What is it? were you just merely tired? I feel a brute for having let you come here.[1] Was it just the bloody flux? I oughtn't to have let you come. Don't you know that there is nothing I wouldn't do to save you a moment's pain, annoyance, fatigue, irritation? and then I go and let you come all this way to see me! I could kick myself—Please forgive me: my only consolation is that you had the motor. My darling, I will try to make up to you for the past weekend. I would ring you up and say all this instead of writing it, but the reason why I don't is obvious. I will dine and fetch you on Saturday. I miss you dearest. Perhaps I will see you on Monday? I'll ring up on Monday at 2.30. I can't get you out of my mind tonight; the corner of the sofa where you sat is haunted for me by your presence, the whole flat seems full of you—

Your
V.

Sussex

1. To Dorothy Wellesley's flat

182, Ebury Street,
S.W.1
[30 November 1926]

It made me wretched to know you were tired yesterday, darling. Do take my scolding to heart! and don't be so social—you'll get like Sibyl Colefax, and develop a bright beady eye, looking for new guests. I hope you're none the worse today; would like to ring you up; but I don't want to bother. So I write.

Just off to Brighton, not looking forward to it much, thank you. I dislike the feeling that one is walking on spikes, with bare feet.

I expect you both Thursday. You couldn't stay two nights, I suppose? no, I suppose not.

We were taken by main force by Mary [Hutchinson] to Mr Kitchin's party.[1] I decided I would never never go to a party again. I saw Clive, looking distraught and scattered.

Well, I must start. Do be good, strong-minded, self protective. I hate it when you get tired and droop. It really hurts me. Bless you, sweet.

V.

Berg

1. Clifford Kitchin, writer and barrister, was the author of *Streamers Waving* (1925) and *Death of My Aunt* (1929), both published by the Hogarth Press.

❧ *Wednesday [1 December 1926]* *[52 Tavistock Square, W.C.1]*

Very nice to get a letter from you, dear Creature—No, it wasn't the people yesterday—I had the shivers, due to getting wet through at Rodmell—that was all—I went to bed, took aspirin, hot bottle, quite all right today, only incredibly sleepy. Still I agree—people are the devil. . . .

Moreover, you cant talk—lunch at Woking, tea Virginia, Cocktail Raymond, dine Mary, supper Kitchin—There I was warm in bed, and glad to hear it was a ghastly failure. And now you're off to Brighton heaven help you! I wish you hadn't that before you, but could drop in and talk—Here I am sitting or rather lying in front of the gas fire in perfect quiet.

Berg

 *Long Barn, Weald,*
Sevenoaks.
Wednesday [1 December 1926]

My darling, is this yours? It is a young cuckoo in my nest, anyway, and I think I borrowed it off you once.

Last night I went to bed very early and read Mrs Dalloway. It was a very curious sensation: I thought you were in the room—But there was only Pippin, trying to burrow under my quilt, and the night noises outside, which are so familiar in one's own room; and the house was all quiet. I was very unhappy because I had had a row with my mother and very happy because of you; so it was like being two different people at the same time, and then to complicate it there was a) the conviction that you were in the room, and b) the contact with all the many people that you had created. (What a queer thing fiction is.) I felt quite light, as though I were falling through my bed, like when one has a fever. Today I am quite solid again, and my boots are muddy; they weight me down. Yet I am not as solid as usual,—not *quite* such an oaf,—because there is at the back of my mind all the time (slightly lifting the top off my head,) a glow, a sort of nebula, which only when I examine it hardens into a shape; as soon as I think of something else it dissolves again, remaining there like the sun through a fog, and I have to reach out to it again, take it in my hands and feel its contours: then it hardens, "Virginia is coming on Saturday." I am going to dinner at Knole tonight, and I shall meet an oil magnate and his wife; but it will be there all the time, a will o' the wisp that lets itself be caught, "Virginia is coming on Saturday."

But she won't, she won't! something will happen. Of course something will happen. Something always does, when one wants a thing too passionately. You will have chicken pox, or I shall have mumps, or the house will fall down on Saturday morning. In the meantime there are three cows staring over the stile; they are waiting for cake. There is a nebula in their minds too, "At four o'clock we shall have cake." And for them, lucky brutes, nothing will happen. But for me there is the whole range of human possibility.

If ever you tried not to have chicken pox, try now. If ever you tried not to be given a headache by Sibyl Colefax, try now. (I remember, ominously, that you said you were going to tea with her on Friday.) Please try with all your might not to let anything happen. I will be responsible for you after you have arrived,—only, please arrive. (I will let you know the trains tomorrow.) Bring your work, I won't interrupt. I so want you to be happy here.[1] I wish, in a way, that we could put the clock back a year. I should like to startle you again,—even though I didn't know then that you were startled.

V.

Berg

1. Virginia came to Long Barn, December 4–6. Vita wrote to Harold: "We talked about Katherine Mansfield, Rupert Brooke, early Bloomsbury. I never knew anyone with so much imagination or gives me so much the impression of a genius." *(Lilly Library, Indiana University)*

❧ *Friday [3 December 1926]* *52 T[avistock] S[quare, W.C.1]*

No—I cant come. I have caught eczema from Grizzle. My hair comes out in tufts. I scratch incessantly. It wouldn't be safe for you, or, what matters more, the puppies. I shall think of you: let that console us.

That joke being done with—yes, I'll come reaching Sevenoaks at 5.22.

It is true I'm incredibly dirty; have washed my head—hair is down—skirt spotted, shoes in holes—Pity poor Virginia dragged off this afternoon by Sibyl to meet Arnold Bennett who abused me for a column in last nights Standard.

Oh I'm so sick of teaing dining, reading writing and everything, except seeing—well it is you, *I admit. Yes it will be nice—yes it will: And shall you be very kind to me?*

Berg

 *Long Barn, Weald,*
Sevenoaks.
Wednesday [8 December 1926]

Pinker and I try to console one another. She sleeps on my bed, and clings to me as the one comparatively familiar thing in a strange and probably hostile world. She was pleased to see me when I came back from London, but ran about sniffing and looking for Mrs Woolf. I had to explain that Mrs Woolf lived in London, a separate life, a fact which was as unpleasant to me as it could be to any spaniel puppy, so she has adopted me as a substitute. I explained that everybody always betrayed one sooner or later, and usually gave one away to somebody else, and that the only thing to do was to make the best of it. I have introduced her to the insect, but he is rather frightened of her because she puts her paw down on him, so he creeps away to his legitimate abode.

So altogether it is rather a desolate party at Long Barn.

Oh, but it was a treat having you here. Such a treat, I haven't yet got over it. I wish I could think you had been one half as happy as I was. Not but what I don't think that I *am* very nice, and very good for you, so you see there is no false modesty on my part. Now I think about Knole, a question over which I am prepared to make myself really disagreeable, simply because I don't think I have ever wanted anything so much, and it will be my last treat before going away. For ever so long. You will come, won't you?[1]

Darling, you will come?

V.

I say, did you remember to send Mrs Dalloway to my mother? White Lodge, Roedean, near Brighton. If you wrote in it she would like that— Sorry to bother you, but you know what she is. I've added 7/6 on to my bill (enclosed). I'll come on Monday, in the undern.[2] Still angry with Arnold Bennett.[3] Did Mrs Cameron boom?[4]

Sussex

1. Virginia spent the nights of January 17 and 18, 1927, at Knole.
2. "Undern" is an archaic word Virginia and Vita used with each other to denote early afternoon.
3. His critical article about Virginia appeared in the *Evening Standard*, December 2.
4. In October 1926 the Hogarth Press had published Julia Margaret Cameron's *Victorian Photographs of Famous Men & Fair Women* with an introduction by Virginia.

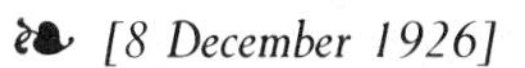

[8 December 1926] *52 T.[avistock] S.[quare, W.C.1]*

Dearest Vita,

(Now why did I say that?) Yes, Monday, undern 2.30. Please come, and bathe me in serenity again. Yes, I was wholly and entirely happy. . . .

But why, darling Mrs N., honourable Mrs N. insist upon Knole? To see me ridiculous, the powder falling, the hairpins dropping, and not a word said in private between us? . . .

Berg

Long Barn, Weald,
Sevenoaks.
Saturday [11 December 1926]

Disaster last night: Pinker, in sportive mood, sprang on to my writing table, upsetting the ink stand, which poured two floods of ink (one red and the other blue) down over the back of the sofa. Pippin was drenched in the blue ink, puppy in the red. Today Pippin looks like a bruise, puppy like an accident. You would have enjoyed the scene. I hope she will have regained her normal colour by January 1st when you have her back.

Oh, and you rang me up. I liked that. But surely you would like to feed stags out of a bucket? I can promise you some good moments at Knole,—and as for no private conversation, why, silly, we should be alone all day practically. We'll stick the powder on with [*paper damaged*] and padlock the hairpins.

It's good of you to say you will write a note to Mother, she likes that kind of thing. By the way she is ordering two copies of Mrs Cameron, to show her appreciation of your advertisements! She says now it is I who make her ill—This I think is a bit hard. Please don't tell anybody of my difficulties with her; I oughtn't really to have said anything about it, ought I? even to you—but it was so on my mind, but it was disloyal of me all the same. Not a nice character.

But a loving one in spite of that,—for Virginia.

V.

Sussex

 *Long Barn, Weald,*
Sevenoaks.
Thursday [16 December 1926]

My lost Virginia, Dottie says she is asking you to dinner on Monday night to read you those incestuous papers; I hope you will go. I shall be there.[1] She isn't asking Leonard because she says she couldn't bring herself to read them to *him*!

My mother has almost forgiven me because yours was so beautiful; I don't follow the logic of this, but there it is. Your correspondence with her disquiets me rather: I hope she hasn't been bothering you? She wants some more of those post-cards,—are there any left?

Puppy very well and happy, in spite of having eaten a whole shoe yesterday.

I am coming to see you on Monday aren't I? but look here, I don't want you to waste your time—Do prepare some job for me to do, good in a corner. It really distresses me to make you idle.

Let's disappear, shall we? and our books will boom. But not to a hydro at Harrogate.[2] Even with you. (Yes, I would, though.)

Such a marvellous day, and all the drops twinkling on the trees. How *can* people live in towns when they needn't?

Your V.

Sussex

1. Vita and Virginia dined with Dorothy Wellesley at her flat in Mount Street on December 20.
2. The detective-story writer Agatha Christie was missing from her home for two weeks, and was discovered hiding in a hotel at Harrogate, Yorkshire, by a journalist.

❧ *Friday [17 December 1926]* *52 Tavistock Square, W.C.1*

Dear Vita,

Here is your mothers letter, to which I have replied in my well known 18th Century style; no, she has been most helpful and emollient. . . . Yes, you are coming on Monday undern: yes, I am dining with Dotty. D'you know what happened to day? I was rushing into a shop to buy a velvet coat, when a woman said Any stains to take out? Good God, I said, I have at least 12 on me at the moment—so I bought her ointment, and all my stains are vanished like snow, and I'd been cleaned unavailingly, so life has turned its rosier cheek, and everything seems possible—except indeed, I had a tooth stopped. Now my lip my cheek, my chin are all boils and blisters. When I say to the dentist, why do you do this to me? He replies, But then, Mrs W. your skin is the most sensitive in London, at which I am flattered, but Leonard paints my skin with zinc ointment which I lick and I daresay its poison and I shall be dead. . . .

Berg

66 Mount Street
W.1.
Tuesday [21 December 1926]

My darling Virginia, look here, overleaf you will find a list of books to be sent—Will you pass it on to Mrs Cartwright before you go?[1] cards enclosed. I'll write to you in Cornwall[2]—This is merely business—

Oh dear—How agitating life is—What *I* think of when I walk

down the Strand is: how fine this would have been if Wren's plans for re-building London after the Great Fire had been adopted. Steps to the river, and all that—and a broad thoroughfare—

I've got lots to say, but it must wait—

Your
V.

Sussex

1. Mrs. Cartwright joined the staff of the Hogarth Press in July 1925 and remained till 1930.
2. Virginia and Leonard were spending Christmas with the Arnold-Forsters at Zennor, near St. Ives.

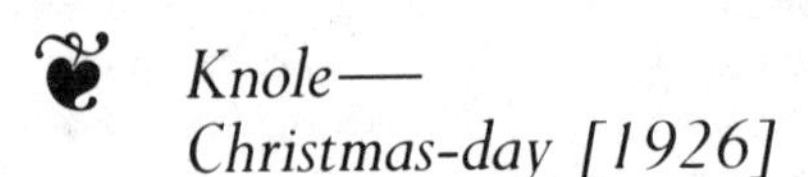

Knole—
Christmas-day [1926]

I am spending my Christmas in bed with influenza. It is very pleasant. I am warm,—and everybody comes in looking blue with cold; an atmosphere of seasonable jocularity prevails, I am sure, in the dining-room,—and I am exempt from it. Kind people bring me grapes. I have a photograph of Virginia,—not a very good photograph,—but better than nothing. I lie in bed, and watch the fire on the ceiling, and hear the clock strike, and think how delicious it will be when you come to stay here—I read Haydon,[1] and an excellent Cruickshank-ish book called Murder for Profit.[2] I have delightful dreams induced by aspirin, e.g. I dreamt that I dined with Eddy, a party consisting of Eddy, Charlotte Brontë, you, and me. Eddy seemed vexed and anxious, and after dinner took me aside to say, "Vita, you must find me *very attractive* to put up with such a dull party on my account?" Altogether it is an excellent way of spending Xmas, and I recommend it.

Are you lugging a spade across the Cornish beaches? Are you happy down there? or rather wistful? When are you coming back?—But my darling you shouldn't have sent me Night and Day; I wanted it to give away! However I am delighted to have it and shall read it as soon as Eddy brings it back. (My pen's run out of ink.) We haven't been able to go to Brighton yet—I see you, don't I, on my way back from Sherfield? on Monday of next week? I can dispose of the boys that afternoon—

A silly letter, because in spite of the charms of 'flu I don't really feel very well—I miss you very much, and am glad I can look forward to your coming here as otherwise I should be really too depressed—As it is, I lie making lovely plans, all firelit and radiant—My bed's at least nine foot wide, and I feel like the Princess and the Pea,—only there is no Pea. It is a four-poster, all of which I like. Come and see for yourself.

V.

Sussex

1. The *Autobiography* (1847) of Benjamin Robert Haydon, the painter and writer
2. By W. Bolitho, 1926, a famous detective story

Knole,
Sevenoaks.
Wednesday [29 December 1926]

Oh Lord! I hope you got my letter at Zennor. They seem to have taken ages.

Brighton tomorrow. . . .

I shiver in my shoes.

Sherfield on Friday, and Clive, and bawdiness, shall I write to you from there?

I've just been down to Long Barn, and got such a welcome from Pinker as I never had from anybody, not even from Virginia. Oh but I do so want to see Virginia, and only a month left to do it in. How frantic life is—Xmas trees and what not—and influenza—and making children write letters to say thank you—The next thing is to settle when you are coming here—that is of the greatest importance—

So many people talking in the room—though not about the League of Nations— [1]

I looked out Zennor on the map.

I miss you—

V.

Sussex

1. Virginia and Leonard had been discussing the League with the Arnold-Forsters.

❧ *Wednesday [29 December 1926]* *52 Tavistock Square [W.C.1]*

Dearest Creature,

I only got your letter this morning, so I rang up a surly butler, and heard Eddy was ill but Mrs Nicolson was better. I do hope so. Not that Eddy should be ill. Only I hate your having flu. . . .

. . . One thing is I dont think Knole is possible; for this reason: I tore all my clothes on the gorse, and cant get any more, and I couldn't ask your butler to wait on me, nor is it for the dignity of letters that I should eat behind a screen, so I dont see how I can come to Knole, all in holes, without a pin to my hair or a stocking to my foot. You'd be ashamed; you'd say things you would regret. But read carefully whats coming. Its this

I am going to America.

Now thats exciting isnt it?

Berg

❧ *[30 December 1926]* *52 Tavistock Square, W.C.1*

America—

*The [*New York Herald*] Tribune's offered me free passages, hotel bills, and £120 to go to New York for a month in the spring and write 4 articles. I've said I will if I can arrange times, and not too much work. . . .*

Knole

I was partly teasing. I dont mind being dowdy, dirty, shabby, red nosed middle classed and all the rest—its only a question when and how—I do want to see you, I do—I do.

Berg

❦ *Sherfield Court,*
Sherfield Upon Loddon,
Basingstoke.
Sunday [2 January 1927]

So you're going to Rodmell on Tuesday. Very well: that involves the natural consequence that I'll come up tomorrow (Monday,) and come to the basement. Now never say again that I don't love you. I want dreadfully to see you. That is all there is to it.

Pinker: I'll send her to Rodmell—quite easy by train from Sevenoaks—in a hamper. I love her, but she ought to go back to you, as now that I am not at Long Barn any more she is apt to follow stray people down the road and I have been in terror of her getting lost.

People are very wearisome, really, aren't they? I mean I feel I know exactly what they're all going to say long before they've said it. Not but what they are not all very nice; and to see Ethel [Sands] dancing the House-Party to Eddy's accompaniment is a great treat. And we went to Steventon, where Jane Austen lived—They also discussed you for the whole of one dinner, a discussion to which Vita contributed not one word.

And then arguments about de la Mare, Fromentin, Derain,—and all the old vocabulary trotted out.

It's time I either lived with Virginia or went back to Asia, and as I can't do the former I must do the latter.[1] I'm feeling, you see, like a person who has eaten too many sweets.

But a very handsome tribute from Mr Drinkwater in the Observer.[2] One is easily comforted.

I shall go for a long walk, alone.

Till tomorrow, then, my dear—and very nice too. You'll be nice to me, won't you? and I'll be nice to you. And we'll arrange about Knole. I shall pin you down.

Your V.

Sussex

1. Virginia spent January 17 and 18 at Knole, and ten days later Vita went for the second time to Persia.

2. John Drinkwater (1882–1937), the playwright, poet, and actor, who presented the Hawthornden Prize to Vita for *The Land* in 1927

❧ *[4 January 1927]* *[52 Tavistock Square, W.C.1]*

Came home to find a letter from Harold, begging me to get you to promise to be inoculated—So don't be a donkey and promise me to do it—or I won't come to Knole. Its absolutely necessary. Why risk death and typhoid and no Virginia for sake of 10 minutes bother?

Harold writes about us too—wont be jealous he says. . . .

Berg

 *Knole,*
Sevenoaks.
Thursday [6 January 1927]

I sent off a furious Pinker,—furious at being put into a basket. By the way may I have the basket back? I could fetch it at Monk's House one day next week when I am at Brighton so you would have no trouble with it.

I am so much amused at Harold writing to you (1) inoculation (2) jealousy. Of course I shall be inoculated. Of course he isn't jealous.[1] But how funny he is, writing to say so. No, you write to him by post:

British Legation
Tehran, Persia—

because the bag won't go for another fortnight now. Please tell him how much you like me—because you do don't you?

The house swarms with children and things—No peace possible—More and more do I marvel at the way everything conspires to chop life up till there is no continuity left. What is making me wild is the thought that these last weeks are slipping by and I am not seeing you. Before we know where we are I shall be gone. Anyway I'll come on Monday—and please, please remember that I shall be in London 27th and 28th—and I simply must see you then, as the 29th is the day I go. You are coming here on the 20th? but oh dear it's a bad date for certain reasons—damn it—you wouldn't, would you, consider the weekend of the 16th instead? but we'll talk about it on Monday.

Your
V.

PERSONAL, Continued.
Blush ye dull and witless Letter Writers of To-day, and hang your heads, for this is the anniversary of the death of the ever adorable Madame de Sévigné.
"De toutes façons vous avez droit
de plaire,
Mais surtout vous savez nous
charmer en ce jour."

S.C.

I didn't know Sibyl Colefax was so great an admirer of Mme de Sévigné.[2]

I feel that the sentiment expressed fits into a nutshell what you feel about me?

Sussex

1. Harold had written to Virginia from Teheran: "I am glad that Vita has come under an influence so stimulating and so sane. . . . You need never worry about my having any feelings except a longing that Vita's life should be as rich and as sincere as possible. I loathe jealousy as I loathe all forms of disease." *(Sussex)*

2. The newspaper clipping was attached to the letter.

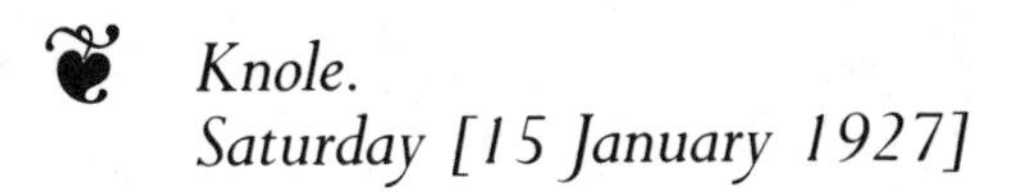

Knole.
Saturday [15 January 1927]

You've no idea of the intrigues that have been going on here to ensure your getting the room I wanted you to have [at Knole],—how I have lied shamelessly, tucked Olive away in a room she never has,[1] bundled her clothes out, bribed the housekeeper, suborned the housemaids. You have a curious effect of making me quite unscrupulous, of turning me into a sort of Juggernaut riding over obstacles. Now all is well,—do I expect you by the 5.18? or when? Telephone Sevenoaks 146 to say. But as early as possible, please. I look on it as a swansong. (Not a permanent swansong; only a temporary one.)

My mother was an angel; I adore her.

I send you lots and lots of money.

Eddy told me he had seen you last night, little pig. He returned, looking rather dissipated and rather charming—I'm going to the film society with him tomorrow—Wish I could come to see you, but you will be otherwise engaged.

I've got a lovely full moon (or nearly) for you—I've just been out looking at the court; it's now midnight; I like the battlements in the moonlight and the frost. You *will* stay over Tuesday night, won't you? and I'll motor you up to London on Wednesday morning. Do remember what a dreadfully long time it will be before I see you again.

I don't know, by the way, why I assume that you won't come till the evening; come any time you can.

I suppose I can manage to exist till Monday but I'm not sure.

Your
V.

Eddie Marsh says I'm the best living poet under 80—so there.[2]

Sussex

1. Olive Rubens, Lord Sackville's boon companion. He wanted to marry her after the death of her husband, Walter, but Lady Sackville refused a divorce.
2. Edward Marsh had edited five volumes of *Georgian Poetry*. The fifth volume (1924) had contained seven poems from Vita's *Orchard and Vineyard* (London: John Lane, 1921).

January–February 1927

On January 28, Vita left London for her second visit to Persia, having spent that morning alone with Virginia. She was again accompanied on this journey by Dorothy Wellesley, and by Leigh Ashton, another friend; they traveled by rail through Germany to Moscow, and from there to Baku, where they took ship across the Caspian to northern Persia. Virginia's grief at her departure was not quite so acute as it had been the year before, and her letters to Persia (sharpening Vita's replies) were among her most brilliant.

 *182, Ebury Street*
Pimlico
[28 January 1927]

Beloved Virginia, one last goodbye before I go. I feel torn in a thousand pieces—it is *bloody—I can't tell you* how I hate leaving you. I don't know how I shall get on without you—in fact I don't feel I can—you have become so essential to me. Bless you for all the happiness you give me. I'll write in the train. Bless you, my darling, my lovely Virginia.

Your Vita

Such ages before I can hear from you, too! Please write by post soon—in fact at once—I can't bear to wait long for a word from you. Please, please. [*in pencil:*] Put 'honey' when you write—

Darling, please go on loving me—I am so miserable—Don't forget me—

Berg

London–Dover
[28 January 1927]

My darling, it's so shaky I can hardly write, we are tearing through my Weald—(see Passenger to Teheran, Chap. 2 passim.) So odd to have all the same emotions repeated after a year's interval—but oh *worse* where you are concerned. I really curse and damn at the pain of it—and yet I wouldn't be without it for anything—I shall remember you standing in your blue apron and waving. Oh damn it, Virginia, I wish I didn't love you so much. No I don't though; that's not true. I am glad I do. I don't know what to say to you except that it tore the heart out of my body saying goodbye to you—I am thankful to have had yesterday, a real gift from the Gods—Oh my darling you *have* made me so happy, and I do bless you for it—and I oughtn't to grumble now—ought I? but I really do feel wretched—You won't be able to read this letter—I sent you a telegram from Victoria—

Your
V.

Berg

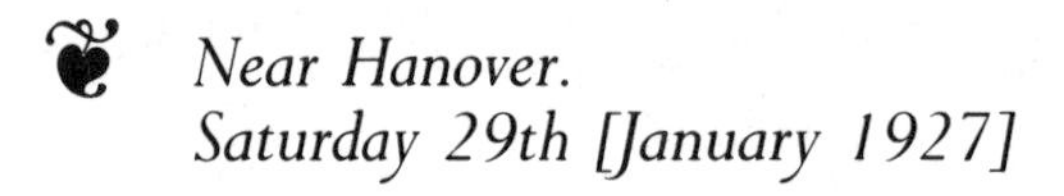

Near Hanover.
Saturday 29th [January 1927]

My darling,

I hoped I should wake up less depressed this morning, but I didn't. I went to bed last night as black as a sweep. The awful dreariness of Westphalia makes it worse: factory towns, mounds of slag, flat country, and some patches of dirty snow. And you are going to the Webbs.[1] Well, well.

Why aren't you with me? Oh, why? I do want you so frightfully.

The only thing which gives me any pleasure is Leigh's get-up.[2] He has bought a short sheepskin coat, in which he evidently thinks he looks like a Hungarian shepherd, but horn-rimmed glasses and a rather loud pair of plus-fours destroy this effect. Dottie on the other hand has appeared in a very long fur-coat, down to the ankles, so thick as to make her quite round; *she* looks like a Russian grand-duke. We are all rather cross, and have rows about luggage. I want more than ever to travel with you; it seems to me now the height of my desire, and I get into despair wondering how it can ever be realised. Can it, do you think? Oh my lovely Virginia, it is dreadful how I miss you, and everything that everybody says seems flat and stupid.

I do hope more and more that you won't go to America, I am sure it would be too tiring for you, and anyway I am sure you wouldn't like it.[3] Come to Beirut instead??

So we bundle along over Germany, and very dull it is—Surely I haven't lost my zest for travel? no, it is not that; it is simply that I want to be with you and not with anybody else—But you will get bored if I go on saying this, only it comes back and back till it drips off my pen—Do you realise that I shall have to wait for over a fortnight before I can hear from you? poor me. I hadn't thought of that before leaving, but now it bulks very large and horrible. What may not happen to you in the course of a fortnight? you may get ill, fall in love, Heaven knows what.

I shall work so hard, partly to please you, partly to please myself, partly to make the time go and have something to show for it. I treasure your sudden discourse on literature yesterday morning,—a send-off to me, rather like Polonius to Laertes. It is quite true that you have had infinitely more influence on me intellectually than anyone, and for this alone I love you. I feel my muscles hardening,

> *"Il poeta è un' artiere*
> *Che al mestiere*
> *Fece i muscoli d'acciaio. . . ."*[4]

Yes, my very dear Virginia: I was at a crossways just about the time I first met you, like this:

You do like me to write well, don't you? And I do hate writing badly—and having written so badly in the past. But now, like Queen Victoria, I will be good.

Hell! I wish you were here—The team of ponies prances with temper. Send me anything you write in papers, and send 'On reading'. Please. I hope you will get my letters quick and often. Tell me if I write too often. I love you.

V.

Berg

1. Beatrice and Sidney Webb, the sociological and political writers, with whom Virginia stayed on January 29 at their house in Surrey

2. Leigh Ashton, who later became director of the Victoria and Albert Museum in London

3. After some hesitation, Virginia declined the invitation of the *New York Herald Tribune* to visit the United States.

4. "A poet is a creator/Who through his work/Makes sinews of steel"—GABRIELE D'ANNUNZIO

❦ *Moscow*
Monday 31st January [1927]

I tried to write to you in the train, but it was so shaky I gave it up in despair. Oh, my head is in a whirl: little patches of snow in Germany, more snow in Poland, all snow in Russia. Dark fir-woods weighted down with snow; peasants in sheepskins; sleighs; green, glaucous rivers immobilised into ice. All very beautiful, and endlessly melancholy. Fancy living in this country, feeling yourself to be only a little black dot in the middle of a flat whiteness stretching away to China. Then Moscow, with gold, green, red, blue roofs above the snow; and the scarlet Soviet flag, lit up from below at night just like the columns of Selfridge's, floating over the Kremlin; and all the traffic passing to and fro over the frozen river as though it were a road; and sleighs everywhere, and coachmen stuffed out with straw. I went to see Lenin tonight. He lies embalmed in a scarlet tomb just below the red flag, and the crowd walks round his glass case two by two. A woman had hysterics just behind me; screamed like an animal; sobbed; screamed again; nobody took any notice—And oh my God, there's a dinner party of 22 people tonight [at the British Embassy]—and I collided with Denys Trefusis in the hall—and is he coming to the dinner?[1] and shall I be put next to him? and then there's to be a concert—when the only thing I want is bed and sleep. I so nearly sent you a telegram, but thought you would think that silly; I had written it out, and then tore it up. Would you have thought it silly? or been pleased? and do you know where I am, I wonder, or have you lost count? It's seven o'clock here, but only five in London—so you're having Sibyl to tea at this moment, instead of me, and *she* won't sit on the floor or say my lovely Virginia, and you won't rumple *her* hair—and it won't be nearly so nice. I hope you miss me, though I could scarcely (even in the cause of vanity) wish you to miss me as much as I miss you, for that hurts too much, but what I do hope is that I've left some sort of a little blank which won't be filled till I come back. I bear you a grudge for spoiling me for everybody else's companionship, it is too bad—

Oh heavens, I must dress for this thrice bloody dinner party, when I want to go on writing to you. And how angry it makes me that you shouldn't be here, and I do ache for you so all the time—damn it—it gets no better with time or distance—and I foresee that it won't—Nor shall I have a word from you for ever so long—oh damn, damn, damn—You would be pleased if you knew how much I minded—

Your
V.

Berg

1. Denys Trefusis, husband of Violet (with whom Vita had eloped to France in 1920). He was an ardent Russophile, and died, more or less estranged from his wife, in 1929.

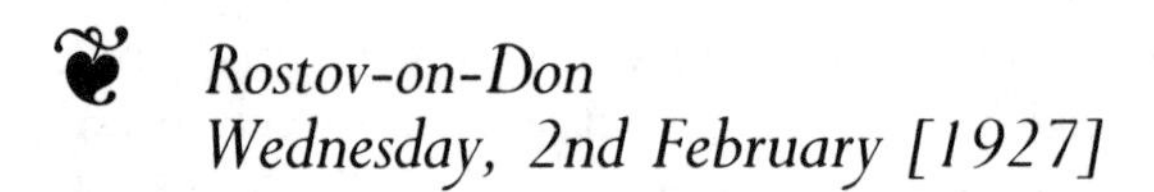

Rostov-on-Don
Wednesday, 2nd February [1927]

Belovèd Virginia—two days of snow-bound steppes, in an over-heated train with hermetically sealed windows, have dulled my fancy. So I have smashed the window with a corkscrew, and a thin shrill pencil of frozen air rushes in reviving us, giving us stiff necks, but bringing with it a blast of freshness reminiscent of Long Barn in winter, where the plaster has retreated from the beams and a smear of pale blue sky squints at one as one lies in one's bath—I don't know if you have ever noticed this—I read Boswell's tour in the Hebrides and speculate agreeably on the probable difference between Boswell's conception of the Hebrides, and yours [1]—The train bumbles along at a pleasantly slow pace,—the Ukraine under snow, the Sea of Azov, then Rostov where Leigh danced the Highland fling on the platform to the great delight of a crowd of Cossacks—who pressed round us saying 'Whisky.' But we hadn't any—but they kissed their hands to us all the same as the train drew out of the station on a fresh lap of its interminable leisurely journey. Meals happen at unusual hours: lunch at 3, and dinner at 5; we manage very nicely, on caviare and vodka. Miss Jebb fits in very well; [2]—a jolly girl, who can swing herself by one hand from the luggage rack,—Miss Elgood fits in less well, [3] but is inoffensive enough,—fetches and carries for us, and has but one standard for everything in life—"Naice," or "Not very naice." I think Leigh will probably propose to Miss Jebb before he has done; I've already told him to—and he agrees he might do worse. But oh my God, I'm glad I don't live in this country. The unutterable dreariness of the little Cossack villages isolated there out in the snows of an endless plain! Dr Johnson [*Journey to the Hebrides*] appears marvellously civilised—I feel he would have been in agreement with Desmond [MacCarthy] on almost every point—except that he had 100% more vigour than Desmond can ever have had—even before he (Desmond) faded away into a mere refinement of himself and became obliterated like a footprint after a fresh fall of snow.

For the rest, it is just the existence one settles down to on a long journey: the sponge-bag has its place, and the bottle of mineral water, and the penknife for sharpening pencils, and the books, and the hold-all—and then the extraordinary mixture of one's thoughts, half one's brain being concentrated on looking out of the window, and not losing the tickets or the passports or the money, and the other half living with a greater intensity in the life one has left behind,—what does Leigh think of? what does Dottie? what does Miss Jebb? what does Miss Elgood? of the museum? Sherfield? Lower Sloane Street? Hurstmonceux? and what do I think of? of Virginia in her blue overall, leaning against the doorpost of Tavistock Square, and waving, while the rapidly greying glass of milk stands in front of the gas-fire in a hopeless effort to get warm, and [George] Gissing lies on the table—That's what I think of, here in the steppes, with a twisted heart and an ache of homesickness, and a regret for the second night at Knole—which now cannot be made up for until Long Barn in May when the nightingales sing outside in the thorn bush and the irises come into flower in the night between sunset and sunrise—My darling, you will be in England, won't you, when I come back? and I can come and see you, the first person in London? You see, I'm already thinking of that—and I shall think of it for the next three months—

Your
V.

Sussex

1. Virginia's *To the Lighthouse* was set in the Hebrides.
2. Marjorie Jebb, the sister of Gladwyn Jebb, third secretary at the British legation in Teheran
3. A Foreign Office secretary who was traveling with them to join the legation staff in Teheran

❧ *Monday 31st Jan [1927]* *52 Tavistock Sqre [W.C.1]*

My dear Honey,

It was nice to get your telegram and letters—write as many as you can. It gives one a fillip. The only good thing thats happened to me is that the moment you left I became involved in a series of telephones, notes, scenes with Clive and Mary, all very emotional which left me so angered, so sordidified, so exacerbated that I could only think of you as being very distant and beautiful and calm. A lighthouse in clean waters. . . . Clive giving champagne suppers to Mary. I was amused to think how angry certain charges made against me by Mary would have made you—God, if you'd been here, what fun we should have had.

But the main good was that I've been kept on the hop the whole time: so I've been restless and scattered; its like taking sleeping draughts: I try my best to put off thinking about you. . . .

. . . D'you know its a great thing being a eunuch as I am: that is not knowing what's the right side of a skirt: women confide in one. One pulls a shade over the fury of sex; and then all the veins and marbling, which, between women, are so fascinating, show out. Here in my cave I see lots of things you blazing beauties make invisible by the light of your own glory.

No: I'm not going to America. They write that they are entertaining me at dinners, but not, apparently paying my hotel bills. So the cost would swallow up all my earnings, and I think we can cry off and go to Greece. . . .

I've not *got a cold in my head, but its like having a cold in the head, sitting here writing to you and everything at sixes and sevens. I feel dissipated and aimless for some reason. . . . Then its you being away—I am at the mercy of people, of moods, feel lonely, like something pitiable which can't make its wants known. How you have demoralised me. I was once a stalwart upstanding woman. Then its not writing novels: this journalism is such a thin draggled straining business, and I keep opening the lid and looking into my mind to see whether some slow fish isn't rising there—some new book. No: nothing at the moment.*

Yes, I like you to write good poetry. My parting lecture was not very coherent. I was trying to get at something about the thing itself before its made into anything: the emotion, the idea. The danger for you with your sense of tradition and all those words—a gift of the Gods though—is that you help this too easily into existence. . . .

Berg

February–May 1927

In Teheran once more, Vita felt acutely homesick, in spite of Harold's presence ("God, the people here!"—by whom she meant not the Persians but the diplomats), and missed Virginia "damnably," proposing that they should meet in Greece on her return journey to shorten the period of absence. She found herself unable to write, even journalism. But after nearly two months in Teheran she embarked with Harold and two friends on an adventure that resulted in her next book, Twelve Days. *They traveled via Persepolis and Shiraz to the wild Bakhtiari mountains in southern Persia and crossed them by foot and on mule to the Persian Gulf. This time Harold returned home with her, through the Mediterranean, and they arrived at Long Barn on May 5, to find, on this its publication day, a copy of* To the Lighthouse. *Only a few days earlier Virginia and Leonard had returned from a month's holiday in France and Italy.*

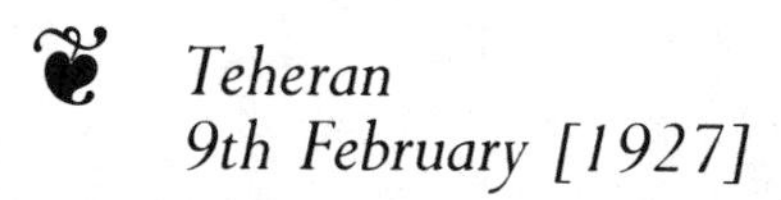

Teheran
9th February [1927]

My darling, I hardly know how to write to you, everything is so confused, so Einsteinian, an effect which I never can hope to communicate to you, so I won't try. Anyway, I am here. I have come over those familiar mountains, and crossed that familiar plain—and it seemed from the first as though I had never been away. My mind adjusted itself instantly to the proportion and shape, smell and colour, of Persia; just slipped click into gear. And now I don't know whether England seems near or far—It is a mixture: England itself seems a dot on the map, populated only by three or four figures of natural size, which makes them bulk unduly large on the tiny island on which they have their being. This, I think, is as it should be: the place dwindles, but the humans remain.

The moment we had arrived we began talking about how to get back. For one moment our [Bakhtiari] mountain expedition seemed in danger, but now it is re-established; for another moment it seemed that we should return by Constantinople and Athens, by ship, in which case I conceived the dizzy idea of meeting you there; but now that is abandoned. Would you have fallen in with that plan? (always assuming that you go to Greece and not to America,) would you have come on board at the Piraeus and found me waiting for you at the head of the gangway? Then we would have returned together through the Greek seas, which would I think completely have unhinged my reason. Greece, with you—in May.

God, the people here! They're still talking about the same things as when I left, only now they have got me as a new victim, "Alors, chère amie, vous avez fait bon voyage?" "Etes-vous contente, chère madame, de vous retrouver a Téhéran?" And I behave so pretty, and answer it all as though it were the most important thing in the world. Dottie says she never knew I had such nice manners. (She has written to you, by the way.) But, darling beloved Virginia, I can't believe that I was intended for the diplomatic career. Harold unfortunately seems to think that he was. This is a theory which I count upon you to dispel.

But what is really odd, is that I should be sitting again at the same table, with the sun pouring in through the plane-trees, writing to you as I used to do last year, and feeling again that helpless sense of impotence, travel being, as you know, the most private of pleasures. And your studio seems so much more real, and you waving on the doorstep. Oh, how I wish you would explain life to me, so that I might see it steadfastly and see it whole, or whatever the quotation is. I find it more and more puzzling as I grow older. I shall read Gide's mémoirs and see if that helps at all.[1]

But at the same time it is very exciting, and I suppose it is good for the soul to be hurt and perplexed perpetually. I know at least that I miss you damnably: that is a good fixed star. I do, Virginia; and would rather be hurt by that, and have something solid to hold on to, than flounder in a quicksand that never bruises but only smothers. Oh dear, you won't understand a word of all this, and small blame to you either.

The bag is going, but I can write by post. Russia was bloody, and I was nearly raped in the train—but for Leigh's timely interference. So he came in useful after all.

Midday: the cannon: the muezzins loosing their cry in the street: the sun: a little flute from an orange-seller—Do you remember once writing to me from Spain, years ago, about a religious procession?[2] How glad I am that you exist.

Your
V.

Sussex

1. *Si le grain ne meurt* (1926).
2. See *VW 1375.*

❦ *Teheran*
19th February [1927]

Virginia, listen. We are coming back by Greece. ("We" means Harold and I, i.e. Dottie is going home earlier.) We arrive at the Piraeus on Thursday April 28th, and leave again the same day for Trieste by Lloyd Triestino. Now, if you go to Greece, I imagine that you would be returning about the same time? Why not make it exactly the same time? Why not make it, in fact, the same boat? I cannot tell you the name of the boat yet, but I shall soon be in a position to do so, and in any case the Lloyd Triestino which leaves Athens on April 28th should not be hard to identify. Now will you give your mind and energies to arranging this matter? I write of it in this practical and business-like way, leaving it to your imagination to reconstruct what it would mean to me if I saw you coming up that gangway; I hope, also, that it would mean something to you—though with a cold fish it is difficult to know for certain. Harold says he would like nothing better, so let's have no silliness about *that*—and do not, oh I beseech you, do not let us miss such a chance through any muddle or mismanagement on your part. It's a good rendez-vous, you'll agree: meet me in Athens on April 28th at dawn.

Now for more practical information: the last bag by which you can write to me here is the one which leaves London on Thursday March 17th. But you can, if you will, write to me c/o the High Commissioner, Baghdad, Iraq, where I shall be for one day on April 20th. I don't know how long a letter to Baghdad takes, but I should think about a fortnight. You can also write to me c/o Sir Ronald Storrs, Nicosia, Cyprus, where I shall be on April 24th.[1] It would be nice to find a letter from you in that romantic place.

For a whole fortnight I shan't be able to write to you or to anybody, while we are camping. You remember when I dragged you to see the film called 'Grass'?

I've had one letter from you, full of mysteries about Clive. What on earth did Mary accuse you of?[2] How unkind to arouse my curiosity and then to allay it. I nearly sent you a telegram at 5/- a word. But I like people who get angry, whether it's Mary or Lord Gladstone, and whether their anger is justified or not. Don't tell me that it was over you that they had quarrelled—however it's no good asking you now—but I'll get it all out of you as we sail up the Corinth Canal.

Darling . . . the queerness of human beings strikes me more and more forcibly here. You see, it is just the opposite of London. In London people meet together because some common interests bind them; here, we are just a collection of people thrown together through a purely fortuitous circumstance, with nothing in common except the place we happen to find ourselves in. So that is the one and only topic. I go to call on some bloody Pole or Belgian, and we know that there is nothing to talk about except the Trebizond road, or the Shiraz road, and whether one has done it or not, and whether one is going away for the summer or not, and whether we may expect more snow. There is nothing else, except the cardinal facts of life, and foreign diplomats do not talk about copulation with the same ease, candour, and readiness as our friends in England. Correctness is the order of the day, so we never get any further. I should like to see how you would manage it. I said to the clergyman's daughter, how was she liking Teheran? and she replied, "Well, really, the theatricals seem to be the only excitement." Persia, Rheza, the swarming bazaars, Asia,—these are not excitements, nor is a civilisation thousands of years old, nor the spectacle of a worn-out nation. But Mrs Fairley comes to tea, and Mrs Wilkinson comes to luncheon,[3] and so it's not so bad, and one can always watch the football, and it *is* possible to get Karmalade though it's more expensive than it ought to be, "but I don't like that pomegranate jam, do you?" Meanwhile I cannot write, so am miserable—Instead of the odder, more angular thoughts I produce exquisite platitudes fit only for the fire. But I looked into my ring today,—an old Persian topaz, pale pink,—and saw there reflected a plane tree, some blue sky, and a white mountain, all tiny and coloured, and this seemed to me worth while, so I daresay there is still something left to write about. And we are going to Shiraz and Persepolis.

If I could know that we would meet in Athens, I should, of course, start writing at a hundred miles an hour, just from sheer joy. By the way, we'll be in London on May 2nd.

Oh, I got a letter from Sibyl. Would I please let her know the date of our return, so that she could arrange a party.

On the whole one can get a certain amount of fun out of the people. There is the fat clerk who says "I don't like gentlemen, Mrs. Nicolson, if you'll excuse my saying so, but I should like my sons to be one." There is the assistant military attaché, whose standard of civilisation is Quetta [India]. There is the governess (Eton crop, hands in pockets,) who says "Oh but you know, Mrs Nicolson, those boys in the Air Force *are* so naughty . . ." And we have bought a new motor car,—big, shut, blue,—which has sent up our credit in Teheran. And everybody refers slily to my book, which is supposed to be kept a secret from the Persians.[4]

I say, will you tell Leonard to make whatever arrangement he thinks best with Doran?[5] I know he'll do the best he can, both for the Press and for me, so I'm more than content to leave it in his hands. I telegraphed at once.

It *is* fun about the bookshop.[6] I hope it won't prevent you from going to Greece though. I never did approve of America and am relieved that you are not going there.

Can you read the inscription on my seal?[7]

The insect is frightfully excited about meeting you in Greece. You wouldn't have the heart to disappoint it,—would you? For you have a kind heart really, and are rather clever at managing what you want to manage. I feel that if I can enlist you as an ally, the thing is as good as done. Please write me nice letters—A week is a very long time to have to wait, from one post to another—and if you go to Greece God knows how long letters will take—oh no, of course they'll go by Constantinople and Khartoum.

Your
V.

Berg

1. Storrs was governor of Cyprus, 1926–1932. But Vita never went there.
2. Clive Bell's long affair with Mary Hutchinson was ending in mutual desolation.
3. Wives of legation officials
4. In *Passenger to Teheran* Vita had referred to the Shah as "a Cossack trooper . . . with a sullen manner, huge nose, grizzled hair and a brutal jaw." Although in the book she never mentioned her connection with Harold or the legation, this was thought to be highly offensive to the sovereign to whom Harold was accredited.
5. George Doran, the New York publisher, was considering an American edition of *Passenger to Teheran.*
6. Leonard was proposing to buy the bookshop in Bloomsbury founded by Francis Birrell.
7. *Nos patriae fines et dulcia linquimus arva* ("We have left the borders and dear fields of our native land").

Saturday, 5th Feb 1927 *52 Tavistock Sqre, London [W.C.1]*

Dearest Honey,

No letter since you were careering through the snow in Westphalia—that is nothing since Monday. I hope this doesn't mean you have been eaten by brigands, wrecked, torn to pieces. It makes me rather dismal. It gets worse steadily—your being away. All the sleeping draughts and the irritants have worn off, and I'm settling down to wanting you, doggedly, dismally, faithfully—I hope that pleases you. It's damned unpleasant for me, I can assure you. I had a sort of idea that I'd cheat the devil, and put my head under my wing, and think of nothing. But it wont work—not at all. I want you this Saturday more than last and so it'll go on.

. . . I sit over the gas in my sordid room. Why cant I write except in sordid rooms? I dont think I could write a word in your room at Long Barn. Furniture that people can sit in implies people, and I want complete solitude—thats at the back of my mind, and so I get sordider and sordider. The Voyage Out was written in comparative splendour [Fitzroy Square]—a maid, carpets, fires; To the Lighthouse was written—as you know. So the next book will necessitate a shed. This fits in with my mood at the moment. I have banged my door on parties, dug myself into a dank dismal burrow, where I do nothing but read and write. This is my hybernating season. . . .

Berg

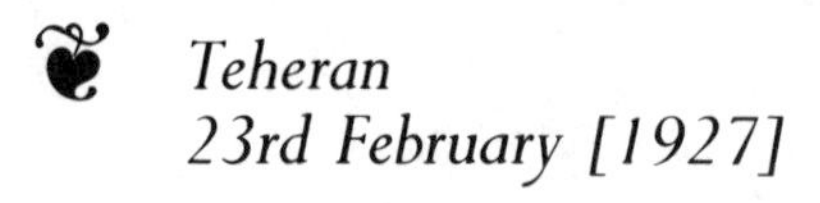

Teheran
23rd February [1927]

Yesterday the Russian post came in; at least, half of it did, for the Persians are incapable of delivering the whole of the post at one go, and think us most unreasonable for expecting them to do so, so that it arrives in driblets, spread sometimes over three days; but it was the right half that came yesterday, for it contained a letter (a nice, long, missing-me letter,) from you. I had been entertaining the Sheikh of Mohammerah, who most disconcertingly called upon me in state at 11. in the morning. He is a superb black-bearded old Arab, with the most beautiful hands I ever saw (always excepting yours,) and a large emerald ring; and then after half an hour of difficult conversation, and endless cups of tea, he took his departure and I was at liberty to read my letters. One from Raymond, one from you. I went down into depths of despair and self-reproach because I had not telegraphed to you. I did want to; then I thought Leonard would open it and be annoyed; then I hoped Mother would let you know, as she did last year. (I say: I can't bear there to be yet a third year of this [Persian] business. But Harold is in a very Empire-building frame of mind. Enormous skill will be necessary to get him out of it.)

I dreamt at great length, having read your letter, about what it would have been like to bring you here. Would you have got very tired on the journey? Do you like travelling? Are you the sort of traveller who constantly says "Oh look!"? Or do you take everything for granted? What would you like best here? Are you so much amused by people,—just as human beings,—that you have no surplus energy left for places? What would it be like to have you sitting in the room now? People become so different once they are taken away from their own surroundings—however well one knows them one discovers that one doesn't know them to the extent of being able to predict how they will react. E.g. Dottie,—I never realised what a luxury-child she was, being accustomed to seeing her always in England, where comforts happen automatically—she thinks Teheran uncivilised,—no electric light, scanty baths,—what would she be like really roughing it, if, for instance, she was allowed to come on our Bakhtiari expedition, which she isn't? Leigh, now,—he gets the hang of the place at once, knows the name of the streets, is full of curiosity. Dottie doesn't; she just allows herself to be taken about as a parcel. It irritates me, and I abuse her for it.

I never allowed myself to indulge in these speculations about you last year,—it was too painful and made me long for you too much,—and why pray do I indulge this year? why, for two reasons, (1) there is the chance of meeting you at Athens, and (2) there is that scheme of yours about Italy in October. Yes, indeed, I should think there jolly well were 'private reasons' against your going to Spain in May with Dadie [Rylands]; I don't think I could ever forgive you that. But come home from Greece with me.

I haven't written a line since I've been here. It is really awful. I don't believe I'm a writer at all,—no, nor even a journalist. If I were, I should at least have turned out a round dozen of articles. And certainly not a poet. This dreadful brain stagnation. But the literary side of one's brain is so odd a thing that one never knows when it won't make a sudden spring and land firmly on all four feet. It's due partly I think to an increase in my sense of self-criticism; but for that, I should no doubt now be turning out another of those lamentable novels. Oh, why hadn't I got you in those days to say "This won't do at all?" Now, ideas come along, and I simply turn them all down, with the result that nothing gets done. I am reading Gide's memoirs, very disappointing I think, so far; I have found hardly anything that pleased me except the marble that had been dropped into the hole in the door. I read Jesting Pilate[1] and liked it. I have tried Arabia Deserta[2] for the fiftieth time, but can't manage it. Yet no doubt it is a more monumental work than Jesting Pilate. What is the secret of the whole business? I wish you could tell me. And then this question of intelligence,—are we too much, too readily impressed by mere articulateness? I mean, is Raymond really a more intelligent person than the subaltern here who has commanded Indians all his life? How would Raymond come out of it, if he were suddenly put into a position of responsibility and authority? How would his appreciation of the finer shades serve him then? And which is the more important? Or is it merely a question of difference, not of degree?

Besides, so far as feeling goes, I suspect there is as much feeling in the terse remarks of the subaltern,—"Jolly day,—jolly the mountains look,—topping view,"—as in any amount of verbiage.

It's all very difficult.

The Union Jack floats languidly over the guard house, a flute player passes in the street, at midday the muezzins let out a yell. There, across the way, are the Consulate and the Chancery, with all their paraphernalia of government,—providing security for us who doze in the sun and speculate on subtleties. Why should Gide's marble in the door give me more pleasure than the sight of active men going in and out of the consulate carrying papers? I wish I knew what life was all about, and what place literature really held in it, to a God's-eye view. I wish at least that I could be content to accept things because they *are*, instead of trying to poke back to their origins and discover *why* they are, and what they are made of.

In the meantime Clive quarrels with Mary, and is reconciled to Mary, and goes to France, and doesn't go to France, and it's all very intriguing, and comes to me in your letters like an echo,—a pleasant echo that makes me smile because I am fond of Clive.

I'm afraid there must have been a long gap between the letter I posted to you at Baku and the first one I wrote you from here. You see, there was no post out for nearly a week after we had arrived. You can't imagine,—you who collect letters six times a day out of the wire mouse-trap at the foot of your stairs,—you can't imagine the enormous importance of THE POST in this place. It is the only thing which punctuates our otherwise eventless weeks. Thus the servant rushes in with a beaming face to say "The post has come!" There is always a spice of the miraculous about it. The post has come; that is, there has been no storm on the Caspian; the ship has not been wrecked; the motor has not gone over a precipice; the pass has not been blocked by snow; the bridge has not been carried by a flood. The post has come!

I have not yet found a coat for you, though I have searched. I think Isfahan will be the better place, and it's more fun to have one from there. Or Shiraz. When will you get this letter? On March 14th I suppose. Remember that the bag of the 17th is the last one which will catch me here—and that indeed won't catch me *here*—but the letters will be brought down by hand to us at Isfahan before we set off for Bakhtiari. I shall try to write something about that Expedition—Persia re-visited? From the Caspian to the Persian Gulf? My God how hot it will be on the Gulf and in the desert. I shall return to you as thin as a rail and as brown as a nut and as muscular as a settler,—at Athens, that is, on the 28th of April. Have you got that date firmly fixed in your mind?

Yes, I *am* glad you miss me, even if it is 'damned unpleasant.' I thought from your first letter that you didn't miss me at all, and was sad about it. Now I am all pleased again. Selfish, isn't one? But I go through it too, you know,—this missing you, and wanting you,—so that I know exactly how damned unpleasant it is, and probably even better than you do. The insect cries sometimes, and I have to mop him up. I think he's a little scared by Persia altogether,—it's too big for him.

By the way, send Pinker to Louise if you want a home for her while you are in Greece. Mlle Louise Genoux [Vita's maid] her name is. She would love to have Pinker to look after.

Now I shall have to stop. Have you got your blue apron on? in your funny sordid room? No I can't believe that a carpet would interfere with your solitude—I want to write a poem about solitude—

Your
V.

Berg

1. By Aldous Huxley, 1926; an account of his tour around the world in that year
2. By Charles Doughty (1888)

❦ *Teheran*
25th February [1927]

The world in which we live is Proustian; i.e. if you did it on the principle of naming race-horses, it would run: By *Proust* out of *Miss Mitford: Teheran.* (Not "also ran" but "tehe" ran. Bad joke.)

Last night, for instance. A dinner of thirty people at our legation. Long dinner table; candles; full length oil portraits of Edward VII and Queen Alexandra; the Minister [Sir Rober Clive], very distinguished, white hair, le type Gainsborough, soft sensitive mouth; too exquisite of manner to show how bored he is; perfect courtesy. A dollop of British colony: the doctor (who hates his wife so much that he wants to commit suicide;) the doctor's sister, with a black eye and swollen nose, the result of playing hockey; the manager of the Imperial Bank of Persia, (Wilkinson,) who has been here 23 years, hates Persia, pines for Godalming; Mr Campbell, very Scotch, agent for the Trans-desert mail; Mrs Drurie, cousin of Yeats and proud of it, ("I always say, Mrs Nicolson,—of course I may be wrong,—that Persia reminds me,—but of course you may laugh at me,—of the west of Ireland;") Miss Bill, long-toothed, horsey; Miss Palmer-Smith,—but Miss Palmer-Smith defies description: She must be seen to be believed in. A dollop of Americans: Mr Poland, who has come to prospect for a railway, ("Now for every citizen of the United States, Mrs Nicolson, 13½ horse power of machinery is at work; and in this country, how many? why, I'll tell you: NIL.") A dollop of Persians: Teymourtasche, the power behind the throne, the Man who has the Shah's Ear, very Parisian, very boulevardier, very moche; wears his black fez on one side, very rakish;[1] his wife, an Armenian, exuding sex at every pore, still conscious that Teymourtasche ran away with her a year ago, under a former husband's nose; Abdullah Khan, very would-be English, talking slang and getting it just all wrong. A dollop of foreign diplomats. . . .

We sit down to dinner. We have too much to eat; too much to drink,—above all, too many different sorts of things to drink: sherry, white wine, claret, champagne, liqueurs. After dinner we play poker,—at least, the more fortunate among us do; the less fortunate engage in conversation. That is, they talk to people in whom they have no interest about subjects in which they have no interest. And what is the net result?

The net result is that next day the doctor's wife asks the secretary responsible for the arrangement of the table, why the doctor was not given a higher place? Why Lady Wellesley was sent in below the wife of the Belgian minister? Why Miss P.S. ("that common little woman,") was asked at all?

In such a world, my dear Virginia, I live and have my being. And behind it all,—just as in Proust, behind the figures of Mme Verdurin and Monsieur de Charlus lurks the stormy tragedy of Dreyfus and perversion and jealousy,—behind it all lurks the storm-cloud of Russia and conflicting interests, and poor Persia, divided, rotted by disease, poverty and helplessness; and the concupiscence of short sightedness, and greed of man.

Berg

1. Prince Meyhpour Teymourtasche, Minister of the Persian Court, "a slightly ridiculous personage, a professed lady-killer and socialite." (James Lees-Milne, *Harold Nicolson*, Vol. I [Chatto & Windus, 1981], p. 270.)

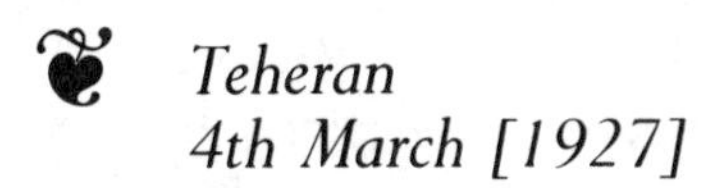

I have a game which I play all by myself. It consists in finding, and piecing together, the scattered fragments of Virginia's world. You see, this world was once whole and complete, and then one day some inner cataclysm burst it into pieces, like the planet which burst into what is now the asteroids, (there is one little asteroid, called Ceres I think, only four miles across, the same size as the principality of Monaco, on which I have often thought I should like to live, revolving in lonely state round the sun. It would be even better than my island in the South Seas.[1] Did you know I had got an island in the South Seas? It has a banana tree on it. But I must tell you more about Virginia's world, and never mind the South Seas.)

Well, Virginia's world was, then, whole and complete, so that it is quite easy to recognise the bits when one comes across them. One bit got itself precipitated into the caves at Cheddar, as you know, and another bit shot into the Shah's palace at Teheran. This bit was made entirely of looking-glass. Some of it flew up and flattened itself against the ceiling of a large room; some of it disposed itself round the walls in the shape of a dado. The ceiling part, of course, reflected everything upside down; not only the room, the carpet, and the furniture, but also the dignitaries who were walking about on the floor or sitting on the chairs; even to the King of Kings himself; all were faithfully reflected, upside down, foreshortened, stumpy, absurd. The dado part also had great fun. It reflected people's legs up to the middle of their calves as they walked past,—big feet, little feet, flat feet, arched feet, thin legs, fat legs. But it wasn't going to be content with doing merely that,—not it. It came, remember, from Virginia's world, and consequently was mischievous, rude, irreverent, poking fun at Grand Viziers and European ladies alike. So it arranged itself in such a way as to reflect the floor going either uphill or downhill, or simply at a tilt, so that the feet climbed a cliff or descended a precipice of carpet, or clung sideways like a fly, all down the length of the great room, right up to the Peacock Throne which stands at the end, and round the corner to the Bed of the Wife of Fath' Ali Shah, which is encrusted with jewels, and which has at its head a clock-like device, with jewelled hands, and the loudest tick you ever heard,—a real joke of a tick,—designed to keep the occupants from going to sleep at inopportune moments. An excellent device, I thought, and one which might advantageously be adopted by Messrs Heal.[2]

Then there were some other looking-glass bits of Virginia's broken world, which had arranged themselves in a facetted pattern in an alcove, so that they reflected only a portion of face at a time,—a nose, an eye, a chin,—endlessly repeated as one looked upward.

Great fun it all was, and I enjoyed myself very much that afternoon.

There is indeed a good deal to keep one amused. There is, for instance, the story of the clergyman who was recently stripped of all he possessed by robbers on the road, but for one garment, which they allowed him to keep on his plea that it would not be fitting for a man of God to enter Shiraz (whither he was travelling) stark naked. This one garment, however, happened to be a cut-away tail coat. The clergyman, after some perplexity, solved the difficulty by putting it on back to front, and made his entry into Shiraz in that guise.

Yes, there is plenty to keep one amused in a small way, but I pine for Virginia, and, to make matters worse (1) the Russian post has run amok now for two weeks, and (2) our bag, which ought to have come in yesterday, has missed the aeroplane and will not be here for a solid fortnight. This means that I get no letters. That I shan't know for ages whether you are definitely going to Greece. That I shan't even know whether you have forgotten me or not. That I shan't know if you are well. All this is damnable. The Russian post will turn up in time; it indulges in these antics occasionally. But I shall send this if possible by a woman who is leaving for England tomorrow.

(Tomorrow! how silly to put 'tomorrow'! It won't be 'tomorrow' or even 'yesterday' when you read of it.)

We've had a series of dinner parties, thank you, one of them indistinguishable from the other. I don't mind so much when I can play poker, which is nearly always. I've written *nothing.* That is hell. Harold, who is kind, says there must always be periods of incubation. But that is just his heart of gold, and it doesn't console me, and I still sit biting the end of my pen. And still the strange meaningless conversations continue, and I wonder more and more at the fabric which nets the world together, so that anything which I do finally incubate out of my system into words will quite certainly be about solitude. Solitude and the desirability of it, if one is to achieve anything like continuity in life, is the one idea I find in the resounding vacancy which is my head.

I had a letter from Eddy about a party he had been to; it made me sick. Do let us try and do something about these young men. *You* could work wonders. I am beginning to feel like Molly [MacCarthy] about them. I wouldn't mind so much if they were more vigorous about it all, but they do so *mince.*

I've read a lot,—Boswell, de Quincey, Tom Jones [Fielding, 1749], Plutarch. One sits in the sun, until the heat of it drives one indoors again. Then we have the telegraph clerks to lunch, and the young men from the Bank. And so it goes on.

How nice it would be, wouldn't it, to get out of the rut of one's own thoughts for a bit; to alter the whole shape of the mind; to walk suddenly into a mental landscape as different as the landscape of Central Asia is from that of Kent.

In the meantime I should be happy if I could get another letter from you, but I can't hope to do that for at least a week. Damn these incompetent posts. It is maddening to think that our mail-bags are lying somewhere in a heap, being of no use to anybody, when we want them so badly. Or, at least, I do.

Your
V.

Berg

1. A tiny islet which she bought for £5 from an advertisement in 1922, but never visited.
2. A grand furniture store in the Tottenham Court Road, London, which also held exhibitions of current art.

❧ *Wednesday, Feb. 16th [1927]* *52 Tavistock Sqre [W.C.1]*

Anyhow, dearest Honey, you are safe at Teheran. I saw Ozzie [Dickinson] who let this pearl fall from his dribbling lips: also your mother has written one of her most gracious letters "Dear Mr and Mrs Woolf, bless you for being so good to my child", to which I have answered, suitably, I hope, in deep humility. Harold is a happy man and I am an envious woman. . . .

Do you realise how devoted I am to you, all the same? There's nothing I wouldn't do for you, dearest Honey. Its true, the other night, I did take a glass too much. Its your fault though—that Spanish wine. I got a little tipsy. And then Bobo Mayor is a great seducer in her way. She has gipsy blood in her: she's rather violent and highly coloured, sinuous too, with a boneless body, and thin hands; all the things I like. So, being a little tipsy about twelve o'clock at night, I let her do it.

She cut my hair off. I'm shingled. That being so—and it'll look all right in a month or two, the hairdresser says—bound to be a little patchy at first—lets get on to other things. Its off; its in the kitchen bucket: my hairpins have been offered up like crutches in St Andrews, Holborn, at the high altar.

. . . You shall ruffle my hair in May, Honey: its as short as a partridges rump.

Berg

❧ *Friday, 18th Feb. 1927* *52 T.[avistock] S.[quare, W.C.1]*

Sweet Honey,

. . . Yes I want you more and more. You'll like to think of me unhappy I know. Well, you can. . . .

We're still talking, you'll be surprised to hear, about love and sodomy. . . . Then Morgan [E. M. Forster] says he's worked it out and one spends 3 hours on food, 6 on sleep, 4 on work, 2 on love. Lytton says 10 on love. I say the whole day on love. I say its seeing things through a purple shade. But you've never been in love they say.

Monday, Feb 21st

It gets worse you'll be glad to hear, steadily worse. Todays the day when I should be trotting out to buy you your loaf, and watching for your white legs—not widow Cartwrights—coming down the basement steps. Instead you're on the heights of Persia, riding an Arab mare I daresay to some deserted garden and picking yellow tulips.

*My solace is what?—dining with Ethel Sands . . . and laboriously correcting two sets of proofs. My goodness how you'll dislike that book [*To the Lighthouse*]! Honestly you will—Oh but you shan't read it. Its a ghost between us. Whether its good or bad, I know not: I'm dazed, I'm bored, I'm sick to death: I go on crossing out commas and putting in semi-colons in a state of marmoreal despair. I suppose there may be half a paragraph somewhere worth reading: but I doubt it.*

Wednesday

. . . Philip Ritchie told me I was the chief coquette in London. "allumeuse" Clive corrected him. Then my suspenders came down, dragging with them an old rag of chemise. . . .

Berg

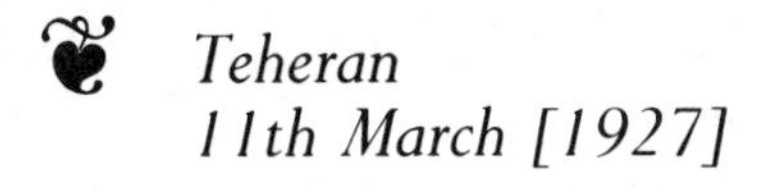

Teheran
11th March [1927]

The posts are all awry and amok; a stray Daily Mail trickles in, then a detective story for Harold, then a letter for me posted on Jan. 30th, but no nice big lumps of post come as they ought to do. As for our missing Foreign Office bag, it hasn't turned up yet. And I haven't heard from my mother for 4 weeks! So Heaven knows when this letter will reach you.

But at least, among the trickles of the Russian post, is a letter from you, of February 16th. I gather from internal evidence that one is missing,—it'll come in the bag next week, I expect. But are you really shingled? is it true? Oh darling, do I like that? I think I preferred the dropping hairpins, that cheerful little cascade that used to tinkle onto your plate. But Mary [Hutchinson] says you look nice shingled, does she? and Mary ought to know. It makes you go all wrong in my mind, and the photograph of you at Knole no longer tells the truth, which upsets me.

Otherwise, yes, you are a very bright bead. What amuses me most is the speculation on what you would be like here. And in Greece: Where shall we go in October? Avignon? Italy? Or are you going to let me down over that? tired of going abroad, after Spain with Dadie!

Meanwhile our plans are ever so slightly changed: we cannot reach Athens on April 28th as I told you before, but on May 5th,—a week later. Is there any hope that you will still be there? We shall be on the Lloyd Triestino (Carinthia, Carniola, or Trento, according to which boat is running,—we can't discover exactly which,) which will reach the Piraeus from Cyprus and go on to Trieste. I dare not hope that you will be able to join it,—or dare I? In any case, we get to London on May 9th, late at night. But oh, if you *could* join the boat. . . .

Do you know that my time in Teheran is drawing to an end? Every night as I walk across the compound and look up at the stars through the planes, I wonder if I shall ever see Teheran again. Everybody asks me if we are coming back. I say "So far as I know." But that is just official discretion: I cannot believe that the swords and silk stockings will exercise their charm much longer. In the meantime I remain wisely silent, observing a struggle going on in Harold, and knowing that an ill-placed word often makes people turn contrary.

What else? Yes, I have read Cowper:

"The stable yields a stercoraceous heap. . . ."[1]

It bears an unpleasant resemblance to The Land, doesn't it? But it has its good moments,

"While fancy, like the finger of a clock,
Runs the great circuit, and is still at home."

I read Les faux-monnayeurs [Gide] too. I remember you said you didn't like it. Yet I wonder you weren't interested by the method of springing decisive events on the reader, without the usual psychological preparation. I thought it gave a strange effect of real life. I liked it better than Si le grain ne meurt, in which I liked only the beginning of the 3rd volume, about the French littérateurs; I was bored by the African part; I don't think lust is interesting *as such*, and it doesn't inspire me at all to know that Gide had an Arab boy five times in one night . . . but the Wilde part was good although revolting. How beautifully unsubtle Gide makes Fielding [*Tom Jones*] appear, with all his knock about fun in Gloucestershire inns, when you read them as I did in conjunction, dove-tailed, Gide in the daytime and Fielding at night.

I have come to the conclusion that solitude is the last refuge of civilised people. It is much more civilised than social intercourse, really, although at first sight the reverse might appear to be the case. Social relations are just the descendants of the primitive tribal need to get together for purposes of defence; a gathering of bushmen or pygmies is the real ancestor of a Teheran dinner party; then the wheel comes full cycle, and your truly civilised person wants to get away back to loneliness. If all my life went smash, and I lost everybody, I should come and live in Persia, miles away from everywhere, and see nobody except the natives to whom I should dispense quinine. It is only affection and love which keep one. But I think Lady Hester Stanhope must have had a good life.[2]

I've been buying, in large quantities, the most lovely Persian pottery: bowls and fragments, dim greens and lustrous blues, on which patterns, figures, camels, cypresses, script, disport themselves elusive and fragmentary. How I am going to get them all home God knows. For the moment they stand round my room, creating a rubbed, romantic life of forgotten centuries. It's like looking into a pool, and seeing, very far down, a dim reflection. I make all sorts of stories about them.

Where will you get this letter? in London? in Greece? I wish I had your address. I told Leigh [Ashton] he might run into you there, he's going to the British School at Athens. Oh God I wish I were going to be in Greece with you, lucky lucky Leonard. Please wish that I might be there. Please miss me. You say you do. It makes me infinitely happy to think that you should, though I can't think why you should, with the exciting life that you have,—Clive's rooms, and talk about books and love, and then the press, and the bookshop, and wild-eyed poets rushing in with manuscript, and all the rest of it.

But I *am* going to Shiraz, it's true. This would be heaven if I didn't so much want Virginia. However, next time I go abroad it will, it shall, it must, be with you.

Your
V.

P.S. I think it is really admirable, the way I keep my appointments. I said I would be back on the 10th of May, and here I am, rolling up in London at 11.50 p.m. on the 9th, with 10 minutes to spare. It's like the Jules Verne man [Phileas Fogg] who went round the world in 80 days, and who had forgotten to turn off the gas in his flat.

Berg

1. William Cowper, *The Task* (1785), Part iii ("The Garden"), line 463
2. 1776–1839. In 1820 she withdrew from English society and for the rest of her life lived in a Syrian convent.

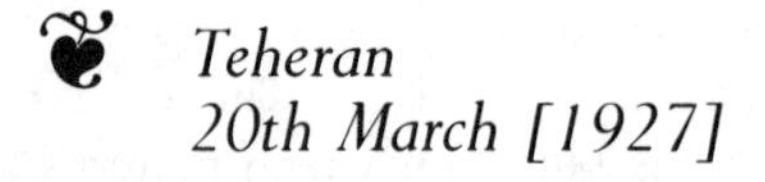

Teheran
20th March [1927]

Post going in ½ an hour—great hurry—beloved Virginia—so this is just to tell you we don't now go to Athens at all—can't get the Italian boat—but are coming direct to Marseilles—arriving in London late on May 5th—a few days earlier than by the other plan. Write to me c/o British Consulate, Beirut, Syria, where I shall be from April 24th to April 28th. Don't write to Cyprus.

Bag in—got two letters from you—but too late to answer by this post. I'll send a long letter by bag on Saturday—

God, here's the man for the letters.

Darling . . . bless you—

V.

Berg

❦ *Persepolis.*
30th March [1927]

The hawks wheel between the broken columns, the lizards dart through the doorways of the palace of Darius; Persepolis towers on its great terrace. I've driven a motor over nearly a thousand miles of Persia within the last week. I am dirty, sunburnt, well. We have got up at dawn every morning and gone to bed (on the floor) at 8.30. We have slept in ruined huts; made fires of pomegranate-wood and dried camel-dung; boiled eggs; lost all sense of civilisation; returned to the primitive state in which one thinks only of food, water, and sleep. But don't imagine that we have nothing but water to drink; no, indeed; we carry a demi-john filled with Shiraz wine, and though we may discard our beds (which we did on the first day, when our Ford luggage-car broke down and we strewed the street of a Persian village with chemises and tea-pots,) the demi-john we do *not* discard. We get up at dawn, we motor all day across plains and up gorges, tearing along, and at nightfall we arrive somewhere or other, and shake out our little diminished camp, and fall asleep. A very good life, Virginia. And now (for I have moved on since beginning this letter at Persepolis) I have seen Shiraz, an absurdly romantical place, and passed again by Sivand, and slept there, a valley full of peach blossom and black kids, and came again to Isfahan, where the post was waiting for us, and a letter from you. (But before I answer it, don't imagine, please, that this life of flying free and unencumbered across Persia is in any sense a romantic life; it isn't; the notion that one escapes from materialism is a mistaken notion; on the contrary, one's preoccupation from morning to night is: Have we cooked the eggs long enough? have we enough Bromo left? who washed the plates this morning, because *I* didn't? who put away the tin-opener, because if nobody did, it's lost? Far from finding a liberation of the spirit, one becomes the slave of the practical—

But anyway, my darling, I found a letter from you. There it was (I've now unpacked the ink and refilled my pen.) We topped the pass, and came down upon Isfahan with its blue domes, and there in the Consulate was our mail-bag full of letters. You were no longer going to Greece but to Rome.[1] You won't like Rome, with its squaling tramlines, but you will like the

Campagna. Please go out into the Campagna as much as possible, and let your phrases match the clouds there, and think of me. I've just been to dinner with a young Persian,—he's in love with me,—such a nice creature,—I knew him last year,—he chants Persian poetry so beautifully—This letter gets interrupted all the time, but I love you, Virginia—so there—and your letters make it worse—Are you pleased? I want to get home to you—Please, when you are in the south, think of me, and of the fun we should have, *shall* have, if you stick to your plan of going abroad with me in October,—sun and cafés all day, and ? all night. My darling. . . . please let this plan come off.

I live for it.

Do you really get the 'Femina' prize?[2] And the Hawthornden.[3] d'you remember our bet? what fun. Yes, let's write about solitude. Oddly enough, by the same post as your letter, I got sheets from Ethel Smyth, largely about that same subject, solitude. She likes it too.

Such a scrawl. By candlelight. The motor leaves at 4. tomorrow morning for Teheran. I'm in a queer excited state,—largely owing to your letter—I always get devastated when I hear from you. God, I do love you. You say I use no endearments. That strikes me as funny. When I wake in the Persian dawn, and say to myself "Virginia . . . Virginia. . . ."

The Common Reader was in my room at Shiraz—it gave me a shock.

Look here. . . . you'll come to Long Barn, won't you? Quite soon after I get back? If I promise to get back undamaged? I'll be sweeter to you than ever in my life before—

Your Vita

Berg

1. The Woolfs were leaving Cassis for Sicily on April 6 by boat from Marseilles. They planned on spending a week in Rome.
2. Virginia received the prize in 1928 for *To the Lighthouse.*
3. Virginia had written: "Oh and about the Hawthornden—take it for granted that they are putting off the presentation till you come back."

❧ *March 23rd 1927* *52 Tavistock Sqre [W.C.1]*

Dearest Honey,

Are you well? Did you enjoy the [Bakhtiari] walk? Were you drowned, shot, raped, tired? Lord! I'd give a good deal to know. But the silly thing is that I'm writing before you've even left Teheran, I suppose. What I pretend to be past is all in the future. Yet to you, reading this, its over. All very confusing, and pray God I may never have to write to you in Persia again.

How you'd laugh to see me stretched out comatose recovering from two days high temperature—all owing to inoculations, and my principles—I know I deserve it. I urged you so lightly into it—how little I pitied you—and now you shall laugh at me. How I wish you'd walk into the room this moment, and laugh as much as you like.

Why do I think of you so incessantly, see you so clearly the moment I'm in the least discomfort? An odd element in our friendship. Like a child, I think if you were here, I should be happy. . . .

Berg

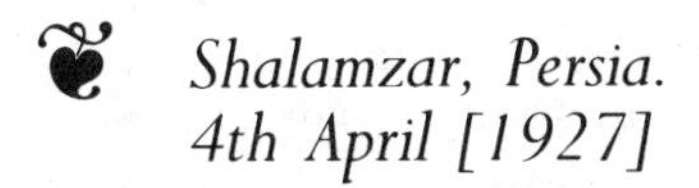

Shalamzar, Persia.
4th April [1927]

I write to you from a purely fantastic place, my lovely Virginia: an oasis at the foot of the snow-mountains, a house belonging to one of the Bakhtiari chiefs.[1] But such a house! Not, as you might suppose, a mud hut, but a sort of Versailles, full of strange objects such as gilt ladies holding lamps and other decorations in the Oriental taste,—and all, of course, falling into decay. I didn't think I should be able to write again, but the cars which have brought us the hundred-odd miles out from Isfahan will be returning to Isfahan tomorrow, and I had the brilliant idea of sending letters back by them.

This is a lonely valley, and behind the house rises the barrier of mountains, with the track leaping in black zigzags across the snow, and disappearing over a little nick in the top. Our fourteen mules are picketed outside, and we have a mounted escort which looks as though they might cut our throats at any moment. Darling, I wrote you a letter from Isfahan; rather excited I was, and over-tired, and wanting you. There was a new moon over the poplars in the Isfahan garden, the slimmest shaveling of new moon, curtseying away from a star like the one we saw when we went for a walk at Long Barn, (the evening you behaved so monstrously,) but in a very different sky; the Long Barn sky was tumbled and stormy; the Persian sky was pale green and cloudless.

I thought of lots of things on the way here which I wanted to say to you, and now I have forgotten them all. I was rather sad, thinking of people who had gone out of my life, though why I should think of them suddenly today I can't imagine. You are at Cassis. I couldn't possibly have written to you there or I would have. Did they like your shingled head? It's just as well you did it while I was away, or I should certainly have got the blame.

Lord, what a funny place to be in—and those wild unknown mountains lying outside—and night coming out—and the sound of the muleteers moving about—and a little snatch of song. Oh if only you were here! I'm alone with four men.

I have millions and millions of things to talk to you about, all very important—general, not personal.

We've got 2 huge bottles of wine with us, I insisted on that. Real jorams they are. They'll dangle on a mule.

Dinner now, and then sleep, and then tomorrow! But do you realise, light of my eyes, that we are *on our way home*? Rather an odd way, but still a way. I can come and see you in the morning, can't I, of May 6th? in the studio? and the grey milk in front of the gas-fire—Because I'll have to go down to Brighton after lunch, only I *must* see you first.

Your, (very much your)
V.

Berg

1. Vita, with Harold, Gladwyn Jebb, and two American friends, Copley Amory from the American legation in Teheran and Lionel Smith from the American legation in Baghdad, walked for twelve days through the mountains of southern Persia where the Bakhtiari tribe migrated annually. The journey was described in her book *Twelve Days* (Hogarth Press, 1928).

❧ *Tuesday, 5th April [1927]* *Villa Corsica, Cassis [France]*

I was in a towering passion—Clive had a long letter from Harold, I none from you. For some inscrutable reason after 4 days two arrived from you and one from Dotty. This has assuaged my rage, which threatened to make our journey one black and bitter pilgrimage of despair. I was very unhappy. . . .

Please darling honey come back safe. We will have a merry summer: one night perhaps at Long Barn: another at Rodmell: We will write some nice pieces of prose and poetry: we will saunter down the Haymarket. We will not *dine at Argyll House. We will snore.*

1. Virginia is completely spoilt by her shingle.
2. Virginia is completely made by her shingle.
3. Virginia's shingle is quite unnoticeable.

These are the three schools of thought on this important subject. I have bought a coil of hair, which I attach by a hook. It falls into the soup, and is fished out on a fork.

Are you well?

Berg

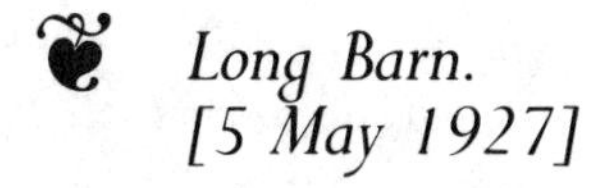

Long Barn.
[5 May 1927]

It is *marvellous* to be actually in England. I passed Cassis yesterday![1] Longed to see Clive.

Darling, darling Virginia, it's quite incredible that I shall see you to-morrow . . .

Berg

1. Vita and Harold returned by sea from Alexandria to Marseilles. Virginia herself had just returned home from a holiday at Cassis in the south of France, where she stayed with Vanessa and Clive Bell, followed by a visit to Sicily and Rome.

May–September 1927

Harold Nicolson was now on leave, awaiting his next diplomatic posting, but his presence at Long Barn and Virginia's undiminished need for her did not deter Vita from falling in love with Mary, the young wife of the poet Roy Campbell, to whom she lent her garden-cottage. Vita still saw much of Virginia, however. They went together to Oxford, often visited each other's houses for a night, and with their husbands traveled north to watch a total eclipse of the sun. Vita was awarded the Hawthornden Prize for The Land, *and wrote at a great pace a short life of Aphra Behn. She and Harold made of their garden at Long Barn a prototype of Sissinghurst and gave many weekend parties there, to which Virginia was not invited because she insisted on being alone with Vita. Vita, too, declared her need for solitude (and began her long poem on the subject), but she enjoyed the company of her friends. This was, indeed, the most social period of her life.*

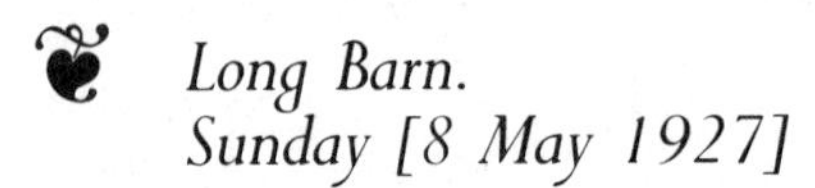

Long Barn.
Sunday [8 May 1927]

Out of the litter of clothes, books, boots, socks, ribbons, bits of Persepolis, letters, string, I rescue a piece of paper and a pen and write to tell you that Pinker and I will come tomorrow afternoon. I am lunching with Sibyl, and will go to Ebury Street after lunch to fetch Pinker, so if you *don't* want us to come will you leave a telephone message for me there? Vic. 5194. Otherwise I'll come with puppy on a string at about 3.30, but put me off if you want to and I'll just leave puppy at Tavistock Square and go sadly away.

I found a heavenly letter here from you. It had been to Teheran and come back again. I also found one from your friend Ursula Greville, which for the sake of the 'mischievous pianissimo' I can't resist sending you.[1] I also found about 150 other letters which entail 150 answers.

Such emotions as I've gone through in the last three days: England, Virginia, Long Barn. . . . I feel like a small cup held under Niagara. But look here, damn it, when are you coming to stay? Anyway I go with you to Oxford.[2]

V.

Berg

1. In Virginia's March 6, 1927, letter to Vita, she referred to the English operatic and concert soprano as "a bad singer."
2. Vita attended Virginia's lecture at St. Hugh's College, Oxford, on May 18. Her lecture was published in the *New York Herald Tribune* on August 14, 1927, as "Poetry, Fiction and the Future."

❧ *Monday [9 May 1927]* *[52 Tavistock Square, W.C.1]*

Dearest donkey West,

Did you understand that when I wrote it was my best book I merely meant because all the pages were empty? A joke, a feeble joke: but then it might get round through Jack Squire, through Hugh Walpole to Gosse: seriously such are your friends.

These things made me shiver like a fish on a hook about 2 a.m. so I am writing.

Then, second: Oxford is May 18th *and I've written to take rooms at the Mitre.*

And shall I see you before? And where does one buy a black coat? I have to broadcast, and think it should be done in broad cloth.

Berg

Tuesday [10 May 1927]

But of course I realised it was a joke;[1] what *do* you take me for? a real donkey? Anyway, it is a marvellous book . . . and I expect you were right. But I haven't finished it yet.

Much as I love Clive (and I have a real affection for the roystering fellow) I prefer being alone with you. I was cross and sulky.

One buys black *velvet* coats (I don't know about broad cloth) at Debenham & Freebody for 25/- Do get one. You'll look nice in it.

Oxford: yes: all right. What time? And do you want to go by train or motor?

Don't, whatever you do, let Mr [Aubrey] Herbert take a room for you at the Mitre and for me at the Randolph.

What are you going to broadcast about? I'll listen to you—or couldn't I bear that?

Oh darling! it is nice being back, and seeing you. Damn Clive though. Dear old Clive.

I've just acquired two goats. They remind me of Persia.

I'm going to Sherfield tomorrow for one night. No London in prospect for the moment.

Harold is writing to Leonard. Don't let Leonard take you away.

V.

Berg

1. Virginia had sent Vita a copy of *To the Lighthouse* in which she had inscribed: "In my opinion the best novel I have ever written." All the pages were blank.

Long Barn.
Thursday evening [12 May 1927]

The clock seems to have been put back a year, for I sit alone after dinner. Harold is in London, but so strong is the habit upon me that I think he is in Persia. But everything is blurred to a haze by your book of which I have just read the last words, and that is the only thing which seems real.[1] I can only say that I am dazzled and bewitched. How did you do it? how did you walk along that razor-edge without falling? why did you say anything so silly as that I "shouldn't like it"? You can never have meant that though.

Darling, it makes me afraid of you. Afraid of your penetration and loveliness and genius.

The dinner is the part I like best perhaps. Then the deserted house, and the passage of time, which must have been so difficult to manage and in which you've succeeded so completely. And odd bits, like the shawl over the skull, and a phrase about the unity of things on page 101—oh, and hundreds of phrases, scattered about, which are so like you (the flesh-and-blood Virginia, warming grey milk by the gas,) that it looks odd to see them in print. And of course the relationship of Mr and Mrs Ramsay. And her shadow in the window. But I could go on for ever like that.

My darling, what a lovely book! I love you more for it. But I still can't think how you did it. It really bewilders me, even coming from you. It's as though you juggled with the coloured stars of a rocket, and kept them all alight, all flying.

Of course it is perfectly ridiculous to call it a novel.

I wonder if you know how like Mrs Ramsay you are yourself? But perhaps that's because she is your mother.

I do really love you more than before, for it. You always said I was a snob, and perhaps that is a form of snobbishness. But I do. Only if I had read it without knowing you, I should be frightened of you. As it is, it makes you more precious, more of an enchanter.

I don't feel that this is a very illuminating letter, but I leave that to your clever friends! it is simply written under a spell—I can't shake myself free.

I tore up to Hertfordshire today; tore back again; and read after dinner. I was greatly moved, when in came Louise carrying a huge dead fish on a platter. They had stuffed the hole with grass, where it had been gaffed. It looked at me with a dead cold eye. But it couldn't bring me back to my senses.

Now I must go to bed, but there will I think be more dreams than sleep. All your fault. Bless you, my lovely Virginia.

V.

Berg

1. *To the Lighthouse* was published on May 5.

❧ *Friday [13 May 1927]* *52 Tavistock Square [W.C.1]*

Darling Vita,

What a generous woman you are! Your letter has just come, and I must answer it, though in a chaos. . . . I was honest though in thinking you wouldn't care for The Lighthouse: too psychological; too many personal relationships, I think. (This is said not of the dummy copy) The dinner party the best thing I ever wrote: the one thing that I think justifies my faults as a writer: This damned 'method'. Because I dont think one could have reached those particular emotions in any other way. I was doubtful about Time Passes. It was written in the gloom of the Strike: then I re-wrote it: then I thought it impossible as prose—I thought you could have written it as poetry. I don't know if I'm like Mrs Ramsay: as my mother died when I was 13 probably it is a child's view of her: but I have some sentimental delight in thinking that you like her. She has haunted me: but then so did that old wretch my father: Do you think it sentimental? Do you think it irreverent about him? I should like to know. I was more like him than her, I think; and therefore more critical: but he was an adorable man, and somehow, tremendous.

. . . I'm rather bothered about my paper; it mayn't suit; it may be dull. Ask Harold whether one can say that God does not exist to Oxford undergraduates? . . .

So dearest, train, Wednesday, to arrive for dinner. I rushed into a whore's shop in Leicester Sqre and bought a coat

Berg

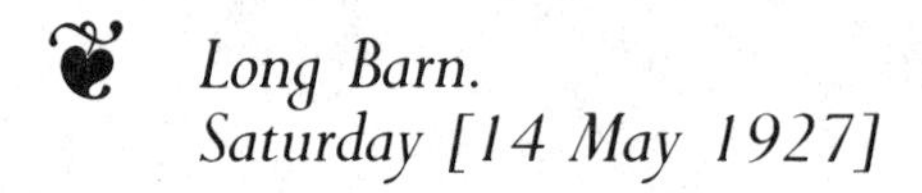

Long Barn.
Saturday [14 May 1927]

But my dearest it's *such* a bad story. However, you can have a look at it, only you're certain to turn it down. I'll bring it Wednesday.[1]

There is a train for Oxford at 4.45 arriving 5.55. Would that do, do you think? The others are all awfully bad. I'll meet you at Paddington, or pick you up at Tavistock Square, whichever you like. Harold says be as rude about God as you would be at Cambridge.

I shall feel rather like puppy, being taken along on a string.

No, *of course* your book isn't sentimental—nor irreverent about your father.

In haste with the whole Colefax clan threatening descent. Blast them.

V.

Berg

1. The Woolfs were planning a story series which resulted in the publication of only one title (Lord Olivier's *The Empire Builder*). Vita's story cannot now be traced.

Sunday [15 May 1927] *[52 Tavistock Square, London, W.C.1]*

All right, dearest donkey. I will be outside the place where one buys tickets at Paddington at 4.35 on Wednesday, carrying a neat bag, otherwise slightly shabby, but distinguished. . . .

Berg

Long Barn, Weald,
Sevenoaks.
Friday [20 May 1927]

My darling, I'm still under the spell of being with you [at Oxford].

This is to tell you that I *am* going to lunch with that old Lesbian on Tuesday,[1] but I have told her I must be back in London by a ¼ to 5. So don't put off Logan [Pearsall Smith] and the rest. It doesn't matter if I come in when they are there, does it? Only don't leave the bell unanswered!

The Vogue editoresses were overpowering.[2] They terrified me. One of them couldn't speak English.

I wish you could see my garden. It is really pretty, and will be over if you don't come till the week after next.

A gentleman writes to know if it is really necessary for him to sow his herb seeds under a waxing moon. Will they fail if he doesn't?

Hordes of people are descending on us over the weekend. Amongst others, Elinor Wylie.[3] She and Hugh Walpole are probably at daggers drawn. Lord help me.

Your
V.

[Pasted in the upper left corner is a fragment from a letter on which is written:] "It must be very pleasant to come home to find such a fine piece of work by Mrs Woolf waiting for you.

Yrs
Leigh [Ashton]"

Berg

1. Ethel Smyth, whom Vita visited at her house in Woking, Surrey, on May 24.
2. On May 19, Vita and Harold went to Knole to meet their friend George Plank, an American employee of *Vogue*; with him were the London editor (Mrs. Chase) and the Paris editor (Mrs. Fernandez).
3. Hugh Walpole stayed the weekend at Long Barn and Vita took him to Knole, where they met Elinor Wylie, the American novelist and poet.

❧ *Sunday [22 May 1927]* *Monks House [Rodmell, Sussex]*

Yes, honey, do come on Tuesday. Only stay longer than they do, whatever happens. I don't like seeing you between the legs and over the heads of Logans and Hendersons. I think it would be a tactful thing on your part if you asked L. to come to Long Barn in person. He probably thinks you dont want him etc: being a modest man. . . .

Berg

 *Long Barn, Weald,*
Sevenoaks.
[26 May 1927]

I thought this absurd photograph would amuse you.[1] Does it?

Oh dear, are you really better? I *know* you were feeling ill, but thought it was too many people.

The book to Mother [*To the Lighthouse*] was a great success, and arrived while I was there. She was delighted. She was too charming for words.

Yes, I'll send back your paper, or give it you Thursday?[2]

Do stay two nights. You know how much I want you to.

V.

Berg

1. Vita sent Virginia a photograph of herself sitting on a Persian mule. It was included as an illustration in *Twelve Days.*
2. Virginia's lecture at Oxford on May 18 about poetry and fiction

❧ *Sunday [29 May? 1927]* *52 Tavistock Sqre [W.C.1]*

Yes, it did amuse me, the picture of you on your donkey, or was it a mule perhaps?

That damned chill has landed me in a damned headache, so I am staying in bed. . . .

You're the only person I want to see when I have a headache—thats a compliment—But its going off fast.

Write, dear honey, a nice letter to me.

Berg

 *Long Barn, Weald,*
Sevenoaks.
Monday [30 May 1927]

It was a mule, of course. One rides donkeys at Margate, not on the Persian mountains.

My poor darling—I do hate these damned headaches that you get. I wish you were ROBUST. I wish also that you spared yourself a little more. I hate to think of you ill, or in pain.

People swarmed like locusts over Long Barn yesterday, and Dada had a party for Eddy's sister [Diana Sackville-West] at Knole which would have amused you: slim young creatures all looking as though they had come straight out of the Tatler, all indistinguishable one from the other, and young men to match.[1] They lay about on the grass, like aristocratic young animals with sleek heads. I was acutely conscious of the difference of generation.

Will you let me know what train you propose to come by on Thursday? and oh yes, Harold says has Leonard got any *books* belonging to him, lent to Desmond? I think it's two volumes of Hobhouse he is fussing after.[2] And his drawings. Would Leonard bring them?

The young man's letter made me smile. What does he mean?

Bring Pinker.

I am terribly excited about your coming here. I hope it won't rain. I don't believe you have ever seen Long Barn in the summer, since the first time you came—and Leonard certainly never has.

Darling, do, do get well.

Your
V.

Berg

1. Including Anthony Asquith, the film-director and son of the Prime Minister, and Lord David Cecil
2. John Cam Hobhouse, 1786–1869, later Lord Broughton, Byron's friend

 *Long Barn, Weald,*
Sevenoaks.
Tuesday [31 May 1927]

My darling, I needn't tell you that it makes me wretched to know that you are ill. I feared the worst the moment I saw Leonard's writing on the envelope. Oh Virginia, I'd do anything to make you well. I wish to God that if you had got to be ill, it had happened here, and then you'd have been obliged to stay, and I could have looked after you. But that's selfish really, because I suppose you'd be miserable away from your own house.

Leonard says will I come and see you towards the end of the week, so you can't be *so* very bad. Of course I'll come any time you like. I shall be here all the week, so you have only to get Leonard to send me a postcard—or ring up.

I send you a few flowers. I fear they won't look as fresh when they reach you as when they leave me. Put 10 grains of aspirin, powdered, in the water to revive them.

Are you in bed? yes, I suppose so. With an aching head. Able to read? Allowed to have letters? I am asking Leonard to let me know how you are. I do worry so about you, and above all can't bear the idea that you should be in pain.

Your
V.
very much distressed.

Berg

 *Long Barn, Weald,*
Sevenoaks.
[1 June 1927]

I thought you'd like the following compliments to cheer you in your seclusion, even though they are only from my poor despised friend Hugh [Walpole]:

"I'm in the middle of the Lighthouse, ekeing it out so that it will last. Why doesn't she publish a book every day? and what fun to be in at the birth of books quite as important as Jane Austen. She is a genius and I would carry a thousand hair-shedding dogs to the gates of Hell for her did she wish it! You're lucky having her for a friend." (Am I?)

Darling, I *know* you are slipping off your pillows, and failing to reach the telephone, having genius perhaps as Hugh says for writing books, but less talent than anybody I ever knew for making yourself comfortable. I hope you may have letters, especially those that need no answer. Such as mine. I worry about you dreadfully, and Mother has sent you a box of chocolates (for you and Leonard) thinking you were coming here tomorrow. So I shall keep them till you do come. I will try not to eat them myself but won't promise.

I wrote 2 poems this morning (both bad) and a bit of my book; so the sap is stirring, if to little purpose.

Oh my dear, I do hope you are getting better.

Your
V.

Berg

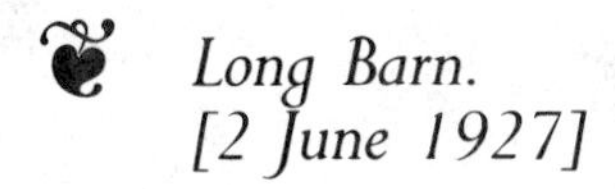

Long Barn.
[2 June 1927]

You said you liked getting letters—

Well, I went round to Raymond's to collect Harold, and collected not only Harold but Raymond also, who ought to have been dining at the Cranium,[1] but preferred to come here (he was coming tomorrow anyway) and enjoyed the thought that he was sneaking away from a lot of people, including Eddy, who were to call for him, drink cocktails with him, go to the dinner with him, etc etc. He allowed himself to be carried off rather in the spirit of a truant than of a guest. Anyway, here he is, and he and Harold have done nothing but argue about vaccination and temperamental anarchism and the Times ever since we arrived, till I am sick of it, and write to you instead. Such a muddle coursed through my mind all through dinner, which made me see how horribly true your lighthouse dinner party was: the red roses in the bowl, the silver shell with the butter, Raymond half deferring and half defiant, Pippin chawing bones under my chair; and then Virginia, so lovely and golden, stretched on two chairs, and more irresistible than ever, with the sparkle gone and only the child remaining.

Your
V.

Berg

1. The Cranium was a dining club in Bloomsbury.

❧ *Sunday [5 June 1927]* *52 Tavistock Square, W.C.1*

. . . *Its odd how being ill even like this splits one up into several different people. Here's my brain now quite bright, but purely critical. It can read; it can understand; but if I ask it to write a book it merely gasps. How does one write a book? I cant conceive. It's infinitely modest therefore,—my brain at this moment. Theres Vita, it says, able to write books: Then my body—thats another person.* . . .

The Seafarers Educational Society has bought 2 copies of The Lighthouse. Its an awful thought that the merchant service will be taught navigation by me: or the proper use of foghorns and cylinders. . . .

Berg

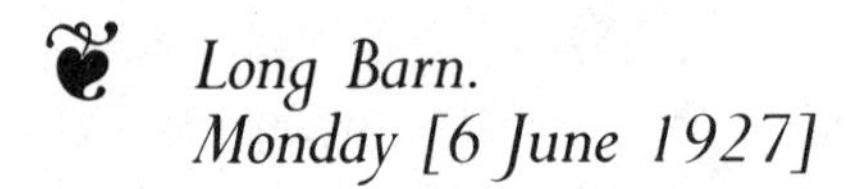

Long Barn.
Monday [6 June 1927]

Damn it, I never knew there was a post on Bank Holiday, and was astonished to get letters this morning, yours amongst them. Or I would have written yesterday. I say, I've had some funny people here since I saw you. Ethel Smyth came to listen to the nightingale. We sat in the wood for three hours. There were at least half a dozen nightingales, despite my fears that the rain and the cold would have silenced them. I was proud and delighted. But . . . *she couldn't hear them.* The poor old thing was deafer than I knew. I was in despair. I kept saying "Hush! Listen!" and darkling she listened, cocking her head on one side, but never a note could she hear. Then one suddenly burst out in a thorn bush not 10 yards away. She heard that all right; and it sang, Virginia, that blessèd little bird, it sang for a solid hour, and she was enraptured. So Long Barn and the evening were a great success: "Belovèd Vita, call me Ethel," all thanks to the nightingale. But she'll never know how many there really were; she thinks there was only one.

It's a very good joke about the Seamen's Union and the Lighthouse. I shall send a presentation copy to the Lifeboat fund. Yes, I do sympathise about John Drinkwater, it is really very humiliating for you. But you'll come and support me on the 16th won't you?[1] or you shan't have your £5. Three o'clock, and they'll send you a card. You know you'll enjoy it, and you know how you like making fun of me. I shall be in London two days,—16th and 17th,—shall I see you at all? I dine with Raymond one night and Clive the next. I suddenly got a letter from Clive asking if he might come here with Mary [Hutchinson] when she returns, so I shall expect a lively visit.

You don't say if you are better, wretch; but as you walked round the square (can one walk round a square?) and are going to Rodmell, I suppose

I may take it that you are. But you were still on chairs,—and look here: I *insist* on your having a sofa. If you won't buy one for yourself, I shall have to buy it for you, and that will make you furious. So if one doesn't appear quickly in your room, I shall deliver an ultimatum. Now do be sensible and pay attention. It is ridiculous for someone who periodically collapses on two chairs under a golden cloak, not to have a sofa.

How you will like being at Rodmell! Dear me, what a lucky man Leonard is. I wish you were coming here instead, though. Bless you, my darling. I shall think of you listening to the ventriloquists [redshanks] on the water meadows.[2]

Your
V.

Berg

1. Virginia had pretended disappointment at not being awarded the Hawthornden Prize, which Drinkwater was to present to Vita for *The Land* on June 16. In any case Virginia was ineligible for the Hawthornden, which was confined to writers under forty-one.
2. See *VW 1761*.

❧ *[7 June 1927]* *52 Tavistock Sqre [London, W.C.1]*

Health.

Better but not quite right yet—I mean I get the jumping pulse and pain if I do anything: Cant write sense. Will you please be rather strict for a time? Its so easy, with this damned disease, to start a succession of little illnesses, and finally be sent to bed for 6 weeks. . . .

Sofa. *Yes. But the difficulty is that few decent sofas can get up our stairs. I sacrificed my old one for that reason.*

Berg

❦ *Long Barn, Weald,*
Sevenoaks.
Wednesday [8 June 1927]

But when have I ever been anything but 'rather strict'? (except, possibly, towards midnight? But that doesn't count.) What counts, is that you shouldn't lavish yourself on people; and this I urge, even when I myself am the people. So do you think I'd better come on Friday? or will you promise to shoo me away like a chicken from your doorstep if you feel in the least tired when I drive up at about 4 on Friday? If you want to stop me, a postcard to me at White Lodge will do it. A disappointment, but no offence. I am afraid you have been worse than you admit. No, indeed I don't think you a molly coddle,—would to God that you were more of one. But I fancy I can solve the problem of getting the sofa up your stairs.

Can we go for a little walk in the water-meadows? with Pinker?

Perhaps I can come round to you with Raymond after dining with him,—but no: you mustn't see people, or be excited. Especially as you dine with Clive next day. Dear Clive, he wrote me such a nice letter; and what an angel to ask me to dinner the same night as you. I like that, because that was where and how I first saw you [on December 14, 1922]. Though no doubt his intention is mischievous, still I am grateful to him, and it provides a look-forward.

Your
V.

Berg

 *Sherfield Court,*
Sherfield Upon Loddon,
Basingstoke.
Sunday [Saturday 11 June 1927]

So you are alone, in your Constable country of elms and meadows, with your blue tit nest ("a wild bird's nest in Helen's breast"?)[1] and your Ouse, and your shingled church tower; and I am here among all these people,[2] just a little bewildered and perplexed by all their talk, as is Harold too, from the fresher air of Asia. It seems to me all a little stale, careful, dead? Are we wrong? or are they?

Do you know what I should do, if you were not a person to be rather strict with? I should steal my own motor out of the garage at 10 p.m. tomorrow night, be at Rodmell by 11.5 (yes, darling: I did a record on Friday, getting from Lewes to Long Barn in an hour and 7 minutes,) throw gravel at your window, then you'd come down and let me in; I'd stay with you till 5. and be home by half past six. But, you being you, I can't; more's the pity. Have you read my book? Challenge, I mean?[3] Perhaps I sowed all my wild oats then. Yet I don't feel that the impulse has left me; no, by God; and for a different Virginia I'd fly to Sussex in the night. Only, with age, soberness, and the increase of considerateness, I refrain. But the temptation is great.

A thin Clive; a haggard Clive.

Oh Lord! They've come to fetch the letters for the post.

Your
V.

Berg

1. This was a quotation from Vita's own poem *The Land.*

2. Clive Bell, Raymond Mortimer, and Dorothy Wellesley

3. *Challenge*, Vita's novel, was published only in the United States in 1923. In it she told, thinly disguised, the story of her love for Violet Trefusis.

[14 June 1927] *[52 Tavistock Square, W.C.1]*

You see I was reading Challenge and I thought your letter was a challenge "if only you weren't so elderly and valetudinarian" was what you said in effect "we would be spending the day together" whereupon I wired "come then" to which naturally there was no answer and a good thing too I daresay as I am elderly and valetudinarian,—it's no good disguising the fact. Not even reading Challenge will alter that. She is very desirable I agree: very. (Eve) [Violet Trefusis]. . . .

Berg

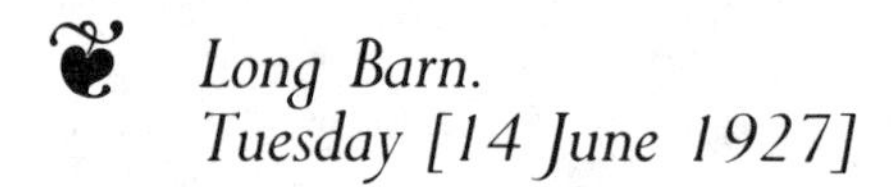

Long Barn.
Tuesday [14 June 1927]

"Chance missed,"—DAMN. We stayed playing tennis at Sherfield and didn't get home till evening.

I say, I'll see you Thursday though. I really rather envy you your fun.[1] I don't envy myself at all. Whenever I think of it, my legs feel like the Charleston.

My mother said something distressing about your being weak. Oh my darling Virginia, are you? Are you not really better? You ought to have stayed at Rodmell you know. Shall I hear from you, I wonder? I am rather worried about you.

Sherfield was a success, and Dottie as good as gold. Clive is a pet; I love him.

I've got nothing to say, except I wish you were here. I could so easily have fetched you this morning . . . but I expect you would have talked more than was good for you.

What about the sofa?

Harold has ordered his book to be sent to you; they had only one copy, a sort of proof for the cover, but it will go to you today.[2] Raymond was delighted with it.

My mother says your handwriting has an extraordinary effect upon her. What *does* she mean?

I think the house is going to fall down—It is squeaking ominously.

Your
V.

Berg

1. At the presentation to Vita of the Hawthornden Prize, Virginia was to be in the audience.
2. *Some People*, published on June 23.

Long Barn, Weald,
Sevenoaks.
Thursday [23 June 1927]

I am furious at not seeing you today. That silly Philip Ritchie has gone and got poisoned, and has put his party off.[1] Harold forgot to deliver my message. What a lovely advertisement [for *The Land*] in the Literary Supplement. I wonder if it will produce any results?

I enclose a letter which I hope will meet the case,[2] and please please, darling, act on it, as I do hate seeing you only in snippets, and people there half the time too. I would so love to have you here.

Your friend Edith Sitwell seems to be entering upon a regular campaign; whichever way I turn, that Gorgon's head springs up on my path.[3] I wish you'd draw her about it next time you see her. I am not annoyed, only vastly amused, and rather puzzled; she says it's "the worst poem in the English language"; now I'm *not* vain, as you know, but I'm hanged if it's as bad as all that!

I say, you are not really well yet, are you? Darling, *what* a curse. And oh damn not seeing you today. I would have come up, but I am getting fussed about Aphra Behn which they want by August 15th, and which I see no prospect of finishing by then. It isn't even started yet.

I did a bit of propaganda for you in Brighton to the Sussex Poetry Society,—told them to read your book.

Your
V.

very melancholy at never seeing you.

Berg

1. The eldest son of Lord Ritchie of Dundee, he was a barrister.
2. This letter is, in all likelihood, the letter of the same date which follows, written for Leonard to read.
3. Edith Sitwell's abuse of *The Land* appeared in the *Weekly Despatch* (January 30, 1927), *T. P.'s Weekly* (March 19, 1927), and the *Daily Mirror* (June 27, 1927).

Long Barn, Weald,
Sevenoaks.
[23 June 1927]

Darling Virginia, I am so sorry about today. I wanted to ask you and Leonard to come for your postponed visit, and was going to suggest the weekend after the eclipse, or any day in the week following that.[1] Will you let me know some time if you can and will?

Harold loved his evening with you. I am glad you thought him nice. He *is* nice. He does so much want you both to come here. You can rest as much as you like,—stay in bed all day if you like!

Vita

Berg

1. Vita and Harold, Virginia and Leonard, with Eddy Sackville-West, Saxon Sydney Turner, and Quentin Bell, traveled north by train to Northumberland to watch the total eclipse of the sun on June 29. The party returned to London without Vita, who was joined by Dorothy Wellesley. Together they went on to Haworth, the Brontë country, and did not return until July 1. Virginia later confessed to feeling jealous about this side excursion, and this of course delighted Vita.

Friday [24 June 1927] — 52 Tavistock Square, W.C.

. . . I think I'm going to see Edith [Sitwell] soon—I like her: she's a character. I dont think you probably realise how hard it is for the natural innovator as she is, to be fair to the natural traditionalist as you are. Its much easier for you to see her good points than for her to see yours. Also, she hates Squire (with some reason—he's the spit and image of mediocrity) and the Hawthornden tars you, you must admit, with that brush; and then you sell, and she dont—all good reasons why being a Sitwell she should vomit in public. . . .

Berg

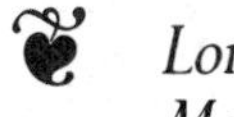

Long Barn.
Monday night [4 July 1927]

See how prompt I am in writing to you now. The truth is, I have missed you horribly this evening. It suddenly turned to summer; we dined on the terrace for the first time this year; there were warm pockets of air; I wished ardently that tonight might be the last night; I sat alone on the steps watching a sickle of moon creep out from behind the poplars; everything was still and scented and soft and romantic; a moth dashed across my eyes. It is all very well, you know, but these snatches of happiness are extremely exasperating.—And why have you such an art of keeping so much of yourself up your sleeve? as to make me suspect that after 20 years there would still be something to be unfolded,—some last layer not uncoiled?

I like making you jealous; my darling, (and shall continue to do so,) but it's ridiculous that you should be.[1]

I'm coming to London on Tuesday of next week, the 12th. Shall we go somewhere nice after lunch? Kew? the docks? the zoo? the ballet?[2] I lunch with Sibyl, but after that am free. Let's do something together. [*Pasted onto the* verso *is an illustration of a dolphin, one of the fantasy animals Virginia used in addressing Vita, with the accompanying text:*] Dolphin (Delphinus delphis) is an agile animal executing amusing gambols

Berg

1. Of Vita's other women friends
2. They went to the zoo, and afterward Vita gave Virginia a driving lesson in Regent's Park.

❧ *Monday [4 July 1927]* *[52 Tavistock Square, W.C.1]*

Yes you are an agile animal—no doubt about it, but as to your gambols being diverting, always, at Ebury Street for example, at 4 o'clock in the morning, I'm not so sure. Bad, wicked beast! . . . But what did I come back to? A message from Dadie [Rylands] and he's coming in next minute, and I'm alone, and Leonards motoring, and we shall have 2 or 3 hours tête à tête—I and Dadie. Hah Hah! Bad Wicked Beast.

. . . You only be a careful dolphin in your gambolling, or you'll find Virginia's soft crevices lined with hooks. You'll admit I'm mysterious—you don't fathom me yet—Who knows what—but here's Dadie:

Honey, could you remember to bring my waterproof (rose pink) and my gloves (scarlet) I flung them down in the hall I think. . . .

Berg

 *Long Barn.*
Wednesday night [6 July 1927]

Slightly light-headed,—my mother kept me up till 6 a.m. this morning,—an all-night sitting. Slightly tipsy,—Harold, dismayed by my appearance, filled me up with port,—sensible man. Slightly exhausted altogether,—a combination of the bloody flux and the all-night sitting. Really my mother is a tragic character.—But there was a letter from you waiting for me; which made up for much. Am I forgiven? and are you discreet?

I'll come on Tuesday. But look here, I'll come *early* unless you tell me not to, i.e. as soon as I can get away from Sibyl's luncheon. That is, about 3. Damn Dadie. *What* bad taste you have. So shop-soiled.

I sent your mackintosh (rose pink) and your gloves (scarlet) today.

Do you think there's any thing in my theory of the barrier of incest between Eddy and me? Or is it a link?

Oh God, I'm so tired.

V.

Berg

 *Long Barn, Weald,*
Sevenoaks.
Sunday [8 July 1927]

Virginia, much as I love you, (and that's more than I like for your peace of mind,) I couldn't possibly go to Hampton Court with you with that party.[1] For one thing, not being Eddy, I don't relish the idea of butting in where I'm not wanted, and then—oh, lots of other things. Why, you might bring Dadie,—who, by the way, asks me to tea on Thursday: why? I'm not going—nor am I going to speak at a luncheon for Miss Gertrude Eileen Trevelyan.[2] I'm coming to London on Tuesday only, to see Virginia and to see her by herself.

Harold is doing nicely: flaming reviews [of *Some People*] in the New Statesman, Observer, and Saturday Review. He is surprised and rather shy.

Clive has asked to come here next Friday. I am glad, as I thought he might be X with me. I am fond of Clive, who is worth a whole bed of oysters. Haven't I provided you with a splendid tease?[3] what a fool I was! But perhaps I wasn't: it's just as well not to buttress you up with *too* much self-confidence and sense of power.

Darling, write me a little note and say you won't take me to Hampton Court. I couldn't endure it—I shall go off at full gallop if you do.

V.

Berg

1. Vanessa Bell, Duncan Grant, and Clive Bell were the party.
2. The winner of the (Oxford) Newdigate Prize for her poem *Julia, Daughter of Claudius* (1927). She was an undergraduate at Lady Margaret Hall, and the first woman ever to win this prestigious prize.
3. Virginia had hinted, teasingly, that Mary Hutchinson ("the oyster") was in love with her (Virginia).

Sunday [24 July 1927] *52 T.[avistock] S.[quare, W.C.1]*

Dearest Creature,

(by the way, why is it that you always come into my presence in letters simply and solely—not even My dear Virginia, whereas I always invent some lovely lovely phrase?) how nice it is of me to be writing to you, when you're not writing to me.

. . . But listen: now what am I to do about powder? Ethel will take it ill if I don't powder my nose. Once you gave me some which didn't smell; . . . Tell me quickly what to get and where. I will rise to powder, but not to rouge. So thats finished. . . .

You'll be glad to hear I've sold 4000 of the L[ighthouse]: in America in a month: so they think I shall sell 8000 before the end of the year. And I shall make £800: (that is with luck.)

Berg

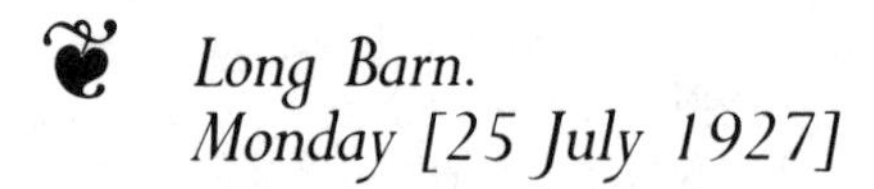

Long Barn.
Monday [25 July 1927]

I never begin my letters, don't I, belovèd Virginia? But as Clive, (who is an authority or thinks he is on such matters,) will tell you, that's the most compromising way of beginning of all.

Well, I sent you a box of powder, same as I gave you before. You must do me credit with Ethel,[1] and without powder or with the wrong sort you certainly wouldn't do me credit. So I telephoned to the chemist and said it must be sent at once. I nearly told him to put in a box of rouge, a bottle of liquid white, a cake of eyelash blacking, and a scarlet lip-stick. I say, may I make you up one day? I should enjoy that.

God, I do wish I were going with you, instead of meeting a horde of boys[2] at Paddington and trying to get too much luggage on to the motor.

But that is capital about Thursdays. You will stick to that? B M has gone to London, so I shall have no Brighton obligations and shan't be made unpunctual.[3] We will walk over the meadows and you will tell me stories.

I went to Canterbury yesterday, and to Wye because I wanted to see where the incomparable Astrea was born.[4] I have killed her off today, which means I have done ¾ of my book. It won't be as popular as the

Lighthouse, with 4 or possibly 8 thousand copies in America. What pearls before swine! I resent their reading it. You don't, but then you are a purely mercenary writer, like Michael Arlen, and think of nothing but your returns.[5]

There.

I shall write to you at Ethel's, just to keep myself fresh and green in your mind. No, my darling, I shan't be in London tomorrow. Coming up Wednesday but you'll be gone.

Your Vita.

Berg

1. Ethel Sands, the American painter, whom Virginia was to visit at her house, Auppegard, in Normandy.
2. Ben and Nigel, on their return from school.
3. B. M. could stand either for Bonne Mama or Belle Mère, and was applied by Vita and Harold to her mother, Lady Sackville.
4. Aphra Behn, about whom Vita was writing a short book. She was born at Wye in 1640, but soon afterward was taken by her parents to Dutch Guiana.
5. Michael Arlen (1895–1956) was born in Armenia and naturalized British in 1922. He is best known for his novel *The Green Hat* (1924).

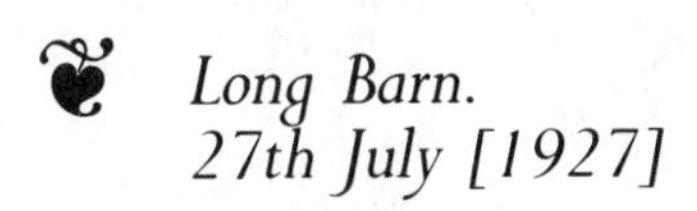

Long Barn.
27th July [1927]

Today as I was driving down Oxford Street I saw a woman on a refuge, carrying the Lighthouse. She was an unknown woman,—up from the country, I should think, and just been to Mudie's or the Times,—and as the policeman held me up with his white glove I saw your name staring at me, Virginia Woolf, against the moving red buses, in Vanessa's paraph of lettering. Then as I stayed there (with my foot pressing down the clutch and my hand on the brake, as you will appreciate,) I got an intense dizzying vision of you: you in your basement, writing; you in your shed at Rodmell, writing; writing those words which that woman was carrying home to read. How had she got the book? Had she stalked in, purposeful, and said "I want To the Lighthouse"? or had she strayed idly up to the counter and said "I want a novel please, to read in the train,—a new novel,—anything'll do"?

Anyhow there it was, one of the eight thousand, in the hands of the Public.

You are in the arms of Ethel [Sands] (metaphorically, I hope,) by now, being motored about Normandy. You will motor through Salcavilla, probably, though you won't know it. You will be taken to see Jacques Blanche.[1] You will be given iced grapefruit when you are called. But there won't be angel fish in your bathroom, nor many of the other delights you find at Long Barn. Please find out for me exactly what it is that one likes about Ethel. Is it the sense of civilisation and silver tea-things? Ethel, in analogy, is certainly a tea-table. But there is a scratch too.

I have got the boys, and the house from being an abode of peace has become noisy. How *can* one write? The door bursts open all the time—"Where is my hammock?" "May we play tennis?" "What can we do now?" Nigel, however, who always likes having situations neatly defined, remarks at breakfast "How nice it is to have a family assembled." I who detest families deplore this domestic sentiment in my younger son.

Darling, *I like solitude*, that's what I like—now do you think my poem on the subject will suffer or improve from my being thus forcibly deprived of it?[2] I don't know when I shall ever write the poor thing. It turns over sleepily in my brain and occasionally lays a little egg in the shape of a line. Besides, most people are so gregarious that it will find no echo in any heart nearer than that of a hermit in Thibet.

My darling, come back soon, I don't like to feel you are out of England. (This comes well from me, dashing off to Persia.) I'll come over to Rodmell when you're alone there. Not on the 6th because that's Ben's birthday. But soon, please.

Your
V.

Berg

1. Virginia met Jacques-Emile Blanche, the portrait painter, at Auppegard. Vita was referring to Sauqueville, the nearby village from which the Sackville family came to England in the eleventh century, when she teasingly wrote "Salcavilla."
2. Vita's poem about solitude was not completed until 1938.

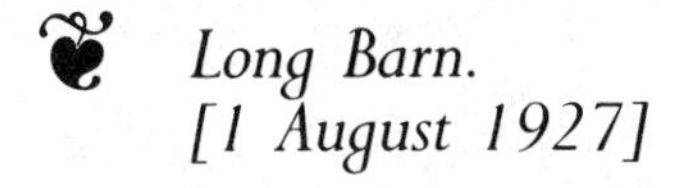

Long Barn.
[1 August 1927]

My darling, I am so upset at your saying you had no letter from me. I wrote you a long letter and posted it myself early on Thursday last. Has it ever reached you?

Desmond [MacCarthy] and Berners here,[1]—Berners painting pictures, and Desmond discoursing delightfully, in great form—

When shall I see you?

V.

Berg

1. Lord (Gerald) Berners (1883–1950), an amateur musician and artist of great talent, a writer of remarkable autobiographies (*First Childhood*, for example), and a brilliant conversationalist

Wednesday [3 August 1927] *Monks House [Rodmell, Sussex]*

Yes, darling creature, your letter was handed me just as we left Auppegard, and caused me, I suppose, to forget my box, so that the exquisite butler had to motor into Dieppe after us. Yes, darling, it was a nice letter. Sauqueville aint a very grand place, all the same. I looked for traces of you. Did your ancestors own a saw mill? . . . Then Leonard goes up on Thursday 11th and comes back on Friday. I shall be alone Thursday night. Could you stay two nights? I dont want to seem as if I had you in secret, though its infinitely more to my taste, exploring about in the recesses secretly. . . .

My God, how you would have laughed yesterday! Off for our first drive in the Singer: the bloody thing wouldn't start. The accelerator died like a duck—starter jammed. All the village came to watch—Leonard almost sobbed with rage. At last we had to bicycle in and fetch a man from Lewes. He said it was the magnetos—would you have known that? . . .

Berg

 *Long Barn.*
Thursday [4 August 1927]

NOT FOR PUBLICATION.
Roshan-i-chasm-i-man,[1]

(You won't know what that means, but you say I never begin my letters, so I try to oblige.)

Tactful letter, or would-be tactful, enclosed. It would in any case be difficult for me to stay two nights, though if you were alone I would certainly do so.

N.B. It is true about the Weald people.

Are you all right? dispirited? over-fed? not fond of me any longer? Something wrong, I feel, by your letter; but still am confident that by this time (i.e. midnight) next week it'll be all right. I'll come after luncheon, about 5, shall I? You can't think how I long to see you. The gaps of time are interminable.

I really *would* stay the 2 nights if I could, if only to make it not seem deliberate,—for your sake if not for my own.

A course of Mrs. A. B. [Aphra Behn] has turned me into the complete ruffling rake. No more than Mrs A. B. do I relish, or approve of, chastity.

V.

Berg

1. A Persian love greeting

❧ *Sunday [7 August 1927]* — *Monks House [Rodmell, Sussex]*

Musha—i—djabah—dal—imam—[mock-Persian]

Which being interpreted means, Darling—West—what—a—donkey—you—are—all my letters in future are going to be addressed to Pippin [dog], since it is clear you cant read them. "Something wrong I feel by your letter."—What do you mean? It was the nicest, lovingest, tenderest letter in the world: a little rasped at not seeing you perhaps, but after all thats to your taste isnt it? Or did you, with the marvellous intuition of the poet, discover what I have tried to keep concealed from you? that I am loved, by a man; a man with an aquiline nose, a nice property, a wife of title, and furniture to suit. The proposal was made the day before I left, and I have a letter now confirming it. What do you wish me to do? I was so overcome I blushed like a girl of 15. . . .

Berg

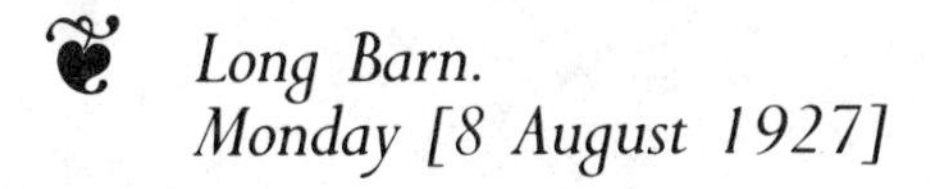

Long Barn.
Monday [8 August 1927]

I was going into Sevenoaks to pick up the boys, when I saw the postman's scarlet bicycle leaning against the village letter-box. That meant that the afternoon's post had arrived. I stopped; went in; and said Are there any letters for Long Barn? There were. Among them was a typewritten envelope which contained a letter from you. I felt myself flush with rage, as I read it,—I don't exaggerate. I didn't know I was so jealous of you. *Who* is your damned man with the aquiline nose?[1] Look here, I really mind. But if it comes to that, I have on my table a letter of the same sort,—which I haven't answered.[2] What sort of answer I send, depends on you. I really am not joking. If you are not careful, you will involve me in an affair which will bore me horribly. If you are nice, on the other hand, I'll send my correspondent packing. But I won't be trifled with. I really mean this.

For the rest:

(1) I'll bring my camera, only my charge is £1 per snapshot, not 2/6.[3]

(2) I won't bring Pippin, I think, because she might be sick in the motor.

(3) I'll come at 4 Thursday.
(4) I'll stay till Friday.
(5) I'd like to lunch at Charleston if you will *promise* to leave directly after lunch so that I may have you alone again.
(6) I will certainly lay myself out to please you.

I do get so angry about you.

V.

Berg

1. Virginia was referring to Philip Morrell, Ottoline's husband, who had renewed his unwelcome advances to her.
2. Probably from Mary Campbell, the wife of the South African poet Roy Campbell, both of whom were living in a cottage near Long Barn
3. To take a photograph of Virginia for an article about her by Jacques-Emile Blanche

Sherfield Court,
Sherfield Upon Loddon,
Basingstoke.
Tuesday [16 August 1927]

My darling,

I had hoped that your photographs would have come this morning before I left Long Barn, but they failed to turn up. I have put in a good piece of work since I saw you: made friends with Lord Gage, and got myself invited to Firle, which might be useful.[1] In the meantime it enrages me to think I might be with you tomorrow.

I have finished with Mrs Behn—and have now only to pack her off. This, in the midst of thousands of people who arrived at Long Barn at all hours of the day and night—Then a quick dash to Sherfield, and Raymond again, and Adelaide Livingstone.[2] The boys splashing about in the swimming bath, Harold writing the history of biography for you, and much tennis. Such is my life—and arguments about feminism, and men and women, and lots of Alella [Spanish wine]—which sharpens the wits even if it undermines the constitution—and Raymond saying "And then Virginia of course who is unquestionably the finest living writer of English prose."

But in the meantime no sign of life from you,—isn't it odd, these sudden, spasmodic, and violent junctions between us, and then these days of complete silence which succeed?

Nevertheless I adore you and am coming on Thursday week am'nt I?

V.

Berg

1. The sixth Viscount Gage owned Firle Place and Charleston, in Sussex.
2. Born in Massachusetts, Adelaide Livingstone came to England when young and was very active in many international and charitable causes, especially during the First World War, when she cared for prisoners of war. She was created a Dame of the British Empire for this service in 1918, and died in 1970.

Long Barn, Weald,
Sevenoaks.
Saturday, 20th August [1927]

As you see, the photographs were not very successful. I have a new film, and can take a new lot on Thursday if you like. I send these for what they are worth.

I like your review of Parson Woodforde.[1] I PROTEST: *never* pay you compliments. My only difficulty is, to repress my admiration so that it may not appear fulsome. If you wrote anything I mistrusted or didn't approve of, I should be down on you like a ton of bricks.

Raymond says I write bad English. I let him read my Aphra Behn, and he pulverised me. I expect you will agree. It will be out in October,—too late for you to review for America, I think. It will be an easy and grateful book to review,—very historico-picturesque.

Why do you typewrite your envelopes to me? They don't look quite like a shop; and then I peer closer, and when I see [L]EWES on the postmark I know it is from you.

If Leonard hears from Adelaide Livingstone about lecturing about history at Heidelberg, I am responsible. But you better not say so to him, or he will think I have designs of getting you to myself. (*N.B.* I have.)

I am reading a delicious book called The Wandering Scholars[2]—I wish I knew Latin. Having actually put Aphra in the post, I feel as free as a lark. Free to read, free to garden, free to think, free to be nice to my children. A delirious sensation,—but already new energies stir in me, 24 hours after Aphra is finished. God damn this energy; thank God for it,—such are my alternative emotions. I can't be happily idle, I sometimes wish I could.

I have lost my fountain pen and am writing with a new one which is more like a pin than a pen.

Shall you see Eddy and Raymond at Charleston tomorrow I wonder?

It is late, the house is asleep, and I sit up alone. Nigel hurt himself today dreadfully on a sharp-cornered piece of furniture and had to be put to bed. Pippin is all lascivious-minded, and goes to Hertfordshire in a hamper on Monday. You are with stockbrokers. I remember you wrote me a letter about them when I was in Persia. I get odd hankerings for Persia from time to time,—painful and queer.

I send you a supplementary photograph [of Virginia], which I had in Persia, and which lived stuck into my looking glass there, and one which I took here the other day. May I have the Persian one back please? it is precious, and I don't know where the negative is. The others do not matter as I have the negatives.

Write to me?

Your
V.

Berg

1. "Life Itself" (*New Republic,* August 17, 1927), Virginia's review of *The Diary of a Country Parson,* vol. 3, by James Woodforde, ed. John Beresford, was reprinted in *Nation and Athenaeum*, August 20, 1927.
2. By Helen Waddell (1927). The book, which was about the study of Latin in the Middle Ages, attracted attention far outside professional academic circles. She followed it with an equally successful novel, *Peter Abelard.*

Long Barn.
Tuesday [30 August 1927]

It wasn't very nice, no, it wasn't, leaving you standing in the gateway on Saturday with Tray [Raymond Mortimer] and Leonard. Lucky Tray. Lucky Leonard. But this is really to say, I behaved with my usual efficiency, caught Mr Harold Monro on the telephone, made him come down here last night, and pushed him and Dottie into each other's arms.[1] It was a great success. They liked each other, and they are going to spend tomorrow afternoon together at the bookshop. I think something may come of it. But Mr Monro takes literature seriously,—likes poets to read aloud,—likes encouraging secondary school teachers in the appreciation of poetry,—and I doubt whether Dottie will be allowed to introduce more than one oyster and one bottle of champagne into the bookshop in the course of a twelvemonth.

She has just handed me her letter to you, to read. I am shocked. I am seldom shocked, but this time I am. I have told her so. She says "Will Virginia be?" I say "Yes," but she is sticking up the envelope and addressing it all the same. The truth is, her head is slightly turned by her success with Mr Monro. He has straight black hair and slavonic cheekbones and a strong mouth. I should think he was a very devil of obstinacy.

My darling, I had lots to say to you. Harold has heard from the Foreign Office this morning. They are all going off to Geneva this week, and they want him to wait till their return, about September 20th, and then go to London to 'have a talk.' Anyhow that is a respite, but I would rather have things definitely settled.

A retired business man wants me to tell him how to be happy living with an invalid wife in a small hotel in Kensington. How should I know? I'm not a novelist. Shall I send you the letter to answer? It seems to be more in your line than mine. He encloses an essay on rabbits.

Dear me, I do wish I had you always in the house. Have you read Oroonoko?[2] Do you like it? Do you like me? Would you miss me if I disappeared? Have you been depressed? Do you still think you are a bad writer? Did you like Harold the other day?

Sheep are bleating on the road outside. That sound whisks me straight back to the Bakhtiari road. How hot it must be there now, and how deserted. I wish I were there in a camp, with you.

V.

Berg

1. Harold Monro (1879–1932), the poet and editor, founder of *Poetry Review* and owner of the Poetry Bookshop, which he hoped Dorothy Wellesley would subsidize
2. Virginia had asked Vita to lend her the most romantic novel Aphra Behn had written. *Oroonoko* (1688) was about a slave whom Mrs. Behn met in Dutch Guiana.

❧ *Friday, Sept 2nd [1927]*

Monks House, Rodmell
[Sussex]

Dearest Mrs N:

Well its all settled. Lady G. Wellesley has bought me. She paid £25 thousand down and the rest on mortgage, so I'm her's for life. I have the use of the Rolls Royce and wine to taste.

Speaking sober prose, however, I wont belong to the two of you, or to the one of you, if the two of us belong to the one. In short, if Dotty's yours, I'm not. A profound truth is involved which I leave you to discover. It is too hot to argue: and I'm too depressed.

Berg

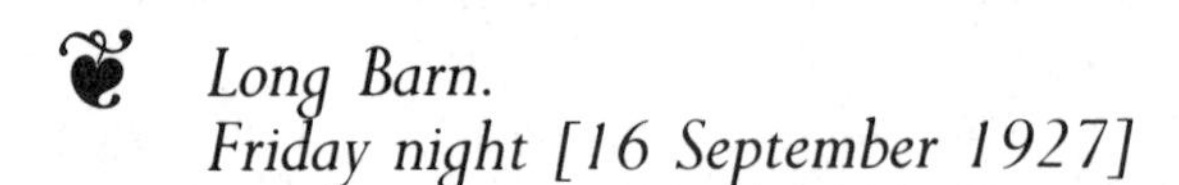

❦ *Long Barn.*
Friday night [16 September 1927]

In spite of Heaven bringing you and Dottie together, she is not coming here before Monday.[1] She is staying till Wednesday morning. So if you and Leonard come, come on Monday or Tuesday, *not* Sunday; that is, if you wish to see her. Come to lunch anyhow, and not at 2.30—a ridiculous hour to arrive at. Telegraph.

I am sorry and shocked about Philip Ritchie.[2] I had no idea he was so ill. I hardly knew him, but he had a good brow and Eddy was fond of him, also Tray. Besides, it is wrong that people of 28 should die.

I am ashamed to say I forgot Mrs [Olwen Ward] Campbell's Shelley. (I don't often forget things for *you.*) I sent it this morning.

I can't come next Thursday damn it because it is the boys' last day at home. They go back to school on Friday. I could come Thursday week if that's any good?

Don't go right away from me. I depend on you more than you know.

V.

Berg

1. Dorothy Wellesley had now given up the idea of taking a share in Monro's bookshop and proposed instead to edit and finance the Hogarth Press series of contemporary poets, a project that succeeded.
2. Ritchie, aged twenty-eight, died on September 13 from septic pneumonia, a complication of a tonsillectomy.

Wednesday [21 September 1927] *Monks House, Rodmell [Sussex]*

. . . Very hurried, so I cant write. And rather melancholy. This I'll explain when we meet, if you are kind.

Berg

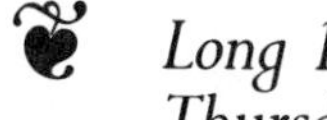

Long Barn.
Thursday [22 September 1927]

My darling, *why* melancholy? I thought you were not quite yourself the other day, and wondered if it was all my imagination. I expect tomorrow in London will be pretty hopeless for me, as (a) I shall have Nigel, and (b) it is B M's birthday so I'll have to go to Ebury Street—but if I can look in during the morning for a minute, even with Nigel (who can be left in the car) I will. Ben has now got influenza, and can't go to school for a few days. I say, I *hope* I didn't give it to you on Monday. My temperature went up to 103½ after you had gone, I was horrified thinking I might have given it to you—did I? I'd have avoided you, if I'd known, and left you to talk to Dottie alone—but I thought I just had a cold.

Tell Leonard I'm sorry my review of Gertrude Bell's letters was so bad.[1] I'm writing an article which I will offer him if he likes.

I wish I were with you today, damn it all; I want to know what is the matter.

Your
V.

Berg

1. In *The Nation*, October 1, 1927

❧ *Sunday [25 September 1927]* *Monks House [Rodmell, Sussex]*

Look here, I want to be told,
(1) how you are, *truthfully.*
(2) any news from Foreign Office?

Hows Ben? Anybody else got it [flu]? My God, I do think you deserve death and disaster for coming to London in that flood after a temperature of 104! . . .

But I own I'd like to see you. Then I'd tell you about my melancholy and a thousand other things Its the last chance of a night before London's chastity begins. . . .

Berg

Vita in 1922

Virginia, photographed by Vita at Monk's House, June 1926

Virginia and Leonard Woolf at Monk's House, June 1926

Vita's sitting room at Long Barn

Vita in 1928,
a photograph
taken by
Leonard Woolf
as an illustration
to Orlando

Knole,
January 1927.
Virginia
with
Benedict (center)
and
Nigel Nicolson

Sissinghurst
Castle
in
1932

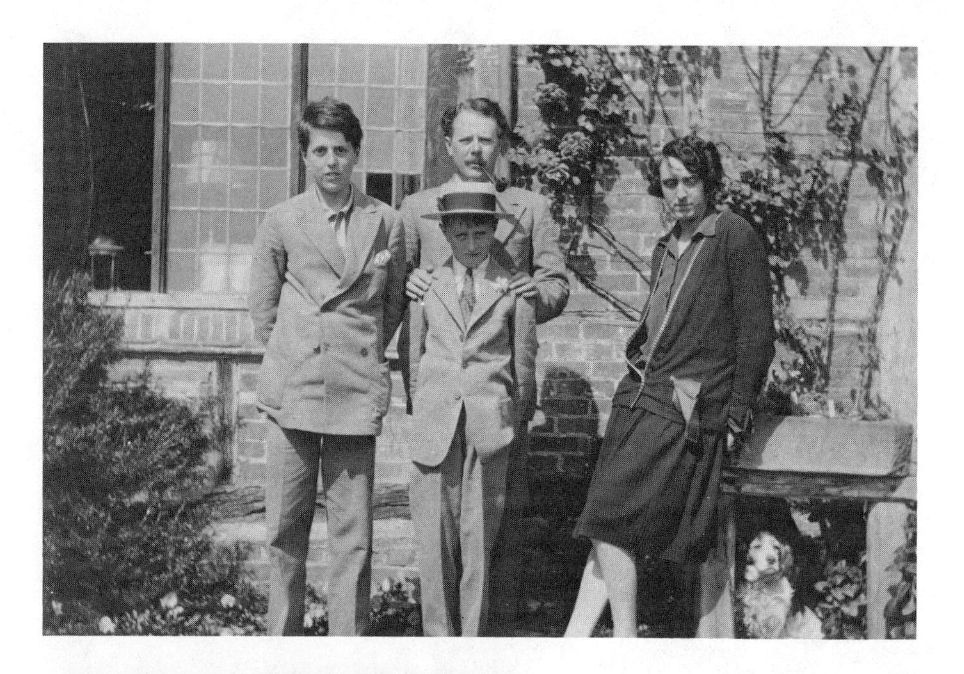

Long Barn,
summer 1929.
Vita and Harold
with their
two sons,
Benedict (left)
and Nigel

Vita
at
Long Barn,
1929

Harold Nicolson
and
Vita
at
Sissinghurst,
1934

Harold
and
Vita
at
Sissinghurst,
1935

Vita
in her
tower room
at
Sissinghurst,
1936

Vita
at
Sissinghurst,
circa
1940

October–December 1927

On October 9, Virginia wrote to Vita, almost casually toward the end of a long letter, that she had decided to write a book about her, to be called Orlando. *Vita was delighted by the idea, and felt no alarm about being publicly identified with the subject by character, dedication, and photographs. She and Virginia returned to Knole for pictures and copy. For the next year the book became a game between them, Virginia demanding details of Vita's past life, Vita trying to prise out of Virginia something more of her intentions, but she was not allowed to read a word of it until the publication day. Meanwhile Vita wrote* Twelve Days, *and continued her affair with Mary Campbell, which hitherto she had attempted to conceal from Virginia (but could not from Roy). On November 10 she made her a full confession, with tears. In mid-December she spent a week in Berlin, where Harold had been posted as counsellor to the British Embassy, then Christmas at Knole.*

❧ *9th Oct. [1927]* *52 Tavistock Sqre. [W.C.I]*

Look, dearest what a lovely page this is, and think how, were it not for the screen and the [Mary] Campbell, it might all be filled to the brim with lovemaking unbelievable: indiscretions incredible: instead of which, nothing shall be said but what a Campbell behind the screen might hear. . . .

Yesterday morning I was in despair: . . . I couldn't screw a word from me; and at last dropped my head in my hands: dipped my pen in the ink, and wrote these words, as if automatically, on a clean sheet: Orlando: A Biography. No sooner had I done this than my body was flooded with rapture and my brain with ideas. I wrote rapidly till 12. . . . But listen; suppose Orlando turns out to be Vita; and its all about you and the lusts of your flesh and the lure of your mind (heart you have none, who go gallivanting down the lanes with Campbell) . . . Shall you mind? Say yes, or No: . . .

Berg

❦ *Long Barn.*
Tuesday [11 October 1927]

My God, Virginia, if ever I was thrilled and terrified it is at the prospect of being projected into the shape of Orlando.[1] What fun for you; what fun for me. You see, any vengeance that you ever want to take will lie ready to your hand. Yes, go ahead, toss up your pancake, brown it nicely on both sides, pour brandy over it, and serve hot. You have my full permission. Only I think that having drawn and quartered me, unwound and retwisted me, or whatever it is that you intend to do, you ought to dedicate it to your victim.

And what a lovely letter you wrote me, [Mary] Campbell or no Campbell. (How flattered she'd be if she knew. But she doesn't, and shan't.) How right I was,—not that it needed much perspicacity,—when I realised at Clive's that here was the most . . . what shall I say? you want duty and devotion, but if I wrote what I really think you would only say that Vita was laying it on a bit too thick. So I better not expose myself to your jeers. But how right I was, all the same; and to force myself on you at Richmond [in January 1923], and so lay the train for the explosion which happened on the sofa in my room here when you behaved so disgracefully and acquired me for ever. Acquired me, that's what you did, like buying a puppy in a shop and leading it away on a string. Still trotting after you, and still on a string. For all the world like Pinker.

Last night was the most beautiful misty moonlight night I ever saw in my life. No, I did *not* go down the lanes. I hung out of my window and listened to the dead leaves twirling down in the stillness. I thought how lovely and lonely it must be at Laughton.[2] I was sorry about Laughton,—a fairy-story place for Virginia to live in.

Moody[3] is writing a novel. About spiritualism.

No, I have never heard of Mr Cecil Beaston [sic] but please do go and be photographed and give me one.[4]

Darling, I can't come up tomorrow, and am sending you a telegram to that effect. I won't tell you why,—a squalid reason. I shall come up next week though, and probably stay a night in London. And what about you coming here one of these days? You said you would, and the advantages are obvious.

Not a word from that bloody Foreign Office. I fear they are plotting something very dark. Harold approaches his correspondence more and more gingerly. Oh, by the way, he finished his book today and it has gone to be typed.[5] So you will have it soon.

I wish you were here. The days and nights are beautiful as only autumn can be. This sounds like Clive when his autumn fires are best, and ripe apples dropping on his head, but I assure you I am not in the same mood as Clive. No. My delight is purely aesthetic, and country bumpkin I am good, industrious, and loving; how long will it be, though, before I break out? I would never break out if I had you here, but you leave me unguarded. Now, none of that means anything at all, so don't imagine that it does. I am Virginia's good puppy, beating my tail on the floor, responsive to a kind pat.

V.

Berg

1. On October 5, Virginia had written in her diary: "And instantly the usual exciting devices enter my mind: a biography beginning in the year 1500 and continuing to the present day, called Orlando: Vita, only with a change about from one sex to another."

2. Laughton Place, near Glynde, was a sixteenth-century moated house that the Woolfs were tempted to buy.

3. George Horne, the butler at Long Barn

4. Virginia twice refused to be photographed by Cecil Beaton.

5. *The Development of English Biography*, published by the Hogarth Press in February 1928

 *Long Barn, Weald,*
Sevenoaks.
Friday [14 October 1927]

Darling, this is a letter written in a hurry and a furious temper to say that Harold is going to Berlin next week.[1] Shall you be free on Tuesday if I come after lunch for a bit? We are so cross, but it appears to be inevitable. We only heard this morning. Berlin for 3 years! Good Lord deliver us.

V.

I shan't go there till the end of January.

Berg

1. He was posted as counsellor to the British Embassy there.

❧ *Friday, Oct. 13th [14th, 1927]* *52 T.[avistock] S.[quare, W.C.1]*

. . . Never do I leave you without thinking, its for the last time. And the truth is, we gain as much as we lose by this. Since I am always certain you'll be off and on with another next Thursday week (you say so yourself, bad creature, at the end of your last letter, which is where the viper carries its sting) since all our intercourse is tinged with this melancholy on my part and desire to be white nosed and so keep you half an instant longer, perhaps, as I say we gain in intensity what we lack in the sober comfortable virtues of a prolonged and safe and respectable and chaste and cold blooded friendship. . . .

Orlando will be a little book, with pictures and a map or two. I make it up in bed at night, as I walk the streets, everywhere. I want to see you in the lamplight, in your emeralds. In fact, I have never more wanted to see you than I do now—just to sit and look at you, and get you to talk, and then rapidly and secretly, correct certain doubtful points. About your teeth now and your temper. Is it true you grind your teeth at night? . . . What and when was your moment of greatest disillusionment? . . .

Please tell me beforehand when you will come, and for how long: unless the dolphin has died meanwhile and its colours are those of death and decomposition. If you've given yourself to Campbell, I'll have no more to do with you, and so it shall be written, plainly, for all the world to read in Orlando. . . .

Berg

❧ *Friday [21 October? 1927]* *52 Tavistock Square, W.C.1*

. . . I'm not afraid of your not wanting me; only of what one calls circumstances. So please say honestly. . . . My questions about your past can wait till you're in London. I should hate forever to be for an instant a burden to you. . . .

Berg

❧ *Sunday [23 October 1927]* *52 T.[avistock] S.[quare, W.C.1]*

Dearest Creature,

I'm afraid you are feeling lonely tonight. I wish I were with you. Harold is a very nice man, and I'm glad I know him.

Would Wednesday, Thursday suit you for me to come, suppose Friday was difficult? But I'm not sure. What used you and Lord Lascelles to talk about? . . .

Berg

Long Barn, Weald,
Sevenoaks.
Tuesday [25 October 1927]

Darling lovely Virginia,

I can't make out from your letter,—do you mean Wednesday or Thursday? because Wednesday I have got to dine with (don't laugh) the

King of Iraq.[1] But Thursday I shall be here. And alone. I shan't stay up in London Wednesday night but shall come down after dinner. I nearly came to see you yesterday, when I was in London, but I thought you might be busy and I didn't want to be a bore. I was so depressed.[2] I was grateful to you for your letter, it was so welcome and badly needed.

I will try to remember what I talked to Harry Lascelles about![3] He was always very tongue-tied, so we didn't get very far. He had nice hands.

Darling I have found some lovely pictures at Knole. I *do* want you to come. Pippin has six puppies. Tell Pinker. Bring her when you come. Oh I do want you to come. Let me know: Thursday or Friday—or Saturday or Sunday if you prefer.

V.

Berg

1. Whom Vita had met in Baghdad on her way to Persia in 1926
2. Harold had left that day for Berlin.
3. Lord Lascelles, who had been in love with Vita in 1912–1913, is the Archduchess Harriet in *Orlando*. In 1922 he married Princess Mary, daughter of King George V.

Friday morning [11 November 1927]

I have been so really wretched since last night.[1] I felt suddenly that the whole of my life was a failure, in so far as I seemed incapable of creating one single perfect relationship—What shall I do about it, Virginia? be stronger-minded, I suppose. Well, at least I won't create any further mistakes! My darling, I'm grateful to you; you were quite right to say what you did; it has given me a pull-up; I drift too easily.

But look here, remember and believe that you mean something absolutely vital to me. I don't exaggerate when I say that I don't know what I should do if you ceased to be fond of me,—got irritated,—got bored. You disturbed me a good deal by what you said about Clive even. Surely you can't mean anything serious? Oh no, that's too unthinkable. I shan't worry about that—There's plenty else to worry about.

Darling forgive me my faults. I hate them in myself, and I know you are right. But they are silly surface things. My love for you is absolutely true, vivid, and unalterable—

V.

Berg

1. Vita had told Virginia about her affair with Mary Campbell, and about Roy's fury when he found out. Vita was reduced to tears.

Friday night [11 November 1927] *[52 Tavistock Square, W.C.1]*

Dearest Creature,

You make me feel such a brute—and I didn't mean to be. One can't regulate the tone of one's voice, I suppose; for nothing I said could in substance make you wretched for even half a second—only that you cant help attracting the flounderers. . . . And I'm half, or 10th, part, jealous, when I see you with the Valeries and the Marys: so you can discount that.

And thats all there is to it as far as I'm concerned. I'm happy to think you do *care: for often I seem old, fretful, querulous, difficult (tho' charming) and begin to doubt. . . .*

Berg

Long Barn, Weald,
Sevenoaks.
Thursday [17 November 1927]

It is absolutely damnable: before getting your letter I promised to go to Brighton on Monday evening, and now I can't get out of it though I have tried. B M was here today, and I left your letter unanswered hoping she would let me off, but it was no good, and now you will think "Oh damn Vita there she is cluttered up again,"—that's just my luck. I shan't blame you if you do think that. What is so maddening is that you say you'll be alone Monday evening. I wish you'd said so the other day—on Monday last

I mean. I better not come to lunch, then? even if I don't steal you from the Press afterwards.

Oxford was a repetition of *your* Oxford: dinner with Mr Aubrey Herbert, and then that assembly at St Hugh's.[1] My paper, and then heckling. A bottle of hock on return to the hotel (the Mitre this time, not the Clarendon,) and so to an exhausted sleep. I wondered why you hadn't been more tired? I felt like a dry sponge—but I remembered that you were as lively as a cricket . . . How I wished you were there. It all came back to me with a painful vividness. Why haven't we got more things to look back upon? The very few days that we have had together away from London stand out for me with just that difference that there is between that stereoscopic photograph I showed you, and an ordinary photograph.

I say talking of photographs I went off with that portfolio of Lenare's by mistake. Shall I send it back? The Kodak people promised that film for today, but I haven't had it yet.

Is this a loving letter? Not very, you will think, and yet there's a lot behind it, if you only knew.

Are you well? are you fond of me? Shall I see you at all on Monday or not? I get into despair when these contretemps happen.

Where is the French that I am to translate?[2] And most important of all, when are you coming here to stay? I feel this is not only important, but vital. Why not come next Saturday and I'll motor you up on Sunday in time for Osbert's play.[3] Give this your consideration, as really I do feel that it *is* urgent. You may not, but I do. I want you to come.

V.

Berg

1. Vita spoke on modern poets.

2. See Vita's letter of 26 April 1928, page 268.

3. Osbert Sitwell's play, *All at Sea*, was performed at the Arts Theatre Club. Although all three Sitwells appeared on the stage, and Cecil Beaton designed the scenery, the play was a total flop, running for only three performances.

❦ *Oxford*
Tuesday [22 November 1927]

I enclose 3 communications which concern you. What are we to do about the Sitwell play? Would you like me to give up my place to Leonard? I don't want to, but will do so if you like—Or could he go in Clive's box? Or could he have a press ticket? They must have sent one to the Nation. I *am* sorry about it.

Ethel [Sands] is a trump, isn't she? I have accepted [an invitation to a party on December 2] and have put off going to Berlin till the 3rd instead of the 1st—all for love of Virginia.

I am not enjoying myself here very much, thank you, but the operation was what they call successful, so that's a comfort.[1] I don't know how long I shall have to stay here, but I should think until Thursday. Rather grim.

What do you make of Sibyl's letter? I think it sounds sinister. She must have a rod in pickle for me.

You were a nice Virginia yesterday—very nice—even nicer than usual. Why? I was glad I had come up.

I say, I do hate being here—and I hate myself for hating it. How selfish one is. I expect it is good for the soul. Is it? I wish you were here, then I should love it.

Bless you, darling darling Virginia—you don't know how much I love you—how deeply—and how permanently.

V.

Berg

1. Benedict Nicolson ("Ben") had had an emergency operation for tonsilitis.

Monday [5 December 1927] *[52 Tavistock Square, W.C.I]*

Shall I come Saturday for the night?—seems the only chance. Let me know. . . .

Should you say, if I rang you up to ask, that you were fond of me?

If I saw you would you kiss me? If I were in bed would you—

I'm rather excited about Orlando tonight: have been lying by the fire and making up the last chapter.

Berg

Long Barn.
Tuesday [6 December 1927]

I am in despair: Saturday is the one and only evening I have somebody coming, Dottie to wit—I have tried to put her off but she says it is the only day she can come. Curse and damn. Could you come either Thursday, Friday, or Sunday, *possibly*? I am going to Brighton tomorrow for the night, so answer to the Metropole please[1]—If you can come, all your questions shall be answered in the affirmative. It is practically impossible to get in or out of the house here, as there is a gaping hole in front of every door,—one has to jump—very dangerous but rather exciting.[2] And stinking men crawling like beetles all over the floor. But no matter—only make a great effort,—come—and see how nice I'll be.

V.

Berg.

1. The Metropole Hotel in Brighton, where Lady Sackville was spending the winter
2. Central heating was being installed at Long Barn.

❧ *[21 December 1927]* *52 Tavistock Square, W.C.I*

. . . I have been buying presents, and feel degraded in consequence—but I bought 2 yards of pearls at Whitworths, or is it Woolworths, for 6d to wear tonight. Shan't I look nice? Heres 12/6. I like writing cheques, it makes me feel more like other women. . . .

Berg

Knole, Sevenoaks,
Kent
Thursday [29 December 1927]

Will this ever reach you? are you completely snowed up? is it very beautiful among the Downs? does Pinker like it? have you perhaps gone back to London? have you anything to eat? Shall I ever get to Sherfield tomorrow? shall I ever see you again? shall I ever write another book? I feel that the answer to most of these questions is in the negative.

I cashed your cheque, not because I wanted the 12/6 but because I thought that would make you feel even more like other women—and I knew it would come back to you eventually with my endorsement on the back, quite as though you were a really grown-up person. Now tomorrow I shall be confronted with Ethel [Smyth] and her eagle eye; I must display, I feel, no enthusiasm about any of my friends; or I say, shall I drag a completely red herring across her path? That would be rather fun. I'll invent a new beauty, whom nobody has ever seen, I'll ask Ethel if I may bring her to dinner, a dinner which on one pretext or another will have to be permanently put off. What shall we call her? You think of a suitable name, something very romantic, like Gloria Throckmorton, or Lesbia Featherstonehaugh. She is only nineteen, has run away from her family in Merioneth, and taken a flat in London. She is more lovely than Valerie,[1] more witty than Virginia, more wanton than Mary, and a better golfer than Miss Cecilia Leitch.[2]

On Xmas day I went to Brighton, throwing up floods on either side, and in torrents of rain. I looked wistfully to the left as I passed through Lewes.

Knole is all soft and white, and the snow falls in great flumps as the men shovel it off the roof. We are quite cut off except by walking. No motors, no telephone. I wish you were here. You're coming to Long Barn, aren't you though? and in no Puritanical frame of mind?

Your
V.

Berg

1. Valerie Taylor, the young actress with whom Raymond Mortimer had been in love
2. Winner of the British Ladies Golf Championship in 1914 and again in 1920–1921. She called herself Cecil, not Cecilia.

January–April 1928

January 1928 was a sad month for Vita. Her father, Lord Sackville, was slowly and painfully dying at Knole. The end came on January 28, and Virginia was her main source of consolation, not only for the loss of a beloved parent but of Knole, too, for as a daughter she could not inherit it. The house, and the title, passed to her uncle Charles. In late February she went to Berlin to be with Harold, and disliked the diplomatic parties even more than she had disliked them at Teheran because Berlin was uglier and the parties smarter. There she met Margaret Voigt, an American writer married to a British journalist, who soon became a rival to Mary Campbell—as Virginia was quick to detect from Vita's letters. Vita began to translate, with the help of her cousin Edward Sackville-West, who was a better linguist, the Duino Elegies *of Rilke. In March she lectured with Harold in Copenhagen. Virginia, though often ill, was making good progress with* Orlando.

Knole, Sevenoaks,
Kent.
Friday [6 January 1928]

Was your telegram intended to convey a command or merely a message? I mean, should it be written "Love Virginia!"—an imperative,—or "Love. Virginia."? Whichever way you read it, it was very nice and unexpected, and if a command it has been obeyed. Darling, Dada has been so ill;[1] we thought it was influenza, and then it suddenly turned to pneumonia. We had an awful fright, and though he is rather better today the doctor still won't say he is out of danger. That is why I am still here, and I think I must stay here all next week—I can't leave him alone with servants and nurses in this big house, he'd be too melancholy. My fingers itch to suggest that you should come down for a night—or more—as I shall be alone; I mean, he'll still be in bed—but I don't know if you would like to? It would be very good for Orlando, (say I tentatively,) and I find that one can very soon have enough of the society of hospital nurses.

Rebecca West wrote an article about the Land which succeeded in annoying me; I resent being told that my feeling for the country is not genuine, but only what I think people *ought* to feel about the country; this is *not* true.[2] Also I was vexed at the Femina prize being given to my bête noire instead of to you; you see, if you had been given it you could never have poked fun at me again.[3] So my literary temper is full of bile. Also I want to see you, but am tied here—Damn it all—

Your
V.

Berg

1. Lord Sackville was ill at Knole with what was thought to be pneumonia.
2. In a review which appeared in *T. P.'s Weekly* for January 7, Rebecca West had described *The Land* as "a poem unlikely to survive."
3. The Femina Prize had not yet been awarded. It went, in fact, to Virginia for *To the Lighthouse*.

❧ *[14 January 1928]* *52 Tavistock Square, W.C.I*

Dearest Creature,

I'm frightfully sorry about your father. Lord! What a time you have of it: I do hope he is better: and for God's sake dont catch it yourself. Please, darling creature, be careful. . . .

Damn Rebecca—who doesn't know a turnip from an umbrella, nor a poem from a potato if it comes to that—what right has she to pontificate about the Land? Let me see it.

Berg

 *Knole, Sevenoaks,*
Kent.
20 January [1928]

Virginia darling, I promised to let you know how Dada was—he is terribly ill, with pericarditis—(inflammation round the heart—) and it is a very slender chance that he may yet pull through. We can only hang on and wait to see what the next two or three days bring forth. I have wired for Harold who arrives this evening. It is a nightmare, especially as he suffers agonies of pain and they dare give him hardly any drugs to relieve it. If he were not in pain it would not be so bad—but as it is, it is simply ghastly to see him—and he is an *angel* of patience and uncomplainingness. The whole atmosphere of the house reminds me so vividly of the end of The Voyage Out.

Don't bother to answer this but I thought you would be wondering what I was up to.

Your miserable
Vita

Berg

 *Knole, Sevenoaks,*
Kent.
Tuesday evening [24 January 1928]

Darling, my father is much better, and I think I can come to London tomorrow—in which case I'll be with you at 5. I'll telephone in the morning if I can't, i.e. if he is not so well. It is absolutely miraculous his having pulled through—as they had really despaired of his life last Wednesday—Telephone before 10. if you want to put me off. I long to see you, and am really coming for that—as otherwise I would send the boys [to school] with Harold—but I do long to see you so.

Your loving (and rather shattered)

Orlando—
ha-ha!

Berg

Thursday [26 January 1928] *[52 Tavistock Square, W.C.I]*

. . . I'm going to keep quiet so as to get back to Orlando as soon as I can. . . . I've been reading the Land—so good, I think, some lines.

Berg

 *Knole, Sevenoaks,*
Kent.
[27 January 1928]

My darling, I am most terribly sorry to know that Hardy and Meredith have been too much for you, between them,[1] but slightly cheered by hearing from Dottie that she is going to see you this evening. Harold was to have left today, and I was going up to London with him, but my father was so unwell yesterday that he put off going, and I am thankful that he did so, as he is very much worse today, and I fear there is now very little hope. His heart is failing at last after the long strain on it. We can do nothing but sit and wait to see what happens. It is all the more cruel after his apparent recovery the other day. I am terribly sorry for poor Olive [Rubens]—it is worse for her than for anybody.

I would have telephoned to ask how you were but don't like to bother Leonard: However, I do hope that the fact of your seeing Dottie means that you are rather better.

Your loving
V.

Berg

1. Thomas Hardy had died on January 11, and Virginia attended his funeral at Westminster Abbey; Virginia was preparing "The Novels of George Meredith," for the *Times Literary Supplement*, February 9, 1928. She wrote to Eddy Sackville-West that she had had to read all of Meredith's novels in a week.

❧ *Sunday [29 January 1928]* *[52 Tavistock Square, W.C.1]*

Darling honey,

This is only to send you my love.—You don't know how much I care for you.

Joanne Trautmann

 *Knole, Sevenoaks,*
Kent.
Monday [30 January 1928]

My darling, thank you for your very sweet little note. I find it difficult to say anything about it all—I will tell you some day.[1] In the meantime nothing but the most grotesque ideas come into my mind, such as What good copy it would all be for Virginia's book. The whole thing is a mixture of the tragic, the grotesque, and the magnificent.

Fortunately one scarcely has time to think. He lies in the chapel, and I wish you could see it. It is very beautiful, and quite unreal.

I am going back to Long Barn tomorrow after the funeral. I would like to come and see you soon if I may. In the meantime, please love me, as you say you do—

Your Vita

Berg

1. Lord Sackville died at Knole a few minutes after midnight on January 28 of pericarditis.

 *Long Barn.*
Thursday [2 February 1928]

My darling, what an angel you are to me. I wish I was dining with you tonight, but I have carried off Olive [Rubens] who is staying here with me and whom I do not like to leave alone. She is going away on Monday, and I think I shall come up to London on Monday, so shall I come and see you then? in the evening. I promise not to be gloomy—and if you would come down for a night any time next week I should like nothing better. I needn't tell you that though. Harold has gone, so I shall be alone. I'm not going to Berlin for about 3 weeks.

I have just come back from Withyham, where the floor of the chapel is completely carpeted with flowers.[1]

Darling, I do love you so, and you are so sweet to me. I do so want to see you—

Your
V.

Berg

1. The village church in Sussex where all the Sackvilles had been buried since the sixteenth century. Vita's own ashes were placed in the crypt in 1962, next to the coffin of her father.

Friday [3 February 1928] *[52 Tavistock Square, W.C.1]*

Yes, darling honey, I shall be in all Monday evening, and shall expect you any time after five. . . .

Don't mind being as miserable as you like with me—I have a great turn that way myself—

A thousand useless but quite genuine loves descend upon you at this moment—which is I know very very horrid, my poor dear honey.

Berg

Long Barn.
Sunday [5 February 1928]

[In pencil]

My darling, there is *nothing in the world* I should like better than to dine with you alone tomorrow night—I did not dare propose it, not thinking that you would be alone—I will come at about 7—shall I?

V.

Berg

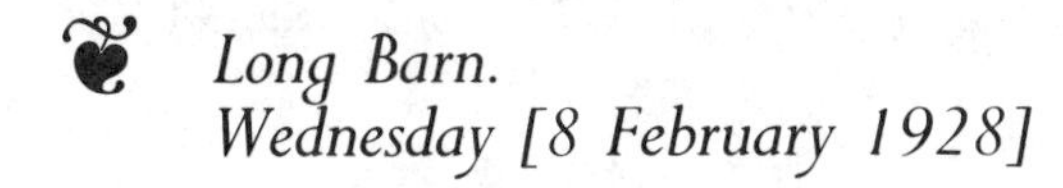

My darling, I think you are not only the most intelligent but also the nicest person I know. I shall never never forget how sweet you have been to me. You have only one serious rival in my affections, and that is Bosman's Potto.[1] I must say he's irresistible, and so are you,—not that I ever made much attempt to resist, from that evening here when you behaved so scandalously, down to the present day.

I can't tell you how much I like the Sun and the Fish, (all the more because it is all about things we did together,) and I am ordering a copy of Time and Tide.[2] If you come on Friday I shall be overjoyed, but I *don't* want you to get tired, and I know you are busy, so don't feel bound, my darling. But if you come, will you bring Vanessa's drawing?

I have written letters all day, and have nearly come to an end, so perhaps tomorrow I may be able to write a gloomy little poem for you, all about mortality.

The N.Y. Tribune says The Land is the dullest poem ever written in that genre . . . I suspect they're right.

It is all very well for Max Beerbohm to talk, but he doesn't know what you're really like—nor what a heart of gold you've got.

I *do* love you.

Your
V.

Berg.

1. Virginia's name for herself when writing to Vita

2. Virginia's article about the eclipse, which she had observed with Vita on June 29, 1927, "The Sun and the Fish," appeared in *Time and Tide*, February 3, 1928

❧ *Thursday [9 February 1928]* *[52 Tavistock Square, W.C.I]*

I shall arrive at Sevenoaks at 1.12 tomorrow . . . and stay till 6.30 so I'm afraid you'll have to give me not only a bun for my tea but a bone for my lunch . . . and by the way I'm now called Bosman's Potto, not *V.W. by arrangement—A finer name, don't you think? . . .*

Berg

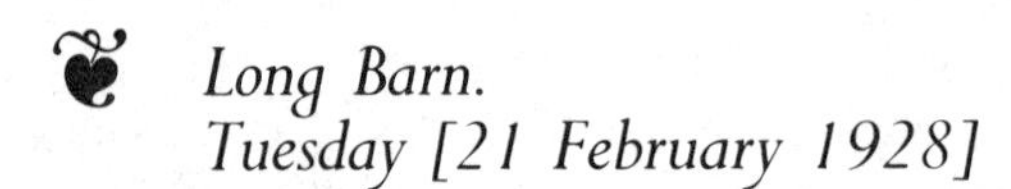

Long Barn.
Tuesday [21 February 1928]

Darling darling Potto—could you *possibly* make it Thursday? I'll tell you why: because if I leave England on Saturday I shall get to Berlin early on Sunday morning, and Sunday is Harold's free day—and if I leave on Saturday I shall have to go up to London on Friday—But if you can't manage Thursday I will put off going—it doesn't really very much matter, but I thought I would ask you on the chance. Will you ring me up tomorrow morning? I would ring you up now, but I always seem to get Leonard—so choose your own time.

I do hope your throat is better.

What a lovely signature. I can't rival that.[1]

I have got the drawing of you [by Vanessa Bell] framed on my writing table.

I can take you up to London by car, whichever day you come—as I shall be leaving then. Mind you ring me up as I suppose I ought to get my tickets. I have got Dada's car and it goes as fast as Captain Campbell.[2]

Your loving
V.

P.S. Now don't say in your high-bred mettlesome way "I won't come at all."

Berg

1. Virginia had signed her last letter "Bosman" and had drawn a circle of loops around it.

2. Captain Malcolm Campbell gained the world's land-speed record in his car *Bluebird* at Daytona Beach, Florida, on February 19, 1928.

 *24 Brücken-allee*
Berlin N.W.23
Wednesday [29 February 1928]

My darling, well, here I am, feeling rather like a jackdaw with a broken wing again—but I have got a lovely sheet of paper, haven't I? to write to Virginia on. Will you, by the way, note the address at the top? and write to me here, as if you write to the Embassy I don't get it till luncheon, whereas if you write here the whole morning is made more exciting by the thought that a post may be brought to me at any moment. This *is* a bloody place, to be sure; and my feelings which if I gave way to them would be all rebellion and despair,—just temper and tears,—are complicated by the feeling that I mustn't hate Berlin because of Harold, i.e. it is an implied criticism of him, and a resentment, and I can't bear to harbour any thought which reflects on him—besides, he can't help it, I suppose—so what with one emotion or another it is all very difficult. Berlin in the meantime is doing its best to look gay with flags: the black flag of Afghanistan.[1] The officials charged with preparing the reception of the Afghans were thrown into an agitation, as they were warned that the King wanted five beds in his room. Was he, then, they asked, bringing four wives? No, he was only bringing one wife, and one lady who for European purposes was known as his sister-in-law. Why, then, five beds? why not three? It then transpired that according to Afghan custom, the remainder of the night may not be spent in any bed in which the act of love has been consummated; therefore, if the King felt inclined to commit that act with either, or both, of the ladies, there must be two spare beds for them to change over into.

The Germans thought this very odd. I think on the contrary that it reveals a high state of civilisation. Ask Potto what he thinks. And do you think that Queen Mary is at this moment supervising the installation of five beds in a bedroom at Buckingham Palace?[2]

I say: I can't be back till the 28th. Is there *any* chance of your still being there? I'll tell you why: because I find that Harold has arranged for us both to go to Copenhagen on the 25th and LECTURE TO THE DANES—ha! ha!—he on Byron, and I on poetry.

I have a new friend here, who for sheer fantasy of nationality and temperament is not unworthy to be a denizen of Virginia's world.[3] (Except that, as we know, it is only your world which is fantastic: your characters are always mild ladies and gentlemen of university education and impeccable refinement.) But as to my friend: born a Greek, with an Italian mother, she was brought up in Italy, naturalised a Swiss, married a Swede who was then naturalised a Belgian. There is also a Russian grandmother somewhere in the background. Very tall and dark, with masses of untidy curly black hair, she decorates her person with apparently every garment in her wardrobe at the same time: large flowered shawls, ribbons, lace, sashes, bows, scarves, mittens; and moreover from her wrists dangle fans and bunches of keys. She cannot move across the room without dropping two or three of these objects on the floor, of which she remains blissfully unconscious. Not content with this remarkable appearance, she lives in a dark house entirely decorated with spurs. Large spurs, small spurs, silver spurs, steel spurs, spiky spurs; and a few stirrups thrown in to fill up. She has no mother-tongue, which is scarcely surprising, but usually talks in voluble and abominable French, and nourishes a posthumous and entirely Sapphic passion for the Lady of Shalott.[4] She is my one amusement and recreation in this dreary city, together with another lady whose morals I strongly suspect, and whose principal link with me is a frenzied admiration for the works of Virginia Woolf.[5] I must tell you that you are the idol of the Berlin intelligentsia; but that the gros public prefer Galsworthy and —Jack London![6] who they think is our leading author.

I propose to translate the poems of Rainer Maria Rilke for Dottie's series, if they have not already been translated—and if you think it would be a good thing to do?[7] They are rather difficult, but very good. I *am* grateful to you for having told me to buy Yeats' poems, they kept me happy in the train all the way. I like the one about Leda,

> "How can those terrified vague fingers push
> That feathered glory from her loosening thighs?"

They are just what poetry ought to be,—but who could have foreseen that Yeats of all people would veer round at the end of his life to your friend Tom Eliot? Rilke is not without a dash of it too,—even to making up imaginary characters like Mr Sweeney [Eliot]. Yet I don't suppose Rilke ever read Eliot.

You will write to me, won't you? I do so hate diplomats—but I'm bound to say that most of the people who come to our house are more or less disreputable journalists—also Sinclair Lewis who is a queer character—and the woman he lives with.[8] All the same I feel an awful fish out of water—and Harold now says he wants to be an Ambassador—but can you see your poor Vita as an ambassadress? I can't—and the prospect fills me with dismay. Really fate does play queer tricks on one, when all one wants to do is to garden and write and talk to Potto—and instead of that one will go to pay calls in a motor with an ambassadorial footman on the box and a cockade in his hat.

Well, well. Poor Orlando.

Your
V.

Berg

1. King Amanullah had been amir of Afghanistan since 1917, and opened his country to Western influences. Among other unprecedented actions, he had established Afghan legations in Berlin, Paris, and London. He was now paying state visits to these capitals.
2. The London visit was from March 13 to the 15th.
3. Else Lasker-Schüler
4. Elaine, the Fair Maid of Astolat in the Arthurian legends, was the subject and title of Tennyson's poem.
5. Margaret Goldsmith, wife of Frederick Voigt, a British foreign correspondent in Berlin, and herself a writer and literary agent
6. The American novelist and adventurer (1876–1916)
7. Vita did these translations with the help of Eddy Sackville-West, and they dedicated the book "To each other." It was not in the Dorothy Wellesley series but was published by the Hogarth Press separately.
8. Harold had met Sinclair Lewis (1885–1951) on his return to Berlin after the funeral of Lord Sackville. The "woman" was Dorothy Thompson, the journalist, whom he married later in 1928, visiting Long Barn on their honeymoon. In 1930, Lewis was awarded the Nobel Prize for Literature.

Tuesday [6 March 1928] *52 Tavistock Square, W.C.I*

For Gods sake, translate Rilke: only be sure of your rights; and that there's no other in English—I read some (prose) in French; and thought it good up to a point; *subtle, melodious; but not quite getting over the obstacle. His poetry may be better; probably, from what they say, it is. Yes, certainly do it. Did you know that I talk French very well? That is with great fluency, some inaccuracy, and a good many words not in use since Saint-Simon? This is the report of my French teacher. . . . I only want you to know this fact: that I do talk French: because you will never hear me; and then I get a little more even with you in real-womanliness—All real women talk French, and powder their noses. . . .*

Berg

 *British Embassy,*
Berlin.
8th March [1928]

I know you are still alive, because Clive mentions you in his letters to Harold, (yes, those documents continue to pile up, and are a source of great amusement to us,) but I don't think you can love me any more because I haven't heard a word from you. Yet I wrote you a long long letter. Have you forgotten me? or are you just busy? or is Potto jealous?

Have you ever heard of a fellow author of yours, called Phyllis Bottome?[1] Hitherto I have always pronounced her name as the part one sits on, but I now learn that the correct pronounciation is Bo-tóme. Anyway, this lady has but one desire in life, and that is to make your acquaintance. As she thinks this is beyond her reach, she has consoled herself by writing a story in which she describes the meeting between you and herself. She describes you as she imagines you to be. Now how much would you give to read that story? Personally I would give a great deal, and am trying to obtain it. (It exists only in manuscript.) Miss Bo-tóme, who apparently is a best seller, does not live here, but in Switzerland somewhere. The friend who told me of this takes it quite seriously, and says it is not funny at all, but extremely pathetic; I have however persuaded her to write for the story.

Darling, could you send me a copy of Seducers and a copy of Passenger to Teheran, by Foreign Office bag? It leaves London on Tuesdays. This is BUSINESS, as I might get Seducer translated. You mark the parcel *By bag to Berlin*.

Any books to review? except that I was so awfully late with the last one that I don't suppose Leonard will ever give me one again.

Oh dear, I *am* so homesick.

Your
V.

Berg

1. Phyllis Bottome (1882–1963), the popular novelist and short-story writer, whom Vita had already met in Berlin

❧ *12th March 1928* *52 Tavistock Square, W.C.I*

. . . I fell in love with Noel Coward, and he's coming to tea. You cant have all the love in Chelsea—Potto must have some: Noel Coward must have some. I played a funny trick. I had no hat. Bought one for 7/11¾ at a shop in Oxford Street: green felt: the wrong coloured ribbon: all a flop like a pancake in midair. Even I thought I looked odd. But I wanted to see what happens among real women if one of them looks like a pancake in mid air. In came the dashing vermeil-tinctured red-stopper-bottle-looking Mrs Edwin Montagu. She started. She positively deplored me. Then hid a smile. Looked again. Thought Ah what a tragedy! Liked me even as she pitied. Overheard my flirting. Was puzzled. Finally conquered. You see, women cant hold out against this kind of flagrant disavowal of all womanliness. They open their arms as to a flayed bird in a blast: whereas, the Mary's of this world, with every feather in place, are pecked, stoned, often die, every feather stained with blood—at the bottom of the cage.

Darling, are you happy or unhappy? Writing? Loving? Please send me a long letter, on big paper, because Potto likes that best. . . .

Berg

24 Brücken-allee,
Berlin N.W.23
14th March [1928]

Here is the nice big paper that Potto likes—I have got some very smart blue paper with the address stamped on it, and telephone number Moabit 37-94, but if Potto likes this best he must have it. I have been coming to the not very original conclusion that Virginia is in every way the most charming person in the world—in fact I have spent the last three or four days thinking of very little else and being very happy in my absorption; it has been like living a little secret life that nobody knew anything about. And listen: I have got Bottome's story for you—and it will follow in a day or two. There must be this delay because the person who got it for me wants to read it again before I send it off. Bottome is so thrilled at the idea of your reading it that she rings up Berlin on the telephone out of Switzerland to know if it has yet been posted to you—and she wishes you to be told that "the idea came to her in a dream." You are called Avery Fleming in the story. You must return it when read.

I have been getting into a row with the Hogarth Press, as you will see by the enclosed bill, the reason being that I thought they would just knock it off my royalties if ever any became due to me; but I hurriedly and apologetically enclose a cheque now. I suppose making up our books means the final withdrawal of Angus.[1] And more business before I go on to any more personal matters or geist-erforschung: there's a woman here called Margaret Voigt-Goldsmith, who is a literary agent and who wrote to you some time ago to ask if she could deal with your books to get them translated into German. You referred her to Curtis-Brown, who sent her an answer which on investigation proved to be inaccurate; i.e. said that Fischer was doing your books here, which it seems he is not. Would there therefore be any chance of Margaret Voigt getting the handling of your books after all? She is extremely nice, and energetic and intelligent; and incidentally a bosom friend of mine. Though I would not recommend her if I was not sure that you would do well by her. Her address is: Mrs Voigt-Goldsmith, 7 Nürnberger-strasse. Really it seems a pity that you should not be translated in German, as they all know about you here; so if you can do anything about Margaret Voigt I think you should.

There. (Now I am going on like Eddy about Kurt Wagenseil.)[2]

I enclose a letter from Louise which will give you her opinion of Clinker.[3] "Clinker et bien bell" is *not*, I think, meant to be a pun. I hope your spelling of French is better than Louise's.

I disapprove violently of your driving yourself through France.[4] I think it is extremely dangerous—and what's all that about flying?[5] Am I to understand that you have left the ground and that that experience is over and need never be repeated? If so, I am thankful. Please write something about it, so that the anguish of terror which I expect you went through should not be wholly wasted. It *is* damnable about my not seeing you before you go, but you see there is Copenhagen, which was not my arrangement but Harold's. Send me your address at Cassis, and *please* don't stay there too long.

My goodness what shoddy people journalists can be. I have just been sitting with some in the bar of the Adlon hotel. There was a woman who told us about the stockyards of Chicago[6]—how the corpses travel round and round on moving platforms, and every few yards something is done to them. There was a blind man who for 35 years had stood there reaching out his hand to pull out a particular bit of intestine as each corpse passed, and he never missed it. She made a regular epic out of it, but I was so conscious all the time of how physically repellent she and her colleagues were that I missed half the pleasure of these succulent facts. But I must say that I prefer this underworld of the international press to the be-starred members of ambassadorial circles. No, Virginia, Orlando may have gone on a mission to the Grand Cham, but his descendant was *not* meant to be an Excellency. I feel that the next person who kisses my hand will get his face smacked.

What else have I to tell you? Our canary has laid three eggs and is sitting on them. My mother has written to my uncle asking to take Knole for two years. The young men of Berlin are engaged in a bicycle race round a track, under arc lights, lasting for six days and six nights. I am going to Leipzig on Monday. We take long walks every afternoon for the sake of our health through the pinewoods. I look at the pines and the sand, and reflect gloomily that this type of landscape stretches away unbroken even into Russia. I try to romanticise Berlin by thinking that Russia lies over there to the east. But the only tangible reminder of Russia is the piercing east wind which comes to us straight off the steppes. I could gladly do without it; but the sun does shine. And it is warm in the flat; I give standing orders to the servants that I am always out if anybody calls; and I make myself happy with Rilke, who is a damned fine poet. That's my life. Not as exciting as yours, no doubt, but I think a lot about Virginia—which makes up for much—and really I have been loving Virginia enormously lately—in an intense, absent way, (absent in distance, I mean,) which has been a great satisfaction to me—like a tide flowing in and filling a lot of empty spaces. Orlando, I am glad to reflect, compels you willy-nilly to spend a certain amount of your time with me. Darling I do love you.

V.

Berg

1. Angus Davidson had been manager of the Hogarth Press since 1924, and was fired by Leonard in December 1927.
2. Wagenseil translated some of Harold's books into German.
3. Clinker was a spaniel puppy which Vita had given to Angelica Bell.
4. The Woolfs went to France by car on March 26.
5. Virginia never flew in her life. Here Vita is referring to Shelmerdine's flight described in the last pages of *Orlando*.
6. Ms. Kuts of the United Press

❧ *[Typewritten]* *52 Tavistock Square, W.C.1*
[20? March 1928]

Dearest, Mrs Nicolson,

O what a curse these translators are! Tell your Bosom friend Mrs Voigt Something or other that all I can say is that I have received a cheque from, and signed a contract with, the Insel Verlag which is I understand the Fischer Verlag by which they are to produce Mrs Dalloway this autumn and The Lighthouse later. But all communications must be through Curtis Brown. . . .

ORLANDO IS FINISHED!!!

[in Virginia's handwriting:]

Did you feel a sort of tug, as if your neck was being broken on Saturday last [17 March] at 5 minutes to one? That was when he died—or rather stopped talking, with three little dots . . . Now every word will have to be re-written, and I see no chance of finishing it by September—It is all over the place, incoherent, intolerable, impossible—And I am sick of it. The question now is, will my feelings for you be changed? I've lived in you all these months—coming out, what are you really like? Do you exist? Have I made you up? . . .

Berg

12 Richelieu Allé
Hellerup,
Copenhagen.
[but from Long Barn]
3rd April [1928]

I am not in Copenhagen. But I was when I secured this piece of paper and wrote the address on the envelope for fear I should forget it. So I feel justified in filling up, although I am somewhere quite different, (at Long Barn in fact,) a piece of paper which originally was meant for you.

I have so much to say that it would fill several volumes. Don't be alarmed: I'll leave most of it out. The train is put on to a ferry, several ferries, because Denmark is split up by the sea. One arrives, to find

Copenhagen itself split up by the sea; one crosses bridges which are liable to open suddenly in the middle to allow passage to ships while all the traffic of the Danes is suspended. A great grievance, and a source of excuse to all the unpunctual people in Copenhagen. "I'm so sorry I'm late, but the bridge was open." I found myself wishing that Piccadilly Circus or the Strand would suddenly gape to allow passage to a Swede. That's because I am unpunctual, and I have a theory that everything conspires to render unpunctual people more unpunctual than they already are,—their taxis break down, they get into 15-minute blocks,—"to him that is given shall much be given, but to him that hath not shall be taken away even that which he hath."

Anyway,—Copenhagen. We fell into a household which was undiluted Ibsen, (how suitable,—though you mustn't let the Danes think that Ibsen, or Norway, have anything to do with them.) Our hostess turned out to be the sister of that Elsie Mackay who had just flown away for ever into the Atlantic, and whose loss had only been accepted 2 days earlier; our host, her husband, was the most insensitive of men. She had, moreover, a baby only a few weeks old.[1] There were all sorts of additional horrors,—such as his collection of rowing caps and oars, (he was once a rowing Blue,) trophies of his athletic prowess enshrined behind glass doors; medals, and silver cups; *her* personality was entirely eclipsed. A horrid man, with a voice like a curate. The whole house was (visibly) dominated by *his* triumphs, as by his evangelical accents; but underneath it all was *her* tragedy, small, crushed, suppressed. We (Harold and I) hated it so much that we bolted; caught the night train as we couldn't bear to wait till the morning.

But it's a whole story, that you ought to write. Incorporating Carl Bodelsen and Else Arnefeldt, and Doktor Jespersen, and Pastor Storm, and Mrs Picton Bagge. All real people.

Well, then, Harold delivered a lecture on Byron which was *most* brilliant and amusing, standing up behind a white-and-gold tribunal; and I delivered a lecture on English poetry which was most boring and stodgy; and so we came back to Berlin by the train on the ferry, and next night I came on to England, and found that Leonard had (a) ruined my life by sending me a book on Afghanistan[2] which is the place I most want to go to, and (b) brightened my life by sending me a most unexpected cheque for £50—will you please give him both these messages? Also I found Pinker, more like a flounced Victorian lady than ever. (She is very well.) I say "Where's Leonard? Where's Virginia?" and she rushes about sniffing as for a mouse. I showed her the drawing of you, but I regret to say that she didn't recognise it. Tell Vanessa that I love it, and that it hangs in my bedroom. (Ha-ha.)

Oh, and I've got so much to tell you: about Berlin, and Else Lasker-Schüler, and Schwichtenberg, and the nigger who was really a man not a woman; but had all the graces of a cocotte, and the temper too; all an ocean in my head. And here is Bottome's story at last, which I forgot to send, but which will be appreciated by your friends and relations who are fortunate enough to be with you, damn them.

And when are you coming back?

No, of course I never saw Sibyl.

How is the umbrella [Leonard's car]?

How cross I was to reach London and to know that you were not there. An empty London, in spite of 8 million inhabitants or whatever it is. Just a desert, but not so nice as a real desert. (I.e. Afghanistan. All Leonard's fault.)

Are you well? Are you in the sun? Oh, and Orlando. I forgot about him. You absolutely terrified me by your remarks. "Do I exist or have you made me up?" I always foresaw that, when you had killed Orlando off. Well, I'll tell you one thing: if you like,—no, *love*,—me one trifle less now that Orlando is dead, you shall never set eyes on me again, except by chance at one of Sibyl's parties. I *won't* be fictitious. I won't be loved solely in an astral body, or in Virginia's world.

So write quickly and say I'm still real. I feel terribly real just now,—like cockles and mussels, all alive—oh.

Will you come and stay with me when you come home? When will that be?

Have you taken Potto to Cassis or left him in Tavistock Square? Was he frightened in the motor?

This is the paper Potto likes, only folded in two.

Your adoring and perfectly solid

Orlando

Berg

1. Their host was Eugen Millington-Drake, first secretary of the British legation in Copenhagen. Their hostess was Lady Effie Millington-Drake. Her sister was Elsie Mackay, who was lost over the Atlantic on an east-west flight on March 13. The baby was James, born January 10, 1928.

2. *Through the Heart of Afghanistan* by Emil Trinkler. Vita reviewed it in *The Nation*, May 19, 1928.

❧ *31st March 1928* *Orange [France]*

Dearest Honey,

Are you back? At Long Barn? Happy? With the dogs? Comfortable? Well?

I can't remember how one writes. Nothing but a heart of gold would make me try to write now—perched on a hard chair in a bare bedroom in a bad inn. . . . I think of Vita at Long Barn: all fire and legs and beautiful plunging ways like a young horse. . . .

*The day before I left I read in the Times that I had won the most insignificant and ridiculous of prizes [*Femina Vie Heureuse*]—but I have heard nothing more; so it may be untrue. I dont mind—you will laugh either way. . . .*

Berg

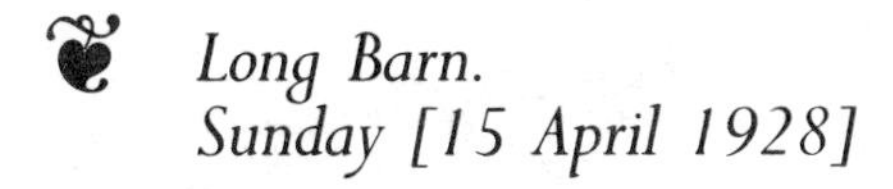

Long Barn.
Sunday [15 April 1928]

I have been wanting to write to you for such a long time, but I thought you would be on your way home [from France]. My God, I shall be thankful when I know you are safely back.

I am coming up on Wednesday; shall Pinker and I come in the evening? I am going to broadcast at 9.15, and they want to give me some sort of rehearsal during the day, but I expect they'll fix a time in the morning, so I ought to be free the rest of the day. Tell me when to come.

And did you ever get Bottome's story?

Now I shall not write more, because you will find this when you arrive—and you will have floods of letters—and you will have to be nice to Nellie [Boxall, Virginia's cook]—so you won't want to read letters.

V.

Berg

❧ *Tuesday [17 April 1928]* *52 Tavistock Square, W.C.I*

. . . Come punctually at 4 with Pinker, or Leonard will be gone. May I come to the broadcasting with you? And aint it wretched you care for me no longer: I always said you were a promiscuous brute—Is it a Mary again; or a Jenny this time or a Polly? Eh?

The truth shall be dug out of you at all costs.

Am I to be wearing my heart out for a woman who goes with any girl from an Inn!

Berg

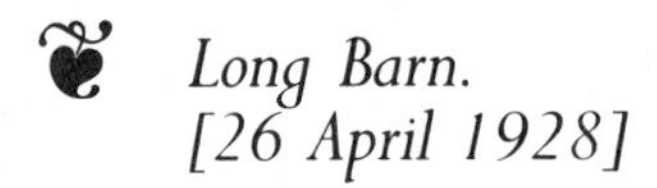

Long Barn.
[26 April 1928]

[Typewritten]
"I think I met a gentleman of your family in Poland last summer."
"Je crois avoir fait la connaissance d'un gentilhomme qui vous était apparenté en Pologne l'été dernier."

"The ladies of the English Court ravish me with their beauty. Never have I seen so graceful a lady as your Queen or so fine a head dress as she wears."
"La beauté des dames de la cour d'Angleterre me met dans le ravissement. On ne peut voir une dame plus gracieuse que votre reine, ni une coiffure plus belle (élégante?) que la sienne."

"Might I trouble you, Sir, to pass me the salt?"
"Voulez-vous avoir l'obligeance, monsieur, de me passer le sel?"

"With all the pleasure in my life, Madam."
"Avec le plus grand plaisir du monde, madame."
"Avec la plus grande joie du monde, madame."

Nauseating mixture: *mélange nauséabond,*
or, *potion nauséabond,* (if you mean *medecine.*)

bumpkins: *lourdauds.* (lit. oafs.)
or: *rustres,* (lit. yokels.)
or: *hobereaux* (lit. country noblemen.)

figure of fun: I cannot think of any absolutely literal translation. You could say *C'est un véritable épouvantail,* (lit. scarecrow.) or *Il a une tête à se tordre de rire.*

Rigged up like a Maypole: *Une grande perche mal fagotée.*
or, *mal ficelée.*

Of wood, of sackcloth, and of cinders. This puzzles me. If you mean 'sackcloth and ashes,' it is *'le sac et la cendre.'* But cinders is really *"escarbilles,"*—what we also call clinkers or breeze. Wood is of course *bois,* or *planches* if you mean boards.[1]
[Handwritten]
The difference between *cendre* and *escarbilles* is, that ashes are fine and powdery; *escarbilles* are lumpy. *'Sac'* seems ambiguous for 'sackcloth', unless used in conjunction with *la cendre,'* as it can also mean bag. Wouldn't it be better to leave it in English? if not essential to put it in French?
"De bois, de sac, et d'escarbilles," sounds very odd!

Darling, is this any use to you? I got a peculiar jump as I realised that the phrases I was copying were phrases out of that unexplored country, your book. I tried to build up whole scenes from them,—scenes into which they could possibly fit,—like an anatomist reconstructing the animal from one bone. I didn't get very far.

The big crab apple has covered itself with blossom since I left yesterday morning, and the nightingales are singing in broad daylight.

How is Orlando's bride in her dress sewn with oranges? and how are the bees? Still busy? And Stella Benson?[2] And all your life? Oh I am writing on the back of the typing, which you were to have cut off for your typist. (A typist in German is called a *Tippfraülein.*) But how is all your life, all the same? Is it really as enchanted as it appears to me? and as full of Authors? people who have printed a Book? Enviable Virginia—full of bees and prizes. I won another prize [for *The Land*] the other day—I forgot to tell you—in America—but it was only a vast anthology of American verse. I had hoped for dollars.

[Several words heavily scored over.]

Now it's no good your trying to read that, because you won't be able to—It was something very interesting.

I have stolen an oak. Put a fence round it. I'll show you when you come—but when will that be? Not for weeks, if you have to do 10 pages a day.

Tell Leonard that Roy has written to Graves, challenging him to a duel, and saying that he shall say exactly what he likes about him and all pipsqueaks of his sort;[3] but tell Leonard not to repeat this, as Roy may change his mind—and we mustn't make bad blood between the poets. I oughtn't to say it but it will amuse Leonard. It's the rudest letter I ever read!

Your Orlando. (quite real)

Berg

1. In *Orlando* (p. 38), Virginia used only the first two of Vita's translations, describing the opening conversation between Orlando and Sasha, the Russian princess with whom he fell in love. Vita was bilingual in French and English, and so was Orlando, but not Virginia.
2. Virginia and Leonard had had Stella Benson to dine. She had been the second choice for the Femina Prize and, according to Virginia, "I had never been so sneered at in my life for getting it." However, Stella Benson won the Femina in 1932 for her last novel, *Tobit Transplanted*.
3. Roy Campbell, the South African poet, had quarreled with Robert Graves, the poet and novelist (*Goodbye to All That*). He had attacked Graves in the first line of his poem *The Georgiad*.

❧ *Friday [27 April 1928]* — *From Monk's House [Rodmell, Sussex]*

I rang you up just now, to find you were gone nutting in the woods with Mary Campbell, or Mary Carmichael, or Mary Seton, but not me—damn you. . . .[1]

Berg

1. "There was Marie Seaton, and Marie Beaton,
   And Marie Carmichael, and me."

From *The Ballad of the Queen's Maries*. Virginia would use these names for her fictitious novelists in *A Room of One's Own* (1929).

May–September 1928

In the summer of 1928, Vita was finishing Twelve Days; *and Virginia,* Orlando. *Vita's intimacy with Mary Campbell and Margaret Voigt gradually drew to an end, to the distress of both women but not of Vita, who had acquired a new friend, Hilda Matheson, talks director of the BBC, for whom Vita frequently broadcast. Virginia came several times to Long Barn and had Vita photographed for* Orlando, *and Vita attended the presentation to her of the Femina Prize for* To the Lighthouse. *They were in common sympathy for Radclyffe Hall, whose lesbian novel* The Well of Loneliness *was declared obscene by the British Home Secretary. For a month in August–September, Vita went again to Germany, where she continued to translate Rilke's poems. The relationship between them at this time could be described thus: Virginia still loved Vita, and Vita venerated Virginia, but there was a partial withdrawal on Vita's side owing to other distractions and the competition of other women.*

❧ *Friday [4 May 1928]* *52 Tavistock Square, W.C.I*

Orlando,

I think I must tell Eddy about you [and Orlando*]. What do you say? He is so passionate about Knole and Sackvilles. I feel it awkward to spring the whole thing without warning—Would he keep it secret? . . .*

I hear Mrs Nicolson and Mrs Woolf gave some offence on Wednesday by coming to the prize dressed as if for a funeral. Still it was *my funeral. . . .*

Berg

 *Long Barn, Weald,*
Sevenoaks.
Sunday [6 May 1928]

Yes, do tell Eddy. He'll be amused, and I hope annoyed. He's coming here to day, to lunch. I think he would be discreet, if you impressed it well on him. The secret has been so well kept, it would be a pity for it to leak out now.

Do you know that I came and stood on your doorstep at 11.15 on Wednesday night? but the door was so firmly shut, and all the windows looked so dark, that I didn't dare ring the bell, but went sadly away like a poor dog, and drove myself home to Long Barn through the night. Yes, the nights are marvellous. Full moon, nightingales, and all that business. But where is Virginia? What about Virginia coming here for a night on Tuesday or Wednesday? before the moon begins to wane. And the garden is so pretty.

Would you ask Leonard, provisionally, if he would like a companion volume to Passenger to Teheran?[1] I think he said the Press had made over it, in spite of a comparatively small sale. I have a good deal of material, and some nice pictures. I think I could probably finish it by July, if that would be early enough for the autumn. But don't let him hesitate to turn it down if he wants to, on the score of friendship. I don't want to be a Polly Flinders to you. [2]

Clive asks me to dine on the 17th. Are you going? If so, I will go; if not, I won't.

You looked so lovely the other day[3]—but I do think it's a mistake not to come and stay at the 1st class hotel.

Your most loving
V.

Berg

1. *Twelve Days*, at which Vita had been working since her return from Germany, was an account of her journey through the southern Persian mountains in 1927.
2. "Little Polly Flinders/Sat among the cinders" (nursery rhyme, c. 1805), i.e., a cause of impoverishment to the Hogarth Press
3. At the presentation to Virginia of the Femina Prize for *To the Lighthouse* on May 2.

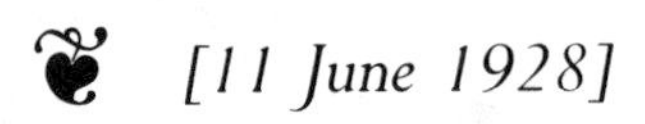

I am afraid I could not go on Friday to Lenare [photographer] but I could go on Monday if that would do as well,—perhaps better, if Vanessa is then more likely to be back? Harold leaves on Monday evening so I shall be in London with him any way that day. Your suggestion of coming here on

Thursday delights me, though it would delight me more if I thought you were coming to stay next week—If you come on Thursday you will find here the [Sir Robert] Clives who were in Teheran (I mean, he is minister in Teheran and is now on leave,) but that would not matter except that it might bore you and personally I prefer to have you alone—But if you are in a hurry? . . . In any case I shall see you tomorrow night, shan't I, if I come in after dinner?

The long letter was to have been about the excitements of wireless,[1] but perhaps it is better spoken.

Do you think that Osbert's Proclamation means that Sachie gets the Hawthornden tomorrow?[2] I bet it does. (Not £5 though.)

We come up after lunch tomorrow.

Are your ears still sore? Have you enjoyed the sensation of twiddling the rings when they have stuck? A new, small, peculiar sensation.[3]

Have you forgotten your poor Orlando already?

V.

Berg

1. On June 4, Harold had broadcast on biography, and Vita on *The Land*. The BBC gave them a dinner party at the Savoy to celebrate the occasion.
2. Sacheverell Sitwell did not receive the prize for his *All Summer in a Day*. It was awarded to Henry Williamson for *Tarka the Otter* and presented to him by John Galsworthy on June 12.
3. On June 4, Vita and Virginia had had their ears pierced for earrings.

❧ *Sunday [17 June 1928]* *52 T.[avistock] S.[quare, W.C.1]*

. . . Oh heavens what a bore Orlando is—worse in his death than in his life: I think: I'm so tired of him.

Berg

 *Long Barn, Weald,*
Sevenoaks.
Tuesday [10 July 1928]

Virginia, will you give your very serious consideration to the possibility of dashing to the [Burgundy] vintage with me between Sept 26th and October? Having got this idea into my head, where it has now been simmering for several years, I want to execute it more than anything.

And, more immediately, could you go to the BBC with me on Friday afternoon? Will you ring me tomorrow morning and tell me, and I'll arrange with Miss Matheson.[1] Then I'd come back to tea with you, and we might also go and look at the things from Ur.

How may illustrations may I have, please? Most of the book [*Twelve Days*] has gone off to be typed. But I expect Leonard will refuse it when he has read it. I might as well know about the illustrations though, because I must get prints made from my negatives.

I've been feeling very much chastened since you were here, but also curiously happy. I am never wholly crushed when you lecture me, because it shows that you aren't indifferent.[2] And really I have a few good qualities. Ask Potto—to whom my love.

Encouraged by your counsel, I've written some lines of poetry in the best Tennysonian tradition.

I say, we must make up for that abortive night soon? But all the same, it had a nice and unusual character of its own.

I got Harcourt Brace's autumn list with Orlando in it. Have you remembered to let them know that you have torn it up?

You were very very charming really in spite of the lecture. And you are definite to me,—my goodness, you are. My silly Virginia. My darling, darling, precious Virginia.

V.

Berg

1. Hilda Matheson, with whom Vita became intimate, much to Virginia's annoyance. See *VW 1969*.
2. Virginia had been at Long Barn on July 6. She wrote in her diary next day: "Lay by the black currant bushes lecturing Vita on her floundering habits, with the Campbells for instance."

Long Barn, Weald,
Sevenoaks.
Monday [23 July 1928]

I was about to write you in protest: on Saturday I caught the gleam of your handwriting among my letters; put it aside as a treat to read last; and then, coming to it full of expectation, discovered that it was for Eddy . . . .

I don't, incidentally, know where Eddy is, so sent it to 41 Gordon Square, the last address I had for him.

Did you know that I was going to marry Eddy? I didn't know it myself, but my mother told Ozzie [Dickinson] so. I am going to divorce Harold and marry Eddy, so as to get Knole. That is why I have stolen all her jewels to give them to Knole.

Will you come to my wedding?

I hear you rang me up. What was it? I don't like to bother you on the telephone, but will you perhaps ring me up tomorrow before 10? Was it to say you would come here?

V.

Berg

Long Barn, Weald,
Sevenoaks.
Tuesday [24 July 1928]

Virginia darling, I am so sorry, I have made a stupid mistake: I quite forgot I had Lady Lindsay[1] coming down for the night on Monday—so I cannot come then. Might I come Sunday instead? or if that isn't convenient to you I could come to lunch Monday and get back here in time. Will you say?

I'm so glad you have escaped from London—which must be a furnace. I do hope you're all right. I don't like you to have headaches.

Your
V.

Berg

1. Elizabeth (daughter of Colgate Hoyt, a New York banker) was the second wife of Sir Ronald Lindsay, British ambassador in Berlin 1926–1928. The Nicolsons remained very fond of them both, and met them again in 1933 in Washington, where Sir Ronald was ambassador from 1930–1939.

 *Thursday [9 August 1928]*

But would you really? Come here, I mean? On Sunday? For the night? If October 11th is to see the end of our romance, it would be as well to make the most of the short time that remains to us.[1] Still, there's that hopeful if problematical week in France, at the end of September. It doesn't seem safe to *count* on that—so I snatch at Sunday—or Saturday. Either. For the night. Only let me know which.

Saturday afternoon I have someone coming here, but she would be gone by the evening. Someone of whom I am rather frightened: Princess Lichnowsky.[2] I don't know why I am frightened of her; I have never set eyes on her. I just feel that she is destined to have a baleful influence on my life—Perhaps Harold will fall in love with her. Perhaps Ben will. Not me. Anyway, she would be gone by the evening.

I was very jealous of Eddy being with you. Very cross about your being together in the telephone box.

I *do* want to see you.

V.

Berg

1. *Orlando* was scheduled for publication on October 11.
2. Princess Mechtilde Lichnowsky (1879–1958), a writer, collector of modern paintings, and a friend of Roger Fry, was the widow of Prince Karl Max Lichnowsky, German ambassador in London (1912–1914), where he had been a close friend of Harold's father, Lord Carnock, then head of the British Foreign Office. Harold had visited them on their German estate just before the prince's death on February 27, 1928.

 *39 Manger-strasse II*
Potsdam.
21st August [1928]

I sit on a balcony overlooking a black lake [the Heilige See] hung with weeping willows. The view is not too depressingly German. By the water's edge there is a little grey pavilion with a domed roof of green copper. Some way off, in the trees, there is a romantic ruin, like something in one of Eddy's books. I live entirely in the company of angels and of obscure but tragic figures from the Italian Renaissance, (whose catastrophes gain by being only lightly hinted at and not expounded,) because I am translating Rilke. The boys have got a young German tutor who has (as luck will have it) devoted the past two years to the study of Rilke, and in particular to the study of the very poems I am translating; his hair stands straight up on end with excitement when he talks about it, and his horn-rimmed glasses descend to the tip of his nose, where they remain balanced by a miracle of gravity. Then he takes the boys off, and I see them dwindling in size as their little boat pulls them further out into the lake. Then I see two white naked bodies, standing up in the boat, and then a flash and a splash, and then only two round heads bobbing in the water. And I return to Rilke.

"How strange it is to live no more on earth;
To make no further use of customs learnt;
No longer to attribute to the rose
Or anything of fair especial promise,
A metaphor of human destiny;
To be no longer that which once we were,
In ever terrible hands; to throw aside
Even our personal name, a broken toy!
Strange, to desire no more the consummation
Of our desires! How strange to see all things
Related to this earth, float free in space!
Death is a weariness so void of meaning
That slowly we conceive eternity." [1]

And next Saturday we give a dinner party to sixty members of Parliament who are touring Europe. "His Britannic Majesty's Chargé d'Affaires and Mrs Harold Nicolson request the honour. . . ." Will you, please, Virginia, consecrate a kindly though sarcastic thought to me at 8.30 on Saturday evening? as you wander out after dinner down to the water-meadows to throw a stick into the Ooze [*sic*] for Pinker?

Any more developments about France?

I found a very very old letter from you in a book, beginning Dear Vita.[2]

The German army, or what is left of it, rumbles its artillery every morning over the cobbles, and the music of a distant military band echoes over the lake. In the intervals of Rilke I think about my novel,[3] and a sort of patch-work counterpane is beginning to form, but so far the patches are only laid side by side and I have not yet begun to stitch at them. Is it better to be extremely ambitious, or rather modest? Probably the latter is safer; but I *hate* safety, and would rather fail gloriously than dingily succeed. Anyhow I don't care about what is "better," for however many resolutions one makes, one's pen, like water, always finds its own level, and one can't write in any way other than one's own. At least I feel confident that the rank growth of my early years has been pretty severely pruned by now—and I hope has made nice strong woody growth instead. We shall see.

Poor Virginia, she will have to read that novel when it is finished—and what's more she'll have to say what she thinks of it—and with the utmost brutality too. I shall join the company of Doris Daglish or whatever her name is,[4] and the pillmaker.

I do miss you so. I do hope we go to France, but I daren't think about it yet with any confidence. Will you write to me?

Your
V.

Berg

1. Vita's translation of part of the "First Elegy" by Rainer Maria Rilke, in his *Elegies from the Castle of Duino* (Hogarth Press, 1931)

2. *VW 1412* (July 1923), the only one so addressed

3. *The Edwardians*

4. A woman from a London suburb who had submitted a worthless novel to the Hogarth Press. See *VW 1588* (September 1925).

30th Aug 1928 *Monks House, Rodmell*
[Sussex]

Why need you be so timid and pride-blown, both at once, over writing your novel? What does donkey West mean about her ambition and failure? . . . surely, for the last ten years almost, you have cut back and pruned and root dug—What is it one should do to fig trees?—with the result that you write sometimes too much like a racehorse who has been trained till his tail is like a mouses tail and his ribs are like a raised map of the Alps. Please write your novel, and then you will enter into the unreal world, where Virginia lives—and poor woman, can't now live anywhere else. . . .

Berg

39 Manger-strasse II
Potsdam.
31st August [1928]

Henry (Pinker's younger brother,) the boys, and I went for a walk in Potsdam. We walked down long, tidy, cobbled streets, with trams squealing round the corners and the dust whirling in clouds before the incessant wind. I felt extremely depressed. Am I for ever, I thought, to spend my life walking the streets of Potsdam, Belgrade, Bucharest, Washington? Then I remembered that I had lost my cigarette case, with a £10 note in it, *and* my motor license, *and* a cheque from The Nation, *and* another cheque, *and* a photograph small but precious of Virginia, *and* a prescription belonging to somebody else. I remembered also that the Foreign Office had refused to pay for the dinner to the MP's, which had cost us something over £100. So my depression deepened. But then we came home and I found in the letter box a letter which I knew to be from you, even though the envelope was typewritten, and my spirits rose. I have now thrown the boys into the lake, and am at liberty for at least half an hour.

I feel very violently about The Well of Loneliness.[1] Not on account of what you call my proclivities; not because I think it is a good book; but really on principle. (I think of writing to Jix[2] suggesting that he should suppress Shakespeare's Sonnets.) Because, you see, even if the W. of L. had been a good book,—even if it had been a great book, a real masterpiece,—the result would have been the same. And that is intolerable. I really have no words to say how indignant I am. Is Leonard really going to get up a protest? or is it fizzling out? (What a conceited ass the woman must be.) *Don't* let it fizzle out. If you got Arnold Bennett and suchlike, it would be bound to make an impression. (Avoid Shaw, though.) I nearly blew up over the various articles in The New Statesman. Personally, I should like to renounce my nationality, as a gesture; but I don't want to become a German, even though I did go to a revue last night in which two ravishing young women sing a frankly Lesbian song.

France. . . . Well, you can get a pale reflection of the matrimonial miseries which *I* undergo. You hesitate to leave Leonard for six days; I leave Harold several times a year for several months. I see him off to Persia. He sees me off to England. We are perpetually in a state of saying goodbye.

By the way, when you say "Ethel Sands advises us," etc, do you mean (by us) you and Leonard, or you and me?[3]

I will leave you to your own fluctuations, which amuse me a good deal. I will only say, that you mustn't come if it's going to make you miserable all the time. But you wouldn't.

Don't tell me that it is a lovely August in England. It is so cold here that I sit with an eiderdown over my knees. It rains nearly every day. It is a foul climate. You mustn't say it is lovely in England, or that the Downs are golden or whatever it is—because then I rebel against my lot.

Your
V.

My love and a kiss to Potto.

Berg

1. Virginia had written to Vita that *The Well of Loneliness* (1928), an overtly Lesbian novel by Marguerite Radclyffe Hall, had been banned as obscene, and British intellectuals were rallying to her defense.
2. Nickname of the Home Secretary, William Joynson-Hicks, who was responsible for censorship matters and had banned the book, a decision that was now challenged in the courts
3. Ethel Sands was advising Virginia about the itinerary of their proposed holiday in Burgundy.

❧ *Saturday, Sept 8th 1928* *Monks House, Rodmell, Sussex*

Concentrate your mind upon this, and give me your answer. Suppose we start (you and I and Potto) on Saturday 22nd. Sleep in Paris. Get to SAULIEU *on Monday. . . . Do you want to go 2nd or 1st (I insist on 1st on the boat) If first is much more comfortable, first is advisable. Not otherwise; because first class travellers are always old fat testy and smell of eau de cologne, which makes me sick. . . .*

. . . But I was going to say that I like your Tolstoy very much. I think it is your best criticism, so far as I've seen. And as I always take credit for your good writing, I'm pleased with myself. . . . The question you should have pushed home—had there been room—is precisely the one you raise, what made his realism which might have been photographic, not at all; but on the contrary, moving and exciting and all the rest of it. . . . But I like you when you write such interesting things—and I have a great deal to say . . . about your novel. I thought out, indeed, a long and it seemed then very profoud essay upon writing novels. . . . I believe that the main thing in beginning a novel is to feel, not that you can write it, but that it exists on the far side of a gulf, which words can't cross: that its to be pulled through only in a breathless anguish. Now when I sit down to an article, I have a net of words which will come down on the idea certainly in an hour or so. But a novel, as I say, to be good should seem, before one writes it, something unwriteable: but only visible; so that for nine months one lives in despair, and only when one has forgotten what one meant, does the book seem tolerable. I assure you, all my novels were first rate before they were written. . . .

As for Radclyffe Hall, I agree: but what is one to do? She drew up a letter of her own, protesting her innocence and decency, which she asked us to sign, and would have no other sent out.

Berg

 *British Embassy,*
Berlin.
Tuesday [11 September 1928]

Your letter has just caught me, as we leave early tomorrow morning. I am absolutely overjoyed to think that our France may really materialise, and I beg you to get the tickets before you have time to change your mind. The only thing is, I would *rather* start on the 24th if it were exactly the same to you, and get back on the 2nd instead of starting on the 22nd and getting back on the 30th—partly because I have my first wireless article to do (I can't do it here, as I have not the necessary books,) and partly because Nigel doesn't go back to school till the 26th and I would prefer to be at home with him as long as possible—but that doesn't really matter—and I *can* do the wireless thing in 2 days I suppose—(I say 2 days, because I shall not have much chance of doing it until I have got Ben off to Eton.) so you decide on the date which suits you. I only made the suggestion in case it was absolutely the same to you.

I don't see, however, why you should bother about the tickets, when I shall find Miss Le Bosquet waiting for me at Long Barn![1] Let me see to it. We'd better go from Newhaven, hadn't we? I'll motor there, and pick you up on the way—and leave the car in a garage there till we come back. I have never travelled 2nd [class] in France and don't know what it is like, but am quite agreeable to do so, but agree with you on insisting on 1st class on the boat AND a cabin. Experience has taught me this.

My congratulations to Pinker.[2] Leonard very kindly asked if I would like a puppy; may I decide when I know whether Pippin has had any or not? I have heard nothing from Louise about it. If Pippin has not had any, as I rather fear, I should love to have a bitch—to keep my stock going.

I suppose you will not be in London on Tuesday 18th? as I must take Ben up on that day and could come to see you for a minute about France. Send me a line to Long Barn where I arrive on Saturday.

I blushed with pleasure because you liked what I wrote about Tolstoy;[3] I wish I could have made it twice as long. I found that I had come to the end of my allotted words when I had only just begun.

No more,—because I must pack and go on—and also because I shall at last really have time to talk to you.

I say: is Potto jealous of the puppies? Leonard, I suppose, is in the 7th heaven—and like a regular old nannie—

Your
V.

I think you'd better get a little basket for Potto, with a mackintosh sheet.

I think Dottie must have been conscious of something wrong, as she wrote to me and said she felt she had been absolutely at her worst![4]

Berg

1. Audrey Le Bosquet was Vita's secretary.
2. Pinker had had four puppies: two male, two female.
3. "Tolstoy," *Nation and Athenaeum*, September 8, 1928
4. Virginia had written that Leonard became enraged by Dorothy Wellesley's behavior during a recent visit.

Long Barn, Weald,
Sevenoaks.
Wednesday [19 September 1928]

I write in a hurry because I am just starting for Eton with Ben.

Monday,—yes. Could you send a postcard to say

(1) what time the boat starts,
(2) how much I owe you for tickets
(3) the name of the hotel at Saulieu.

According to the time the boat starts, perhaps I may decide whether to come Sunday night or Monday morning? I'll come by train anyhow, and not by motor.

No clothes. A fur coat certainly. The other objects mentioned,—I hope unnecessary. Potto's basket. A bib for Potto.

I was in a bookshop in London yesterday and the bookseller said to me knowingly, "I saw an advance copy of Orlando."

I also am interested in this journey, but not wholly as an experiment.

Will you tell Leonard I was under the impression that the Bookman [weekly trade magazine] was merely a publishers' rag? He can leave the quotation in if he likes.

I must go. Poor Ben.

V.

Berg

October–December 1928

At the end of September, Vita and Virginia went on a week's holiday to Burgundy—their only journey alone together—scarcely mentioning Orlando, *which was published on October 11, a few days after their return. Vita's reaction to the book (see her letter of October 11) was total delight. It received from the critics almost unanimous praise (the only person appalled by it was Vita's mother), and Vita, to her pleasure, was soon publicly acknowledged Orlando's model. In October, Virginia, accompanied by Vita, gave at Cambridge the first of two lectures on which she based her next book,* A Room of One's Own. *Vita began her short study of* Andrew Marvell, *and ended the year again in Berlin.*

 *Long Barn.*
Friday night [5 October 1928]

My darling,

I was enjoying the melancholy pleasure of looking through your letters this evening, when it occurred to me that it was some time since I had had one from you,—not, in fact, since I was in Berlin. And now you are in London, besieged by Sibyls and Tom Eliots, not to mention packing up parcels of Orlando, and you won't have time to write. Besides, if I have not had letters from you it is because I have been with you, which is better than ink and paper. And you were here, dear me, no later than yesterday.

It was queer, reading some of your letters, in the light of having been with you so much lately. A fitful illumination played over them,—a sort of cross-light,—(do you realise that at Auppegard one is always in a cross-light? a symbolic fact which would, I feel, have had more influence on you or on me, had either of us chanced to live there, than it has had on the relatively unimaginative natures of Ethel [Sands] & Nan [Hudson][1].) Well, a sort of cross-light, as I say, played across them, projected half from the rather tentative illumination of the past and half from the fuller illumination of the present. I couldn't stop to wonder which illumination I preferred, because I saw at once that in their union they created a very lovely limpid light in which I was bathed and in which I felt extremely happy. However, no more of this, or you will think me sentimental (which I swear

I am *not*,) and I am still sufficiently respectful of you not to wish to be despised by you.

This letter is principally to say that Potto is not very happy; he mopes; and I am not sure he has not got the mange; so he will probably insist on being brought back to Mrs Woof [*sic*] on Wednesday, but I have explained to him that if Valerie [Taylor] is here I shall scarcely be able to go to London. No word of Valerie so far, but I suppose she is liable to walk in any day now, and God knows how long she will expect to stay. I shall lock her into her bedroom until luncheon-time.

Pinker, on the other hand, has taken kindly to her old home—and poos bark as though they were the official watch-dogs of the establishment. Oh yes—and I've sold one of them—the dog—to Dottie—for 6 guineas. She had wanted one of Pippin's—so will have one of Pinker's instead.

Burgundy seems a dream. "Before, a joy proposed; behind, a dream."[2] I was very happy. Were you? I read Walter Pater on Vézelay.[3] I say, that narthex that I kept worrying about is one of the glories of France, it seems. And we never saw it. But I feel as though I had seen enough to make up for a dozen narthexes. Anyhow, I've returned home a changed being. All this summer I was as nervous as a cat,—starting, dreaming, brooding,—now I'm all vigorous and sturdy again, and ravenous for life once more. And all thanks to you, I believe. So you see that this letter is a Collins.

It is a ¼ to 1,—nearly 2 hours after Virginia's bedtime. My dearest, I do love you. All the Sibyls and Tom Eliots in the world don't love you as much as I do. I do bless you for all you've been to me. This is not a joke, but very sober truth.

Your
V.

[A capital P *enclosed by two circles of loops drawn in red ink.]*

I dine with you on Tuesday 16th, don't I? if our friendship has survived?

Berg

1. Vita and Virginia had dined with Ethel Sands and Nan Hudson (her American painter friend) at their house, Auppegard, near Dieppe, on September 30 before returning home after their Burgundy trip.
2. Shakespeare's Sonnet 129
3. In his *Studies in the History of the Renaissance* (1873)

❧ *Sunday [7 October 1928]* *[52 Tavistock Square, W.C.1]*

Dearest Creature,

It was a very very nice letter you wrote by the light of the stars at midnight. Always write then, for your heart requires moonlight to deliquesce it. And mine is fried in gaslight, as it is only nine o'clock and I must go to bed at eleven. And so I shant say anything: not a word of the balm to my anguish—for I am always anguished—that you were to me. How I watched you! How I felt—now what was it like! Well, somewhere I have seen a little ball kept bubbling up and down on the spray of a fountain: the fountain is you; the ball me. It is a sensation I get only from you. It is physically stimulating, restful at the same time. . . .

Berg

Long Barn, Weald,
Sevenoaks.
Tuesday [9 October 1928]

My dearest,

I think I won't come up tomorrow, because (a) my uncle [Charles Sackville] is at Knole and (b) Valerie [Taylor] is here. Besides I am sure you are full of people and busynesses, and don't want Vita—or Potto—who seems to be settling down. (Pinker was suffering from constipation—It wasn't that she missed Leonard. She has now had a pill, and is quite happy again—as indeed we all are when we have had pills.)

But you will send me Orlando? before 4. o'clock? I need hardly say that I can hardly exist till I get it. Valerie is very sweet—and tells me stories of her early life, which you would enjoy.

It is dreadful to think that this is the last friendly letter I shall ever write to you.[1]

Your
Vita

Berg

1. *Orlando* was to be published on Thursday, October 11.

Long Barn, Weald,
Sevenoaks.
11th October 1928

My darling,

I am in no fit state to write to you—and as for cold and considered opinions, (as you said on the telephone) such things do not exist in such a connection.[1] At least, not yet. Perhaps they will come later. For the moment, I can't say anything except that I am completely dazzled, bewitched, enchanted, under a spell. It seems to me the loveliest, wisest, *richest* book that I have ever read,—excelling even your own Lighthouse. Virginia, I really don't know what to say,—am I right? am I wrong? am I prejudiced? am I in my senses or not? It seems to me that you have really shut up that "hard and rare thing" in a book; that you have had a complete vision; and yet when you came down to the sober labour of working it out, have never lost sight of it nor faltered in the execution. Ideas come to me so fast that they trip over each other and I lose them before I can put salt on their tails; there is so much I want to say, yet I can only go back to my first cry that I am bewitched. You will get letters, very reasoned and illuminating, from many people; I cannot write you that sort of letter now, I can only tell you that I am really shaken, which may seem to you useless and silly, but which is really a greater tribute than pages of calm appreciation,—and then after all it does touch me so personally, and I don't know what to say about that either, only that I feel like one of those wax figures in a shop window, on which you have hung a robe stitched with jewels. It is like being alone in a dark room with a treasure chest full of rubies and nuggets and brocades. Darling, I don't know and scarcely even like to write, so overwhelmed am I, how you could have hung so splendid a garment on so poor a peg. Really this isn't false humility; *really* it isn't. I can't write about that part of it, though, much less ever tell you verbally.

By now you must be thinking me too confused and illiterate for anything, so I'll just slip in that the book (in texture) seems to me to have in it all the best of Sir Thomas Browne and Swift,—the richness of the one, and the directness of the other.

There are a dozen details I should like to go into,—Queen Elizabeth's visit, Greene's visit, phrases scattered about, (particularly one on p. 160 beginning "High battlements of thought, etc" which is just what you did for *me*,) Johnson on the blind, and so on and so on,—but it is too late today; I have been reading steadily all day, and it is now 5 o'clock, and I must catch the post, but I will try and write more sensibly tomorrow. It is your fault, for having moved me so and dazzled me completely, so that all my faculties have dropped from me and left me stark.

One awful thought struck me this morning: you didn't, did you, think for a second that it was out of indifference I didn't come to London yesterday? You *couldn't* have thought that? I had got it so firmly fixed in my head that Oct. 11th was the day I was to have it, that I was resigned (after all these months) to wait till then. But when I saw it in its lovely binding, with my initials, the idea rushed into my head and utterly appalled me. But on second thoughts I reflected that you could not possibly so have misunderstood.

Yes, I *will* write again tomorrow, in a calmer frame of mind I hope—now I am really writing against time—and, as I tell you, shaken quite out of my wits.

Also, you have invented a new form of Narcissism,—I confess,—I am in love with Orlando—this is a complication I had not foreseen.

Virginia, my dearest, I can only thank you for pouring out such riches.

V.

You made me cry with your passages about Knole, you wretch.

Berg

1. Virginia had sent Vita a specially bound copy of *Orlando* on its publication day. On receiving this letter, Virginia sent Vita a telegram: "Your biographer is infinitely relieved and happy."

❧ *Friday [12 October 1928]* *52 Tavistock Square, W.C.1*

What an immense relief! . . . It struck me suddenly with horror that you'd be hurt or angry, and I didn't dare open the post: Now let who will bark or bite; Angel that you are—But I'm rather rushed: and wont write, except this line. Sales much better. Enthusiasm in the Birmingham Post [Mail]. Knole is discovered. They hint at you.

Berg

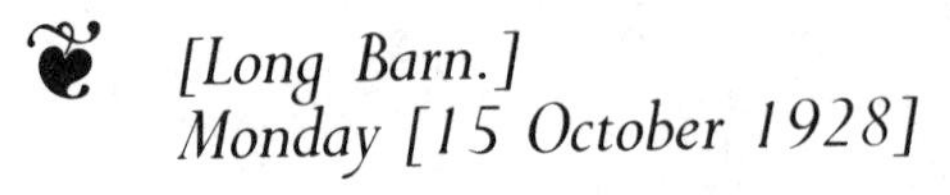

[Long Barn.]
Monday [15 October 1928]

This is only to send you extracts from three letters I had this evening:

(1) "As a work of beauty and genius it is magnificent—it leaves one breathless with admiration. The descriptions of Knole are too beautiful—they must surely equal in beauty anything that has ever been written or said about Knole. I feel you will be happy with those descriptions. . . ."

(2) "How lovely your pseudobiography is. It is one of the most exquisite pleasures that one could want, to read it. I must think that the form is peculiarly adapted to her genius and that this is the greatest of her imaginative works. The language is so lovely."

(3) from Harold. "What a wonderful book! The whole thing has a beauty which makes one catch one's breath—like that sunset before Dilijan. (the reference is to Persia.) It is so far *more* than brilliance. I simply cannot believe that such a book will not survive. The whole world of life has been poured into it, flashing with molten flames."

My darling. I am reading it all through again from the beginning. I'll come at 6.45 tomorrow, or a little before perhaps.

V.

Berg

❦ *[Long Barn.]*
Wednesday night [17 October 1928]

Rabbit Ears herewith. (But there are no flower spikes this time of year.)

And my mother's letter returned.

And one from Hugh Walpole. I have said I could lunch on Oct. 30th. Will my "new creator" PLEASE come too? Yes? No?

Yes. She will.

A letter from Clive too. Will Harold (oh genius of tact that Clive is!) dine to meet Bertie Russell on Oct. 26th? An invitation Harold would never dream of resisting—even were it not for the night I want to go to Cambridge with Virginia *on.*[1] (You see, I am no stylist, though you are.)

"Salt is what makes potatoes nasty if you don't eat them with."

Pippin was pleased to see me. I kissed her nose.

Darling, I love you.

V.

Clive adds a brief postscript: "Orlando is a masterpiece."

Harold says: "Lots to say about Orlando but shall keep it till Friday. It is lovely and glittering *and* profound."

Berg

1. At Girton College, a Cambridge college for women, Virginia delivered a lecture on which she later based *A Room of One's Own*.

[Long Barn.]
Sunday [21 October 1928]

I shall never never speak to Squire again.[1] I never read anything like it for sheer idiocy. I go back on the first sentence: I should like to speak to him just once more, to tell him what I think, and then nevermore.

V.

very angry.

Berg

1. J. C. Squire called *Orlando* "a pleasant trifle" in his review in *The Observer*, October 21, 1928.

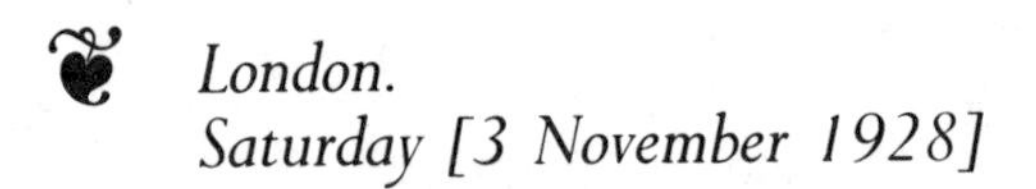

London.
Saturday [3 November 1928]

My gentle genius,

This is just to tell you that I rather lost my heart to Mrs Richmond yesterday.[1] She must have been lovely. In a way, she reminds me of you a little. Mr R did not come, as he had had to go to Scotland.

I have been asked by Clive to dine on the 13th for your opening night.[2] Do you not want me to come, for any reason? If so, will you say so? Otherwise I will come. But as you did not say anything about it yourself, perhaps you did not want me to know.

You missed Bernard Shaw the other evening, who came after you had left and made a long, paradoxical, witty, and entirely destructive discourse.[3] I was sorry you went away. The company grew bolder and more outspoken as time went on, and the little waitress from Harrods sitting behind the buffet nearly exploded with excitement. "There," I thought, "is another young life gone wrong." Not very much conclusion was arrived at, I'm bound to say.

Thank you so much for the poster [of *Orlando*]! it amused me—and I liked the advertisement

Orlando is
Orlando is
Orlando is
" "<br>" "<br>" "<br>" "<br>" "[4]

Berg

1. Elena Richmond, wife of Bruce Richmond, editor of the *Times Literary Supplement*
2. Of her "Tuesday Evenings," Bloomsbury after-dinner parties at Vanessa's house in Gordon Square
3. On November 1, Vita and Virginia attended a meeting in the studio of Clough Williams-Ellis, the architect, to discuss giving evidence on behalf of *The Well of Loneliness*. Their offered evidence was disallowed, and the book was finally declared obscene on November 16.
4. This advertisement by the Hogarth Press appeared in several newspapers: "'*Orlando* is another masterpiece', says Hugh Walpole; '*Orlando* is . . .'," followed by other favorable quotes, and ending, "*Orlando* is by Virginia Woolf."

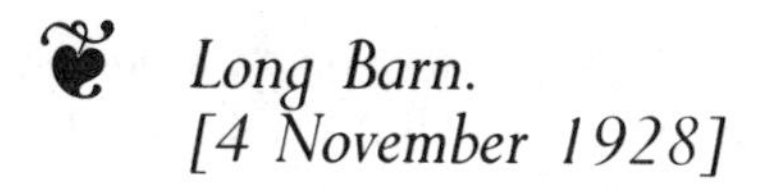

Long Barn.
[4 November 1928]

Harold's father is still alive—and we don't know what will happen. H. is putting off his return to Berlin. That infernal Foreign Office charges him £2 a day for every day he outstays his leave! but he dare not go, as he would probably be sent for again at once.[1]

I've finished writing about Virginia's Tom Eliot.[2] I think I'll submit it to you—shall I?

Did you see your Lord David [Cecil]? Did he sit at your feet? literally? metaphorically?

Your loving
Orlando.

Berg

1. Harold's father, Lord Carnock, died on November 5, and Harold returned to Berlin on the 15th.
2. Vita had been giving a series of broadcast talks on modern poets. Her talk on Eliot was printed in the *Radio Times* on November 30, 1928.

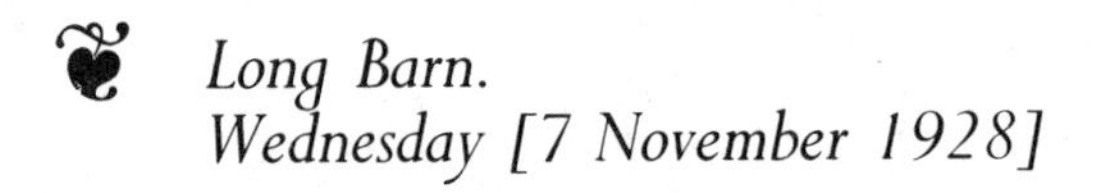

Long Barn.
Wednesday [7 November 1928]

Boski was rather baffled by Desmond:[1] he went so fast, and people came in and disturbed her at her hieroglyphics, but I enclose as much as she was able to get. There was more; all very complimentary.

I found a nice, nice letter here from you—at least, it was so nice in parts that I think my ally Potto must have held your hand. If you are all right, I will come tomorrow Thursday at any time you like, and we will dine together. I must be at Savoy Hill [BBC] by 9.15. Would you ring up Mount Street (Grosvenor 184.) tomorrow morning *before* 10—(because at 10 I must go to Lord Carnock's funeral) and say if you are all right, and if I am to come? I am going up to Mount Street tonight after dinner.

I see Rose Macaulay has the sense to like Orlando.[2]

I do hope you are better. I had such a longing to see you on Monday night, and nearly cried when Nellie said you were out. But the fireworks were lovely, through the fog. Did you see them?

Your very very loving
V.

Berg

1. Desmond MacCarthy had been dictating to Audrey Le Bosquet, Vita's secretary, his review of *Orlando* which appeared in the *Sunday Times*.
2. Rose Macaulay (1881–1958), novelist and essayist. Her review of *Orlando* appeared in *T. P.'s Weekly*, November 10.

 *Long Barn, Weald,*
Sevenoaks.
Tuesday [20 November 1928]

Damn Eddy. *I* refrain from writing to you because I think you already have more than enough to do—and then the brat goes and bothers you.[1]

Yes, of course I mentioned the pictures to Uncle Charlie. I didn't tell him the exact purpose for which they were wanted, because Orlando was then a secret. I just said "for her new book." He said "Of course—naturally—delighted," and all those things. Your letter to him is quite all right. You can say if you like that I told you I had asked him to confirm the permission Dada had given, and that he was agreeable to do so. What idiots people are. Dada would NEVER have thought of this.

As for Eddy's own private grievance, it just shows what his egoism is, to think that everybody would immediately associate the initials S.W. with him. One's own initials are familiar to oneself, but not to anybody else. I should tell him this, if indeed you answer his letter at all.

I went off into fireworks with temper with Eddy. Puppy. Squealer. Imp.

I am coming up next Tuesday. Have been summoned by Molly [MacCarthy] to go and see her. Shall I look in on you after the BBC? or shall I come more at leisure any time on Wednesday (28th)? Clive asked me to dine again on Tuesday but I can't: I'm dining with Ethel. He murmured something about a farewell party to Raymond on Tuesday night, and suggested that I should come on from Ethel's. If you are going to be there I will come, but I don't know where it is,—at Vanessa's house perhaps? Clive sent me two pheasants; nice of him.

Shall I bring up the remaining puppy on Tuesday? The one that is sold? It is so attractive, and it seems a pity that its owners should miss its

1. Edward Sackville-West had complained that Mr. S. W. in *Orlando* might be mistaken for him. (Virginia explained that the initials stood for Sydney Waterlow, the diplomatist.) His father, the new Lord Sackville, complained that the pictures from Knole in the book had been used without his permission.

youthful charm. I could bring it to you any time before 3.30 on Tuesday, especially if I lunch with Raymond as I thought of doing. Unless you would come and lunch with me somewhere alone. RSVP. Postcard would do.

Berg

Long Barn, Weald,
Sevenoaks.
Thursday night [29 November 1928]

I am feeling something like (I imagine) a fisherman must feel between a gale and a gale. On a calm day he can go out and catch lots of little silver fishes. But there is this difference: in a gale, he can sit at home and smoke his pipe, (unless he is also a member of the lifeboat crew,) whereas a gale to me represents London, Eton, Oxford,—just a being blown out to sea, the little fishes all scattered. In other words, I managed to get myself home this morning, only to start off again tomorrow, early; and what sort of life is that, I ask you?

Anyway, there was a HUGE dinner,[1] and I made a speech, in great alarm; but after dinner was somewhat consoled by a vision of pink and silver bearing down on me; rather moved, I was.[2] I didn't much take to Mr. B. R. [Bruce Richmond]—rather soapy I thought? and a bit too plausible? but I was most cordially pressed to come to Robertsbridge etc etc—so that's all right. Such a lot of people—at least 300—and flashlight photographs—and a microphone—and Mr Winston Churchill with whom I would gladly elope if asked—and me rather miserable in the midst of it all—and wondering why I was there—and then suddenly a speech about Knole—and Jack Squire very drunk with a cold in his head. Dear me, I don't like public life. I like toasting buns over the gas-fire in Virginia's bedroom.

I tried to read [Herbert] Read on poetry—Words words words,—and all polysyllabic.[3] That isn't poetry; nor even the explanation of it. I dreamt that I understood space-time, which came much nearer to the truth than all the redes of Read.

"I saw eternity the other night
Like a great Ring of pure and endless light
All calm, as it was bright . . .
Yet digged the Mole, and lest his ways be found,
Worked underground. . . ."[4]

In Oxford I shall dine with John Sparrow[5]—and Sunday I shall come back here—and Thursday Virginia will come and we shall all the pleasures prove. Would it be better to be dead than all confused? as I am? and life never synthetic? But I do enjoy life.

What an egotistic letter—as bad as Eddy—only *not* about my initials.

Darling, you're my anchor. An anchor entangled in gold nuggets at the bottom of the sea.

V.

Berg

1. Given by and for the National Trust (for the preservation of historic houses and attractive landscape)
2. Elena Richmond
3. Herbert Read (1893–1968), the poet and critic of literature and art
4. Henry Vaughan, *Silex Scintillans (The World)*, 1650
5. John Sparrow, who was to become warden of All Souls College, Oxford, 1952–1977, was then an unusually brilliant undergraduate, aged twenty-two. He had visited the Nicolsons with Maurice Bowra in Potsdam earlier that year.

❧ *Sunday [2 December 1928]* *52 T[avistock] S.[quare, W.C.1]*

So you are just back [from Oxford] I suppose, it being after dinner, and I had mine alone. What a good letter you wrote me! Do you know I think about your writing with interest? All your feet seem to be coming down on it now, not only the foreleg. Very few people interest me as writers; but I think I shall read your next poem with care.

And I like the way you stand up resolute in the full flood of Tom's [Eliot] and Reads: a British Grenadier. I forget what I was going to say now—something frightfully exciting, something that hit me between forehead and hair this afternoon: . . .

Coming down with all her feet at once—thats what I like in a writer. Desmond shuffles, and I'm a jumper: never mind, I'll think it over and tell you.

Lord! what a pleasure you are to me

Berg

 *Long Barn, Weald,*
Sevenoaks.
Monday [3 December 1928]

How maddening. There was I sitting alone at Charing X. from 7. to 8.30 last night, having missed my connection; and there were you dining alone the other side of London. I could have come so easily, and taken an even later train. Damn, damn, damn. But you were reading Chaucer.

Harold writes this morning: "He (a friend) took me to a [Berlin] bar which he said was quite respectable, but the proprietor showed me pornographic photographs, which are things I absolutely loathe and abhor. So I went away in a dudgeon and read a chapter of Orlando to cleanse my mind. That book is the cleanest thing I know,—like very clear and deep crystal." Yes. It is. It is. Harold's quite right.

Are you really coming to Berlin in January? Really and truly? And you won't let Eddy absorb you? I hope your quarrel with him deepens, so that by Jan 15th you will not be on speaking terms. I am always, you know, a little jealous of Eddy's friendship with you. Spiteful . . . .

Oxford was littered with Orlando. I nosed into all the bookshops. Such a time I had; and am slightly in love with an undergraduate, which is a sure sign of middle-age.

Darling, I'm no poet, I think. I am a lump of dough, so far as poetry is concerned. But I'd like to talk to you about it. I am rather sad about it; and think of going into mourning for my dead Muse. She died in youth, poor thing, before she had learned to talk. Or do you think she has merely been spending a few years in retreat, and will emerge again someday, grey haired but wise? I read The Land for five minutes and thought it damned bad. Not a spark in it anywhere. Respectable, but stodgy.

Boski says she would be DELIGHTED to do any letters for you; so if you have any which could be met by just a typewritten acknowledgment, bring them,—the more the better,—and you can sign them on Friday morning. It would save you a power of time and trouble. Please.

I enclose a list of trains. *How* I am looking forward to Thursday to be sure, light of my eyes and delight of my soul that you are.[1]

There was an awful muddle over Vanessa's sketch: it was by Duncan. I am feeling rather badly about it. I'll tell you on Thursday. But Dottie has bought 3 of Duncan's pictures for 200 guineas. I envy her. They are lovely.

I wish it was Thursday. Yes,—what a pity you cannot work magic on time in real life as you can in books. Then we could make Thursday last for 300 years. Marvell seems to have had much the same idea. I now realise fully and for the first time exactly what he meant.[2]

Bring Potto. He shall have a smelt all to himself.

Your Orlando

Berg

1. Virginia stayed that night at Long Barn, bringing with her the bound manuscript of *Orlando* as a present to its subject. Vita bequeathed it to Knole, where it is now on display as the property of the National Trust.

2. Vita was beginning to read for her book on Andrew Marvell, published in 1929 by Faber & Faber. By "exactly what he meant," she is referring to Marvell's poem *To His Coy Mistress.*

❧ *Friday night [14 December 1928]* *[52 Tavistock Square, W.C.1]*

Dearest Creature,

I was very much upset to think you had been angry (as you said) that I didn't go to the bloody womans trial—(and yet I rather like you to be angry). . . .

And now Leonard has cut up rough about my having Elena to tea on Tuesday if I lunch out and dine with people. So I won't ask Elena; and then again you'll be angry. But the truth is I've been rather headachy. . . .

Berg

Sunday [16 December 1928]

My dear Potto,

I wasn't angry—I was only disappointed not to see Mrs Woolf. You know how much I like seeing her. *She* doesn't know it, but you and I know.

Could you give her a message from me? that I will come on Tuesday at 1.5. and I don't a bit want to see Elena [Richmond]. Tell her this and she will understand. Or would she rather I came to dinner instead, and let her have lunch alone in peace? as we are both going to the same party after dinner. Will she send me a postcard? I could come to either—or both—

Tell her I had a nice talk with Mrs [Mary] Hutchinson, who would like to come and stay here one day with Mrs Woolf.

Dear Potto, you will explain to her that I wasn't angry? only sad?

Berg

24 Brücken Allee
Berlin N.W.23
26th December [1928]

I would have written to you days ago, but for the first few days I was too splenetic to be fit for human society, whether on paper or in the flesh, and then I got laid up with a sort of influenza from which I have just recovered, retaining only wobbly knees and a still rather gloomy outlook on life. Partings are very odd and unpleasant: I still have a sense of having torn myself suddenly from your side and gone away into the night with scarcely a word to anybody. Now, however, I begin to look forward instead of back, and to reflect that in very little more than a fortnight you will be here. That will be nice, and I promise to be as tactful as my delight at having you will allow. Could we once, do you think, (here the promised tact breaks down) go out alone together of an evening? But I leave that entirely to you.

Eddy plays a large part in my life; he is very happy and in his nicest mood; he has acquired a large black ring and a thin gold bracelet, and his conversation consists almost entirely of the most idiomatic German exclamations and interjections; but we are getting on very nicely together.

Did Boski remember to send you the amber beads? and will you wear them? and not scold me? and look on each of them as a kiss from Orlando? and I will think of you as a fox, a melon, or an emerald, or anything else you can devise?

And you are at Rodmell today, inventing your new room? very happy, with Pinker rushing about the garden?

And shall I write again? My malady has left me quite witless—so I'll say no more today except that I love you.

V.

Berg

❧ *29th Dec. 1928* *Monk's House, Rodmell, Lewes [Sussex]*

That wretched Potto is all slung with yellow beads. He rolled himself round in them, and can't be dislodged—short of cutting off his front paws, which I know you wouldn't like. But may I say, once and for all, presents are not allowed: its written all over the cage. It spoils their tempers—They suffer for it in the long run—This once will be forgiven: but never never again—The night you were snared, that winter, at Long Barn [18 December 1925], you slipped out Lord Steyne's paper knife, and I had then to make the terms plain: with this knife you will gash our hearts I said and the same applies to beads. . . .

Berg

❧ *31st Dec. [1928]* *Monk's House, Rodmell [Sussex]*

Please be an angel and let me have one line on receipt of this to say how you are. . . .

If I dont hear, I shant sleep; then I shall get a headache; then I shant be able to come to Berlin:

So you see Love, love: and its the last day of the year by the way.

Berg

January–July 1929

In January 1929, Virginia visited Vita in Berlin, with Leonard, Vanessa, Duncan Grant, and Quentin Bell. Edward Sackville-West also joined them. It was too large a party to be a success. They got on one another's nerves. Virginia contrived a few hours alone with Vita and seems again to have declared her love, to which Vita responded cautiously. Virginia fell ill on her return to England, and Vita was almost her only correspondent. The paradox was that Vita's love, but not her affection, had been altered by Orlando *and there was little she could do about it. Virginia was obliged to recognize this. She was beginning the first draft of* The Waves. *Vita had embarked, much more rapidly, on her best-known novel,* The Edwardians, *and, after a short visit to Italy with Harold, continued it when she returned to Long Barn in early March. They made some "funny little expeditions" together, to Keats's house in Hampstead and to Richmond. They met at Long Barn, Rodmell, and Bloomsbury parties. In June, Virginia and Leonard paid a short visit to Vanessa at her villa in the South of France.*

24 Brücken Allee
Berlin N.W.23
2nd January [1929]

I was just beginning to wonder if you were cross with poor Towser,—whether the amber beads had been so many cannon balls fired against your heart, or what,—and then this morning I got a nice nice loving solicitous letter—and Towser's tail began to wag again.

I have recovered, if that is recovery in which cigarettes taste like chipped sandstone and one's limbs feel like picked oakum,—all gritty and stringy. But everyone is ill here; no sooner do I get up, than Harold goes down; but he was sick, and I wasn't. It is unpleasant but not serious.

I send you this in an envelope which Nigel had begun to type for my mother, as I thought the Dogware [Dowager] Mrs Woolf was a nice title for you. I am glad the Times says Orlando was the most important piece of fiction of the year.

I am now going to sit down in patience and wait for the long letter. (But, my angel, British Embassy Berlin is quite an easy address to remember! and you remembered with an efficiency that never failed to impress Harold's much more complicated ones in Iraq Syria and elsewhere.) Oh dear how funny that you will see Brücken-allee. I am getting rooms for you all,—is that right?—8 marks a night, I think—but tell me if it's on the 15th or 16th that you arrive—and mind you tell me at what time (i.e. by what route you are coming—) so that I can meet you, *and what station* (Friederichstrasse is best). If you come Harwich—the Hook [Holland] you have to get up at 4.45 in the morning, and don't let them book your seats in a non-smoking compartment which they will do unless told to the contrary. I got caught over this once.

How nice of you to have sent Boski the Common Reader—she is delighted.

I went to tea with a lady lying on a divan playing with a parakeet. I went to tea with another lady,—an old one this time,—who lives with a nephew who is expected to commit a crime at any moment. She consoles herself with 3 Aberdeen terriers. A real Balzac household—plus a sister-in-law with a broken leg. When not in Berlin they all live in a XIIth century castle near Hannover, all at sixes and sevens, and no money, so that the roof is falling in. Another sister in law has just died of a broken heart, and a son-in-law of appendicitis.

I will write again when I have had the long letter. This is really to say that I am all right, and that you must tell me exactly when you come—because of the rooms. Five single rooms—is that what you will want? Perhaps all this is in the long letter.

I am still full of spleen, but it will diminish as the 15th draws near. I shall cry, quite frankly, when you leave, with sorrow, envy, and despite.

But really it is marvellous that you should actually be coming in a fortnight. I only wish you were going to stay at Brücken-allee. Will you come to Long Barn in March?

Your faithful Towser.

Berg

24 Brücken Allee
Berlin N.W.23
Sunday 6th January 1929

But you see, that there Potto (when you weren't looking—you know what a sly little beast he is—though I don't like to sneak on him behind his back) that there Potto, I say, stole a copy of Orlando and had it bound for me in Niger leather—and not content with that, he also stole the MS of Orlando and had *that* bound too—so I thought I really might give him some yellow beads this Xmas—without getting into a row—because I like giving Potto things—and am ordinarily so severely controlled that I never dare to. Am I forgiven? and is Potto forgiven? for having rolled himself in them?

I am taking a special housemaid's cupboard for Potto, plus your five rooms, at the Prinz Albrecht.

Another ten days, and you will be here. Shall I see lots of you? every day? Wagenseil,—yes, I'd queered Wagenseil's pitch before I ever got your letter.[1] I told Eddy firmly that you didn't wish to meet anyone, least of all Wagenseil. Then I met Wagenseil myself. He is a beautiful, brown, lean, young man like a Spanish captain, with melancholy eyes and a twisted mouth; very attractive. But still I was obdurate. A wall has been built between Wagenseil and you. You are safe.

I had to read your letter several times over before I extracted all the meaning from it. What is all that about the 3rd and 4th rib and one's loves? Whose loves? Yours?[2] but you are said to have none. Mine? but everybody knows I am Virginia's Towser. So what's all that? But there was one remark at the end of your letter which encouraged me a lot: did I love you, you asked, particularly and not reasonably? So you do know (at any rate in theory) that there is a distinction. A la bonne heure! How Clive would chuckle. Anyway, I shan't give you the answer till you come to Berlin,—except that you know it already.

I say: it's awfully cold here. I recommend gaiters. Colder than anything we ever get in England. But of course it may have changed by the time you come.

Do you know, I am looking forward to the 15th (or is it 16th?) as the faithful look forward to Paradise. Only I can't bear the thought of your going away again. Silly to think of that before you have even arrived; but it weighs on me. I met a nice man at dinner two nights ago; a German. He stared at me when I was introduced; stared hard. "Orlando!" he cried then. Then he said it was the most wonderful book ever written.

Is it true,—can it be true?—that you are coming to Berlin? Heavens, I wish you were coming alone. But Virginia in Berlin . . . Very odd. It almost reconciles me to Berlin, that Berlin should be going to contain Virginia. The red tongue creeps across my calendar, eating up the days: only ten days more. Don't oh don't get ill and be prevented from coming. As pants the hart for cooling streams [3] . . . Because, really, you have no idea how miserable I am here. I almost cease to exist. I shall revive when you come, like a watered flower.

I shall meet you at the station.

I'd better stop now, or I should write you too wild a letter of love and longing.

V.

I am so glad Julian [Bell] likes the Land—so glad he thinks me a poet. I wish I thought so too. But I do like the young to like The Land—and I like to be told it is a good thing not to resemble Tom Eliot.

Berg

1. Kurt Wagenseil was a friend of Harold's who also translated some of his books.
2. Virginia had written: "The image of one's loves forever changes; and gradually . . . from being a sight, becomes a sense—a heaviness betwixt the 3rd and 4th rib; a physical oppression."
3. Nahum Tate (1652–1715) and Nicholas Brady (1659–1726), *New Version of the Psalms* (1696)

❧ *Tuesday 8th January 1928 [1929]* *52 Tavistock Sqre, WCI.*

What station it will be I will tell you later. Vita will say Hullo Virginia! Leonard will stoop and pat the dog. He will compare her with Pinker, and if you are tactful you will say "But Pinker's a much better colour, Leonard" and then we shall all feel happy.

. . . Orlando has now sold 13000 copies in America: thats the last time I mention him.

The [Berlin] station will be Friederichstrasse.

Berg

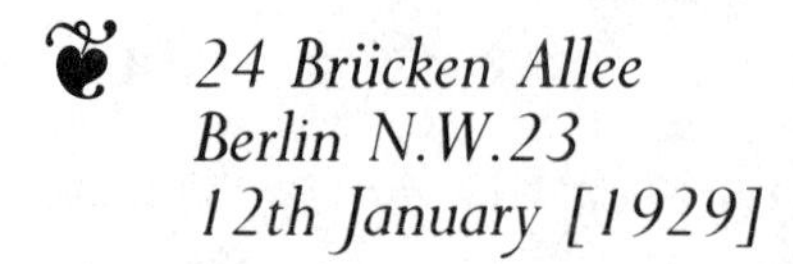

24 Brücken Allee
Berlin N.W.23
12th January [1929]

Henry [Harold's spaniel] and I will meet you at 5.9. p.m. on Thursday the 17th at the Friederichstrasse. We shall be very pleased to see you. Your address in Berlin is:

> Hotel Prinz Albrecht
> Prinz Albrechtstrasse 9.
> Telephone Zentrum 88-74. Telegraphic address,
> Hustersäle, Berlin. Price, 9 marks a day per room.
> H. and c. Lift. Two rooms reserved
> for the 17th; three more for the 18th.
> Amen.

Meanwhile I count the days, for you don't know the full pathos of how I devise little schemes for making January and February go; and with your advent a whole block of time resolves itself, from the bright 17th to the black 24th. But after the 24th there is only a week to February; and once February is here I shall begin to prick my ears once more. Also I've been pulling strings, which has resulted in a charming letter from Lady Lindsay today, saying that she has told Sir Ronald that Harold would like to come back to the Foreign Office as soon as a vacancy presents itself, and he has promised. . . .

I have confessed to Harold, practically alienating his affection thereby, ("I won't have my career arranged by women,") but what do I care, if I can only get him back to London? Meanwhile he is pretending to be cross.

We went to the sodomites' ball. A lot of them were dressed as women, but I fancy I was the only genuine article in the room.[1] A very odd sight. We also went to a bicycle race which lasts for 6 days and 6 nights, round and round a banked-up track under arc-lights. There are certainly very queer things to be seen in Berlin, and I think Potto will enjoy himself.

Now I won't say any more, except that there are 482000 seconds between now and your arrival, and that that is the moment I am living for.

V.

Berg

1. It was called the *Ball der Jugend*. They were accompanied by Mario Panza, Victor Cazalet, and Edward James, all long-established friends of Harold's.

24 Brücken Allee
Berlin N.W.23
Monday [14 January 1929]

If you could bring me a copy of Seducers [*in Ecuador*] . . . You won't be leaving London till Wednesday night, so this ought to reach you in time. And it won't take much room. I am terribly excited. Yes, there is a lot of influenza, but a very mild variety. Bring plenty of warm clothes. It is warmer today, but has been incredibly cold hitherto. I recommend gaiters.

Does Leonard skate? if so, bring skates.

Your coming is quite the most exciting thing that has ever happened to me in Berlin. Do you speak German? i.e. will you want to go to the theatre?

Oh God, I don't believe, I can't believe, that you'll ever arrive. That I shall ever see you get out of the train at Friederichstrasse. Will you and Leonard like to dine with us that night, or will you be too tired? Anyway I will meet you.

Your coming is simply saving my life and my reason. I do hope you won't get the influenza. I do long for Thursday, I do, I do, I do.

V.

Berg

 *24 Brücken Allee*
Berlin N.W.23
Friday [25 January 1929]

My darling lovely Virginia,

It is so empty here without you. I went to lunch today to meet Pirandello; a little elderly man with a goatee beard.[1] He was ¾ of an hour late for lunch; and why? Because, having come to Berlin for a lawsuit, he had been suddenly visited in his hotel by two enormous German policemen, who had taken his watch from his pocket and his rings from his fingers,—which, his knuckles being rather swollen by gout, had hurt him considerably. A regular scene. He was very calm about it on the whole, but his hitherto admiration for the Germans had turned within the space of half an hour to hatred.

You won't get this, thanks to the English non-Sunday post, till after you have been to Long Barn, which I hope will have reminded you of me a little and perhaps revived in you something of those feelings to which you gave such startling and disturbing expression in the Funkturm.[2] I say, you don't know what a difference your week here has made to me. It just shows how little the actual duration of time really counts. Formerly, the whole of Berlin was pure loathesomeness to me; now, there are just a few places which are invested with romance. Prinz Albrecht-strasse, Potsdam, the Funkturm; even Brücken-allee holds something of your flavour. So your transporting of 4 people to Berlin has not been wasted—and I settle down with comparative philosophy to my remaining month. THEN, comes Long Barn and the spring, and the nightingales and your big bedroom, and all the rest of it. But will you be in a different frame of mind by then? or unfaithful to me? Mary [Hutchinson]? Christabel?[3] God, I'd never forgive you— No—save yourself for your own

Orlando

Berg

1. Luigi Pirandello (1867–1936), the Italian dramatist and novelist
2. The Berlin radio tower where Vita and Virginia had dined
3. Christabel McLaren, whose husband succeeded as the second Lord Aberconway in 1934

Sunday [27 January 1929] *[52 Tavistock Square, W.C.1]*

Well, here I am in bed. I had to be hauled out of my berth at Harwich—a mixture of the somnifeine [Somnifène], flu, and headache—apparently. Quite drugged. But I'm better. Only of course the dr. makes me stay in bed and do nothing. I wish it had happened in Berlin. I wish I could see you. Do write. I'm much better today. Berlin was quite worth it anyhow.

Berg

Tuesday evening [29 January 1929]

My poor, poor Virginia,

I am so dreadfully sorry—and so angry that IF you had to catch 'flu at all, you didn't do so in Berlin. We would have carried you here, and looked after you so beautifully—and you could have stayed on for at least a week—banked up with hot bottles—and your Towser trotting in and out—sorry about the 'flu—but happy to have you to look after. Are you all right again? and no headache left as a legacy? Did you feel very miserable? oh dear oh dear, what it is, to be far away, and to hear of things days after they have happened—What a wretched journey you must have had—and Harwich at six o'clock in the morning—with the 'flu—it just doesn't bear thinking about. I hate you to be ill; it matters more for you than for other people. I say, look here: if you'd like to escape to the country, (and there is only Mrs. Bartholomew at Rodmell,[1]) you know that all the servants are at Long Barn twiddling their thumbs, and you could go there and be comfortable, (the comforts of a 1st class hotel etc.) and nothing in this world would make me more happy than to think you were benefitting by my empty idle little house—except to be there with you myself: so if you feel inclined, will you ring up and say you and Leonard and Pinker are coming. I really would love you to—but I needn't say that: you know that I mean it, and Louise would spoil you—and they would all be delighted to have something to do.

When I wrote to you, did I tell you we were going to Rapallo for a week on the 9th? No, I don't think we had thought of it then. Harold says he shall die if he doesn't escape from Berlin—so we are going. You may imagine if I am delighted. After that it will be a very short time till I come home—so my time-plotting scheme is working beautifully. You will never know what you did for me by coming to Berlin, and so I feel it is somehow my fault that you caught the 'flu and were hauled out of your bunk.

I heard a lot more about Kessler:[2] he is very rich, owns a copper-mine in Mexico, and is a bugger. I thought as much. I had such a lot to say to you, but it has all been driven out of my head by the idea of your being ill. I shan't be happy till I know you have recovered, and if I thought you would go to Long Barn I would be *truly* happy. Just think of that nice room—and huge bed, and get into the Umbrella and drive off. Darling, do. And miss me a little.

Think what I owe you! I got a great sheaf of white lilac suddenly, with a card: "For Orlando." I felt I ought to pack it all up and send it to you.

Darling I do feel so worried about you; are you all aches and miseries? have you recovered?

Your very very loving and concerned

V.

Berg

1. Rose Bartholemew, the daily help at Monk's House
2. Count Harry Kessler, who supervised the printing of Vita's translation of Rilke

❧ *Tuesday [29 January 1929]* *[52 Tavistock Square, W.C.1]*

Dearest Creature,

Here is another selfish invalids bulletin, but I like to write to you, and you won't mind it all being about myself.

I am really better today, only still kept in bed. It is merely the usual headache which is now making me rather achy and shivery but passing off. . . . Its odd how I want you when I'm ill. I think everything would be warm and happy if Vita came in.

Berg

 *24 Brücken Allee*
Berlin N.W.23
Thursday [31 January 1929]

Your little shaky pencil letters simply wring my heart—oh, how damnable space and time are—you see, all my pictures of you are at two days' remove. I know you were in bed still when you wrote, but what I don't know is whether you're still in bed *now*—or whether you've been promoted to the sofa—anyhow I gather that you have been rather bad—you always understate your ills—and that is quite disturbing enough for me. Berlin did that to you—the fiend—The coffin of Berlin is becoming absolutely studded with nails—nails with big brass heads—like the Lord Treasurer's [Thomas Sackville] chest at Knole—and the biggest nail of all, so far, is that it made Virginia (who is more precious to me than a whole Lord Treasurer's chest full of pearls and rubies) ill. Yes, I wish I could open your door suddenly—instead of your painted Mary [Hutchinson]—and talking of Mary I saw the most marvellous photographs of her. . . . but I'll go back to the beginning, because I had a funny day yesterday—the sort of day that amuses Virginia—beginning with low life and ending with high—beginning with a rakish little ghost from Teheran [1] and ending with a Papal Nuncio [2] and a red headed Lesbian in the middle.

The ghost from Teheran suddenly appeared, having come to Berlin to see me—*not* from Teheran but from Sweden—a squalid rather amusing Montmartre sort of person—always full of fantastic stories which may be true and on the other hand may not. I had been bored with her in Teheran but was pleased to see her here—and she wanted to see the Aquarium so we went—heavily haunted by memories of Virginia it was—and then I took her along to tea with the red headed Lesbian [3]—where we found Pirandello and his two little tarts that he travels about with—and several other very shady-looking people.

Red-head is a photographer—and there on the walls amongst the photographs of every conceivable European celebrity from Hindenburg to André Gide was our Mary [Hutchinson] marvellously portrayed. Red-head manoeuvred me into a dark little room where she showed me photographs of Josephine Baker stripped to the waist,—very beautiful,—and other photographs of an indecency which I won't describe; leered at me; made me take my hat off; and finally pestered me into saying I would sit to her tomorrow morning. She fair gives me the creeps. I came home and had a bath. Then finished up the day by despatching my Teheran friend off to Paris, and going to a great huge dinner at the Embassy—footmen in knee breeches; a sort of Suisse holding a silver topped pole which he banged on the floor every time the door opened; stars and ribbons; a lady who has had 5 husbands, including a Persian prince, and a final husband who is the nephew of the first one,—she changes her wig, too, according to her mood, so that it is sometimes grey, sometimes black, sometimes red—; gold plate in rivers down the table; and the Papal Nuncio in rose-red silk with a great gold cross on his breast. (He'll probably be the next Pope.)

Potto *would* have wagged his tail.

And all the time I thought of Virginia lying upstairs in Tavistock Square, and wished I were there.

And Frau [Katie] Stresemann got hold of Harold and said "I know you think I'm a fool, because whenever you see me you ask me if I have been dancing much lately, but I'm not a fool, and I can tell you that you are wasting yourself *and* your wife on this idiotic profession." Which improved my opinion of the lecherous Katie.[4]

Did I tell you we were going to Rapallo for a week on the 9th? Yes, I surely did.

Oh my darling do be good and look after yourself—Leonard sees to that, I know—but I simply can't bear you to be ill. I *wish* I were there—

Your
V.

Berg

1. Baronne Frachon, who had lived for a short time in Teheran and was self-appointed leader of diplomatic society there

2. Eugenio Pacelli, later Pope Pius XII

3. Her name was Frau Riess. (See Victoria Glendinning, *Vita* [1983], p. 212.)

4. The wife of Gustav Stresemann, German foreign minister, 1923–1929. Harold described her as "a vulgar, eager woman, haggard, ill-dressed, bony and pretending to be young." (See James Lees-Milne, *Harold Nicolson*, Vol. I, p. 333.)

Thursday [31 January 1929] *[52 Tavistock Square, W.C.1]*

I shall now have my little treat of writing to Vita, I say to myself.

I wish I'd heard from you, but perhaps I shall. No I am not to see anybody—not Mary [Hutchinson] even. Dr Rendel can't imagine why I want to see Mary, (her cousin). There is such a thing as womanly charm I reply. Anyhow it aint allowed. I console myself by thinking that they wouldnt allow you either. I have been rather giddy, and have to keep lying down. It is something to do with the spirit level in my ears. There is a kind of mouse which turns for ever, because its ears have no spirit level. Would you like to see Potto turning for ever? Everything is put down to Berlin. I am never to walk round a gallery or sit up drinking again. All my adventures are to be lying down—which will suit, in some ways. Really I am rather better, and make up a book to be called The Moths [The Waves] *hour after hour.*

Berg

24 Brücken Allee
Berlin N.W.23
2nd February [1929]

How is my poor dear invalid? Does Potto sit under the sofa,—the Knole sofa,—feeling miserable just out of sympathy? So would Vita, if she were there.

Potto has a stary coat and a hot nose. His tail doesn't wag. It just moves, but only just, when he sees the toe of a shoe he knows, under the flounce of the sofa. If he saw the toe of Mrs. Hutchinson's shoe, he would growl.

Truly I am very unhappy about you. Being strictly kept for rather a long time has a sinister ring. It is only from these chance phrases that I can deduce how bad you must have been, since you never complain. Shall you go to Long Barn? I told Boski to ring Leonard up and urge the case. You see it is so silly and so exasperating for all those servants to be there doing nothing, and they don't like it themselves. However, it's boring for you to have me maundering on about how much, how very much, I would like to think of you at Long Barn, and I do trust you to know how passionately I mean it, and act on it the very minute you felt inclined.[1]

We went for a really lovely walk with Eddy through a pine wood; the snow was bright blue in the shadows, and bright pink in the sun; deer bounded across our path, and there were people on skis; at the end of the walk we came down on a lake. Now that January has turned into February I am able to find comfort once more in the beauties of Nature. But I am menaced by a growing danger: the wall-paper in my bedroom is becoming detached from the walls owing to the heat and dryness; I hear a loud report like a pistol-shot, and lo! a fresh section has broken away and hangs loosely bellying. One night the last piece will give; the whole will come down, like a rose suddenly falling to pieces; and I shall be buried under the pheasants and the peonies.

Grand Hotel & Europa, Rapallo, Italy, should you still feel disposed to tell me how you are, will be my address from next Saturday the 9th to Saturday the 16th—and I know you've written to me because you promised—angel that you are—ill or not ill—it *is* appreciated. But you mustn't get tired. Heavens, what a comfort it is to think of Leonard and his beefsteaks. But I wish you were at Long Barn. No parties, no romances—poor, poor Virginia. Although I am all for the kennel (with a little wire run) I don't like it to be for that reason;[2] would rather have Virginia well and naughty, than Virginia ill and good. Much, much rather.

What about the photographs [Lenare's]? I long to see them. I had a good tease for my red-headed photographer, who mentioned you, by telling her you had just been here. She nearly died of it. As a matter of fact I am rather sorry, because she might have made some lovely photographs of you, and had I seen them I might have taken you there. But Lenare! Lenare!

I say, would it be any help to you to use Boski for your letters? If so, telephone to her to come up—and in any case make use of her if you go to Long Barn. Oh damn, it is so tantalising to be such miles away, and not be able to do anything for you, except make suggestions which I greatly fear you will scorn. But everything which is mine is yours, as you very well know—even to my heart.

Your
V.

A wretched letter from Raymond [Mortimer], who is hating New York!

Berg

1. Virginia did not accept this invitation.
2. "You want Potto and Virginia kept in their kennel," Virginia had written.

❦ *24 Brücken Allee*
Berlin N.W.23
Monday [4 February 1929]

In bed for another week! my precious Virginia, what horrors are happening to you? It's all very well saying there's nothing wrong with you,—and I don't believe it was Berlin really, I think it was the 'flu that started it, which you might have got anywhere. *Did* you feel very tired here? If so, you concealed it marvellously. I have seldom wished so much that I was in England; only, as you say, you wouldn't be allowed to see me. But I could sit on the doorstep. The only thing that consoles me is your saying you will go to Long Barn if you want to, and anyhow perhaps you'll come for a little spoiling in March, to convalesce? you know I'm a good nurse and very severe. Yes—by the way, talking of nurses, I laughed a good deal over Mrs Clive's "sombre *nurse*" in my review of novels in the Nation this week—when it should have been "sombre *muse*"—but still perhaps I'm lucky that they didn't print "sombre *mouse*"! [1] There's a terrible packet of misprints in that wretched review (and one sentence which doesn't make sense at all, because a "not" has been omitted)—tell Leonard I love him, but that he's a bad man.[2] Well, if you come to Long Barn I'll be a sombre nurse or mouse or muse or anything you like—and give you soup—not coffee—in the middle of the morning. Truly, my darling, I am wretched that you should be ill, and have pains, and a headache, and I wish for nothing in the world so much as that I might look after you—short of being able to work a miracle to make you instantly better. Instead of that, we have to go to The British Colony Ball! But there are compensations: a chemist[3] came to lunch and told us that within two years war would have become impossible, thanks to the absolute deadliness of the new gases, and he has also invented a device for getting your motor out of difficult parking places—so the world seems to be progressing towards civilisation after all. Then there was a party at the Embassy, which we attended, and we went to 'The Squeaker' [by Edgar Wallace] in German—and what else? we had 41 degrees below zero, Réaumur—and all the windows of the motors are cracking with the cold which has returned with all the fury of a horde of Tartary. But mostly I think of Virginia, lying in lovely silks making up stories about moths [*The*

Waves]—but not, not happy or well as I would have her. "Variable and therefore miserable condition of Man: this minute I was well, and am ill this minute; I am surpriz'd with a sodaine change and can impute it to no cause." That's Donne; not me. In this cold, I find one must proceed with caution: a sudden touch on metal, fur, or water produces an electric shock; I feel one could light a gas-jet by snapping one's fingers. And at Rapallo I expect we shall get sheets of rain and a raging grey sea. But we shall work very hard, and Max Beerbohm will draw a picture of Harold. I'm told Edith and Osbert [Sitwell] are at Rapallo! but I don't believe it. I still haven't got over Francis Birrell thinking my handsome tribute to the Sitwell genius, bitter.[4] It doesn't seem to me to make sense.

Do my rambling letters bore you? but they're written with so much concern about you and so much desire to hear that you really *are* better—which in spite of all your assurances I don't believe. Not so long as you are kept in bed and given bromide which clamps your head to the pillow, and allowed to see no one. Those facts speak for themselves. Only when I hear that you have had Sibyl to tea shall I regain any confidence. Meanwhile I am your very worried and infinitely loving V.

Berg

1. The review (February 2) was of Mrs. Archer Clive's *Paul Ferroli*, originally published in 1855.
2. Leonard Woolf was literary editor of *Nation and Athenaeum* until early 1930.
3. Frederick Lindemann (1886–1957), later Lord Cherwell, and scientific adviser to Winston Churchill in World War II. Since 1919 he had been professor of physics at Oxford University.
4. Francis was the son of Augustine Birrell and a favorite friend of Bloomsbury people, especially of Raymond Mortimer. He owned a Bloomsbury bookshop and edited the series in which Vita's *Aphra Behn* appeared. Vita's "handsome tribute to the Sitwell genius" was included in her lecture to the Royal Society of Literature in November 1928.

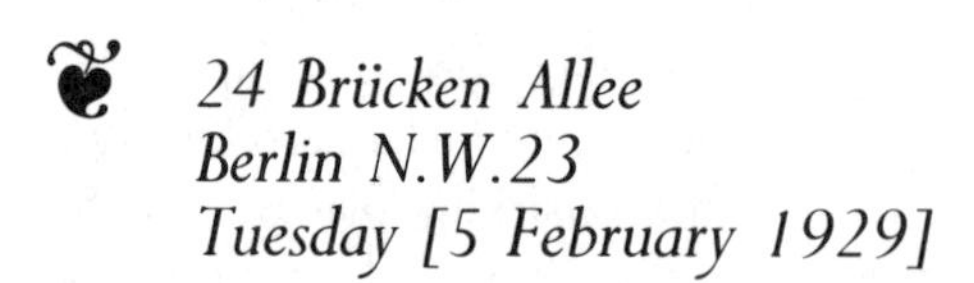

24 Brücken Allee
Berlin N.W.23
Tuesday [5 February 1929]

I came in just now, having been to Wertheim's to buy a pair of gloves for 4 marks, and meant to go on with my story of the bank clerk who loses his memory, but having stopped at the book shop on the way and bought

Orlando in Tauchnitz I began to read, and so lost myself that the evening is already nearly gone. Do you know, I never read Orlando without tears pricking in my eyes? You may believe this or you may not, but it is true. Sometimes they even spill over. Whether it is the mere beauty of the book, or whether it is because it is you, or because it is Knole, or because it is all three, I don't know; anyhow you like facts, and there is a fact for you. There never was a book that so bewitched and moved me. All this, in spite of my being forbidden to mention O——o. Perhaps today the effect was heightened by the damnable fact of your being ill. When I am old and dying I shall cause Orlando to be read aloud to me.

Meanwhile are you better? which seems to be the only thing that matters. I had a note from Leonard but there was not as much information about you in it as I should have liked. He said "You will have heard from Virginia," but surely he knows by now that Virginia is an arrant liar who always says she is better whether it is true or not? Even Potto and I know that. Potto cautioned me long ago to disbelieve simply every word that Virginia uttered in that connection. I thanked him, and said I knew it already. So I should have welcomed a little enlightenment from Leonard whom I take to be a truthful (although prejudiced) man. But he did say you were improving, though it was a slow process, and I was glad of that crumb.

A dinner party tonight, Lord have mercy upon us. But on Saturday the cage opens and the birds take flight.

Your loving loving
V.

Berg

❧ *Monday [4 February 1929]* *[52 Tavistock Square, W.C.1]*

Dearest—What a time your letters take to come! One posted Thursday comes this morning—to my great delight. You can't think what a difference it makes when they bring in a blue envelope. I'm still in bed. . . . And no pain for two days and no sleeping draughts, only Bromide. I've had this sort of thing before, especially after flu, slight though that was and it always takes some time to go off—Also the sea sick draught, which was veronal, made me more susceptible. But of course the dr and Leonard say its all the Berlin racketing (I daresay it was) on the top of the others.

. . . A woman writes that she has to stop and kiss the page when she reads O:—Your race I imagine. The percentage of Lesbians is rising in the States, all because of you.

Berg

 *24 Brücken Allee*
Berlin N.W.23
Wednesday evening [6 February 1929]

Harold is writing the Life of Lord Carnock [his father], and I have been reading a German war-novel which is creating a great commotion here,[1]—70,000 copies sold in three weeks, so they say,—ha ha,—but this Teutonic language tramples like an elephant on my brain, so I prefer to write to Virginia—not that I have anything to say except that I love her and wish she were not ill. I can't believe it's the 'racketing' of Berlin; really, you might have spent every night for a week till 5 in the morning indulging in orgies—to hear you talk—or Leonard talk, rather, and the doctor. No, no; it was the 'flu, but whatever it was it's very distressing. Now look how well you were when I brought you back from France; all round and rosy, and Potto's coat a treat to see. Do you know what I believe it was, apart from 'flu? it was SUPPRESSED RANDINESS. So there—You remember your admissions as the searchlight went round and round [on the Funkturm on January 19]?

No, darling, I didn't succumb to the red headed lady [see Vita's letter of January 31]—nor to anybody else. I am as good as a snowdrop—and just about as cold. Industrious, too: I've finished Rilke. But oh! the trials that you expose me to! We dined last night with the Sibyl of Berlin [Mrs. Thelwall],—but you must multiply Sibyl's crudity by 1000, and then remove all her brains. She bore down on me after dinner. "Oh *won't* you come and sit in the next room? We're all dying to talk to Orlando." That's what I have to suffer for your sake. But Orlando wouldn't play. Was sulky and disobliging.

I wish my letters didn't take so long. I've written every day—a blue

mouse in the mouse-trap, and the necessary spirit-level in its ears. No, indeed, I shouldn't like to see Potto turning for ever. Would ear stoppers help?

Your
V.

Berg

1. *All Quiet on the Western Front* by Erich Maria Remarque

24 Brücken Allee
Berlin N.W.23
Thursday [7 February 1929]

Do you know what? In tramped Marta [German maid] with a parcel—a big flat parcel—registered—"aus England." Would I sign the receipt? Torn from sleep, I scrawled my name—burnt the string with a match—and there was my Virginia looking mischievous [Lenare photographs].

Oh Virginia, darling, they are good. I have stuck them up all round the room. I don't know which I like best. May I keep them till tomorrow? absurd question, since you can't say either yes or no—and by then perhaps I'll have decided. (Of course there's nothing to prevent my ordering them all from Lenare myself if I want to!) Do you like them yourself? does Leonard? You will find that they are a source of perpetual expenditure to you, as people will ask you for them. You are an angel to have sent them—I was longing for them. Very tidy you were, that day, and I'm glad you had no hat on. What with your letters and now the photographs I have been spoilt—hullo, here's the second post, and a note from Leonard—and a postscript from you—'rather tired'—oh dear—but Leonard says you are really better thank the Lord—and you say will I bring the photographs back with me and not send them—of course I'd much rather do that. Tell Leonard yes I will do the novels—but on no account let him send me one called 'Belated Adventure'[1]—as it's partly about me and so I couldn't possibly do it. Grand Hotel et Europa, Rapallo, but he mustn't let the printer make me create purely imaginary characters such as Mrs. Clive's sombre nurse this time!

Now I have to go and lunch with a man like a Borzoi—but am all excited and happy.

V.

Berg

1. By Margaret Goldsmith Voigt. Vita appears in it as "Hester Drummond." (See Victoria Glendinning, *Vita*, p. 212.)

 *24 Brücken Allee*
Berlin N.W.23
Saturday 9th [February 1929]

This is a farewell letter, to be stamped with my last German stamp, before we leave for Rapallo. Harold has treated himself to a new despatch case and at least three guide-books (with maps.) We are very much excited. We get to our destination at 7 tomorrow evening. On Monday we go for a long walk, in the sun? snow? among the aloes. And shall I get a letter from Virginia? It is foggy in London isn't it? yellow, thick. Lord!

Will you and I ever go to Cassis, do you think?

Can I come and eat my bun loaf with you on March 4th? I shall get back on the 2nd, but Ben arrives simultaneously for the weekend so I'll have to go straight to Long Barn. The 4th is Monday. I don't know what time he has to go back to Eton. I could come to dinner perhaps? but it all depends on how you are. It would be dreadful if I made you ill, by recalling the racket of Berlin.

How exciting to think of crossing the Alps—Hannibal and Napoleon—and of descending on Liguria—and seeing the sea—and saying to the concierge Are there any letters? My standards have rushed so contemptibly down the scale, in Berlin, that it seems just as exciting as setting off for Baghdad. Thus is one's spirit broken, or at any rate diminished.

Have you been taken for a little drive yet? and have you thought about moths? Darling, I send you all my love, you know. I think about you all the time, and with huge concern. Leonard's note was reassuring.

But I don't like you to be ill.

V.

Berg

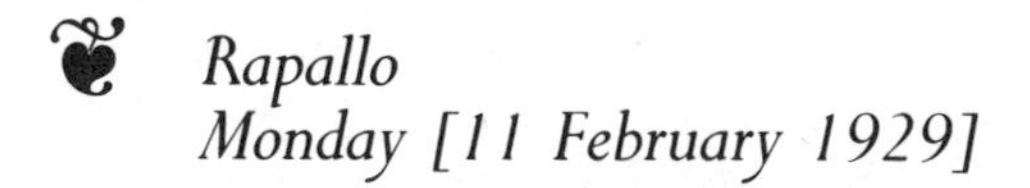

Rapallo
Monday [11 February 1929]

What a lovely Italianate address you invented for me. Yes, I found your letter here last night, when, after a triumphal progress across Germany and Switzerland, during which our dining car burst into flames and had to be abandoned, we arrived. And it was warm. We went out after dinner without any coats on, and strolled under the orange trees and the mimosa, while the Mediterranean sighed upon the beach. The Alps had really been very beautiful; all the cascades were frozen, and hung like iridescent beards down the face of the cliffs; sunlit peaks pushed themselves through the mist, and in the valleys the willows were all golden. The truants were exuberantly happy. It is a great thing, Virginia, to be mobile; to take advantage of trains, and not to say that a week's truancy is not worth a 30-hours journey. It *is.*—Lord, if I say that, you'll be dashing off to Spain with Leonard.

I was pleased to know exactly what had happened to you. I don't think it was really the fault of Berlin. I don't want to think it was, because then I feel I must bear a part of the guilt; otherwise, I should be only too glad to fasten any crime on to Berlin. I expect it was the seasick cure. I've known people as strong as horses be made ill for weeks by those things.

Later. We have been for a lovely walk, and discovered a little green and white house which said Pensione [Villa Cuba]. We are going to move into it tomorrow, and I telegraphed to Boski and told her to let you know, but I shall come to this hotel to fetch my letters for the next three days. It is a beastly hotel, and the Pensione is so nice: its toes are practically *in* the sea, and there are big plain wooden rooms with big windows looking right down the coast almost to Spezia. It appeared to be completely empty, as we were shown room after room to choose from.

Then we walked on, and everything was blue and gold and dusty. This part of the coast is much less sophisticated than the French part. The effect of coming down on this blue sea and sunny headlands, after the snow and hideousness of the German plain, is simply extraordinary.

About Lady Bessborough: Harold says he can't remember for certain, but he knows the correspondence you mean and he thinks you will find it referred to in the Life of Lord Granville.[1] He is very cross at not being able to remember exactly. Anyhow he says he thinks Lord Granville would at any rate provide you with the necessary reference.

Oh how I wish you were here, it would be so good for you, (no racket,) and there *are* olive-terraces and all the rest of it. Why does one live in England? Why does one live anywhere but in the South?

Your
V.

Berg

1. By Lord E. Fitzmaurice (1905). Harold was correct about Lady Bessborough's correspondence.

Villa Cuba,
San Michele di Pagano,
Rapallo.
Wednesday [13 February 1929]

I should like to go on telling you of blue skies, but having a great respect for truth I am bound to confess that it has snowed. It is, in fact, bitterly cold. Everybody says to us "È proprio straordinario," and tells us how up to last Sunday they were sitting out basking in the sun,—which I believe for we did get one day of it,—and this irritates us to such an extent that Harold will I am sure commit murder if anybody says it to him again. With coats wrapped round our knees we sit and shiver, a truly pitiable sight. Personally I don't mind so much, as anything is Paradise after Berlin, but I'm so sorry for Harold, whose days of escape and holiday are counted.

Leonard's novels arrived yesterday, not a very exciting lot. Why is it that novels are all so ghastly competent nowadays, with just about as much life in them as an expiring fish? It depresses me to the extent of quite preventing me from trying to write one myself. The ordinary novel has been reduced to a mere formula; they're like those beastly illustrated papers, Vogue and so forth,—yes, I know what's happened to novels: they've become to literature what *good taste* is to art. (I shall put this in my review!) Everybody has it, so that one now welcomes a blue china kitten and antimacassars, as a change from grey pile carpets and Coromandel screens. But I did read one that I liked: Sergeant Grisha.[1] Moreover this feeling that the novel has become a formula, drives people to go straining after something different, and you get either the deliberate artlessness of people like Bunny Garnett and Dorothy Edwards [*Rhapsody*, 1927], or else the fireworks of Ronald Firbank. However, I daresay you'll clear up the whole matter when you are allowed back to write about fiction, much as you may dislike it.

We haven't done anything about Max Beerbohm yet, but we shall.[2] Now there's a man who can write, don't you think? When I come home, will you make me out a synopsis of solid reading? I have recently been appalled by my own ignorance. You see, you know all about people like Sterne, and I don't. I go worrying on, without having enough background of good standards to use for purposes of comparison. There's no doubt about it, I'm lamentably ignorant. But I do love literature, and I do *hate* the secondrate.

Presently we shall walk into Rapallo, our heads held down against the blizzard, to fetch such letters as may be at the hotel. It was such a beastly hotel. We found this tiny villa on Monday when we were out for a walk; it would be delicious in warm weather, for it is practically *in* the sea, and from the windows you can see right down the coast as far as Spezia. Did I tell you this? I forget. But now the sea lashes the rock on which it is built, and the oranges look simply silly. Southern countries look much sillier in wintry weather than northern ones do in summery. I don't quite know what I mean by that, but I know I mean something.

My darling are you better?

Your

V.

Berg

1. *The Case of Sergeant Grischa*, by Arnold Zweig

2. Virginia had asked Vita to "give my humble duty to Max B. if you see him." He lived at Rapallo.

❧ *Tuesday, 12th Feb. [1929]* *52 T.[avistock] S.[quare, W.C.1]*

You have been an angel—letters every day and today a letter from Le Boski with your new address. . . .

I have been out. I have twice walked round the square leaning on L's arm—very cold and ugly it was, and a cat had chosen to die on the path. Then I undress and lie on the sofa.

Today I have lain on the sofa—not dressed, and feel now much brighter and clearer and less inclined to curse God for having made such a crazy apparatus as my nervous system. Is it worth it? . . . L. wrapped me up warm; and I am very cheerful again. Its awfully difficult to say how long its going to take though. I agree it was the flu; but I think I was foolish also in Berlin—you dont realise what a valetudinarian life mine is, usually, so that what's nothing to anybody else is rackety to poor Potto. Never mind. I shall be in robust health by the 4th. But cant you look in for a bite on the 2nd? And I'm awfully tempted by the notion of a few days at Long Barn—as Le Boski insists.

Berg

Villa Cuba,
San Michele di Pagano,
Rapallo.
Saturday [16 February 1929]

(I enclose a photograph
which I think may bring
you some comfort.)

Every morning while I still lie in delicious sleep in an enormous *letto matrimoniale*, (but alone,) I am aroused by a clash of opening shutters next door, and then a figure dressed in canary-yellow pyjamas bursts into my room, and, saying 'You simply *must* look,' opens my shutters with an equal clash. I turn a sleepy and reluctant eye upon the dawn. I see a dark, purple sea; dark, purple promontories; and above them a primrose sky. There are a few little clouds in the sky. They are pink. They turn from pink to gold. A scarlet rim appears above the promontories. It changes into a scarlet disc with the suddenness of an ejaculation. The sun is up. The whole coast floods with light; the sea turns blue. Another day has begun.

Now this is true, while your Thames freezes and your pipes burst. Why does one not live on the Riviera? Harold, at all events, is determined to; "a little pink house," he murmurs, "among the olives." So, if Leonard in one of his dramatic moments smashes the Press, murders Mrs Cartwright, sacks Nellie, and, putting Pinker into a basket and Virginia on to a lead, removes his camp to the south of France, there is quite a good chance of your finding Harold and Vita encamped a little way down the coast. Indeed it seems insane not to live here, at any rate for the winter. I admit, that for two days while the Italian Press burst into headlines about "Il tragico governo invernale," we had a snowstorm. But almost immediately the climate recovered itself. The Ligurians ceased to pelt one another with snowballs, and resumed their normal occupation of drinking vermouth at round tin tables on the pavement, examining and criticising meanwhile the ankles of the strolling women.

Max Beerbohm is not here; he is in England. We walked to his villa; a horrid little house, as closely sandwiched in between his neighbours as the ham between the bread.

What's this about "a few days at Long Barn"? Before I return? or after? Consider: I return the week after next, which is not so very long to wait, and you know I'd look after you like the most expensive of Scotch nannies with a new baby to powder. Seriously I would. You see, I have just had your letter addressed here, and oh dear I fear you aren't as well as you should be—a long business—but do say that it wasn't I who tired you in Berlin? No,—it was all those galleries, to which I didn't come. Sans Souci perhaps? but you would have gone there, me or no me. My poor darling—I mind more than you know. I mean, I keep feeling I haven't the right to be well and in the sun, when you are lying on the sofa with a headache. I would exchange with you, if only an archangel would appear and give me the chance.

We share this little house with five other people. A young Italian, whom I took to be a poet (at least,) when I saw him tearing his hair over sheets of foolscap. But it turned out that he was only trying to write a letter to his mother. An elderly Italian couple, she rather beautiful, he very absent-minded, continually murmuring to himself "Ah, bello! bello!" about nothing at all,—unless his own thoughts. An English couple, mother and daughter, name of Smith, with the best British accent in Italian I ever heard. Harold and I study the English virgins in this place with great interest. They have the most pronounced family look. A tight, disapproving mouth,—ah, the joys we have missed!—let us make up for it by condemning them. And so they knit, since they may not love.

We go for long walks, either along the coast or else up the hills into the olives. We leave here on Tuesday, not very much encouraged by the newspaper accounts of what happens to trains in Central Europe,—to be snowed up is nothing, but what about the wolves? And do you see what the temperature has been in Berlin? For once, I think, the whole of Europe has talked about the weather as unanimously as do, habitually, the English.

I say: would you tell Leonard, I had already sent my review of his novels to Boski to type, when two more arrived this morning. What am I to do? Re-write my review? cut out two books, and substitute the two new arrivals? Return the two new arrivals to him, to be put into his next batch? I await his orders.

Lord! I wish I could see you. But I shall soon. On the 4th. I shall have to go straight from Dover to Long Barn on the 2nd, on account of Ben, I think. I'll let you know if I change my plans. I hope Potto is nice to you?

Your
V.

Berg

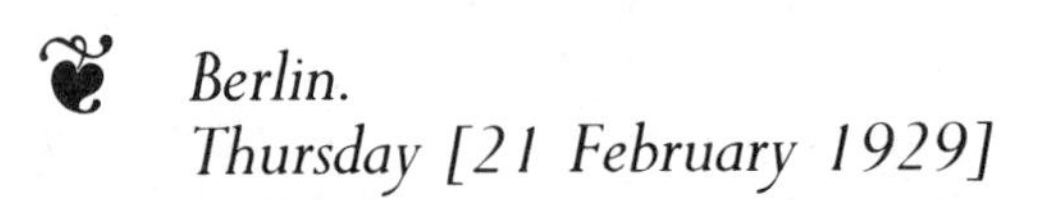

Berlin.
Thursday [21 February 1929]

I wish I could tell you that we had got stuck in a snowdrift and been set upon by wolves, but it just merely wouldn't be true; our train was, indeed, draped in curtains of ice, but apart from being two hours late our return journey was without incident. We left San Michele in a blaze of sunshine, and almost immediately after turning our backs on Genoa were swallowed up by the snow. Yes of course it was true about the mimosa and being warm. Do I ever tell anything but the truth? If I didn't, I might be a better writer,—less plodding, humdrum, pedestrian. But never mind: I've thought of a novel, and I'm going to write it this summer and make my fortune [*The Edwardians*]. Such a joke it will be, and I hope everybody will be seriously annoyed.

Everybody in Berlin looks mediaeval: they have evolved every sort of extraordinary garment against the cold,—which is pretty fierce. Old women with their heads tied up in dishclouts, men in Rembrandtesque fur caps, great felt boots, sheepskins, ear-caps, huge gloves. For two days, apparently, hardly anybody went out, and no motor could be made to start, so the streets were empty and Berlin a city of the dead. Of course it is all your fault; I thought of that long ago; so will you please now write a description of how the Gulf Stream boiled and the English climate became torrid? (TORRID, not HORRID.) I hear your disastrous passages on the Great Frost [*Orlando*] were read on the wireless, so I suppose there'll now be a fresh boom in your sales,—book-stall novelist that you now are!

This letter is only really to say we've got back—and that I found your letter here, and that I am coming back next week and shall I be allowed to see you on Monday? and are you really and truly better? and still fond of me?

By the way, Tauchnitz has come out strong with your works: Mrs Dalloway and Orlando rub elbows with The Squeaker [Edgar Wallace] in all countries,—Germany, Switzerland, and Italy. Truly. At all the stations along the line I saw them, and waved a friendly hand. But they cut me, no doubt ashamed of the low company they were keeping, as an English gentleman (so I understood) pretends not to see a respectable woman he knows when he's dining with a whore.

My darling I shall see you soon,—hooray.

Your
V.

Berg

 *British Embassy,*
Berlin.
Saturday [23 February 1929]

My darling Virginia, I have been feeling so grim about Berlin that I have not had the heart to write any letters. If I wanted to describe what I felt about it, I should have to enlarge my vocabulary. And the cold! Thick snow, and the thermometer fallen to nothing. I feel completely atrophied. Now, as I write this, I shall probably be in England by the time you get it, and next morning I shall see you,—shan't I?—so that's a nice thought—but my poor Harold . . . However, he doesn't hate it as much as I do.

True, there are the museums, and the Planetarium. I'll tell you about the Planetarium. I wanted to have one at Long Barn, but on enquiry I discovered that they cost £20,000. I am therefore going to devote all my energies to getting one put up in London. It is another aspect of Virginia's world. I shall try to write an article about it, but it is a subject for you, not for me. There is also a lovely aquarium, and they play ice-hockey by artificial light,—have you ever seen ice-hockey?—and the pictures are intoxicating—so you see I am trying to make the best of Berlin—also I have discovered a bookstall which deals entirely in homosexual literature, which sounds even funnier in German than it does in English. These are my compensations—but the rest is just black misery, and I shall have to be petted and coaxed back into equanimity. As for the idea of three years interlarded with large slabs of Berlin, it doesn't bear contemplation. You will *have* to come and stay with us here. I feel as though the top of my head were coming off,—a wild, helpless feeling.

I met an admirer of yours, one Mr Cohen-Portheim, a gentleman lacking in charm but of some discrimination in literature.[1] He knows Leonard, he says. When he let drop your name, the room (for me) became suddenly irradiated. I have met thousands of people, and scarcely had a moment to myself.

Oh, I must bring this letter abruptly to a close, as my old friend

Kühlmann has called.[2] Damn him. Bless you, my lovely Virginia—Wednesday morning!

Your
V.

Berg

1. Paul Cohen-Portheim, a German Anglophile writer, whose best-known book was *England the Unknown Isle* (1930)
2. Baron Richard von Kühlmann (1873–1948). He was German foreign secretary, 1917–1918, and thereafter employed by the Weimar Republic as a roving diplomat.

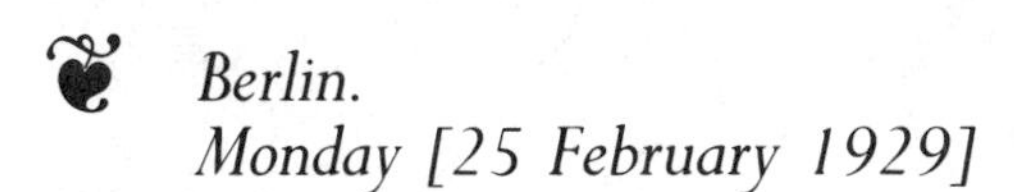

It snows and snows,—Berlin has now been under snow since the beginning of December. One's brain, or at any rate mine, becomes completely atrophied; but what really horrifies me is the prospect of leaving Harold here while I come frisking home to England. You wouldn't like to leave Leonard in similar circumstances? no, of course you wouldn't.

An echo of Virginia: Dottie went to see you. I heard about that. If she thinks everyone hates her, it is my fault. I scolded. I orated. Now you, as I have reason to know, like scolding people and making them cry, whether beside gas-fires or among currant bushes; but I don't, and am sorry about Dottie. One cannot unsay what one has said, least of all if it happens to be the truth. Things said in a temper can be unsaid; not the cold things, the meant things. Besides, your scoldings and corrections (though not said in temper) are deserved; they are opportune; they are salutary. Mine, to Dottie, may be deserved, and richly; but opportune they are never—and salutary seldom. Therefore I had better keep them to myself. Whereas your scoldings of me have the effect of inducing 12-months chastity on me, both physical and moral. Very good both for my soul and my nerves.

Do you know what we are doing? Harold is reading about Harmann, The Butcher of Hanover,—an unbelievably horrible book which I recommend by the way to the Hogarth Press, in translation,—and I am writing to you, and over us both hangs the immediate prospect of putting on our pretty evening clothes and sallying out to a party. Not a diplomatic party; but a party at which Yvette Guilbert will perform;[1] Yvette Guilbert whom I have not heard since I was 17, and went to a party I had been forbidden to go to, in London. Little by little our determination is ebbing. We have come to the stage of saying, "If we don't go, we shall be sorry afterwards,—Yvette Guilbert will die,—and it will be like [Eleanora] Duse, when we were too lazy to go up to London to see her." So I write to you, expecting at every moment to hear Harold saying from the next room,—tearing himself from the Butcher of Hanover,—"We must go and dress;" or else to hear myself saying severely "Harold, go and dress." She wore long green gloves when I saw her, and I had, very acutely and humiliatingly, the impression of not understanding one-third of what she sang. But tonight, if I go, I shall understand it all. So one grows up, and I suppose one is the better for it? or not?—Yes,—of course.

Meanwhile how is my Virginia? I say, may I ring you up on Saturday evening? On principle, I never ring you up; but I think I'll make an exception? Between 7 and 8? You will be on the sofa, perhaps, not yet gone to bed. Because you see I do want to know how you are, and I don't think I can wait till Monday. So shall I?—Oh, I am so torn. Long Barn, Virginia, my own room, Pippin, England,—and my Harold left behind in Berlin, hating it. Ugh. You'd hate it too. I should be so happy to come back, whole-heartedly, if only he were coming too.

Your
V.

Berg

1. She sang some "faded songs" (Harold's description) at the Goldschmidt-Rothschild reception. Born in 1869, she was the French *diseuse* who in her youth won great fame by her songs of the Quartier Latin.

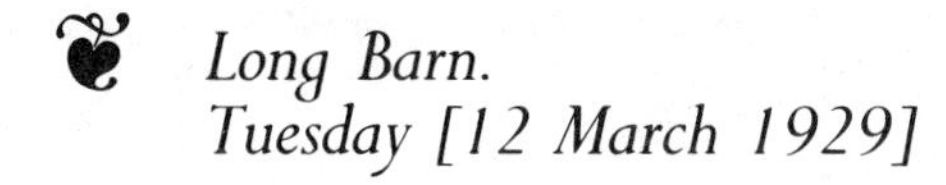

Long Barn.
Tuesday [12 March 1929]

"You might write," you said; and the days have drifted, and I haven't. Like the happy nation, I have no history. But do I dine with you on Friday? Clive asked me to dinner that night, and I refused. Will you send a postcard on receipt of this to say where and when I am to come?

It has been warm, and I have wished you were here—It would have done you so much good. My only companion has been Andrew Marvell; and not such a bad companion either; but I should have preferred Virginia. In the intervals I have gone out and watched the irises growing. On Saturday I adventured out into the World,—went to Penn's, in fact, where I found Christabel [Maclaren]! . . . lunched there, stayed to dinner, and came home to find Pippin wagging all over, thinking I had gone back to Berlin. Dottie has lost Vanessa, who answers neither telegrams nor letters—What has happened to her? She was by way of going there to see about the painting.[1]

I feel as though a thick curtain had come down between me and the rest of the world: I've seen nothing, heard nothing; I know Major Segrave won the world's speed record,[2] and that's about the nearest approach I have made to humanity. I go for long walks over fields the colour of hayricks; everything is the same colour just now; it is very beautiful. I enjoy it immensely, and am ceasing to be a person and am turning into some natural object such as a scratching post for sheep.

I do hope it's all right for Friday evening, and that you are well enough? and fond enough of your

V.

Berg

1. Dorothy Wellesley had commissioned Vanessa Bell and Duncan Grant to decorate her dining room at Penns-in-the-Rocks, Sussex.
2. Sir Henry Segrave in his car *Golden Arrow* gained the world land-speed record (233 mph) at Daytona, Florida, on March 11, 1929.

 *Long Barn, Weald,*
Sevenoaks.
Wednesday [3 April 1929]

You know, or, rather, you don't know, how dilatory I am, except when writing books for the Hogarth Press, and that's because I am frightened of Leonard. You know, for example, that it took me 15 years to get my ears pierced, not wholly due to cowardice; and things lie about the house for five and seven years before anything is done about them. But when I get two [Lenare] photographs of Virginia they go straight to Sevenoaks to be framed, which is where they now are. Now I consider that I am free to give you 2 guineas worth of presents, even unbirthday presents, since not only did I *ask* for the photographs but made you go to have them done, which you will find to be a permanent item of expenditure in your future years. Darling, I love them. I wish Potto had been sitting on your knee, that's all.

We have all been suffering from a mysterious complaint here, a mixture of neuralgia and rheumatism it feels like. I have recovered, and now watch the members of my household going down one after the other. When am I going to see you? I shall be in London on Tuesday next,—is that any good? Should we perhaps go to Kew if it was a fine day? or you once said you would take me to Keats' house at Hampstead, or are you busy? I am lunching with Francis Birrell; otherwise free, and would like to see Virginia, whom I have been missing rather badly lately. But the photographs helped to keep me happy.

Your
V.

Berg

❧ *5th April [1929]* *Monks House, Rodmell*
[Sussex]

In God's name: yes: I have several sentences addressed to you with that beginning:

I.G.N. Come on Tuesday; to the basement, not a wink later than 3:

I.G.N: Do NOT *bring Francis [Birrell]—a dear old rattle headed bore.*

IGN. Do NOT *bring Dottie: This I feel strongly about. Twice lately she has utterly ruined my serenity with you; and I wont have it. Choose between us. Dottie if your taste inclines that way by all means; but not the two of us in one cocktail.*

. . . I told Nessa the story of our passion in a chemists shop the other day. But do you really like going to bed with women she said—taking her change. "And how d'you do it?" and so she bought her pills to take abroad, talking as loud as a parrot.

Berg

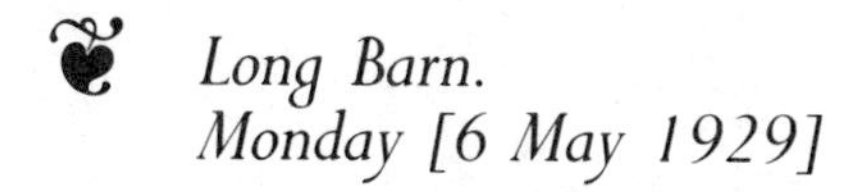

Long Barn.
Monday [6 May 1929]

And am I ever going to see Virginia again? A despair has settled down upon me about it. My own fault, no doubt; but I have had Harold, who went back to Berlin last night though I urged him to play truant. I am now here solitary, and oh so busy: writing a novel, writing about Marvell, writing a little poetry in between whiles; and with a new piece of furniture [book-trough] at my elbow which ought to be part of every writer's equipment. It has solved ½ the problems of life.

But seriously: shall I come up one day not Friday or Saturday and we'll go to Keats and dine together—or must I wait till Thursday 16th when I shall be released from the dentist at 3.30 and free till 7. when I broadcast? It depends on how busy you are.

I had a letter from Leonard this morning; will you tell him I have no wish to let Doran [American publisher] deal with Canada? He will understand.

I say, the novel is about the Edwardians,—a fascinating subject, if only I can do it justice. It is absolutely packed with the aristocracy. Shall you like that? I feel that for snobbish reasons alone it ought to be highly popular! I hope so, because Leonard's offer was very handsome, and I should hate to ruin the Press, towards which I feel avuncular as you know.

How is the pump?[1] I am still worried about it, and you.

Pippin so full of puppies. Jane less mangy. The aviary full of nests. The woods full of nightingales. But where's Virginia? On every hoarding, but not here.

Your
V.

Berg

1. A machine in Tavistock Square, used in the building of a vast new hotel, which caused the residents of the square much annoyance

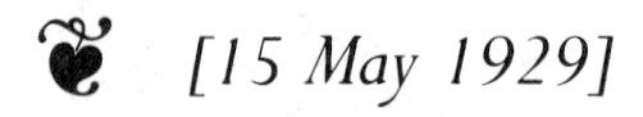

[*In pencil*]

This is too tantalizing! I would rather you had come to tea, which would have been hopeless, but to miss you by an hour is dreadful.

I'll come tomorrow at 5.

V.

Berg

Long Barn.
Monday [10 June 1929]

Virginia, my angel, is Potto very busy just now? Because a young man called Kenneth Rae, who is in Cobden Sanderson is terribly anxious to get you to write 300 to 400 words for a "Forget-me-not Calendar," illustrated by one Rex Whistler, and I thought Potto might do it for you. They have got your admirer Max (Beerbohm), your friend Hugh Walpole, your friend [Edmund] Blunden, your brother-in-law Clive, Siegfried Sassoon, your poor shaggy sheep-dog [Vita], and your friend Maurice Baring, amongst other distinguished contributors—any subject, they say, provided it would fit into Autumn or Winter, and suggest 'Influenza' or 'Weekends.' I said I did not think there was any chance of your consenting, but I would ask you. They can only pay £5. The only thing is, they must know at once—so could you like an angel send a telegram? to them direct would be best, KNOXYNOX, Westcent, London is their telegraphic address.[1]

You said I was to write an intimate letter, and this is the result! I have been working like a black. Finished and despatched Marvell, and done various oddments, so that now I turn with a sigh of relief towards my novel. Oh yes—and Pinker. We've given her two doses for worms, once in a powder and once in a pill—and each time she has sicked it up again before it could work. Will you tell Leonard? She had a fine fight with Pippin, in which Pippin got the worst of it, and the puppies had diarrhoea in consequence. Otherwise she is charming, though a little wistful,—I think she misses you both. Four little budgerigars, quite naked, but with parroty noses; two little doves hatch out. Harold comes on Saturday.

I forgot to say, the Cobden Sanderson people would have to have your words by the middle of next week. They have been longing to ask you, but did not dare, and then I happened to meet this young man who is bursting with keenness about his calendar,—his first venture on his own since he joined the firm—So I can't help hoping that you will, though I scarcely expect it.

I shall feel forlorn in London with no Virginia when I go up to broadcast on Thursday. Shan't go up till the evening in consequence. No nice expedition or anything. No bunloaf—no affection—no Potto to stroke. Damn. Shall you go to Sibyl's on Monday night? Harold and I are going—~~we're going to~~ no, I shan't tell you that: you'd laugh.[2] You'll find out for yourself fast enough. I could bring Pinker up on Monday, unless you would like to come and fetch her before then?

Did you give all my messages to Vanessa? Do please come back soon, because I miss you.

Your
V.

Berg

1. Virginia did not contribute to this Miscellany.
2. On June 17, Vita and Harold broadcast a discussion on marriage. The discussion was printed in part in *The Listener* of June 26.

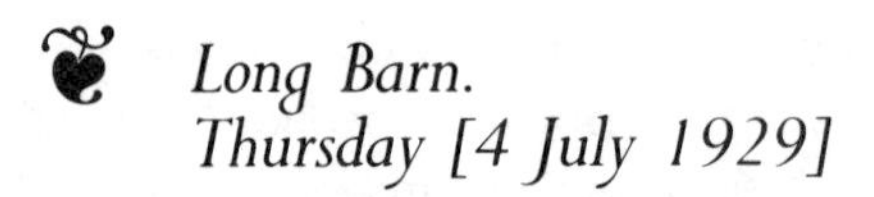

Long Barn.
Thursday [4 July 1929]

Ha, ha! there's a surprise: you didn't know that envelope was going to contain a letter from me, did you? This is to ask: do I see Virginia next Thursday? or is she so surrounded by a cloud of moths [*The Waves*] as to be quite inaccessible? If so, I might take Potto for a walk on a string instead. I dine with the Keyneses on the Wednesday night; shall sleep at Mount St. and be in London all Thursday.

Are you writing and very happy? I am very, very miserable, because Pippin has disappeared. All efforts to trace her have failed. I am left with Jane and the five little orphans, and a gnawing anxiety at my heart to know what can have happened to her. Is she lying hurt in some trap in a soaking wood? Is she poisoned? Do you think the BBC (which I look on as my pocket borough) would broadcast an S.O.S.?[1]

A friend of mine has discovered two unknown and exceedingly obscene poems by Byron, all about his relations with his wife. He found them in his father's safe. He has been put into touch with Desmond. Desmond had never heard of the poems. Have you? They are called 'Don

Leon,' and 'Leon to Annabella,' and are quite unpublishable, but throw a good deal of light on the bed-life of the Byron ménage.

Did Clive remember to bring you my flowers?

Will you let me know about Thursday? I wish you were dining with the Keyneses too; I shall be shy. *What am I to wear?* please, I want to know. A smock? a tiara? Some hint, please. Shall I come and see you just for a minute before dinner, as it is so close, or will you be having a party?

And what about that visit to Long Barn?

Your
↑ *V.*
very much

Berg

1. Pippin, Vita's spaniel, was found dead on July 7.

❧ *[9 July 1929]* *52 Tavistock Square, London, W.C.1*

Darling, we are so unhappy about Pippin. We both send our best love—Leonard is very sad.

Nigel Nicolson (copy)

July–December 1929

In the second half of 1929 two events coincided to effect another slight adjustment in the relationship. Vita's walking tour in Savoy, alone with Hilda Matheson, caused Virginia a spasm of jealousy which she could not hide. It was sharpened by Vita's submission to the Hogarth Press of several poems of a lesbian nature, which Virginia knew were not intended for her but had been written for Mary Campbell. Secondly, Harold decided to leave the diplomatic service and work for a higher salary for Lord Beaverbrook's newspapers. He would live permanently in England with Vita, to whom their constant separations for long periods had given acute distress. His new job would also free them from financial dependence on Lady Sackville, who was becoming increasingly difficult.

Col de l'Iseran [Savoy, France]
24th July [1929]

I am writing to you in an Alpine hut with a thunderstorm imminent outside. We are at the quite respectable height of 9300 feet, surrounded by a ring of white peaks. Up here grow gentians and other lovely little creatures, which seem to become brighter and more fragile the higher one climbs. And there are butterflies and beetles which would rejoice your entomological heart.

By this time I have a good many miles of Savoy in my legs. One meets funny people in these huts, who would amuse you. And Val d'Isère,—which is our headquarters,—is full of 'characters.' We live in the curé's house, which we share with the curé, Théodorine his servant, and Marquise his cow. Every morning at 6. Marquise goes out to pasture with a bell round her neck; every evening Marquise returns, and enters the house by the front door. It is all very familiar, friendly, and slightly smelly. A nice smell of stable.

Hilda is an admirable companion; is content to read for hours together; can make a pudding out of apricot jam and snow, and a waste-paper basket out of the Times. Also she can read maps, so we do not get lost as we cross the hills.

But how does one write a novel [*The Edwardians*]? I have come to the conclusion that I am a good walker but a bad novelist. One writes and writes, and at the end of the time one re-reads and decides that it might all just as well have remained unwritten. I take my foolscap out in my pocket, and, propping my back against a rock from which I can survey Savoy, try to remember exactly the smell of the 'bus that used to meet one at the station in 1908. The rumble of its rubberless tyres. The impression of waste and extravagance which assailed one the moment one entered the doors of the house. The crowds of servants; people's names in little slits on their bedroom doors; sleepy maids waiting about after dinner in the passages. I find that these things are a great deal more vivid to me than many things which have occurred since, but will they convey anything whatever to anyone else? Still I peg on, and hope one day to see it all under the imprint of the Hogarth Press, in stacks in the bookshops.

This is perhaps not what you call an intimate letter? but I disagree. The book that one is writing at the moment is really the most intimate part of one, and the part about which one preserves the strictest secrecy. What is love or sex, compared with the intensity of the life one leads *in* one's book? A trifle; a thing to be shouted from the hill-tops. Therefore if I write to you about my book, I am writing really intimately, though it may not be very interestingly Q.E.D.? But you would rather I told you I missed Potto and Virginia, those silky creatures with a barb under their fur—and so I do, and wonder very much whether they will come and stay with me when I get back? Potto would like the puppies, Virginia would like her nice big bed and coffee at eleven,—and all the affection that would be shown her at hours licit and illicit. I get back on the 4th, I think. A letter addressed to me British Embassy Berlin would be brought to me in Harold's pocket, for I join him somewhere in South Germany in a few days' time.[1] That would be very nice,—a letter, I mean. I've had no letters forwarded, which will mean a tidy pile when I do return!

I watch the beetles,—winged, black splotched with red,—at their amours on hot slopes here, and would like to enclose one of them. But it would get squashed in the post. So I just send you my love, unsquashable.

Your
V.

Berg

1. The purpose of this sudden meeting, in Karlsruhe, was for Harold to discuss with Vita the offer he had just received from Lord Beaverbrook to leave diplomacy and join the staff of the *Evening Standard*. He accepted.

❦ *Val d'Isere [Savoy, France]*
30th July [1929]

What does Potto think about Lord Beaverbrook? I gather that Harold has been writing to you and Leonard on the subject and receiving encouraging replies which have helped him to make up his mind. When I last wrote to you, I had heard nothing of it, so it has burst on me as a happy bombshell during the last few days. I am terribly excited and can hardly contain myself till I see Harold tomorrow. So now Harold becomes a journalist. Well, well! life is very exciting to be sure. Plus the mountain air, it has all gone fairly to my head. If you are at Rodmell I must come and see you, though I don't forget a phrase in one of your letters about coming to Long Barn for a night. I expect to be home on Monday—shall I find a note from Potto waiting for me, do you think? I have done a lot of my novel since I have been here; it is a very honest little book, quite straightforward with no fal-lals, and I fear you will find it devoid of all interest save for a few details about the servants' etiquette, which is of a nature to please you. What with one thing and another, I feel like a boat in a maelstrom—only not in any unpleasant sense—and looking forward terribly to seeing Virginia again.

Your
V.

Berg

 *Long Barn, Weald,*
Sevenoaks.
Friday [9 August 1929]

Oh dear I posted my letter in the blotting book, where I have just found it, and now it is all out of date, containing as it does messages about trains. So I don't send it. I am however sending my proofs,[1] which will you glance at? I'm very doubtful about the poem called Nocturne on p. 56 & 57; shall I cut it out? It seems to me meaningless now, though pregnant enough when I wrote it!

And look here you *will* put me off if you feel any worse? Otherwise I'll come (by car) in time for luncheon Sunday. I promise not to get in the way, but only to look after you and to eclipse myself if you get tired. I am longing to be with you, but shall understand if you say you would rather be alone, or if Leonard thinks you ought to be.

V.

Berg

1. Of *King's Daughter*, Vita's new volume of poems. In her diary entry of August 10, she expressed her anxiety about the "Lesbian poems" in the book. (See Victoria Glendinning, *Vita*, p. 219.)

❧ *Monday [12 August 1929]* *[Monk's House, Rodmell, Sussex]*

Dearest Creature,

I dont think I shall be able to come this week—I've had to retire to bed with the usual old pain, not very bad and the price of the value I set on your honesty. Lord! . . .

Meanwhile will you send at least a line to say what happened about Hilda—I particularly want to know the situation with respect to Janet [Vaughan], as I have anyhow to write to her. And please make Hilda see that it was all your donkeyism. . . .

Berg

 *Long Barn, Weald,*
Sevenoaks.
Tuesday [13 August 1929]

Oh dear, oh dear, oh dear. I feel so miserably responsible, you can't think. Poor, poor Virginia,—and that means you can't write—can do nothing in fact except stroke Potto's ears. But I love you enormously,—more, if possible, since this incident.

No harm was done by my impulsiveness. H[ilda] M[atheson] had the sense not to write to Janet Vaughan, so there is no need for you to make any allusion to it unless you wish to. I have told her it was mostly due to a misunderstanding on my part, and she says she will not say anything either, when she dines with the Vorn [Janet Vaughan]. So although a donkey I have not been a mischievous donkey, and there is no need for you to take any action.

Darling,—how I hate you to be ill. Have you put off all your visitors? I wish I could come and look after you. I am a cripple myself, as my back gave way again, and I can only hobble from room to room on two sticks, or else drag myself along the floor like Porgy, but I don't expect it will last long. I wasn't doing anything violent,—just walking upstairs. Silly Vita.

Oh you will never know what miseries I went through before seeing you. I couldn't bear to see your manuscript on its shelf or your photographs in my room. They were all like so many daggers. What *should* I have done . . . but my imagination revolts. All having ended well, I must admit that the incident was very illuminating. Only I cannot feel it has ended well if your headache is really due to it; if that is true, then it has ended disastrously. Will you let me know if you are better? I fret about you more than you know but not more than you might expect if you thought about it at all.

Your
V.

Berg

❧ *Aug 15th [1929]* *Monks House [Rodmell, Sussex]*

And now I see Geoffrey Scott is dead, at my age—no a year younger. Do you mind? Does it bring back the hot afternoon when the Salvation Army called, and the mews where he almost strangled you when you were late, and the scene on the downs? I didn't like him; at least I didn't trust him for some obscure reason. . . . But I took up my pen to say that I hope, if you see Hilda, you will make her understand, not merely superficially, that Janet Vaughan was as blameless as anybody could be—mere joking and affectionate at that,—I mean I shouldn't have minded to hear what she said of me; and to show how casual and lightly meant it was, she never even gave me a hint that Hilda could seriously entertain those passions. It was merely Oh how amusing it would be if Hilda could fall in love—and then nothing more, but what I took seriously—that the plan had been made many weeks or months.

Berg

 *Friday [16 August 1929]*

Eddy rang up to say he was back from Charleston and had heard you were better, though he had not seen you. I hope that he and his informant both speak the truth.

I have been in bed for the last three days [with lumbago]. It would be incorrect to say I was better, but I am getting more ingenious: i.e. I have learnt what positions are to be avoided, and I have got a rope slung round a beam, by the aid of which I can raise myself at least two inches. Jane [Vita's spaniel] has now slept solidly on my bed for 72 hours. I have read a great number of books, as it is difficult to write and I cannot remain on my elbow propped for more than five or ten minutes at a time—So you see that even had you been able to come today. . . . . it would have been dull for you—let us say.

Geoffrey (Scott) has died of pneumonia in New York, which has upset me a good deal.[1] How horrible to die alone in a foreign hospital away from all one's friends—Poor Geoffrey—what a disastrous life—

It is rather interesting, being physically incapacitated, provided one knows it will not last for ever. Having all one's normal activity taken from one—Even turning over in bed becomes an adventure—and takes a damned long time—Normally I could walk half the way to Sevenoaks in the time it takes.

I wish I knew REALLY how you were—at least I have my head left free, whereas your aches—or ached—

Here is Louise for the post.

Your
V.

Berg

1. Geoffrey Scott had been in love with Vita in 1923–1924. His wife divorced him because of her. He was author of *The Architecture of Humanism* and *The Portrait of Zélide*. He was forty-six at the time of his death.

Sunday 18th Aug. [1929] *Monks House [Rodmell, Sussex]*

I am very much distressed about your back. I wish you would answer, if only in pencil on a card, these questions. 1. Have you seen a doctor? 2. What does he say? 3. Are you better? Surely it has never been anything like as bad as this. Have you got rheumatism in it? Is it very painful? . . .

Anyhow, my dear Creature, let me know truthfully and exactly how you are. Potto kisses you and says he could rub your back and cure it by licking.

Berg

Long Barn.
Thursday [22 August 1929]

Miss V. Sackville-West is announced as broadcasting on New Novels at 7. tonight, but Miss V. Sackville-West is a poor lame thing what can just crawl on two sticks, and will be unable to appear at the microphone.

Therefore her paper will be read for her, and she will lie on the sofa in the big room and listen and curse the reader for missing all the points. It is a very queer thing, being ill, when you are not used to it. I suppose in the course of time, if one became really bed ridden, one would evolve ingenious methods of dealing with the difficulties of bed-life,—one could have little nets everywhere, like in a wagon-lit, to keep things in and prevent them from getting lost, for at present everything either seems to fall on the floor or else to become submerged under blankets and sheets. Also litter—what does one do about litter? My room is like Hampstead Heath after a Bank Holiday. And the worst of bed is that it is not really comfortable, except to sleep in. Trying to prop oneself up in bed is misery, isn't it—What do you do about it, you who must have spent so many months of your life in this situation? On the other hand the sense of retirement is pleasant, one has a sense of Buddhistic gravity, and feels oneself superior to the active people who irrupt into one's room from a strenuous world—Then there is the question of sleeping badly,—familiar to you but a new experience to me,—and rather an interesting one. One's mind seems to extend itself into different directions when one lies awake and everybody else is asleep—not unhappy exactly, but speculative and enlightened in a calm way. One thinks about dying. I find also that one thinks (with some distress) about the falsity and difficulty of one's relations with people; how there is probably nobody in the world who knows *all* round one; how one shows separate sections to different people, not on purpose, but willy-nilly, and the best one can hope for is that they will guess the rest. Besides one would probably not like it if anybody did see all round and all through. And what does it matter anyhow—which brings one back to dying again, and to the extinction of one's own absorbing microcosm, which then becomes easier to believe in than *not* to believe in,—its extinction, I mean. The reverse is the case, when one is normal and well.

But about knowing people, I have read the two volumes of Miss Mayne's life of Byron [1]—and that's illuminating: being presented with first one letter and then another, both written the same day and flatly contradicting each other, to two different people. That shows you up more than anything. To Tom Moore, for instance, and to the Guicciolli; or to Augusta and to Lady Byron. Instead of seeing just one flat section of his mind at a time, you see right through (so to speak) down into the next section, in a way that his contemporaries couldn't do. Now you write to me, and how do I know that next minute you won't snatch up your pen and write something completely different to Vanessa? And even you yourself don't know which you really mean. There is nothing to prevent me from writing to Harold in an hour's time, and swearing at the horrors of illness, whereas to you I have written of its charms. But that's a thing you would never know unless you had second sight.

Anyway I should be very glad if I could write letters like Byron's. . . .

Emily Brontë too I have been thinking a good deal about,—Leonard's fault because he sent me a book on them.[2]

When will you come, I wonder? for I really am recovering and ought to be restored by the beginning of the week, if not before. Any day but Monday, when I have an aunt,—Aunt Cecilie, of whom Eddy has told you,—the one who always says, "Oh, but that's classics."[3]

Have you been persecuted by an American woman friend of Vernon Lee's, who caught Clive and wants to draw you? Beware of her: she is the most voluble talker in creation, and will tire you. I discouraged her by saying you were ill.

Look at my sticky fingers all over the paper. I have been eating peaches. *"Le jus des pêches que tu coupes,"* etc—

Oh I do so want to see you—

Your
V.

Berg

1. Ethel Colburn Mayne's *Byron*, 2 volumes, 1910, reprinted 1924
2. *A Short History of the Brontës* by K.A.R. Sugden, reviewed by Vita in *The Nation*, September 4, 1929
3. Vita's father's sister, Lady Cunliffe

❧ *Saturday [24 August 1929]* *Monks House [Rodmell, Sussex]*

Might I come on Wednesday for the night?—could you let me know?

. . . And how are you? The best sleeping draught is audit ale at bedtime: any fellow of a college will get it, and if you don't like it, I will drink it.

A thousand different varieties of love are rained upon you, like the showers from a gigantic watering pot by Virginia and Bosman.

Berg

❦ *Long Barn.*
Monday [26 August 1929]

Wednesday is perfect,—unless, indeed, you would prefer to wait till next week when I can drive the motor? I am very much better, but I can't quite drive it yet. If you *would* rather put it off, let me know. Thursday of next week I have to go to London, and Friday Harold comes; otherwise all clear.

My unfortunate children have just gone off to Streatham to see my mother. . . . .

Of course I may be so much better by Wednesday that I may be able to drive again; in which case we might go somewhere on Thursday? and I'd take you home.

In any case, crippled or not, you shall have a warm welcome. There, wasn't that nicely put?

Your
V.

Berg

❧ *[27 August 1929]* *[Monk's House, Rodmell, Sussex]*

Well then, I think I had better come next Tuesday, instead of tomorrow, for the simple reason that if I come tomorrow you will certainly drive the car and risk your back again. Admit that my psychology is correct. . . . All this is very well reasoned; but I admit I am rather disappointed. . . .

Berg

❦ *Long Barn.*
Friday [30 August 1929]

I, too, was disappointed, but I expect it is a better arrangement really, as by next Tuesday I shall be as lively as a flea. At present, rather like a lame jackdaw. So come on Tuesday, my blessing, and on Wednesday we'll go somewhere nice, and I'll take you home.

I don't know what Dottie means.[1] I may have said you said something or other in a letter,—I don't remember,—anyhow it wouldn't be that she oughtn't to have 4 gardeners!

I've had an awful blow: Harold says he doesn't think these poems of mine are good enough to publish[2]—So I am holding up the proofs till Friday next, when he comes home, in the hope that I can talk him round—Will you tell Leonard? I can't make up my mind if he's right or not—and would like your advice please—or Potto's. Potto's would perhaps be better—

It will be nice, Tuesday—Very nice—Your impatient

V.

Berg

1. Virginia suspected Vita of showing her letters to Dorothy Wellesley.
2. *King's Daughter*

❧ *Sunday Sept 1st 1929*

Monks House [Rodmell, Sussex]

Damn Harold. And why should you attach any importance to the criticism of a diplomat?

Have you got your proofs? I will read them. . . .

Berg

 *Long Barn, Weald,*
Sevenoaks.
13th September [1929]

I have several things of the highest importance to tell you:

(1) Harold has resigned from diplomacy.

(2) He has engaged himself to Lord Beaverbrook from Jan 1st 1930.

(3) We have written to my mother telling her we will be dependent upon her no longer after the end of this year.

(4) Harold has withdrawn his objections to 'King's Daughter' so that's all right.

Now there is a fine packet of news for one letter.

Harold will be here till Nov. 1st and will then probably have to return to Berlin for a month.

And did you sign your name 500 times? And has Hugh [Walpole] sent you his new book in which you figure under the name Jane Rose?[1]

We have got 12 goldfish in the pond.

We are feeling very proud and free.

I suppose there is no chance of your being in London next Thursday when I am coming up? No, I suppose not. But I have a longing to see you.

Your
V.

Berg

1. *Hans Frost*. Of Jane Rose, Walpole wrote: "She had in her last novel spoken of the beam from a lighthouse 'stroking the floor of a lodging-house bedroom'—so her art illumined, gently and tenderly, the world that he knew. The debt that he owed her could never be paid."

❧ *Sunday [15 September 1929]* *[Monk's House, Rodmell, Sussex]*

A thousand congratulations from us both.
I daresay these are the happiest days of your life.
No, alas, I go to London on Friday not Thursday.
Yes, very pleased about Kings Daughter.
Thank Goodness, no more dealing with Lady S.
Yes I've signed my name 600 times.
Yes, I've read Hugh.
Why need he say all his characters are dead, when its true?
How business like this letter is!
And looks like a sonnet.

Berg

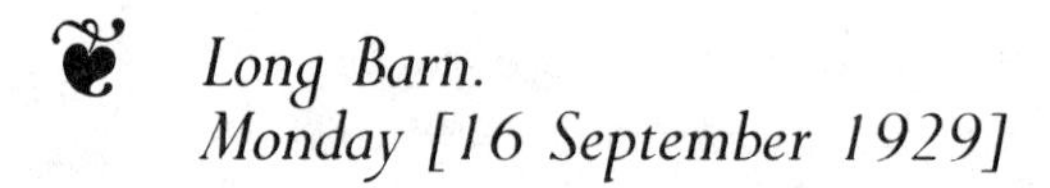

Long Barn.
Monday [16 September 1929]

I dreamed last night that you and Leonard had never been really married, and that you decided it was high time to hold the ceremony. So you had a fashionable wedding. You were dressed in a robe of mediaeval cut, made of cloth-of-gold, and you wore a long veil, and had an escort of bridesmaids and pages. You did not invite me to the wedding. So I stood in the crowd, and saw you pass on Leonard's arm.

For some reason or reasons (not far to seek) this dream made me extremely miserable, and I woke in tears, and have not yet thrown off the effect of it.

Will you tell your bridegroom that I sent back the proofs of King's Daughter to Mrs. Cartwright last week? I am sending him a flea-comb, enclosed, which is better than Keatings [dog powder].

We are going up to London this evening to dine with Lord Beaverbrook.

I wish you had said something illuminating about Hugh's novel,—except that there is nothing illuminating to say,—because I must talk about it I suppose on Thursday on the wireless.[1] I say, has Rebecca West's book come your way? It is unreadable. It is a brew of Meredith, Orlando, and Amanda Ross. Here is a phrase from it:

"So hastily had the old house been converted to feed the house-hunger that raged after the Great War, so far faster than any fast bowler had the contractor hurled in staircases and partitions of wood that had he left them alone had become matchboxes, that some problems of architecture had inevitably gone unsolved."

Am I prejudiced, or have some problems of style here gone unsolved.

My brother-in-law[2] thinks he can get us a flat in the Temple.

Will I ever see you again? I have a great and urgent craving to. But you seem very remote. "There was something terrifying in her gentle remoteness." No, it isn't that,—not your gentle remoteness,—that terrifies me, but merely geographical remoteness,—just that you are at Rodmell and I at the Weald. Anyhow I may be living at the Temple this winter— That would be nice. Anything may happen now that we have kicked over the traces. It is like being twenty (years old) again. Are you going to Cassis? I think of going to Barcelona for a week in November to see the exhibition, if I can prevail upon Dottie to motor me there. Or if you were still at Cassis I might come and see you there, on the way from Barcelona? Is it on the way? More or less? But you want to be alone there. And the exhibition may be over by then, for all I know. At any rate, all sorts of different landscapes seem to open, whichever way I look, not just the vista of a dinner table with gentlemen in gold-braided uniform and ladies in low dresses. Oh Christ, how much I always want to see you when life becomes exciting.

Your Orlando.

The fact that I don't see *you* prevents these from being (some of) the happiest days of my life.

Berg

1. On September 19 (see *The Listener*, September 25). Vita was broadcasting on New Novels every other week. In the same talk she reviewed Rebecca West's *Harriet Hume*, not favorably.
2. Frederick Nicolson, now second Lord Carnock. The flat was in 4 King's Bench Walk, Inner Temple, London E.C. 4, and Harold lived there from 1930 till 1945.

❧ *Tuesday [17 September 1929]* *[Monks House, Rodmell, Sussex]*

And when shall we meet? I'm a little dismal. Another of these cursed headaches. How I get them I can't imagine—Whether its writing, reading, walking, or seeing people. Anyhow its not been bad at all—only it makes Leonard gloomy, and tightens my ropes—I mustn't walk, or do anything but sit and drink milk—you know the old story.

Berg

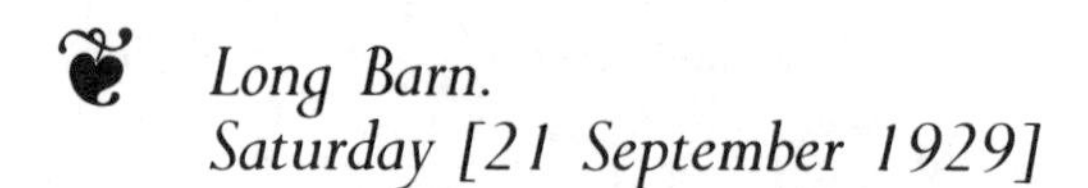

Long Barn.
Saturday [21 September 1929]

I am so miserable to think you had a headache again, poor poor Virginia—and Potto laying his snout along his paws. I wish I could come over on Oct. 5th but I don't quite see how I can, do you, with Harold here—as he will be away again in Berlin for two months. If he were permanently at home in his new job it would be different. He doesn't take it up till Jan. 1st, and it is on the Evening Standard; it is not quite settled yet what he is to do exactly, as they will try him on several different things first to see what he is best at,—the Londoner's Diary, for instance, and leading articles. He is to get £3000 a year, but Lord Beaverbrook wants this kept dark. It sounds an awful lot; but as a matter of fact, after we have paid income and super tax, and £800 a year for the boys, and £100 to Lady Carnock, it will leave us with only £1500 between us, to keep Long Barn on and Harold's rooms in London (perhaps in the Temple,) so we shall have to supplement it by a lot of writing—Long Barn costs so much. (This sounds like a 3 a.m. conversation "and how much do you pay the cook?") Anyhow I am very pleased, but the situation is being complicated by my mother refusing to accept any of our arrangements.

Harold would like very much to see you—If you are better, i.e. *quite* recovered,—would you stop here for dinner one night on your way back from London? or will Leonard not allow you to go to London any more? If Harold is away in London for the night towards Oct. 5th could I perhaps come and stay with you? by your hot sea or elsewhere? I don't know where Lyme Regis is—is it the same as King's Lynn?[1] My poor Virginia I do hate your having these headaches—and the moths [*The Waves*] will all fly away for the moment—

I've got your collected works—and very pretty they are too, in their green covers.[2]

Have you seen the 'Punch' joke: "Mrs Harold Nicolson is the Orlando of Miss Rebecca West's remarkable book of that name. *Weekly Paper*

But if she sees this, Mrs. Virginia Woolf will probably become an Orlando Furiosa."

Tell Leonard I have resumed my novel [*The Edwardians*]—as a publisher he will be interested to hear this perhaps.

Will I see you? shall Harold and I come over one day? But not to tire you and not till you're better. I wish I knew that you were. I can't tell you how I mind your being ill. This time it wasn't *my* fault.

Your
V.

Berg

1. Lyme Regis is in Dorset, King's Lynn in Norfolk. Virginia canceled plans to go to Dorset.
2. The Hogarth Press was reissuing Virginia's novels in a uniform edition.

❧ *Thursday [26 September 1929]* *Monks House [Rodmell, Sussex]*

No, I didn't mean I was ill—only an ordinary headache, and I'm perfectly all right again. . . .

I'm reading an Oxford undergraduate ms novel, and his hero says "Do you know these lines from The Land, the finest poem, by far the finest of our living poets—" but for all that, we shan't publish him.

I have only one passion in life—cooking. I have just bought a superb oil stove. I can cook anything. I am free for ever of cooks. I cooked veal cutlets and cake today. I assure you it is better than writing these more than idiotic books.

. . . Well, God knows when we shall meet. You'll be off to Barcelona. . . .

V.

Berg

❦ *Long Barn.*
Saturday [28 September 1929]

Did I, or did I not, detect a note of annoyance in your letter? a quick scratch?[1] Anyway you are quite wrong: if I go to Barcelona at all, it will not be with Hilda Matheson but with Dottie, in her motor, and in any case I don't think the scheme will mature. I am so glad you are all right again, and a cook. If I can find a receipt book I will send it to you! Meanwhile I have made the acquaintance of an old man you would like, and have persuaded him (I think) to write his autobiography. He furnished me with some notes on his career. He is a professional life-saver,—in the intervals of life-saving, a rag-and-bone merchant,—he has been saving life and performing other philanthropic actions for 49 years and 9 months, so he has a further 3 months to run before he has completed fifty years, and then he is going to stop. Here are a few items from his autobiographical notes:

> "Taking poor girl off spiked fence in the Park.
> Falling over a boiling well by myself.
> Assisting a dear lady being drowned, near Tonbridge.
> Assisting first-aid to dear man killed by an apple-tree.
> A lady's pony that could not walk for years,—I made it walk.
> Taking expectant mothers to hop fields free of charge.
> Eventually found walking-sticks for the Blind.
> Also I have given mothers a pram.
> Catching my son from a very high ladder.
> Taking a dear sheep's head hung on some staples.
> A blacksmith masterman got kicked, he died, he lent me his apron.
> Looking for an old lady to have a Christmas, and succeeded.
> Caught squirrel in lady's bedroom.
> Caught 86 rats with my own hand.
> Also other items not mentioned, all worked by the Dear Spirit. Can be illustrated at any time by request."

Who is the Oxford undergraduate, and what is his novel? By the way, Harold and I both liked Clifford Kitchin's murder book, and I shall recommend it on Thursday, so tell Leonard to notice if it affects sales.[2] Will you ask Leonard if I may have a few days' grace for reviewing his poets?[3] His blue slip said Oct. 1st, but we have had SO many people—and I have had several novels to read, I have had no time—Also I have to go to London on Monday—but I will hurry up, tell him.

I think I could come Friday or Saturday—may I let you know? Tell Potto I would like to come, if I can provide company here for Nigel Nicolson.

How good your Beau Brummell was![4] and I like the artful way it linked on to Cowper.

My novel is so commonplace, so thin—

The fields are lovely, we go for walks with the puppies, for the sake of our health. They run after pheasants. How tame pheasants are, before the 1st of October. Impossible to alarm them.

We have 12 goldfish, and four little new naked budgerigars.

Rodmell seems a long way from the Weald, but I expect you are very happy.

We had Sir Victor Sassoon to dinner[5]—he has 14 millions, and a wrist-watch that winds itself up every time you move your arm.

Your
V.

Dottie says her dining-room is a vision of loveliness.[6]

Berg

1. Vita heavily scored out five lines at the end of Virginia's letter of September 26. They may have hinted at Hilda Matheson.
2. *Death of my Aunt* by C.H.B. Kitchin (Hogarth Press) was reviewed by Vita in her broadcast of October 3.
3. "New Poetry," *The Nation*, November 2
4. "Beau Brummell," *Nation and Athenaeum*, September 28, 1929
5. Chairman of the Sassoon merchant bank. He was then aged forty-eight and unmarried.
6. Decorated by Vanessa Bell and Duncan Grant

❧ *[30 September 1929]* *[Monk's House, Rodmell, Sussex]*

No, no, no, I meant Dottie, not H.M. (about going to Barcelona) and the reference was to your late travels and it was only a joke and Potto made it and said hah hah to show it was a joke and only Donkeys bray. . . .

Berg

 *Long Barn, Weald*
Sevenoaks.
Saturday [5 October 1929]

Darling, it was so difficult yesterday—Yes you were quite right, I had said I might be able to come, as I thought Harold might be in London; then he asked somebody here whom he wanted me to meet,[1] and there were other things (all very dull, also b. flux) which in the aggregate made me have to decide I couldn't. It is always complicated when he comes home. But look here, I shall be in London on Tuesday—can I come and see you? We come up late on Monday evening and dine with Sibyl—(yes! That's Harold's fault again,) and on Tuesday we look at a flat we have been offered in King's Bench Walk—very nice—but not so near you as one which we saw in Taviton Street—or another in Tavistock Place. But that had been let already when we got there. King's Bench Walk is very romantic though,—panelled,—and absurdly cheap—with plane-trees and pigeons outside. I shall spend all January and February in London at any rate—perhaps longer—with weekends here. Will that be nice, do you think? Will I see you? will we go on more London expeditions?

We are rather excited, and I remained impervious to *24* pages of abuse which I had from my mother last night.

I did think Beau Brummell and Mary Woll—(can't spell that) so good.[2] God I wish I could write like that.

Your
V.

Berg

1. Maurice Bowra, the Oxford classics don and prolific author
2. "Mary Wollstonecraft," *Nation and Athenaeum*, October 5

1930–1931

For the years 1930 and 1931 no letters from Vita to Virginia survive, although in the same period Vita kept more than seventy of Virginia's. The affectionate tone of Virginia's replies removes any suspicion that she no longer thought Vita's friendship worth cherishing or her letters worth preserving. They were lost at some later stage of Virginia's life, or after her death. But Vita's changing mode of living was gently widening a gap between them. Early in 1930 she discovered, purchased, and restored the near ruined Sissinghurst Castle, twenty miles from Long Barn, and the Nicolsons left Long Barn to live there permanently from 1932 onward. Vita became increasingly withdrawn from social life. At Long Barn there had been five guest rooms. At Sissinghurst there were none. Virginia spent only a single night there, while Harold was away, in his bedroom. But this distancing between them must not be exaggerated. Their diaries show that in the four autumn months of 1930 they met eight times, and in the first four months of 1931, nine times—in London, Rodmell, and Sissinghurst. In these same years Vita published her two best-selling novels, The Edwardians *and* All Passion Spent, *both with the Hogarth Press, and she began to create at Sissinghurst, with the collaboration of Harold Nicolson, a garden that fifty years later is still among the most famous in England. Virginia published* The Waves, *and made a new friend, Ethel Smyth, the composer and prolific autobiographer, who never replaced Vita in her deepest affections, but came to be her most frequent visitor and correspondent.*

1932

In the spring of 1932, Virginia and Leonard, with Roger Fry and his sister Margery, went to Greece. On her return Virginia led a far more sociable life than did Vita at Sissinghurst. Vita wrote for the Hogarth Press another popular novel, Family History, *and Harold, having left Beaverbrook's employment and made a disastrous start in politics by joining Oswald Mosley's New Party, settled down at Sissinghurst to write a novel,* Public Faces, *and a trilogy of books on diplomatic history. Virginia was now fifty, Vita forty.*

 *Sissinghurst Castle,*
Kent.
Sunday, 25th April [24 April 1932]

My dear, remote, romantic Virginia—yes, indeed, I see the moon in English muddy puddles, and I wonder where you are: sliding past the Dalmatian coast (I think at one moment,) passing Corfu and Ithaca, (and oh God! what associations they all have for me!) and then the Piraeus and Athens [1]—(more associations,) and then what happens to you? for I simply don't know,—the hinterland of Greece, I suppose, which is a closed country to me so far—and is likely to remain closed unless I go there with Ethel [Smyth], which God forbid. Why didn't you ask me to come with you? I would have thrown everything to the winds, and would have come. But you didn't.

In the meantime I cultivate my garden and April cheats me of all its advertised joys: the wind is howling at all hours, and the rain is raining at most of them. A bloodier April England never saw. So be glad that you are in the sun (I hope) of Greece.

I am glad for your sake, but England is empty without you.

Will you come here when you come back? Shall you be dazed by all the things you have seen? You have been to Greece before, and your recollections will be strong, I know. It is rather appalling, to think what things people live through,—people one loves,—when one isn't there with them. Yes, I do wish I were with you.

The book of stamps *was* mine,—at least, I had lost one out of my cigarette case, so I suppose it was the one you found under the chair. Thank you.

You will be seeing those lavender and tawny slopes, I suppose, and all the wild spring flowers which I have never seen,—for I was in Greece in

1. Virginia and Leonard had left for their month's holiday in Greece on April 15. In the letter that follows, Virginia recalled her first trip to Greece in 1906, the holiday from which her brother Thoby returned to England with typhoid fever, and died.

October [1923]. How I envy you. How I envy the people who are with you.

Life is too complicated,—I sometimes feel that I can't manage it at all.

Your
V.

Berg

May 8th [1932] *[Hotel Majestic] Athens*

Well I have just got your letter, and it was very nice to get your letter though I cant help feeling, being as you know a very polyp for emotion, that you're somehow rather saddened worried, bothered—why? Why is life so complicated at the moment? Money? Dotty [Dorothy Wellesley]? Writing? God knows. . . .

Yes it was so strange coming back here again I hardly knew where I was; or when it was. There was my own ghost coming down from the Acropolis, aged 23: and how I pitied her! . . .

Berg

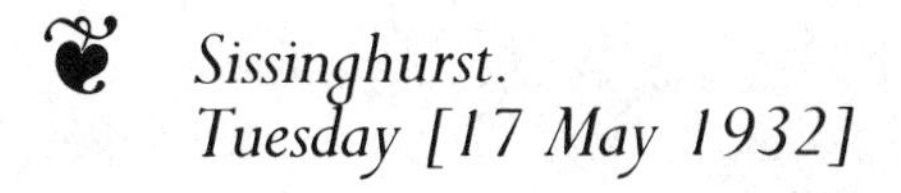

Sissinghurst.
Tuesday [17 May 1932]

We've had no posts here since Saturday! The consequence was that I only got your letter this morning. DAMN. I was in London yesterday and could perfectly well have come, but I never thought you'd be in London on Bank Holiday. I got a lovely lovely letter from you from Greece,—two, in fact,—yes, it sounds ravishing and I wish you'd taken me with you in your pocket.

When shall I see you now? I shan't be in London till the 30th, unless I come up for the flower-show. I am tempted to come up, but I ought to stick to my book. What would be really nice, would be if you and Leonard motored down here on a fine day. Telephone and say you are coming, *Sissinghurst 250*—but our number is a deep dark secret, so tell it to no one.

Sissinghurst really is looking nice just now,—but of course you are spoilt for our simple English beauty. Still, the bluebell wood is really a dream.

No, I'm not depressed and I certainly didn't mean to write a depressed letter. I may have been feeling rather harassed, and you always know when my coat is at all ruffled. I do long to see you.

V.

Berg

❧ *Wednesday [25 May 1932]* *[52 Tavistock Square, W.C.1]*

Dearest Creature,

. . . Theres only one person I want to see, and she has no burning wish for anything but a rose red tower and a view of hop gardens and oasts. Who can it be? Its said she has written a poem and has a mother, a cow, and a moat. I'm so illiterate—I've seen so many people—life offers so many problems and there's a hair in my pen.

Berg

❧ *Friday [9 September 1932]* *Monks House [Rodmell, Sussex]*

I meant to ask—and forgot—if you would lend me the [Lenare] phogh which I gave you (of myself). . . . Could you bring it—but doubtless now, with your other attachment, its down the coal hole. Oh alas.

Berg

❧ *Wednesday [12 October 1932]* *52 T.[avistock] S.[quare, W.C.1]*

I've just bought the 6,000th copy of Family History—6000 sold before publication—my God! And my fingers are red and whealed with doing up parcels for 3 dys incessantly. Miss Belsher ill—orders pouring in—we all working till 7.30—thought we were just finished—then a last batch of orders discovered hidden in a drawer another hours work—clerks panting—telephones ringing carriers arriving—parcels just finished in time to catch the vans—Oh Lord what it is to publish a best seller. . . .

Berg

 *Sissinghurst Castle,*
Kent.
Sunday [16 October 1932]

Oh dear, not content with making you tie up six thousand family histories, I made you tie up the common reader too.[1] An extra parcel. I won't apologise, though. If you knew what pleasure it gave me, you wouldn't want me to apologise. . . . Lord, you ARE a good writer, aren't you? and a good critic. I take off my hat; I sweep it off, so that its plume raises the dust.

I've got an extra broadcast talk to do tomorrow, and am scrapping three books in order to put yours into it.

That is why this letter is not longer: because I've got to write my talk.

Your
V.

Yes, do please come to Sissinghurst soon. Remember, I'll be in America for nearly four months [January–April 1933].

Berg

1. Vita's *Family History* was published on the same day, October 13, as Virginia's *The Common Reader: Second Series*.

❧ *Tuesday 18th [October 1932]* *52 Tavistock Square [W.C.1]*

Oh I was in such a rage of jealousy the other night, thinking you had been in love with Hilda that summer you went to the Alps together! Because you said you werent. Now were you? Did you do the act under the Dolomites? Why I should mind this, when its all over—that tour—I dont know. But I do. D'yu remember coming to confession, or rather justification, in my lodge? And you weren't guilty then were you? You swore you werent. Anyhow my Elizabeth [Bowen] comes to see me, alone, tomorrow. . . .

Berg

1933

In the first four months of 1933, Vita and Harold went on a lecture tour of the United States, the only time Vita visited America (Virginia never did). Vita wrote to Virginia letters that show she much enjoyed herself and was amused by the curious incidents to which her celebrity exposed her, but she concealed from Virginia her capacity, in spite of her reserve, to charm a crowd of strangers—to which newspaper clippings bear unanimous witness. It was her last sustained public performance. She withdrew to Sissinghurst, published her Collected Poems, *and cultivated her garden. Although they wrote that they missed each other "very much indeed," she and Virginia met only half a dozen times in the year. Virginia published* Flush, *and was writing* The Years.

Denver and Rio Grande Western Railroad
En Route Through the Rockies
16th March [1933]

This writing paper appeals to me so much that I must write you a letter on it. This is a Thursday; I left New York on Monday and have been travelling ever since through unending prairies until this morning when I woke to find a semi-circle of snow mountains edging the horizon, their peaks just turning pink as the sun rose over the opposite rim of the plain. Then we got to Denver, at the foot of the Rockies, and by breakfast time we were climbing right up into the mountains and are now some 7000 feet up. It is very beautiful, very desolate, the sun is hot, and I've seen a cowboy. So I'm very happy. It is all, quite suddenly, un-American and subtly Spanish.

We don't reach San Francisco for another three days and two nights. I never realised the size of this darn country till I came here. I hope California will have stopped quaking by the time we get there,[1] and that I shan't again have to live up to the reputation you ascribe to me, for producing convulsions of nature or whatever it is.

Later. I find I can post this right up at the top of the mountains—so you must look at the postmark, which apparently is a special one. The scenery is altogether too scenic for my taste,—terrific gorges and roaring rivers—it gives me claustrophobia and I am scarcely consoled by knowing it is the old Covered Wagon Trail. I preferred the open uplands and distant ranges which reminded me of Persia—

Salt Lake City—March 17th—It was so shaky I couldn't write any more—so instead of posting this on the Great Divide I must post it in the home of the Mormons. The Great Divide worked perfectly, and all the streams suddenly started running the other way—and made us feel like stout Cortes—

The time keeps on changing, which is very disconcerting; from "Mountain Time" we have now got to "Pacific Time," and there is 6 [*sic*] hours difference between us and you. Do you realise that California is more than twice as far from England than Persia?

Harold wants to go for a walk now, as we have an hour here.

Your
V.

Berg

1. The earthquake in Los Angeles had been minor, but the inhabitants were very frightened. Vita and Harold saw no sign of damage on arriving there.

❧ *March 18th 1933* *Monks House [Rodmell, Sussex]*

Well, do you remember me? I wrote you a very long and passionate letter the other day, but stuck it in my case, forgot it, left it, and found it so out of date—it was all about earthquakes and banks failing—that I can't send it. . . .

I saw Sibyl the other day; and she had seen Harold, and Harold had said you are a roaring raging success; which, I said, dont matter a straw with Vita. She'll shake her coat, and the grease and the oil will run down her. A great compliment to you. Shall you net anything after all—with the dollar collapsed?—There'll be the experience, as they call it—all those virgins you've ravished—teas you've eaten, shrines you've visited, fat old women you've intoxicated. . . .

Please Vita darling come back soon. We shall be off in the car to Italy if you dont—we want to try the fluid fly wheel on the Alps. Please come snuffing up my stairs soon, just the same, in your red jersey. Please wear your pearls. Please bring

Sarah [dog]. And then ask me to Sissingt. Lord, how you'll love your first night there and sun rise seen from the pink Tower! Write to me.

Berg

Smoke Tree Ranch—
South California—
[near Palm Springs]
28th March [1933]

I have been trying to write to you for days and days, but life has been too thickly populated with movie stars and so forth. I am now in a three-roomed cottage in the middle of the desert (I send you a photograph of it,) with nothing but a few cowboys and a stray coyote to interrupt. Magnificent stars overhead, and mountains all round. The desert itself is carpeted with rosy verbena. It is exactly like Persia, and we are as happy as larks.

I have several things of importance to tell you. (1) That I went to see the Huntington Library in Pasadena, and, observing that their collection of manuscripts had been brought so up to date as to include George Moore, asked them if they wouldn't like A room of one's own. They were much excited, and I think that if you were to write to

Captain Hazelton
Manuscript Dept.
The Huntington Library,
Pasadena, Los Angeles, California,

there might be a quite good chance of their buying it. Don't be too optimistic though, for as you know the Americans are very hard-hit just now. (2) The second thing is that I met your friend Brett and gave her your love.[1] She blushed all over. I met her in a crazy household at a place called Carmel, where she is living with Mabel Dodge Luhan. Mabel D. Luhan is the woman who gave the ranch in New Mexico to D.H. Lawrence. She wrote a book about it all, called 'Lorenzo in Taos' [1933]. She is married to a Red Indian, but is now in love with Robinson Jeffers, who was also there.[2] A handsome man; you know him. Mabel Luhan sat and gazed at him, while he pretended not to notice, and while I shouted into the sort of Kodak which Brett holds on her knees and which is connected by wires with the telephone arrangement she wears over her ears. Every now and then she stops one from talking while she changes the battery, like putting a new film into a Kodak. She is very pathetic; avid for news of England and her friends. She is getting herself naturalised as an American, but has to pass an exam on the American Constitution first, which alarms her. (I have a sudden feeling that I have already written to you about all this.)

I can't remember if I wrote to you from a place called Pasatrimpo, Santa Cruz, which I was carried off to by a golf champion [a Miss Hollins],—to this day I don't know why. After that I went back to San Francisco and then down to Los Angeles. Mr William Randolph Hearst asked us to stay at his ranch (250,000 acres, plus a Spanish Castle [San Simeon] which he removed bodily from a hill-top in Andalusia) and offered to send an aeroplane for us, but we were proud and refused, partly because it was 300 miles away and partly because Shaw was going to be there, and we thought we couldn't stand that. So after having been conducted round Chinatown in San Francisco and taken over the prison, we departed for Los Angeles. We just missed the earthquake; there was a little one while we were there, but we were both asleep and didn't notice it. Nature seems to have been pursuing us with vengeance ever since we left England: hurricanes in the Atlantic, blizzards in Chicago, earthquakes in California, a sand-storm here, and a meteor which lit up five states for half an hour and came to rest in Arizona. In spite of all this the climate of California is divine; an average temperature here of 80 in the shade, perpetual sunshine, and incredible wild flowers. I enclose a photograph of them just to annoy Leonard. It really is a photograph, although coloured. I mean, it really *is* like that.

Los Angeles is hell. Take Peacehaven, multiply it by 400 square miles, sprinkle it all along the French Riviera, and then empty the Chelsea Flower Show over it, adding a number of Spanish exhibition buildings, and you have the Los Angeles coast. The Americans have an unequalled genius for making everything hideous. Hollywood however is fun. It is pure fantasy,—you never know what you will come on round the corner, whether half an ocean liner, or Trafalgar Square, or the façade of Grand Hotel, or a street in Stratford-on-Avon with Malayan houris walking down it. We were taken round by Mr Gary Cooper. And then we went to a party at

Clemence Dane's,[3] —but it's all too long to tell. Anyhow there was the loveliest creature there, called Diana Wynyard. If Cavalcade comes to London you must go and see her in it.

A young lady rushed up to me in Pasadena and said she was writing a book about you and me. Isn't that nice for us? Would I give her an interview to tell her our (yours and mine) views on Imagery? Fortunately I was able to say I had only just time to catch my train.

Then I saw Elsa Maxwell [the American columnist noted for her parties], and the loveliest fish in an aquarium. The aquarium in London can't hold a candle to that one. They are all the Pacific fish. And there were seals on the beaches, and humming-birds, and mocking-birds, and trees 5000 years old, and acres of cactus, like phallic symbols or else like pre-historic reptiles, and miles upon miles of orange groves,—Sunkist,—and such queer reversals of nature as plants that have to be taken up in November and put into cold storage because the winter is too hot for them. I doubt whether I shall ever recover from all this. At any rate I shall never be quite the same again. That's certain.

We get back on April 21—shall you be in London? for I MUST come and see you. You can't answer this question of course, for you won't get this letter very much before we sail. But you might perhaps send me word to Sissinghurst. I haven't had any English mail for ages, so there may be a letter from you wandering somewhere about America. It will reach me eventually.

From here we go to Arizona and then to New Mexico, and then to Milwaukee, and then to South Carolina, and then to New York, and then to that blessèd Bremen [German liner] which will bring us home. Battered but enriched,—not only by dollars.

Lord, but I am dying to see you.

Your
V.

Berg

1. Dorothy Brett, the painter, a daughter of Lord Esher. She had been an intimate friend of Katherine Mansfield and D. H. Lawrence, and followed Lawrence in Taos, New Mexico, where she remained until her death, in 1977, at the age of ninety-three.

2. Robinson Jeffers (1887–1962), the American poet, owned the house in Carmel, California, where he lived in semi-seclusion. (Harold recorded in his diary that when they arrived they found a notice, "Not at Home," hung across the door, which Jeffers then opened from inside.) Mabel Luhan lived in another house two hundred yards away.

3. Pen-name of Winifred Ashton (1888–1965), the English novelist and dramatist, who was then living at Santa Monica

❧ *April 1st 1933 (fools day)* *Monks House [Rodmell, Sussex]*

I had a very nice letter from you the other morning, written from top of a mountain, where all the streams run backwards. I deserved it, because while you were seeing the streams, I was seeing Mr Scaife [of Houghton Mifflin]. No I dont think I altogether like Mr Scaife. He's a blotchy looking toad like man, who tells stories about his dog's tricks. However he seemed consumed with admiration for you and Harold, and didn't stay long. He seemed to have an idea that I should write a life of my father. Good God!

. . . Now I must put our dinner to cook; oh why dont you swoop down the road, and draw up at the gate, with a great washing basket full of figs, as you once did, when your mother loved me, and sent me a bottle of vermouth!

Berg

Charleston,
South Carolina.
9th April [1933]

In spite of the picture at the top of this paper,[1] I am really writing from South Carolina, quite a considerable distance away. We have been amusing ourselves by reckoning up the distance we shall have travelled by the time we get home, and find that it comes to over 33,000 miles—We've been to 72 different cities, and have spent 63 nights in the train. I hope you are impressed by these statistics.

I am now waiting for Mr Dubose Heyward[2] (did you ever see 'Porgy'?) who is going to take us to supper with Cornelia Otis Skinner.[3] So you see that Charleston, S.C., has its celebrities no less than Charleston, Sussex, Eng.

I found a lovely letter from you waiting for me in Chicago, and I am in hopes that this one may reach England two days before I do, since I shall send it by the Empress of Britain in company of Mr and Mrs Bernard Shaw. We ourselves sail on the 15th, and are nearly sick with excitement.

Yes, I have known Ivy Davison all my life.[4] She is very nice indeed, and I believe has sub-edited the week-end Review very efficiently. However her fate so far as the Hogarth Press is concerned will have been settled long ago. She is a young woman of some enterprise and independence, having been born into a perfectly conventional English family and having shaken herself free of ready-made traditions, to the dismay of her parents, in order to earn her own living on the Saturday Review. She had an unfortunate love-affair lasting some ten years with a married man, I don't know who it was. Her people are decent to the last degree; her father was a great friend of mine. Very handsome they both are—and so is Ivy, I think. She has no money except what she makes. I shall be amused if I return to find her installed in Miss Scott Johnston's place.

Oh, the things we've seen and the people we've met! I don't think I wrote to you from the Grand Canyon which is the most astonishing thing in the world. We are going to come back to America in order to motor all through Texas, Arizona, California, and Mexico, taking tents with us in order to camp in the desert. You can't imagine, Virginia, what the Painted Desert is like. It is every colour of the rainbow, broken by great-pink cliffs the colour of the rocks in Devonshire. And the sun blazes every day, and the air makes you want to leap over the moor. Why don't you and Leonard come with us? January, February, and March would be the time to go, and the first bit of April. Nor can you imagine the desert flowers, although I think I sent you a picture of them. You would escape then from Sibyl *and* from Mr Scaife,—for whom I apologise more than I can say.[5] There would be nothing but a few Indians. We propose to take ship to Panama, land there, buy a car, and drive straight off, taking ship again at New Orleans. Doesn't it appeal to you? If you liked, you could give a couple of lectures which would practically pay for your expenses.

Yes, I think that is a good plan.

Charleston is the home of azaleas. They grow wild in all the woods; bushes about 20 feet high in the gardens.[6] They are all out now, in fact

1. Of Grand Canyon National Park, Arizona

2. DuBose Heyward, American novelist, poet, and playwright (1885–1940). His first novel, *Porgy* (1925), about blacks in Charleston, was an instant success and was the basis for his play of the same title and for George Gershwin's opera, *Porgy and Bess*.

3. The actress (1901–1979) also wrote plays and biographies, as well as a number of very popular books of humorous essays.

4. Journalist and editor of *The Geographical Magazine* in the 1940s. She had applied for a job with the Hogarth Press.

5. Roger L. Scaife was managing director of Houghton Mifflin, Harold's American publisher.

6. Among other gardens, Vita visited Middleton Place, about which she wrote the poem "Stand I in England? Do I dream," published later in 1933 in her *Collected Poems*, p. 214.

some of them are already over. It is the home of magnolias and camellias too, and giant ilexes. It is utterly unlike the rest of America.

Lord, I must stop. But think, next week—*next week*,—we shall be home.

Your
V.

Sussex

Wednesday [19 April 1933] *Monks House [Rodmell, Sussex]*

I say this is exciting!

You're back—Thank the Lord my porpoise is in the fishmonger's again! But when shall I see her? We are here (Lewes 385) till Sunday afternoon. Then London for 10 days: then Italy. Could you ring up—dont tell me you've changed your voice too—and suggest any time, which I'll keep even if it means murder. . . .

Now you must attend to your world. Lord how I envy you the pink tower after all America

Berg

V. Sackville-West
Sissinghurst Castle,
Kent.
Monday [24 April 1933]

Yes your porpoise is back on the marble slab.[1] But with four months accumulation of stuff to deal with,—a real nightmare. I don't feel I shall ever get straight. I can hardly find 8 inches × 8 inches of space on my table to put this paper on. And there isn't a chair to sit on,—all loaded up with books and papers and cowboy hats. I sit on the floor mostly, and Sarah wriggles onto my lap, upsetting everything.

Yes it's very nice—but I've only had one day—Saturday—at home so far. Yesterday I went to see my mother—taking Harold with me. He started by losing his temper and told her he would shoot her—they ended up by Harold sitting at her feet while she fingered his curls into Little Lord Fauntleroy ringlets. A great success. She recognised a kindred spirit, and was amused. I sat by, as a mere spectator, quite left out in the cold.

—Interrupted here by Eddy, who is going to have his appendix out tomorrow.

So you're going to Italy.[2] Well, well. Damn. I shall come up to London to see you before you go. I enclose a postcard for you to tell me *when* you go. (American business methods.) Observe the address. I have become so much attached to my own name, that I now use it always. Note for future reference.

I can't come on Thursday, as the income-tax man is coming then. Otherwise free.

Your bewildered, happy, home-unsick,
V.

P.S. You are the one and only person I want to see. Where is the promised Flush?[3]

Sussex

1. Vita and Harold arrived home from America on April 20, 1933.
2. Virginia and Leonard were driving to Italy in their new car at the beginning of May.
3. Virginia finished the typescript of *Flush* in January and it was published in October 1933.

❧ *Tuesday [25 April 1933]* *52 T.[avistock] S.[quare, W.C.1]*

Well, Victoria West, here's your horrid little post card.

What I say is come and dine then next Friday? Can you? Only I should like to see you alone also—Could you come early? Would another time suit better?

. . . Ring me up, dearest Porpoise West, and say when.

Lord how nice to see the shops pink again!

Berg

 *Sissinghurst Castle,*
Kent.
17th May [1933]

Well, you have disappeared,—vanished from my ken,—lost in Italy,—staying, I daresay, at this moment with Iris Origo among the chestnut woods of Montepulciano or wherever it is she lives.[1] And I expect it is so lovely,—Italy in May,—that I won't even tell you about the bluebell woods here, which are better than anything in the Middle West, I promise you. Nor will I tell you about our charcoal-burner [heating system],—a new denizen of Sissinghurst,—nor about the two swans which have miraculously appeared on the lake, swimming about in white majesty throwing lovely long-necked reflections into the water. No, you have abandoned me, and I am left with nothing but Pinka for consolation—and do you know what? she won't take any notice of me. Pinka who can sniff me even while I'm still on the doorstep in Tavistock Square, and makes a piss, you'll admit, when I come in, won't have a thing to do with me when my guest. All her love is for Louise, whom she never leaves for an instant. I feel very crushed indeed.

She's been having copious doses for worms, tell Leonard. Louise calls her Mrs Pinka, I don't know why.

Are you very very happy? I am sending Ben to Italy for two months—wouldn't you like to be eighteen and going off to Italy alone for two months? I would. He is very nice, is Ben. How I love the young. I should like you to see him again now. You know his admiration for you; that ought to dispose you kindlily towards him, or are you sick of admiration?

And Cimmie Mosley is dead.[2] So beautiful, so young. I am sorry.

Darling, it does seem a bit hard that you should have vanished like this just when I have travelled 33,000 miles in order to see you again. But of course I can't hope to rival the attraction of a fluid fly-wheel.[3] You'd better come back soon though, or I shall begin exploring London for a divertisement. I have to go there tomorrow, and just fancy, I'm lunching with Sibyl.

Ethel wants me to go to Guildford to hear The Bosun's Mate. . . . I think not.[4]

Sorry my ink is going wrong. It is called Higgins' Eternal Ink, and was given me on Shakespeare's birthday the other day by a friend. It is nicely black, but I haven't quite learned how to manage it yet.

Would it surprise you to learn that I miss you very very much indeed? In order to console myself I am thinking of taking up with Marlene Dietrich. So don't linger too long at Montepulciano if you value the rather touching fidelity of your old sheep dog.

Berg

1. Marchesa Iris Origo, daughter of Lady Sybil Scott by her first marriage to Bayard Cutting. She lived in Val d'Orcia, south of Siena.

2. Cynthia, second daughter of Lord Curzon and Mary Leiter, had married Sir Oswald Mosley in 1920. She died on May 16, aged thirty-four, of acute appendicitis.

3. In February, Virginia had boasted of owning a new car—"silver and green, fluid fly wheel, Tickford hood—Lanchester."

4. Ethel Smyth's opera *The Boatswain's Mate,* which was first performed in 1916

❧ *May 20th [1933]* *Spotorno, Italy*

This is a strictly business like (only I happen to be tipsy, having drunk more than my half bottle tonight)

Yes. I am half dazed with travelling, so many cities have I seen, and smelt: now its the waves breaking, and the scent of stocks in the garden. . . . We're so brown cheeked red nosed and altogether dusty shaggy shabby—what a state my clothes are in—even I rather hesitate to wear them—for we lunch in the fields, under olives off ham, and its my duty to wash up, which affects my clothes. . . .

Berg

 *Sissinghurst Castle,*
Kent.
Whit Monday [5 June 1933]

Virginia, darling, you are an angel,—an angel, I mean, to understand so unfailingly when one really minds about something as I minded my mother telling Ben about my morals and Harold's.[1] Not that I am in any way ashamed of my morals or H's. Only Ben might have had a horrid imprint sealed on his mind. Luckily he didn't—a tribute, I think, to our bringing up of him? (That's a boast. But you, also, even you, boast sometimes. Your boasts mostly concern Princess Patricia[2] or some American publisher; mine, merely the way in which I have brought up my sons, so that they should accept without wincing the revelation that their father and mother are both to be numbered among the outcasts of the human race.) Anyway you are a darling to have realised that I minded.

I am slightly and unseasonably tipsy, for I went to a party at my tenants here, to celebrate their golden wedding, and had to drink to their health at lunch. It was the sort of party you would have liked: the old lady, who is just on 80, had tied a yellow ribbon round her neck, with the most coquettish little bow just behind her ear, and kept assuring me how happy her husband had looked on this day fifty years ago. The whole house was draped in Union Jacks. Why is it that patriotism must play a part in the most intimate family gathering? Their son had returned from Australia for the occasion,—they hadn't seen him since the war.

I enjoyed it more than any party I've been to for years. They were all more like characters in a novel than any character in any novel I've ever read. The old lady said to me, rather grimly, when I congratulated her, "Well it's better than divorce, anyhow."

And oh my God, Lady Northampton is coming to tea.[3] How much I prefer my tenants the Gosdens of Sattins Hill, to Lady Northampton of Castle Ashby or whatever it is.

And how much I prefer Virginia to either.

When am I going to see Virginia?

I haven't been to Brighton over Whitsun, or I would have come to Monk's House with a basketful of figs.

I'm writing poetry—but Mr [A. E.] Housman's theories have upset me. Have you read Mr Housman? If one adopts his theories, what becomes of the Prelude [Wordsworth], or the Testament of Beauty [Robert Bridges]?

Your
V.

Sussex

1. Virginia and Leonard lunched at Sissinghurst on May 28, and Ben Nicolson told her that Lady Sackville had spoken to him "about M. [Vita] getting hold of women and D. [Harold] of men—about Violet Keppel, Virginia Woolf etc." While Ben told the story, Virginia "listened . . . with her head bowed. Then she said: 'The old woman ought to be shot.'" For Ben Nicolson's description of the incident, see *Portrait of a Marriage* (1973).
2. Lady Patricia Ramsay, a granddaughter of Queen Victoria, who abandoned her title of princess on her marriage to Admiral Ramsay in 1919. Virginia had been seeing her occasionally in 1933.
3. Lady Emma Thynne, daughter of the Marquess of Bath, whom Lord Northampton married in 1921 but divorced in 1942. Castle Ashby was their splendid house in Northamptonshire.

Thursday [8 June 1933] *52 Tavistock Square, W.C.1*

Would you dine with me alone *upon my honour, on Monday next* MONDAY *12th—anytime you like. It is only that I shall be alone. Otherwise, I dont think its worth anyone's while to come to London. Could you angelically ring the telephone? . . .*

Forgive scrawl
Potto is the writer

Berg

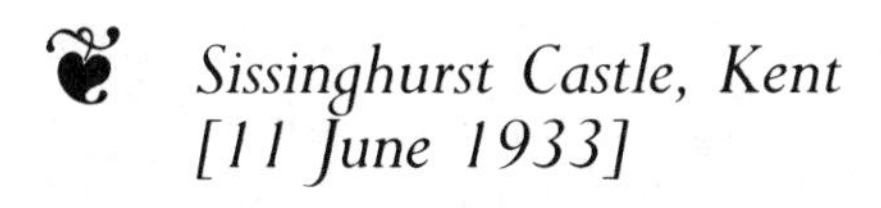

Sissinghurst Castle, Kent
[11 June 1933]

Isn't it enraging that of all people in the world your own particular Ethel [Smyth] should be the one to prevent me dining with you tomorrow? But there it is,—the engagement has been arranged for weeks past,—I get letters fairly trumpeting with excitement from Ethel by every post—supplemented by post cards and telegrams,—and so I felt I simply couldn't put her off—much as I longed to. Anyone else,—any herring griller,—could have gone to hell. But Ethel, I reflected, is 75 and one cannot play fast and loose with the old.

She's coming for the night. . . . . Says she wants to hear all about America. My God.

You haven't got another evening available, have you? I won't tell you how much I want to see you, because you wouldn't believe me—cynical woman that you are—not knowing the meaning of love.

I've been so lazy. I've pulled up millions of groundsel, and written a line of poetry (no, verse,) now and then, but serious literature such as a novel for the Hogarth Press, devil a bit—as a matter of fact I started one today. Didn't start it, so much as returned to a bit of vomit I spewed in America—the novel you said I was to write—all about deserts and hurricanes.[1] I don't know if I can make anything of it.

Now this letter will reach you in the evening, and either you'll be alone or else having someone to dine with you instead of me—and I shall be shouting at Ethel about the Middle West,—Harold shouting into one ear and me into the other,—whereas I might be sitting on the floor at your feet,—physically instead of metaphorically. I really do feel bitter about this.

I mustn't forget to provide a po for Ethel.

Alex [de Froissard] (our new secretary) has just come in to say may she borrow a novel? What sort of novel do you want, I say? Well, she says, shyly, might I have Orlando? So she has gone off with Orlando, and I wonder what she will make of it, being only twenty-four and never having been allowed hitherto to read any modern novels at all with the sole exception of Mr. Galsworthy, whom, to do her justice, she can't abide.

I can see the light in her bedroom window across the courtyard, and so suppose that she has taken Orlando to bed with her.

She has got a kettle which whistles like a nightingale, when it boils. It is audible all over our encampment.

Our encampment has been very lovely lately, with a peculiarly big moon and two planets. I wrote a poem about the two planets, which I think of calling 'Stellar Sodomy.' I'll send it to you if on further consideration I decide that it's proper enough for Alex to type.

Tell Leonard to read Harold's new book.[2] It is more in his line than yours, being political, but I think you would be amused by some passages in his diary, which is the second half of the book. I have a great admiration for

Harold,—quite unprejudiced. I like his lucid mind, and his ease of expression. He is like a person who knows how to use a scythe,—rhythmic, sharp, and sure.

Oh damn Ethel! I really am cross. Father, forgive them, for they know not what they do. She doesn't know that she has defrauded me of an evening with you.

Your
V.

Berg

1. Perhaps *Grand Canyon*, which wasn't published until 1942
2. *Peacemaking*, about the Paris Peace Conference of 1919

❧ *[23? June 1933]* *[52 Tavistock Square, W.C.1]*

Potto's love and 10/- to buy him shoes with: and a peasant womans hat. (But not not not *if theres a pressure or a rush or a difficulty) Lord how happy I was to see you!*

Berg

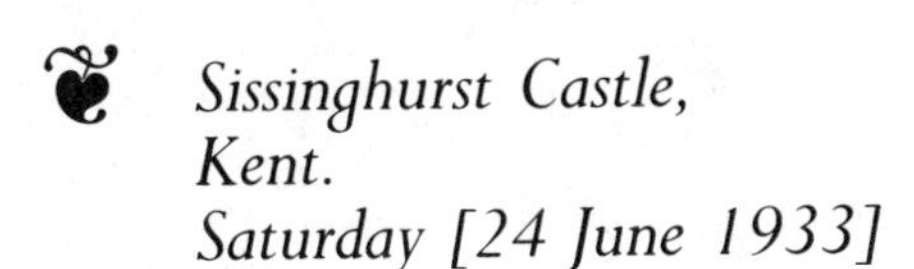

Sissinghurst Castle,
Kent.
Saturday [24 June 1933]

Really, Mrs. Woolf, I think you must have brought Potto up very badly, to let him send 10/- to an old friend for a pair of shoes. To mark my disapproval, I've cashed it and shall give the proceeds to the local cricket club. But I won't forget the shoes for Pott.

So Valerie [Taylor] is back, is she? Last time I heard of her,—in Hollywood it was,—she was just about to have her hips (HIPS, not LIPS) removed,[1] also the enamel from her teeth. That is the kind of thing that is done to people in Hollywood. I think of spending a winter there myself.

Yes it was nice to see you, but I feel rather like a starving man given one solitary crust. Oh I've got so much to say to you—but it takes hours—I mean, the sort of things I want to say to you require prolonged intimacy before they can squeeze themselves out. (That sounds horribly like Ethel.) Do you remember a night in Burgundy,—"Do you remember an inn, Miranda?"[2]—when I came along the dark passage to your room in a thunderstorm and we lay talking about whether we were frightened of death or not? That is the sort of occasion on which the things I want to say to you,—and to you only,—get said.

Well, I go off to Italy on Monday, and if you felt inclined to write and say you still had some affection for me, a letter would reach me at

Hotel Brufani
Perugia

on Monday July 3rd. That is about the only address I know of.

I have now got to go and see The Land performed at Chilham.

Tell Leonard I've been looking over my poems, and making indexes of them, and have achieved over 300 pages already,—quite enough for Vol I,—and that if he really wants a collected edition of all that tripe for the autumn, he can have it.[3] I daresay he is right, in saying that it would prepare the ground for any longish poem I might write later. Still, I can't rid myself of the idea that it is all a little pretentious,—much worse than becoming a Litt. Doc. of Manchester.[4] However. . . . .

Your
V.

Berg

1. "Rolled" was Harold's phrase, in his diary.
2. Hilaire Belloc, *Tarantella*
3. *Collected Poems*, Hogarth Press, London, 1933
4. An honorary degree that Virginia had just refused

 *4, King's Bench Walk,*
Temple, London, E.C.4.
Friday [14 July 1933]

Darling, I've just rung up the press, but hear you're away till Monday. We got back from Italy yesterday and were immediately sent for to go to Eton as Nigel was suspected of having appendicitis. We brought him straight up to London and he was operated on within the hour,—a frightfully bad case, very urgent, with the complication of an abscess, last night. He is dangerously ill, and they won't be able to tell till tomorrow how it will turn out. Harold and I are terribly worried as you may imagine. IF all goes well, can I come and see you both early next week? say Monday or Tuesday? Would you send me a line here (King's Bench Walk) to say when you will be back?

V.

Berg

 *Sissinghurst Castle,*
Kent.
Friday night [21 July 1933]

Virginia, I've come down here—going back to London on Wednesday morning.

You leave London on Thursday, don't you? for good? So would there be anything doing on Wednesday or not? Lunch? dinner? Would you come out to either of those functions with me? Come and lunch with me at the Café Royal on Wednesday? Or will you be too busy?

Still, you *must* lunch somewhere.

Will you tell your husband, please, that I return his announcement herein with two suggestions—and tell him please that I shall be a terrible bore to him about this edition [*Collected Poems*], because it is the only book of mine I shall ever have minded about—I.e. I don't give a damn for my novels, but I do give ½ a damn for my poems,—which is not saying much.

Normally I don't think I'm much of a bore as an author, vis à vis my publisher. But on this occasion I may become one.

HELL—I've just remembered: I'm lunching with Sibyl on Wednesday. Can you make it dinner or not? If not, I shall understand, as you are leaving London the next day.

Lunch Thursday if you like.

A postcard here—to Sissinghurst—

Main point: I do want to see you—but don't want to be an incubus.

V.

Berg

Wednesday [16 August 1933] — *Monks House [Rodmell, Sussex]*

Poor Virginia has been in bed; and thought how nice it would be to see Vita!: and is now up and says How nice it would be to see Vita! And L says (this is a terrific compliment) "I should like to see Vita." What about coming one day next week for the night? Could it be?

And who's Lady Roehampton in the Edwardians? Please tell me. . . .

But can you come?

If so, Ill write a long long letter. This is only Potto's scrawl

Berg

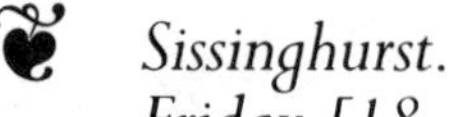

Sissinghurst.
Friday [18 August 1933]

Dear Mrs Woolf

(That appears to be the suitable formula.)

I regret that you have been in bed, though not with me—(a less suitable formula.)

About next week. I am more flattered than I can say by your suggestion that I should come to Rodmell, knowing how much you dislike invasion. I am all the more flattered by Leonard's support,—yes, I really do take that as a compliment. But next week is rather difficult, though not impossible. The point is, that I've got my sister-in-law staying here,[1] and she's been ill, and I am supposed to provide the cure. Country rustication and all that. And Harold is writing a book about Lord Curzon,[2] whereas I'm not writing any book at all, so I am free to look after his sister,—which I like doing, because [*five words omitted*] she is editing a book [*The Family Book*, 1934], at the moment, on advice to Parents, which I find fascinating,—I mean, I like seeing a really expert mind at work technically on such difficult matters. We sit on the steps of the tower discussing why some women get their physical satisfaction interiorally or exteriorally, and what connexion there may or may not be between the inner part of the nerve and the outer—and what connexion there may be between perversion and normality—and so on.

A very interesting question.

I might tell you more about it at 3 in the morning—but not in cold blood. Anyhow, it's a better subject for 3 in the morning than the butler's wages.

Well,—anyhow,—net result: can I come to Rodmell on Tuesday August 29th? for the night?

The Edwardians,—oh, that bloody book! I blush to think you read it. Lady Roehampton is Lady Westmoreland,—a lovely sumptuous creature who came to Knole when I was eight, and who first set my feet along the wrong path, I fancy, but who died, herself, relatively young, of drugs and a plethora of lovers. (No, it wasn't Lady Westmoreland who set my feet along the wrong path, now I come to think of it, but the Queen of Roumania who appeared in my schoolroom one day.)

Here is the post going.

Your
V.

Berg

1. Gwen St Aubyn, Harold's younger sister. In 1940 her husband, Francis (Sam) St Aubyn, succeeded his uncle as Lord St Levan.

2. *Curzon, the Last Phase*, about Curzon's period as foreign secretary, 1922–1924

❧ *Wednesday [30 August 1933]* *[Monk's House, Rodmell, Sussex]*

Just to say that I've been talking to Raymond, and I'm glad to say things aren't nearly as bad as it seemed. Francis [Birrell] has been to an expert, who says the growth is small, and he thinks on the outside of the brain. He is going to have the operation next week, but they think he ought to recover completely, though it is of course serious. He's up and about at present only with two paralysed fingers. This I write in haste, thinking you'd like to hear.

Berg

Sissinghurst Castle,
Kent.
1st September [1933]

They are shooting all round the place,—partridges of course,—first of September,—and I said "Rabbits" dutifully this morning when I woke up,—so now we can eat partridges and oysters,—and so another season opens,—"oh sweet monotony of the year." I forget who summed it up so neatly—but suspect myself—My memory, however, is so bad that I mistrust my own quotations.

(I am really getting rather worried about my memory: it is bad beyond all reason.)

It was nice of you to write to me about Francis—I really minded, thinking of that twinkly face in danger of complete extinction.[1] Raymond [Mortimer] writes this morning that they have reason to believe that the growth is on the *outside* of the skull—and that the operation itself would not be fatal. How horrible the body is, when it goes wrong. I wish I didn't mind so much about my friends,—not that Francis was ever an intimate friend of mine. He was just a person I liked, and God knows there are few enough of those.

Interruption: there is a man waiting to ask me about ancient pack-ways,—and there is one in my wood, which I must go and show him,—he also makes bricks and pottery.

When are you coming here on the way to Ellen Terry's house?[2] any day next week, except Thursday and Friday—RSVP

Tell Leonard a rival publisher is trying to bribe me away with £1000—but I won't be bribed, and have said so.

A faithful sheep dog? nicely trained to heel?

Your
V.

Berg

1. Francis Birrell died on January 2, 1935.

2. Smallhythe, ten miles from Sissinghurst, a cottage that had belonged to the famous actress from 1899 to 1928, and which she bequeathed to her daughter, Edith Craig. It now belongs to the National Trust.

❧ *15th Sept [1933]* *Monk's House, Rodmell, near Lewes, Sussex*

Dearest Creature,

I am a wretch never to have written—not that you care But there has been such a rain of visitors on my head that I couldn't escape. Next week is hopeless . . . but after the 23rd Heaven be praised, there'll be no one that I know of. . . .

My word, what a nice woman you are! Thats the very words I said, on reading your letter to Leonard. Moreover, they confirmed my own saying. He was rather in a stew, and thought we were making demands on your honour, integrity, friendship, magnanimity and so on. I said, Oh but Vita is like that. Then your letter comes to confirm it. It was a noble act though, tossing 1000 guineas into the duckpond, or cesspool, for to tell the truth, I dont like [Rupert] Hart Davies in the flesh, nor [Jonathan] Cape [publishers] in the spirit.

Berg

❦ *Sissinghurst Castle,*
Kent
Saturday [16 September 1933]

I had begun to wonder if you were X with me—though I didn't know why, and had a clear conscience. "After the 23rd" fits in beautifully, because it appears that they are producing "All passion spent" at the Croydon Theatre on that date, (with Jean Cadell as Lady Slane,) and I suppose I'll have to go and see a rehearsal one day next week, in order to prevent them from committing too many howlers. You might tell Leonard, would you, about this, if he doesn't know? because he would probably like to arrange with the theatre to have the book on sale there,

Croydon Repertory Theatre
Wellesley Road,
Croydon

is the address—as he did for The Edwardians.

Any day after the 23rd will do for you to come here,—I mean, I've no engagements, thank God. Try to come before Oct 4th when Ben goes to Oxford, because Ben likes you. Isn't that odd?

No, it wasn't [Jonathan] Cape who offered me the 1000 guineas. It was Cassell. Cape was quite a separate bribe. We had [*name omitted*] here, and I decided I couldn't bear him,—hairdresser's block that he is,—smug snob,—sparrow brain,—and too amiable by half. Anyhow, you can tell Leonard that no temptation to desert the Hogarth Press is any temptation at all. ~~One of the reasons I~~ No, I won't say that. It was going to have been a spiteful remark,—no, not spiteful exactly, but resentful on your behalf.

You will send me Flush, won't you? I shamelessly keep you to that promise.

I say: my poems are so *thin*. It really appals me, re-reading them all in a bunch, and thinking "Is that all I've got to show for half a life's experience?" I can hardly hope that you won't even glance at them, in your capacity as ½ my publisher, so I shall send you a copy in which I shall mark the only specimens I could bear you to read, and shall trust to your honour not to eavesdrop on the others.

My mother refuses to let me dedicate the book to her, so I think of dedicating it to Edith Sitwell instead.[1]

Lord, I must go and plant fritillaries.

When will you come?

V

Berg

1. But it was dedicated to Lady Sackville.

❧ *Saturday [30 September 1933]* *Monks House [Rodmell, Sussex]*

. . . we dined with Mary [Hutchinson], and her Jeremy wants to meet your Ben, so I said I would hand on the message.

Mary makes love to me—yes: other people dont. I daresay at this very minute you're couched with some herring griller in the straw God damn you. . . .

Berg

❧ *Wednesday 1st Nov. [1933]* *52 T.[avistock] S.[quare, W.C.1]*

"I saw Vita lunching at the Café Royal today" said Jack Hutchinson last night.

Oh such a pang of rage shot through me! All through dinner, and the supper . . . And it burnt a hole in my mind, that you should have been lunching at the Cafe Royal and not come to see me.

How pleased you'll be! You did it on purpose I daresay. But who were you with? You knew I should get wind of it—yes and it was a woman you were lunching with, and there was I, sitting alone and and and . . . . .

. . . Dearest Creature, do write and tell me who you were lunching with at the Cafe Royal—and I sitting alone over the fire! . . .

Oh the Cafe Royal! When Jack said that—not to me, but to the company, you could have seen my hand tremble; and then we all went on talking . . . and the candles were lit, and I chose mine, a green one, and it was the first to die, which means they say that out of the 8 or 9 people there, I shall be the first to wear a winding sheet. But you'll be lunching at the Cafe Royal!

Berg

 *Sissinghurst Castle,*
Kent.
Friday [3 November 1933]

My lunch at the Café Royal! Well, I was taking Gwen [St Aubyn][1] to a nursing-home, and took her to have some luncheon there first. We didn't then know if she had to have her head cut open or not. Thank goodness, it turns out to be *not*. But they say she won't be well for a year; perhaps not for two. She's having treatment for it,—a red-hot rabbit-hutch that they put over her head twice a day, and which makes her faint. They seem to think that this will dispel the injury to her brain.

I go to Wales on Monday and shan't be back till Saturday because I am going to stop at Oxford on the way back to see Ben, and Gwen is coming with me (if they will let her out of her hot hutch) to see her little boy [Giles St Aubyn] who is now at Summerfields [school] where Ben and Nigel were. I shall be in London on Monday Nov. 13th when I MAY have to lunch with your own Ethel—and have to give a lecture at 5 somewhere—but shall we dine together that night? Write to me here, and say.

I couldn't stay up in London yesterday, (Thursday) when I had suggested your telephoning to me; but I left a message for you with Gwen in case you rang me up.

I can't tell you how gratified I was by your annoyance (as you predicted) on discovering me in unknown company at the Café Royal—but if I hadn't been on so grim a mission you may be sure I should have let you know. As it was, I was with doctors and specialists all day—and didn't dare make any other appointments because of them and their erratic movements.

I've been worried—but am now slightly relieved.

I say! it's a shame for you to have my book [*Collected Poems*] in your hands, and me not.

I'm so sorry about Quentin—I am afraid that means he is ill—and if he is ill Vanessa will mind—and if Vanessa minds you will mind—and if you mind I mind.[2]

Damn—you won't get this letter till Monday if you're at Rodmell.

How lovely the woods are—brown, green, red, and gold.

Poor Francis [Birrell]—how sorry I am about him.

Tell me about dinner on the 13th—if you still have any affection left for a rather shabby sheep dog that gnaws its bone at the Café Royal.

Berg

1. Harold's sister had been in an automobile accident.

2. Quentin Bell had a persistent form of pleurisy and was going to spend three months in Switzerland.

22nd Nov. [1933] *52 T.[avistock] S.[quare, W.C.1]*

Oh faithless—why has everybody got a book and not I? Didnt I give you Flush and Orlando? Arent I a critic too—arent I a woman? Dont you care what I say? Am I nothing to you, physically morally or intellectually? . . . Look here, Vita, you may be putting off humanity and rising, like the day star, a dog—but do let your last act, in the guise of humanity, be to pack a book, called V. Sackville West Collected Poems *and sign it for me. . . .*

Do you know a woman called Phyllis Bottome?

And another called Jean Cadell?

Berg

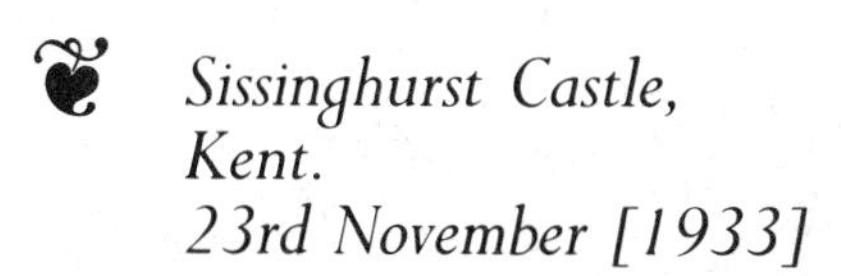

Sissinghurst Castle,
Kent.
23rd November [1933]

I have, as you may observe, been printing, and send you this my first effort.[1] It started by being Sissinchurst Gastle, Xent, but I have improved on that. But my God! what a complicated game! And does one ever get clean?

Do you know, it was my native modesty which prevented me from sending you my book [*Collected Poems*]. I couldn't believe you really wanted it. However, here it is. I wish somebody would review it, as at present it seems to be completely still-born.

No, I don't know Phyllis Bottome, except by name as a writer of (I think) magazine stories.[2] I do know Jean Cadell. She took the part of Lady Slane in All passion spent at Croydon the other day.[3] She's a very good actress—and I rather like her. She's Scotch. Why do you want to know about her? Sandy-haired; plain.

What about Dec. 15th? Shall you be in London? and shall I see you? Not dinner, because I am dining with Charles Siepmann[4] and going to Poil de Carotte [French film]—but how about tea-time?

Such a lot of gardening going on here—we are planting the loveliest shrubs—and Sissinghurst is going to be a riot.

Is it true that Berners is going to marry Violet?[5] I suspect the rumour of being a joke either on his part or on hers. Lord, to think how angry I should have been once!

Tell Leonard that never has a man been pined for as I pined for him yesterday when trying to print. He would have been flattered.

Have you read Michael Sadleir's book about Lady Blessington?[6] you would like it.

Ethel has sent me her book.[7] . . . . . . I lunched with her the other day—you weren't in London.

Now I must go on printing to make a cleaner job of it. I never realised that ink could be so ubiquitous.

Your
V.

Berg

1. An arrow is drawn in, pointing to a smudged imprint of "Sissinghurst Castle, Kent," where Vita and Harold had been attempting to print on the old Hogarth press, which Virginia had given her in 1930.
2. Phyllis Bottome (1882–1963), the novelist, who in 1917 married A. E. Forbes-Dennis. Vita had met her in Berlin (see her letter of March 8, 1928, and several following).
3. *All Passion Spent*, Vita's novel, was dramatized by Beatrice Kelston under the title *Indian Summer* and first performed at Croydon, with Jean Cadell as Lady Slane, on September 23.
4. Charles Siepmann succeeded Hilda Matheson as director of talks at the BBC, 1932–1935.
5. Lord (Gerald) Berners, a lifelong bachelor, had no intention of marrying Violet Trefusis, nor she him.
6. *Blessington-D'Orsay: A Masquerade*, 1933
7. *Female Pipings in Eden*, Ethel Smyth's latest autobiographical book

❧ *Sunday [26 November 1933]* *[52 Tavistock Square, W.C.1]*

And the book came. And I've read one or two of the new ones. And I liked them yes—I liked the one to Enid Bagnold; and I think I see how you may develop differently. You're an odd mixture as a poet. I like you for being 'out-moded' and not caring a damn: thats why you're free to change; free and lusty. . . .

Oh dear me, I wish I could read behind some of the poems!

Berg

1934–1936

Only three of Vita's letters to Virginia survive from these years, but as an indication of how far they maintained their friendship, Vita preserved twelve of Virginia's replies in 1934, eleven in 1935, and nine in 1936. Vita wrote two books: The Dark Island *and a life of Joan of Arc. Virginia, one:* The Years. *Harold entered Parliament in 1935. Vita's mother died early the next year, her death easing not only their financial situation (for Lady Sackville was a wealthy woman), but personal strains, for she had become increasingly eccentric. Yet Vita loved her. For Virginia, Ethel Smyth was still the most intimate among her friends. For Vita, her sister-in-law, Gwen St Aubyn.*

Castello,
Portofino.
6th February [1934]

I am writing to you on the terrace of a tiny old castle perched above the sea.[1] Two great stone-pines shield me from the sun, which is almost too hot. There is a rustle of lizards among the aloes. The sea sparkles three hundred foot below. In the distance are snow-mountains. A Franciscan monk with a rope round his waist and a vast grey beard has just been to call on me. A large bottle of golden wine stands at my elbow. I write and write and write,—which reminds me, would you please tell Leonard that I can probably give him my book by May or June.[2] I want to serialise it if possible, before publication, so that (if he wants it at all?) he had better regard it as an autumn feature. It is, at present, called *The dark island*, and I would be more than grateful if he could ascertain in any way if any book of that name already exists. Perhaps there is some catalogue of fiction available to him as a publisher? I don't know. But it sounds to me suspiciously like a title which has already been taken?

So much for business.

You see, I couldn't resist the castle. I started in a little hotel down in the village, and every evening I used to watch the castle turning pink in the sunset. So I made enquiries; found it was empty and to let; rang up the agent in Genoa, and in five minutes had arranged with him for immediate occupation. There is only a path up to it, so half the population turned out to carry our luggage up on their backs. And we were greeted at the door by the gardener with a large bunch of irises and narcissus, and by two perfect Italian servants called Teresa and Angela, who are 'characters,' and, as all 'characters' are apt to be bores.

No doubt about it, this is the way to live.

You might write to me, I think. But not here, for we leave alas on Sunday. Write to Hotel Majestic, Marrakesh, Morocco.

Your
V

Berg

1. Vita, with Harold and Gwyn, had taken a short lease of the Castello at Portofino in northern Italy, featured by Elizabeth Russell in *The Enchanted April* (1923); they then went to Morocco for three weeks.
2. Vita's *The Dark Island* was published by the Hogarth Press in October 1934.

❧ *18th Feb. [1934]* *52 T.[avistock] S.[quare, W.C.1]*

Yes it certainly sounds very nice, your castle. But you will have left it by now. You will be at Marrakesh, with the Princess Royal and Lord Harewood—this piece of news stares me in the face in Sundays paper. . . .

I've been laid up on the sofa in my dressing gown almost ever since you left—what a bore! I hope I didnt infect you that day in the car: the usual little chill; then the usual damned headache. . . . And I've dipped into ten thousand books. That reminds me—I told L., who shouted for joy, to find out about the dark island, and he says he's written to you. We both shouted for joy. Our list was looking very lean and dry—now nature's plenty has descended on it. What a blessing!

Berg

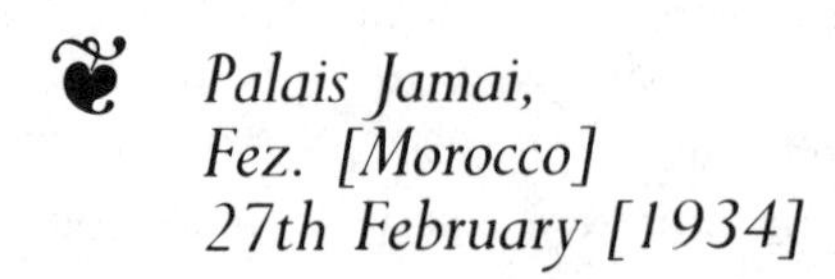

Palais Jamai,
Fez. [Morocco]
27th February [1934]

Darling, I am miserable to hear you have been ill; I learnt it from your letter which I got here yesterday, forwarded from Marrakesh, and also from Ethel [Smyth] sandwiched in between remarks about wishing men wouldn't force one to think them all rotters. I do, oh I do, hope you're better. You always seem to do this at this time of year, like when you returned from Berlin [in 1929]. Do send me even a postcard to the British Consulate General, Tangier, to say how you are; but say it truthfully.

We didn't really like Marrakesh as much as we expected to, so we came here, and are delighted to have done so, for Fez is one of the most enchanting places I have ever seen. We are lodged in an old Moorish palace [Palais Jamai], all blue and green tiles, fountains, terraces, weeping willows, and running water. It opens straight on to the old city, a secret and mysterious labyrinth of narrow streets where no wheeled traffic can ever come, and where majestic Moors ride by on scarlet saddles on tall mules or Arab horses. At dawn one is woken by the muezzins calling from a dozen minarets; and then somebody takes up with a snatch of song, and innumerable birds begin, and the storks clap their beaks like castanets on the house-tops. Incidentally we have shaken the royal party off our tracks,[1] and so far as I know there is no threat here in the way of acquaintances except Evelyn Waugh who is here for the purpose of writing a book.[2] My own book [*The Dark Island*] hasn't got on as well as I intended it to, for there is something in the air of Morocco which makes one stupid; Harold the ever-energetic complains of the same thing, which rather reassures me, as I had begun to think I should never be able to write a line again. Even large doses of Carter's Little Liver Pills don't seem to help, usually an infallible remedy. It is maddening, because one can't go sight-seeing all day, and so one has a good deal of time left over. But how disgusting of me to grumble, when *you* have to stop writing in order to lie on a sofa and feel hurt and wretched.

I see your books everywhere in Morocco, both in French and English—the latter in Tauchnitz. It's odd to meet Orlando in Marrakesh and

"*La promenade au phare*" [*To The Lighthouse*] in Rabat. I'm sure you like this!

Did I tell you I was going to motor home from Marseilles? If you and Leonard are going in the contrary direction, perhaps we shall meet on the way,—in Avignon, say, or St Rémy. I've sent for the motor to come and meet us.

Well I must go and have my luncheon, but I shall toss off a large glass of Moorish wine (which is rather good) to your recovery. My darling Virginia, my poor darling Virginia, I am really deeply unhappy to think of you ill in the fogs of London.

Your V.

Berg

1. Princess Mary, daughter of King George V, and her husband, Lord Harewood (previously Lord Lascelles when he had loved Vita in 1911–1912), whom they had spotted and avoided in Marrakesh
2. *A Handful of Dust*

❧ *5th March [1934]* *52 Tavistock Square [W.C.1]*

Yes, I am ever so much better. It was only the usual little temperature, which makes the headache hang about. But I am back in my room again, writing. . . .

However the fog is over . . . heaven be praised Ethel's mass has been played—but it was a joke to see her sitting in her triangular hat by the Queen's side in the Royal Box, among all the court. Afterwards she gave a tea party at Lyon's—a more sordid 6d. affair you cant imagine; marble slabbed tables, thick bread and butter, and the populace munching their cream buns. . . . and Ethel bellowing, as red as the sun, entirely triumphant, and self satisfied . . . .

And I'm flirting with a rather charming—oh dear me, this wont make you jealous, sipping roses at Fez. . . .

Berg

❧ *Friday [15 February 1935]* *52 Tavistock Sqre. [W.C.1]*

. . . I'm longing for an adventure, dearest Creature. But would like to stipulate for at least 48½ minutes alone with you. Not to say or do anything in particular. Mere affection—to the memory of the porpoise in the pink window.

I've been so buried under with dust and rubbish. But now here's the spring. . . .

My mind is filled with dreams of romantic meetings. D'you remember once sitting at Kew in a purple storm? . . .

So let me know, and love me better and better, and put another rung on the ladder and let me climb up. Did I tell you about my new love?

Berg

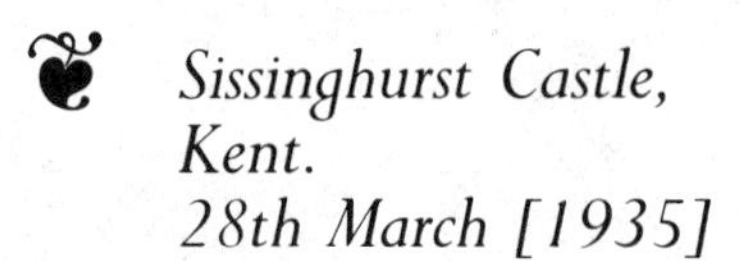

Sissinghurst Castle,
Kent.
28th March [1935]

Darling Virginia,

I hate to bother you, but Ethel [Smyth] has taken to writing me such extraordinary letters (and also to Gwen [St Aubyn],) that I thought I would warn you and also ask you if you can throw any light on her attitude? As you know, she dined at Gwen's house a short time ago,—to be exact, on the 8th of this month,—and was then perfectly friendly and her usual self. I was alone with her for a short time, and she made no critical remarks whatsoever. Next day Gwen sent her a present of oysters and I sent her a case of wine, because we had both felt so sorry for her in her troubles. She wrote to thank for these in her usual friendly way. Then, absolutely out of the blue, we both got letters from her in a very different strain, accusing Gwen of 'ruining' me; saying that we were leading 'a rotten life'; and were not fit to write the life of Joan of Arc (I had told her that Gwen was helping me with the actual research work.)[1] We both answered her letters as patiently as we could, but today I get another one, which begins "I tried to answer your letters—but I had such terrible things to say that I felt it is no good. We live in such totally different worlds of ethics, have such different ideas on the subject of sanity, truth, honesty, clean living, duty, religion, kindness . . . that there is no common language between us," and so on.

Now what does all this mean? and what has happened between that dinner and now to have put her into that mood?

Of course I know she is an outspoken person who always says, and says brutally, what she thinks; I know also that she has written you letters which have made you very angry, telling you what she conceives to be home-truths. I should not take so much notice if I thought she would confine her remarks to me, but it does worry me to think she may be chattering and discussing me and my affairs with all and sundry. I shouldn't mind her talking to *you*, because you know me and you know Ethel—and I am quite happy to leave the judgment to you—but to other people who don't know either me or Gwen she may be giving a very dangerous impression. Have any echoes of anything of the sort reached you? If so, I know you will tell me, and I know also that if you do see Ethel and she starts on the subject, you will tell her firmly that gossip of the sort is a very poor form of friendship,—for she still professes to have a genuine affection for me. I must say, it's an odd way of showing it!

The only thing which I have always known her to hold against me, is that old story of Christopher St John[2]—but that subject has long been closed—Ethel never could see my point of view, so we agreed to drop it—so I don't think that that can have anything to do with her latest move.

I am going to Greece next week (Thursday),[3] so do be an angel and send me a line before then.

Your rather worried

V.

Sussex

1. Vita's *Saint Joan of Arc* was published in 1936 by Cobden-Sanderson.
2. Christopher St John, Ethel's friend and future biographer, had fallen in love with Vita, her neighbor in Kent. Vita reciprocated her affection, but not her love. The Ethel-Vita friendship was soon mended.
3. A Mediterranean cruise with Harold, Gwen, Hugh Walpole, and Nigel

❧ *Friday [29 March 1935]* *52 T[avistock] S.[quare, W.C.1]*

Lord what a nuisance about old Ethel!

I'm afraid I cant throw much light on it because I dont understand it myself. . . . Certainly, I've heard no echoes; if any should reach me, I will let fly at her. Or would you like me to write to her? I dont expect to see her until after Easter. But to do her justice, I dont think she would ever abuse one to enemies or acquaintances, only to old friends, whom one hopes can be trusted to discount it. But its always worrying I know. . . .

Berg

1937

Although, in November 1937, Vita began a letter "My (once) Virginia," and told her not to answer, Virginia did, reassuringly, "saying, in effect, that she would always be there for Vita, and life and meaning returned to their letters and meetings" (Victoria Glendinning, Vita, *p. 291). One event had brought them together again. In July, Virginia's nephew Julian Bell was killed in the Spanish Civil War. Vanessa Bell sent a message to her sister, through Vita, that nobody but Virginia had consoled her more. At the same time, Vita paid tribute to her own mother with* Pepita, *a dual biography which was instantly acclaimed. Vita was now a major writer, in popular, if not critical, esteem. She was forty-five.*

Sissinghurst Castle,
Kent.
15th January [1937]

Oh you wretch! first you tell Ethel I'm going to London—and then you tell her I've *been* to London—and I've thereby hurt her feelings without meaning to—but not irremediably I hope, as she has found a new puppy which I am to give her. It has either two mothers or two brothers, I can't read which—Anyhow she seems happy again, which is all I wish for, for I do believe she has made herself truly miserable over Pan V.[1]

As for my London season, it was entirely wrecked by

(a) your brother-in-law [Clive Bell]
(b) the telegraph clerk at Lewes,
and
(c) yourself, by being away from Tavistock Square.

Still, I gave a very nice cocktail party which was attended by several of your friends, and you were much missed—

I will appear punctually at 1. on January 22nd and we will do anything you like until Mrs ex-J. Chamberlain claims me at 5. I'll tell you then why I am going to tea with your ex-love.[2] (Why have you so many ex-loves, by the way?) It's something to do with you, indirectly.

I saw your portrait in the floor at the National Gallery.[3] Do I much like the idea of the feet of London's and America's millions trampling over you? No, not much. Sheep dogs growl when they see such things.

V.

I have run out of envelopes—

Sussex

1. All Ethel Smyth's sheep dogs were named Pan. This was the fifth.
2. Mary Chamberlain (*née* Endicott, of the United States) was the widow of the British statesman Joseph Chamberlain. After his death she married William Carnegie, sub-Dean of Westminster Abbey, in 1916. Virginia had known the Chamberlains when her half-brother George Duckworth was secretary to Joseph's son, Austen, but the idea that Virginia and Mary were ever lovers was pure fantasy on Virginia's side.
3. A mosaic by Boris Anrep, completed in 1933, which represented several prominent women as classical figures, including Virginia as Clio and Greta Garbo as the Muse of Tragedy.

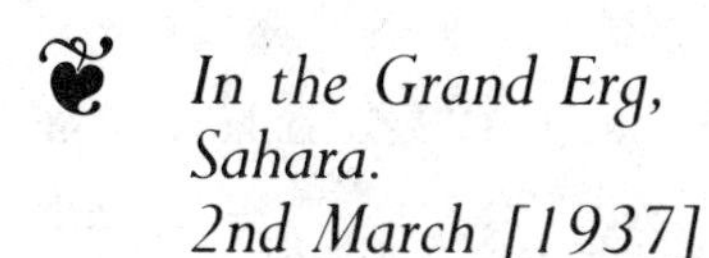

In the Grand Erg,
Sahara.
2nd March [1937]

I write to you sitting at the door of my tent. All around us are the sand-dunes. But what can that convey to you? or how can I convey it to you? It is like nothing else. Just a strange geography of valleys, hill ranges, ridges, peaks, slopes pure as snow, all formed of golden sand. Golden, yes, in the sun; but in the shadows it turns pink or violet, and all the time it changes both its shape and its colour. We have seven Arabs (nomads) with us, two camels, a mule, a sheep (to eat), and a sloughi [Saluki] which is used for hunting gazelle. Every now and then one of the Arabs plays his flute, or sings a brief snatch of melancholy song.

We had meant to start on this expedition yesterday, and had indeed set out, but a sudden sand-storm arose and instantly the whole landscape was obliterated in clouds of sand, thick as a white fog. So we had to turn back. It lasted all day and most of the night. Our tents and provisions had been sent ahead, and during the night one of the tents blew away, and so did the live chicken, which has never been seen again. It was last seen sailing away across the Sahara.

We have been hunting little pink salamanders with one of the Arabs. They bury themselves in the sand, and you trail them by their tracks; then you dig suddenly, and pounce. Leonard would like that game. I am bringing back a tin-ful, to try and keep in a greenhouse at home. Unfortunately the Arab knows only about six words of French, so we had to communicate by smiles and gestures.

Tonight we have a feast of the sheep roasted whole. Our drinks are kept as cool as in your frigidaire by being buried deep in the sand; our bread is baked in the sand, so you see it serves all purposes.

From here we move on to a curious region ever further out into the desert, which is inhabited by people who are said to be the descendants of the ancient Carthaginians.

Back in England on the 13th.

I don't feel like a person who can write letters at all. I do however feel very much more like a person than I ever do in England; I mean, I am just a thing that eats, sleeps, lies in the sun, and forgets time and everything else.

Next day. The whole sheep was dumped on the dinner table (a rickety affair at best) last night, wrapped in a sheet of brown paper. We had to unwrap it, and there it was, head, horns, genitals and all, exposed before us. Then we had to tear it to pieces with our fingers and eat. After dinner the Arabs made a fire in the sand, and we sat round while they danced and sang to the flute. The desert stars blazed above us, and after a while the moon came up.

I've also given a dervish party. They stuck daggers and hammered nails into their naked stomachs. It was a fine party. They danced holding flaring torches to their chests and faces. Then I spent a week in a ruined Roman camp [Timgad, Algeria]. Oh, it's fun, being abroad! How smug it makes our island seem. It hasn't rained here for three years. I shall be back by the middle of March.

You are lavishly represented in the Tauchnitz edition everywhere. I brought The Waves with me, and re-read it with emotion. I like the 2nd half the best,—lovely, lovely pages.

By the way, Ben (I say "by the way" because he so likes The Waves,) is living in London, 72 Gloucester Place. If ever you had people in after dinner, would you let him come? He would love it. He is writing a book on Seurat![1]—rather ambitious, I think, but I'm all for the young biting off more than they can chew.

Will I see you when I come back?

Your
V.

Sussex

1. This book never progressed beyond the research stage, but Benedict Nicolson developed into a distinguished art historian as editor of the *Burlington Magazine* and author of several scholarly books covering a wide field of art history.

Sissinghurst Castle,
Kent.
14th June [1937]

Shall you be in London on July 1st? a Thursday. And if so, should I come to lunch with you? The worst of it is, I have to broadcast at 3.15, so would have to leave you in time for that—Still, it would be better than nothing. May I?

Will you tell Leonard I am sending an ultimatum to Mr Curtis Brown, to the effect that if he doesn't produce a definite offer for serialising my book within the next ten days, I shall take it that serialisation is definitely off, in which case Leonard will receive the typescript by June 30th as per agreement, for autumn publication.[1] I am fed up with Mr Curtis Brown.

I liked getting your post card of Georges [*sic*] Sand.[2]

I have found a portrait of an ancestor of mine who is far more like me than any which we found for Orlando! It is a frightening likeness. I will try to remember to bring it on July 1st, if I may come to you then, as I HOPE.

Tell Leonard, too, that I've got eight Alsatian puppies—5 weeks old—and does he want one, or are Sally's puppies too imminent for him to contemplate any others?

Your loving
V.

Berg

1. Vita's dispute with Spencer Curtis-Brown, the literary agent, concerned the serialization of *Pepita*, her biography of her grandmother and mother, which the Hogarth Press published in October 1937. Lady Sackville had died in January 1936.
2. A portrait of the French writer by Charpentier, which Virginia had sent Vita from near the Chateau de Nohant, George Sand's home. Vita always misspelled "George" as "Georges."

❧ *June 17th [1937]* — *52 Tavistock Square, W.C.1.*

Yes, it would be better than nothing—lunch July 1st—one o'clock, so as to spin it out.

Ah hah! (This refers to Curtis Brown). But this business matter must be left for you and L. As for The Alsatians—no: no: What have we spent the last days doing? Rigging up a lying in bed in L's study [for Sally]; the event comes off this Sunday. Thus we cant go to Rodmell. Dogs enough; if dogs there be. Some say she's still virgin. George [Sand] (not an S) certainly wasnt. Have you read her Memoirs? Do: But no more now—

Berg

❧ *Wednesday [21 July 1937]* — *[52 Tavistock Square, W.C.1]*

Dearest Creature

I wired to you because Julian was killed yesterday in Spain. Nessa likes to have me and so I'm round there most of the time. It is very terrible. You will understand

Berg

 *Sissinghurst Castle,*
Kent.
22nd July [1937]

My darling Virginia

I am so terribly sorry. You know how often one says one is sorry, and one is, but there is a difference between being very sorry and sorry-to-matter. I am sorry-to-matter about Julian.[1] He was such a charming alive person,—do you remember when you took me to tea with him in his rooms at Cambridge?—and he might have done so much and enjoyed life so fully, and now! . . . Then apart from him as a person I mind about you, for I know you were fond of him; and about Vanessa. I mind for her own sake, and also for yours, for you must suffer to see her suffering. And Clive too. I wish I could tell you how much I mind.

I couldn't come to see Leonard, and anyway I didn't feel that in the circumstances I should be anything but in the way.

Darling Virginia—I wish I could do or even say something. You are so very dear to me, and you are unhappy—and I can do nothing—except be your ever very loving

V.

Sussex

1. Julian Bell went to Spain as one of a team of ambulance drivers on the Republican side in the Civil War. He was attached to a British medical unit based in the Escorial Palace near Madrid, and was mortally wounded by a shell on July 18 outside the village of Villanueva de la Canada. He was twenty-nine years old.

[26? July 1937] *52 Tavistock Square, W.C.1*

Dearest Creature,

I was very glad of your letter. I couldnt write, as I've been round with Vanessa all day. It has been an incredible nightmare. We had both been certain he would be killed, and the strain on her is now, perhaps mercifully, making her so exhausted she can only stay in bed. . . .

Lord, why do these things happen? I'm not clear enough in the head to feel anything but varieties of dull anger and despair. . . .

Berg

 *Sissinghurst Castle,*
Kent.
21st September [1937]

My only Virginia,

First, for an intelligent woman, which every American magazine which I open assures me that you are, I must say that you betray a singular lack of even ordinary sense in describing yourself as 'visitors who interrupt and bore.' Don't you know how I *love* seeing you always? and what an especial joy it is to have you here? and what a benefit you confer on me, a lasting treasure, by coming?

Second, thank you for the letter.[1] I return it. I agree with Leonard that it is the effusion of a maniac, else why should the poor man go into his wife's past history? I hope you won't follow his advice, but still I have a certain secret pride in the thought that "your affair with V. S-W." should enable you to write with authority. Would it? There is much to be said on that subject, but perhaps it would be better said by firelight on a winter evening when one had omitted to turn on the lights.

If you are really in Paris in October, I shall be there on the 14th, 15th, and 16th I *think.* I say 'I think,' because you know how one's dates are liable to alteration when one motors—but these dates are pretty certain. Hotel Crillon, Place de la Concorde, will find me there then, so perhaps I shall find a note from you? . . . By the way, Gwen will be with me; I don't suppose you mind that, but I thought I'd better tell you. It would be fun to dine at the Exhibition?[2] Harold is in Paris till tomorrow, when he returns, so I shall have heard about all the most amusing places from him.

I have spent a lovely day with the game-keeper from Knole, who came here to fish—and also Nigel and I have been excavating the foundations of the old castle, out in the [Sissinghurst] orchard.

Your loving
V.

This is a private postscript. I had a note from Vanessa which ends thus: "I cannot ever say how Virginia has helped me [after Julian's death]. Perhaps, some day, not now, you will be able to tell her it's true."

Perhaps I ought not to quote this to you, but I don't see why not. In any case, please keep it to yourself.

Berg

1. Virginia had received a letter from an American asking her to write an article about Vita, adding that Virginia's "affair with V. Sackville-West" should make her an authority on the subject.
2. The major International Exhibition staged in Paris that year. Virginia did not join them.

❧ *Oct 1st [1937]* *Monks House [Rodmell, Sussex]*

We have been so ridden with visitors that I never had a moment to write. In fact I was so touched by your letter that I couldnt. Isnt it odd? Nessa's saying that to you, I mean, meant something I cant speak of. And I cant tell anyone—but I think you guess—how terrible it is to me, watching her: if I could do anything—sometimes I feel hopeless. But that message gives me something to hold to. . . .

Berg

 *Sissinghurst Castle,*
Kent.
13th November [1937]

My (once) Virginia

You said I was a fool not to write to you when my pen wriggled to do so.

Well, it wriggles now. I write from the pink tower, which you like.

I hear echoes of you—from Eddy for instance, who says he went to tea with you. I felt envious. I felt I could have come to tea with you on far closer terms than Eddy. Why don't I? Just because I am not in London—and Eddy frequently is. Isn't it a pity that geographical distance should make such a difference?

Anyway we are going to have some jaunts of our own liking in January, aren't we? Where shall we go? To Kew? Do you ever think of me?

If you do, please imagine a Sissinghurst very muddy, with busynesses going on, such as gardening (ask Leonard, who *is* a gardener, and he will tell you that all gardeners have an orgy of planting and transplanting at this time of the year. You may have seen him and Percy busy at it.[1])

Such an unpleasant party of people came here, their hands shaky from drink or drugs, I don't know which; I hated them; they made the sort of impression one doesn't forget.

Is this just a letter to be put up behind your paper-weight on the mantelpiece, to be answered some day? If so, I'd rather you didn't answer it at all. Or among Ethel's letters? What an awful thought!

No, Virginia, please don't answer it. I shall know it has arrived and that you will recognise it as a thought of love from your Orlando.

The servants made such a lovely bonfire here on Guy Fawkes' day [November 5]. I thought of you, as the flames shot up. They had fireworks too, and turned the whole front of Sissinghurst pink as though it blushed. They put the fireworks into a dustbin, and blew the lid up into the sky.

Behind all this nonsense, is the horror of Spain [Civil War]. I do mind about it so much. And all the rest of the world too—Only, Spain is in the foreground for the moment.

A rather inconsecutive letter, I fear, (I've just read it over,—you know how one does, at the bottom of the page,) but somehow I always turn to you when I feel like the dustbin with fireworks inside it.

Your
V.

Berg

1. Percy Bartholemew, gardener at Monk's House

❧ *15 Nov. [1937]* *52 T.[avistock] S.[quare, W.C.1]*

Why 'once' Virginia? Why mayn't I answer your letter? That of course is the way to make me sit down at once and answer it. Why are you a dustbin? And why shouldn't we go for a jaunt? Why, why, why?

Just because you choose to sit in the mud in Kent and I on the flags of London, thats no reason why love should fade is it? Why the pearls and the porpoise should vanish. . . .

So no more—But if your pen should again take to twisting, let it.

Because, my dear Vita, whats the use of saying 'once *Virginia' when I'm alive here and now? So's Potto if it comes to that*

Berg

❧ *[26? December 1937]* *Monks House, Rodmell*
[Sussex]

Its not due to you that I'm alive today: I've eaten the whole pie practically myself!

Heaven above us, what immortal geese must have gone to make it! It was fresh as a dockleaf, pink as mushrooms, pure as first love. (but first love conveys nothing to the hardened and battered—this I put in by way of an aside) It was so divine, I could forgive any treachery. My word what a pie! Tom Eliot was dining with us the night it came. Complete silence reigned. The poet ate; the novelist ate; Even Leonard, who had a chill inside, ate. Nothing of the least importance was said. Where do they come from? Could one send a card and have one at will? It seems incredible. . . . oh did I tell you I'd been offered an Order?—I forgot—they thought I'd come from Buckingham Palace. A kind of Order of Merit.

But Orlando, pink porpoise, isnt it against our Covenant to do this sort of thing? Dont you remember offering me Thackerays wine cooler or ash tray [paper knife] or something in the days of the fishmonger and how I said: Unhand me Sirrah?

. . . Ethels in ecstasies over her pate. 12,000 copies of Pepita sold.

I'm thinking of buying a fur coat

Berg

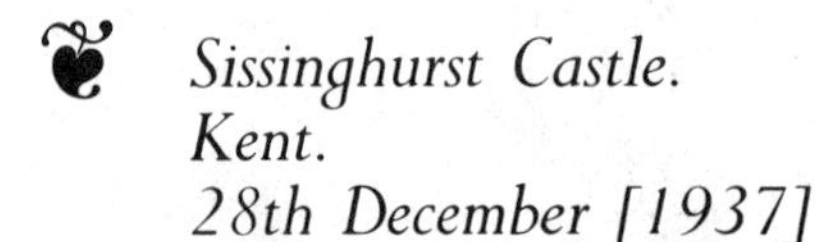

Sissinghurst Castle.
Kent.
28th December [1937]

Yes, of course a postcard will produce a paté at will. You send it to

M. Robert Gerst
7 rue des Frères,
Strasbourg (Bas-Rhin,)

and if you wish to give a reference as to your respectability, (assuming M. Gerst not to be a man of letters,) you mention my name. He will no doubt accept it as a guarantee, for he has known both my mother and me for many years. M. Gerst has an enchanting catalogue, which he will send you on request, but once you get into his clutches you are lost: your life becomes one vast truffle and your cooking is based entirely on paté de fois gras.

What's all this about your being offered an Order? I should like to know more, please. Could you rival Ethel as a Dame?[1] Or what? I am really intrigued, and should like a post-card if you have no time for more.

Glad Pepita is going to furnish you with a fur-coat. I continue to get the oddest and nicest letters about her. Hugh [Walpole] is the latest recruit among her admirers. Is it true by the way that someone threw an all-in wrestler over the ropes at Hugh and injured him severely?[2]

You sized up my ex-temporary-secretary nicely,—the one who rang me up about the dogs while I was dining with you. When I returned here next day [*fifteen words omitted*] I had to sack her on the spot. No fault of mine. (N.B. this is not to be repeated, as I shall be had up for libel.)

Sibyl was to have come here today for luncheon, but has met with a street accident,—been knocked down, in fact. So do be careful when you go for your London walks. It is not a safe place, and I am glad I have the wisdom not to live in it. All the same I regret not being nearer to Virginia whom I love. Lord, how lovely you looked the other night in your black and scarlet!

Your pink porpoise
Orlando.

Berg

1. Ethel Smyth was created a Dame of the British Empire in 1922. Virginia was not offered an Order. It was known that she refused all titular honors offered to her, and here she was joking.
2. This curious incident occurred in Los Angeles in February 1936.

1938

International tension mounted, and achieved a temporary respite in the Munich agreement in September 1938. Virginia published Three Guineas, *a condemnation of male vanity and aggression with which Vita could not wholly agree. Her accusation that Virginia had employed "misleading arguments" led to the only quarrel between them, and it was soon mended. Vita wrote to Harold after a visit to Rodmell: "Oh my dear, what an enchanting person Virginia is! How she weaves magic into life!" The recollection of their past love irradiated their continuing but more distant friendship. In her new poem,* Solitude, *published by the Hogarth Press in this year, Vita hinted at the contrast between her ephemeral love affairs ("Those cheap and easy loves") and what Virginia still meant to her.*

 *Sissinghurst Castle,*
Kent.
1st April 1938

It is a mangy sheep dog that writes to you, Virginia, but I thought I had better write in case you got given some garbled version of my disasters [illness] and thought them worse than they were. Also I feel I owe you an explanation for never having followed up the alluring suggestion that we should go to Mourning becomes Electra together, as I had fully intended to do.

Well . . . . You know I was ill in January with what was thought to be jaundice and internal inflammation? Well, I went on getting attacks of it, and having to take to my bed with pains, and I lost 2 stone in weight, and altogether felt wretched. So they decided it must be gallstones, and during the last attack 10 days ago they rushed me up to London by ambulance to be X-rayed etc—and then, having put me in a nursing home and taken pints of blood out of my arm, they discovered it wasn't gallstones at all, but lead-poisoning. How I got it is not yet clear; the cider-press [at Sissinghurst] is suspected, though as that hasn't got a particle of lead in it I can't see how it can have come about; anyhow, there it is: I am full of it. I daresay my aunt Amalia[1] has something to do with it, with her Borgian ancestry.

I escaped from the home yesterday and am perfectly all right, except for being a bit shaky,—rather like a newly born lamb, wobbly at the knees. Otherwise I am as well as usual, and within a short time it will all have disappeared out of my system. In the meantime I have a lovely sylph-like figure, and have to keep my clothes up by means of safety-pins.

I would have let you know I was in London, but (1) I didn't want to bother you, (2) I was only there for 5 days, (3) I scarcely had a minute to myself owing to a procession of specialists, X-ray, and so on.

So there is my little explanation, and you must forgive the total egotism of this letter, which could be excelled neither by Eddy nor by Ethel. I am fully aware of that.

Any chance of your passing this way? The garden has gone mad,—everything out—

Your
V.

Berg

1. Sister of Lady Sackville; both were illegitimate daughters of Pepita and Lionel Sackville.

❧ *Tuesday [5 April 1938]* *52 T.[avistock] S.[quare, W.C.1]*

. . . I am miserable to think how bad you've been; and going through all that torture of waiting for results. Are they sure they've spotted it now? And why lead from Cider? Isn't it from painting a greenhouse?—But if you have a moment let me have a word. We both sit up like begging dogs, with our paws up, sending our faithful humble sympathy. And how do they de-lead you? . . .

Berg

Sissinghurst Castle,
Kent.
11th May 1938

Ben has just returned from London and tells me he met you lunching with Clive and that you asked after me. This makes me feel very guilty, as I have been meaning to write to you for some days. I am all right for the moment, though I am told that fresh attacks may leap on me without warning. However, I think not. I think my extraordinarily robust constitution will defeat the grim prognostications of the doctors. I shall feel I have scored, if I do escape without further attacks.

So you are going to the Hebrides! So am I, but not until August. I am going there to lunch with Nigel on his own island,[1] a somewhat doubtful undertaking, as the storms are frequent and the fishing-boats tiny. So we may get held up for days, but I hope for good luck in weather.

Would there be any chance of seeing you here? No, I suppose not. That is too much to hope for. But what a delight it would be! I suppose I must hope only for a day at Rodmell (sandwiched in between Ethel and Sibyl) some day in September. Still, I would love to see you and Mitzi [Leonard's marmoset] and Sally [dog] and Leonard here.

By the way, my Jacob's Sheep had twins apiece, and my dear dear Mrs Staples [Vita's cook] had a daughter two days ago, who is going to be called Josephine after Pepita. Isn't all that nice for me?

What did you think of Ben? I am so cross with him at the moment, for having missed his train, that I can't see straight about him. Normally, I like and even love him. I hope he doesn't go Bloomsbury.

Your loving
V.

Berg

1. The uninhabited Shiant Islands, north of Skye, which Nigel had just purchased. Vita never went there. Virginia and Leonard went to Skye in June of that year.

❦ *Sissinghurst Castle,*
Kent.
30th May 1938

I thought I must have committed some crime when I saw a typed letter from you signed "yours faithfully Virginia Woolf," but I quickly saw it was all right, and have sent a small donation to the library.[1] As it happened, I got a letter from a French friend of mine by the same post,[2] bothering me to ask you for your autograph for her collection. This I should have refused to do, but as fate has delivered "yours faithfully Virginia Woolf" into my hands, do you mind if I cut it off and send it to her? I wouldn't do so without your permission. Although a bore, she is quite respectable,—is a princess by birth, a countess by marriage, and a great-grand-daughter of Mme de Stael by descent. She prides herself on never having bought an autograph for her beastly collection.

May I send it? I enclose a postcard for your reply, to save you trouble.

What about your book?[3] I thought it was coming out this month, but have seen no more about it.

How very nice it was, coming to dinner with you. You know, I like your house better than any other house; its atmosphere, I mean. I always come away feeling that life is more worth while. This sounds like a phrase, but is the right truth. Will you let Ben come in after dinner one night when you have got people there any how? I mean, if you have got people to dinner anyhow, he wouldn't be wasting your time, and he would so love it. Only don't tell him I suggested it, or he would half murder me.

I went to Edy Craig's barn-theatre yesterday,[4] and she made an

1. The feminist library in Marsham Street, Westminster, founded by the London National Society for Women's Service, of which Virginia was an enthusiastic patron, appealing to all her friends for subscriptions.

2. Probably Princess Anne-Marie Callimachi

3. *Three Guineas*

4. Edith Craig lived with Christopher St John in the house of her mother, Ellen Terry, at Smallhythe, Kent, where she had organized a society for the production of plays in a converted barn.

appeal to the audience to obtain new members, so (knowing that you had been flirting with the idea for several years) I told them to send you the necessary information.

For their next show they are having marionettes. You need not do anything about it unless you want to, but I do think it would be fun if we could go there together, or meet there. You could come to luncheon at Sissinghurst first.

Your loving
V.

Sussex

❧ *1st June [1938]* *52 T[avistock] S.[quare, W.C.1]*

The book [Three Guineas] comes out tomorrow. Its only a piece of donkey-drudgery, and as it repeats in still soberer prose, the theme of that very sober prose The Years, which, rightly, you didnt like, I hadn't meant to send it. But I will, by way of thanks, and you need neither read it nor write and say you have. Both those books are now off my mind, thank God. Why did I feel I must write them? Lord knows.

Berg

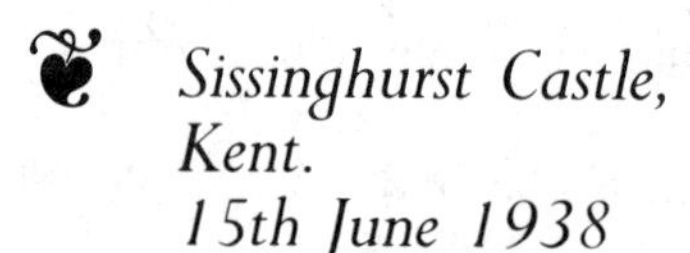

Sissinghurst Castle,
Kent.
15th June 1938

If I haven't yet written to thank you for your three guineas, it is only because I knew you were going off to Skye, not because I didn't savour it. You are a tantalising writer, because at one moment you enchant one with your lovely prose and next moment exasperate one with your misleading arguments. You see, so provocative a book can't be thanked for in a mere letter; it would need a reply as long as the book itself, and that would mean a publication by the Hogarth Press. And far be it from me to cross swords with you publicly, for I should always lose on points in fencing, though if it came to fisticuffs I might knock you down. So long as you play the gentleman's game, with the gentleman's technique, you win.—I am not explaining myself very well, indeed very badly and confusedly, so shall we leave it till we meet? In the meantime, let me say that I read you with delight, even though I wanted to exclaim, "Oh, BUT, Virginia . . ." on 50% of your pages.

What a little imp of mischief Jeremy is.[1] Ben has now secured a tenement in Soho, and his address is 47 Dean Street, Soho, W.1. He would jump at any invitation you proffered.

Did you like Skye? Did you go to Sligachan? Did you see The Old Man of Storr and the Cuillins?[2]

Your
V.

Thank you for the autographs, in the super plural[3]—I sent one to my French princess.

Berg

1. Jeremy Hutchinson, son of Jack and Mary, who had been a close friend of Ben at Oxford and later became a distinguished barrister
2. Sligachan was a hotel on the Isle of Skye where Virginia had expected to stay; "The Old Man of Storr," a remarkable pinnacle of rock on the island; and the Cuillins, the main mountain mass of Skye.
3. In her response to Vita's request, Virginia had sent her a card inscribed with her autograph written seven times over.

❧ *19th June [1938]* — *George Inn, Chollerford*
Northumberland

. . . Of course I knew you wouldn't like 3 gs—thats why I wouldn't, unless you had sent a postcard with a question, have given it you. All the same, I dont quite understand. You say you don't agree with 50% of it—no, of course you dont. But when you say that you are exasperated by my "misleading arguments"—then I ask, what do you mean? If I said, I dont agree with your conception of Joan of Arc's character, thats one thing. But if I said, your arguments about her are "misleading" shouldn't I mean, Vita has cooked the facts in a dishonest way in order to produce an effect which she knows to be untrue? If thats *what you mean by "misleading" then we shall have to have the matter out, whether with swords or fisticuffs. And I dont think*

whichever we use, *you will, as you say, knock me down. It may be a silly book, and I don't agree that its a well-written book; but its certainly an honest book: and I took more pains to get up the facts and state them plainly than I ever took with any thing in my life. . . .*

Berg

❧ *22 July [1938]* *52 T.[avistock] S.[quare, W.C.1]*

Leonard says you have sent a poem, and would like to know what I think of it. Now I would like to read it and normally would fire off an opinion with my usual audacity. But I want to explain: constituted as I am (not as I ought to be) I feel I cant read your poem impartially while your charges against me, as expressed in a letter I have somewhere but won't quote, remain unsubstantiated. I feel, I mean, that you thought me dishonest in 3 gs: You said something about its being "misleading" and suggested that if only you weren't incurably clumsy honest and slow witted yourself you could demolish my specious humbug. You could knock me down with your honest old English fists and so on. And then you sicklied me over with praise of charm and wit. . . .

Berg

Sissinghurst Castle,
Kent.
23rd July [1938]

But my darling Virginia, never in my life have I ever suspected you of humbug or dishonesty! I was absolutely appalled by your letter this morning. Obviously you have never had a letter I wrote you while you were away, and perhaps foolishly sent to Skye. I of course cannot now remember exactly how I expressed myself in it, but it was to the effect that I had never for a moment questioned your *facts* or their accuracy in 3 guineas, but only disagreed in some places with the deductions you drew from them. And this, after all, is a matter of opinion, not of fact. By my unfortunate allusion to the elegance of your style I meant that you almost succeeded in convincing one in spite of oneself, until one stopped to reflect afterwards in cold blood. To take an example, I question very much whether any Englishwoman feels that England is not her country because she will lose her nationality if she should happen to marry a foreigner (p. 196.) Again, on p. 194, you suggest that "fighting is a sex characteristic which she cannot share," but is it not true that many women are extremely bellicose and urge their men to fight? What about the white feather campaign in the last war? I am entirely in agreement with you that they ought not to be like that, but the fact remains that they frequently are. The average woman admires what she considers to be the virile qualities.

However, it is boring to go on adducing examples, but I hope I have said enough to show you that your honesty, integrity, and good faith were never for an instant under suspicion. I am truly upset to think you may have been nourishing this idea for the last weeks, and I wish to God you had got the letter I wrote to Sligachan. You know there are few people in the world whom I should hate to hurt more than you, and few people whose integrity I respect or trust more. That you should feel you can't read my poem because of some barrier between us shows me that I must have hurt you, though God knows I never meant to, nor was there any cause for offence in my mind, only I must have expressed myself clumsily. At any rate I know you will believe me. Your very contrite and entirely devoted

V.

Sussex

❧ *Saturday [23 July 1938]* *[52 Tavistock Square, W.C.1]*

What on earth can I have said in my letter to call forth your telegram? God knows. I scribbled it off in five minutes, never read it through, and can only remember that it was written in a vein of obvious humorous extravagance and in a tearing hurry. . . .

But, as I say, lets leave it: and I apologise, and will never write a letter so carelessly again. And I've no grievance whatever; and you need say no more, because I'm quite sure, on re-reading your letter, you didn't mean that I was dishonest: and thats the only thing I minded. So forgive and forget

Berg

 *Sissinghurst Castle,*
Kent.
25th October 1938

Now what is the etiquette? Do I give a book to the publisher who publishes it? Oh, I forgot: you're no longer a partner in the press, so that's all right.[1]

Anyway I am asking Mrs Nicholls to give you a copy of 'Solitude' from me,[2] as she has not sent me as many as I wanted, and I thought you would probably be back in London by now, so she could hand it straight over. I do wonder what you will think of it,—not much, probably.

A large bundle of roses is waiting for me to go and plant them. If you are in London I am sorry for you, as these days have been amazingly lovely.

Shall you be there on November 17th? and if so could we meet? I should like that.

Your loving
V.

Sussex

1. John Lehmann had bought Virginia's half share of the Hogarth Press and had assumed equal partnership with Leonard in April 1938. Vita's book was *Solitude*, a lengthy poem.
2. Mrs. Nicholls was the new manager of the Hogarth Press.

❧ *27th Oct [1938]*

Monk's House, Rodmell,
near Lewes, Sussex

*Yes, Mrs Nicholls has handed me a copy of your book [*Solitude*]: which I certainly consider my due, with an inscription. I dont believe you care a damn what I think of it. However, I'll tell you when I've read it, if you want to know. . . . We plan to retire here for ever: in which case I should sink as deep in solitude as even you could wish. . . .*

Berg

 *Sissinghurst Castle,*
Kent.
19th December 1938

Virginia mine—This is to bring you my love—and to say I have ordered a paté for you for Christmas—and also to say I hope you weren't bored at luncheon [1]—and how much I regretted that you weren't there when Father d'Arcy [2] and I went to admire the lizard Freya Stark has brought back from Arabia, a magnificent animal which spends its life in England lying on a hot water bottle under an electric light globe, surrounded by relics of Ur dug up by Leonard Woolley. And was the Freudian dinner a success? [3]

I would have liked some moments alone with you after luncheon—but all I got was compliments about you from Miss Stark, who thought you very beautiful. . . . So did I, if I may be allowed to say so,—very beautiful indeed in your brown fur cap and your exquisitely ethereal slenderness.

Well, well . . . . . . I had better conclude with wishing you a happy Christmas, like any old housekeeper. And to think how the ceilings of Long Barn once swayed above us! . . and dolphins sported on the marble slabs [in 1925–1926].

Your
V.

Berg

1. On December 14, Virginia was Vita's guest for lunch at Antoine's, a London restaurant. The other guest was Freya Stark, the author and traveler in Middle East countries.
2. The distinguished Jesuit priest, Master of Campion Hall, Oxford, 1932–1940. Vita took him and Gwen St Aubyn (who was a Catholic convert) to Sissinghurst that night.
3. To celebrate the Hogarth Press publication of Sigmund Freud's works. Virginia met Freud in person in January 1939, when he was a refugee from Austria in London.

❧ *Xmas day 38* *Monks House, Rodmell*
[Sussex]

Well that was a princely thought—the pate, and better than a thought, it practically saved our lives; pipes frozen; electric fires cut off; nothing to eat, or if there were, it couldnt be cooked; and then behold the parcel from Strasbourg! So we dined and then lunched and then dined off that—I can eat it for ever—I could have been content to freeze almost, if I could eat such gooses liver for ever. But what an extravagant Prince you are! How tremendously in the vein of the pink, and the pearls and the fishmongers porpoise this pink cream with the black jewels imbedded is—or was. . . .

. . . and Mitzi died in the night of Christmas Eve.[1] *It was very touching—her eyes shut and her face white like a very old womans. Leonard had taken her to sleep in his room, and she climbed onto his foot last thing.*

But enough—dont die—

Berg

1. Leonard Woolf's marmoset

1939

Vita consoled herself for the approach of war by beginning her long, reflective poem, The Garden, *and in writing* Country Notes *weekly for the* New Statesman. *When war came in September, the emotion and anxiety generated by it (both Vita's sons were in the army) brought her closer to Virginia, for although they shared "grief and despair at the folly of it all," of the two, Vita was the more exhilarated by shining patriotism. They met more frequently, though travel between Kent and Sussex was made more difficult by petrol rationing.*

❧ *Friday [13 January 1939]*

Monk's House, Rodmell,
near Lewes, Sussex.

*A woman, Victoria Okampo [*sic*], who is the Sybil (Colefax) of Buenos Aires, writes to say she wants to publish something by you in her Quarterly "Sur". She is in Paris, has heard you are going there to lecture—I presume wants to meet you. I've told her to write to you: but that I would explain. She's immensely rich, amorous; has been the mistress of Cocteau, Mussolini—Hitler for anything I know: came my way through Aldous Huxley; gave me a case of butterflies; and descends from time to time on me, with eyes like the roe of codfish phosphorescent: whats underneath I dont know. . . .*

Berg

 *Sissinghurst Castle,*
Kent.
14th January 1939

Well, it was nice to see your writing again and of course I should be delighted to oblige the Sibyl of Buenos Aires, in other words she's welcome to publish anything of mine so long as Leonard doesn't mind. (I presume she means to reprint something?) I remember you did tell me about her once before, saying she was a fan of yours or words to that effect, and I know the case of butterflies; so if I hear from her I will answer civilly as befits a friend of yours.[1] Perhaps she will turn up in Paris, but as I shall be there for one day only she will have to be nippy.

I have several things to say to you—First that I was deeply distressed for Leonard on hearing of the death of Mitzi. Please give him all my sympathy, and tell him he'd better acquire a lemur as soon as possible—they are the most enchanting pets, and said to be more closely allied to the human race than any other animal. I find this hard to believe, judging by their appearance, but biologists affirm that it is so. By the way, has Leonard got Julian Huxley's sound records of animal noises?[2] If not, he should. You get 2 double records and a book full of lovely photographs for 1 guinea.

Second, that I lost my heart to a friend of yours the other day, Margery Fry.[3] I want to know more about her from you some day, please. What a lovely face and sense of humour.

Sussex

1. The case of butterflies that Victoria Ocampo gave Virginia is still at Monk's House.
2. Huxley was secretary of the London Zoo.
3. Vita had met Margery Fry, Roger Fry's sister, on January 6, after lunching with Freya Stark.

❧ *Sunday 19th Feb [1939]* *Monk's House, Rodmell, near Lewes, Sussex.*

It is rumoured that a large shaggy sheepDog was lately seen in Piccadilly. On being questioned, it answered to the name of V. Sackville West.

I dont know why it came into my head to tell you this fact; except that I think its time V. Sackville West answered to her name. What happened in Paris? I never heard. Did you meet Ocampo? Did you effect any shall we say intimacy with her? . . .

You have a ladder: on which rung am I?

Berg

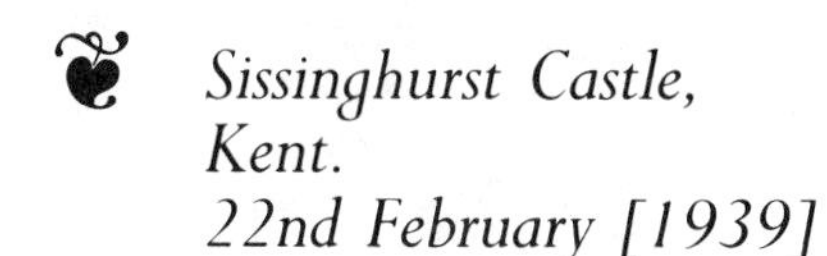

Sissinghurst Castle,
Kent.
22nd February [1939]

How funny: I had just thought to myself overnight, "It is a long time since I heard anything of Virginia,—I will write to her tomorrow,"—and then your letter came.

So our thoughts clashed and clicked—

Well, it can't be true that the shaggy sheepdog was seen recently in Piccadilly, because it hasn't gone near London since Feb. 2nd—when it suggested coming to have a meal of rabbit and dog-biscuit with you—and you replied that you would be going away to Rodmell that day—so that suggested appointment was off.

The sheepdog did, however, go to Paris, and met Victoria Ocampo there, by whom it was presented with an enormous bunch of most expensive orchids, and was driven about in a most luxurious car. I then got a letter from her, saying how ardently she craved for the country and the wide, open spaces of the pampas etc—Well, I thought, why doesn't she go there? what stops her? if she really pines for it as she says, why does she spend her time in Paris and London?

I have no patience with such humbug.

Anyhow, listen, Virginia mine: will you be in London on Friday, March 31st? And if so could I dine with you—or would you dine with me? I will stay up in London for the night if you will consent to do this.

Harold is flying to Egypt on April 4th—This worries me out of all proportion.[1] I tell you this because I know you will understand. Damn, damn, damn,—I wish flying had never been invented. I shan't know a restful moment until he gets back. Nor would you, if it was Leonard.

You wish somebody would write a long poem, although you won't read any new poetry for a year. Well, I am writing a new poem [*The Garden*]—a sort of companion to The Land—but I won't ask you to read it—only you might tell my publisher Mr Leonard Woolf that perhaps he may be offered a new poem sometime in 1940.

And tell him also (which he will be more interested in,) that I am in the process of buying a neighbouring farm [Bettenham] with 200 acres.

Lord, how rich life is, when one takes it the right way! Acres of farm-land, and a new poem in a big foolscap book,—what more could anyone ask from life?

> "Now more than ever seems it rich to die . . ."[2]

I would like to correct that into,

> "Now more than ever seems it rich to live. . . . ."

But if Harold gets killed by Imperial Airways, flying to Egypt, everything will go black.

Your loving
V.

Let me know about dinner on March 31st.

Berg

1. Vita must have misunderstood Harold. He had no intention of going to Egypt, by air or sea.
2. John Keats, "Ode to a Nightingale"

Sissinghurst Castle,
Kent.
23rd April 1939

This is Sissinghurst 250—is that Museum 2621?—Is that Virginia? This is Vita speaking,—yes: Vita,—a person you once reckoned as a friend—Oh, had you forgotten? Well, dig about in your memory and perhaps you will remember a porpoise on a marble slab.—Yes, it is pronounced Veeta, not Vaita—Now you remember, do you? You remember a thunderstorm at Vézalay [September 1928] and the ceilings of Long Barn gently swaying round?

The purpose of this message is manifold. Its principal object is to say that I don't like being cut off from you and thus am making an attempt to get into touch. Will you and Leonard ever come here, on your way down to Rodmell? I would so like Leonard to see my garden. You, I know, are no gardener, so I confine this interest to Leonard. I do wish you would both come.

Signed
Sibyl Colefax

Secondly: I am being set on by various publishers as a fox by a pack of hounds—Tell Leonard I have resisted all bribes, and until now have avoided being torn into pieces. Leonardo da Vinci is clearly out of the picture—as a new biography of him has recently been translated into English—What about Jane Carlyle?[1] I feel she's NOT my subject. Then I was offered another idea: a life of my own old ancestor, Thomas Sackville—It is a very good idea, and I think I could do it—but would it be fair to adopt the idea suggested by another publisher, and then give the resulting book to the Hogarth Press? Especially as the person who suggested it has got large files of notes about T. Sackville, which he offers to lend me, and which would of course be invaluable for my biography, but equally of course I couldn't take advantage of this offer if I wasn't going to give the resultant book to his firm.

It is all very awkward.

You see, I think I might write quite a good life of T. Sackville—bringing in Knole, and all that—but as I stupidly never thought of it for myself, but had to have it suggested to me by somebody else, am I committed to the person who did suggest it, and who is associated with another publishing firm?[2]

What an idiot I was not to have thought of it on my own—and Leonard will also regret that he didn't think of it either—Of course it is a subject absolutely made for me:

(1) Family tradition
(2) Poetry
(3) Knole
(4) Elizabethan splendour

Damn—damn—that neither Leonard nor I ever invented this idea.

I am worried about this and would very much like to talk to

Leonard. You see, I would really like to do this book (which is much more in my line than Jane Carlyle) but would like the Hogarth Press to have it, and no one else—

Well, to pass on—

Thirdly: Ben has returned from America and has got a job. He is now Deputy-Surveyor-of-the-King's-Pictures[3]—which means that he is responsible for all the pictures at Windsor, Buckingham Palace, Hampton Court, Balmoral, Holyroodhouse, Sandringham, Osborne—He is rather appalled by this responsibility. He has an office in St James' Palace—High life, in fact. One of his duties is to teach the Queen something about pictures, she knows nothing but wants to learn. I only hope Ben will prove adequate, also that he won't fall in love with the Queen whom he already describes as the most charming of women—

Your loving
V.

Berg

1. Vita wrote on neither subject.
2. Thomas Sackville was first Earl of Dorset (1536–1608), Queen Elizabeth's Lord Treasurer, and co-author of the tragedy *Gorboduc*. Vita never began the book.
3. Under the surveyor (and director of the National Gallery) Kenneth Clark and, after World War II, Anthony Blunt. Ben remained deputy until 1946.

❧ *Tuesday [25 April 1939]* *52 Tavistock Square, W.C.1*

Well Sibyl Colefax, this is a queer go. I'm addressing the lady who has an ancestor, and wants to write a book about him. The queer go is that the very same idea flashed into my head about 3 weeks ago—and I put it to Leonard and John at lunch; and it also had flashed in L's head. But he's writing to you on the morals of the case; so I won't; only try, as you say, to get into touch with you—thats the other you, sheepdog Vita.

. . . Yes, I well remember buying rolls for breakfast at Vezelay.

Berg

❧ *19th Aug: [1939]* *Monk's House, Rodmell,*
near Lewes, Sussex

Isn't it nice sometimes to write a letter one doesn't have to write? So this is one. I've been walking on the marsh and found a swan sitting in a Saxon grave. This made me think of you. Then I came back and read about Leonardo—Kenneth Clark—good I think: this made me also think of you. And in a minute I must cook some macaroni.

. . . Are you tackling the old ancestor—whats his name [Thomas Sackville]? Now I've enjoyed writing when I needn't; thats not to say you've enjoyed reading. And which rung are we on—my poor Potto and V?

Berg

 *Sissinghurst Castle,*
Kent.
Friday 25th August [1939]

Virginia darling, you are very high up on the rungs—always—

Harold has gone off to join his boat again,[1] and I have asked him to telegraph to me when he is likely to get near to Newhaven. He wants me to fetch him from Newhaven—with the car—so if we aren't at war before then (Monday or Tuesday) I will telephone to you and ask if I may come for the night.

I find one's war-psychology very strange,—don't you? Up to 12 o'clock noonday I am the complete coward, dreading air-raids, bombs, gas, etc—then after 12 noonday I become all brave and British again—and remain brave until the next morning—when the whole thing starts up again in its terrifying cycle of fear, dread, and shrinking cowardice.

I think you are much braver than I am; or should I call it more philosophical? I don't know what you feel.—What strange stages of feelings one passes through, these days! I could not write about this to anyone I did not love as I love you. It is all too private and secret.

I have got Eddy coming here for the weekend. I fear he is very wretched for various reasons. I respect him enormously for volunteering to drive an ambulance or a car in London during air-raids. That seems to me really brave, for a person of his type especially—and delicate at that—He goes up in my estimation—

Your loving
V.

I'll telephone on Monday if . . . . .

Berg

1. A small yawl named *Mar* which Harold had extravagantly purchased for occasional weekend sails. It was destroyed by bombs in 1940.

❧ *Tuesday 29th Aug. [1939]* *Monk's House, Rodmell, near Lewes, Sussex*

But I dont think I'm philosophic—rather, numbed. Its so hot and sunny on our little island—L. gardening, playing bowls, cooking our dinner: and outside such a waste of gloom. Of course I'm not in the least patriotic, which may be a help, and not afraid, I mean for my own body. But thats an old body. And all the same I should like another ten years: and I like my friends: and I like the young. . . .

. . . and indeed, my dearest creature, whatever rung I'm on, the ladder is a great comfort in this kind of intolerable suspension of all reality—something real.

Berg

Sissinghurst.
1st September 1939
Partridge-shooting begins

Virginia darling,

Harold came back. So my Newhaven scheme fell through. I had meant to ring you up and ask if Nigel and I might come to luncheon tomorrow, but my best-laid plans have gone agley and seem likely to go agley-er and agley-er for some years to come. So what can one say? I know you must feel all that I feel, and that millions feel. I keep thinking of Vanessa, with Quentin as a young man and Julian already gone. Perhaps she will now not feel so bitter about Julian's lost life, because he did at least sacrifice it voluntarily for a cause he believed in, which is nobler than being conscripted against his will into a general holocaust.

I do sympathise with you in the minor but still exasperating worry of removing from Tavistock to Mecklenburgh Square.

Well,—there it is,—and I must now go and arrange to darken our windows. Luckily there is a certain amount of comic relief always—and I find myself still able to laugh over ludicrous things which occur. This is called "Keeping the brave British smile" by the Daily Sketch, but I find myself keeping it at moments without conscious effort. I wonder how much longer we shall keep it?

Your
V.

I do hope Potto doesn't mind the Second German War too much.[1]

Shall you stay at Rodmell? It would be folly to go to London unnecessarily.

Berg

1. Hitler had invaded Poland, and Britain and France declared war on Germany on September 3.

❧ *[2 September 1939]* *[Monk's House, Rodmell, Sussex]*

Yes, dearest Creature, come at any moment you like and share our pot. Alone today and what a mercy!

I did like your letter. And if I'm dumb and chill, it doesn't mean I dont always keep thinking of you—one of the very few constant presences is your's, and so—well no more. Yes, I sit in a dumb rage, being fought for by these children whom one wants to see making love to each other.

So come: and I'll write to you, if to no one else, when ever I've a moment free. dearest creature, how I go on seeing you, tormented.

Berg

 *Sissinghurst Castle,*
Kent.
16th September 1939

How much I liked getting your letter. Let us write to one another sometimes: I find that there are few people these days who give me any sense of real contact, but you certainly do; I suppose one's sorrow sifts out the rest. You ask what I feel, and I can tell YOU: on the top I mind what you call the incessant bother of small arrangements,—no physical solitude; people constantly about the place; questions, responsibilities, voices; five six seven eight people to every meal; the necessity of having my mother-in-law to stay here for God knows how long; never knowing who is coming or who is going away; the whole house upside down with people sleeping on sofas,—all this is very trying on the surface and makes one realise how profoundly selfish one has always been about one's private personal life. Perhaps it is salutary no longer to be able to indulge oneself in one's own idiosyncrasies?

Then, underneath this, on the second layer, come the anxieties: the young men one cares about whose lives are upset and who are probably going to lose them in a horrible manner, Ben with an anti-aircraft battery [at Rochester], learning to fire low, at 600 feet, in case of aeroplanes swooping down with machine guns; Nigel waiting, waiting, to be called up into the Guards; Piers [St Aubyn] (aged 18) already with the H.A.C. [artillery]; John [St Aubyn], my nephew, aged 20, waiting to be called up at any moment; Harold fretting because no job has as yet been allocated to him; and when he does get a job it will mean his living in London more or less permanently—with air-raids and all that.

Then on the third layer, deepest of all, comes one's own grief and despair at the wicked folly of it all—

One is very unhappy, and very tired always, don't you think? I have never felt so tired,—physically and spiritually,—in all my life. I think this is the dominant impression I get, so far, from the Second German War: complete exhaustion and weariness. Terror no doubt will come later on, within a fortnight or so, when they have finished with Poland.

I would like to see you. May I telephone in the morning and ask if I can come to lunch? Petrol is still available—or would you prefer to come here, in order to get away from your clerks?

Bring Potto.

"Où sont les neiges d'antan?"[1]

Your
V.

I am glad at any rate that Quentin should be safe—I am glad of that both for Vanessa and you—[2]

Berg

1. François Villon: "Where are the snows of yesteryear?"
2. Quentin Bell had been rejected for military service on medical grounds and was working on a farm.

❧ *Dec. 3rd [1939]* *Monk's House, Rodmell, near Lewes, Sussex*

*That was nice of you—to send me your book [*Country Notes*]. It really touched me. I've not read it (and I dont suppose you'd care a damn to know what I thought, if I thought about it considered as a work of art—or would you?)—but I dipped in and read about Saulieu [Burgundy] and the fair and the green glass bottle. . . . I shall keep it by my bed, and when I wake in the night—no, I shant use it as a soporific, but as a sedative: a dose of sanity and sheep dog in this scratching, clawing, and colding universe. . . .*

Berg

1940–1941

The Woolfs' London houses were made uninhabitable by German bombing, and they retreated permanently to Monk's House, where Vita visited Virginia three times, both thinking that each visit might be the last. The air battles were taking place over both their homes. A German invasion of Britain was expected daily in the summer of 1940, and Rodmell and Sissinghurst were both in the front line. Vita sent Virginia presents from her farm to supplement her food ration. They last met at Rodmell, on February 17, 1941.

❧ *12th March [1940]* *Monks House [Rodmell, Sussex]*

Oh what a pleasure to get your letter! And how odd!—I was saying to L. I felt that you felt we were out of touch: as for myself, I never *feel out of touch with Vita. Thats odd but true. . . .*

Here I am in the week of influenza—cant get normal, but hope to be up by the end of the week. A d—d sore throat.

And this is the only scrap of paper I can find.

But my dear how nice to get your letter! How its heartened me! And how I long to hear from your own lips whats been worrying you—for you'll never shake me off—no. not for a moment do I feel ever less attached. Aint it odd? And so I didn't write but waited—Yes, do, do come. What fun, what joy that'll be.

Berg

❧ *March 19th [1940]* *Monk's House, Rodmell, near Lewes, Sussex*

Dearest,

I have a horrid little fear, as you've not written, that I said something idiotic in my letter tother day. I dashed it off, I was so glad to get yours, with a rising temperature, and perhaps said something that hurt you. God knows What. *Do send one line because you know how one worries in bed, and I cant remember what I wrote.*

Forgive what is probably the effect of the flu. . . . This is to show why I'm being, as I expect, foolish and exacting. It also shows how much I depend on you, and should mind any word that annoyed or hurt you. One line on a card—thats all I ask.

Berg

❦ *24th April 1940*

Thank you for letting me come to stay with you and for being so permanently loving towards me—

Your friendship means so much to me. In fact it is one of the major things in my life—

Would you please tell Leonard that I inadvertently told him wrong about the plant I brought him: it should be Lewisia HECKNERI, not TWEEDII—

Isn't this a nice bit of writing-paper I have found for you?[1]

I am so grateful to you: you sent me home feeling that I really ought to go on with my novel—Before I came to you, I was in the dumps about it.[2]

Then I told you something about it, which I would never have said to anybody else, and you said just the right thing.

So instead of despairing about it, I fished it out again this evening instead of trying to avoid it.

Did I leave a little golden box on your breakfast table?[3] Don't send it, but keep it for me against the day we meet at Penshurst.[4] I apologise. There is nothing more tiresome than a guest who leaves something behind. All the same I must ask you to save my little box for me, as it is rather a treasure: Irene Ravensdale gave it to me once in Rome on our return from Greece.[5]

Don't forget about Penshurst, and our picnic.

Your Orlando.

Berg

1. The stationery was printed with a picture of Grand Canyon National Park, Arizona, where Vita had been in March and April 1933.

2. *Grand Canyon*, set in Arizona. Leonard rejected it for publication by the Hogarth Press after Virginia's death.

3. For saccharine tablets

4. Penshurst Place, Kent, the ancestral home of the Sidneys. Virginia, Vita, and Leonard visited the house on June 14, the day Paris fell.

5. Irene Ravensdale was the second daughter of Lord Curzon and Mary Leiter.

❧ *Sunday [28 April 1940]* *Monk's House, Rodmell,*
near Lewes, Sussex

Oh Potto was so glad to huddle upon the Rung again. Yes, it was a great treat having you. In fact, isn't it a duty, in this frozen time, to meet as often as possible? so that even in the cold night watches, when all the skeletons clank, we may keep each other warm? . . .

Please dearest Vita, come soon again. You've got a hoard [of petrol] in your tank.

Berg

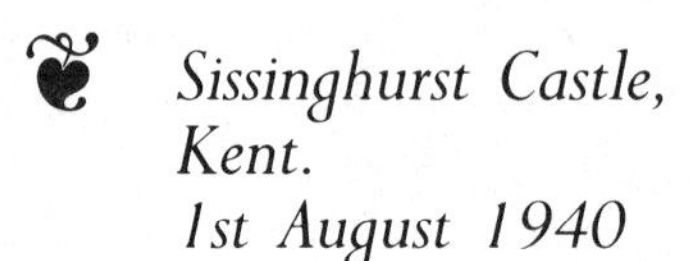

Sissinghurst Castle,
Kent.
1st August 1940

Virginia darling, you were an angel to send me your book which has just arrived.[1] And I am forwarding a parcel to Ben, which I take to be a copy for himself. This is really lavish of you and I needn't tell you how delighted he will be. It will reach him as a birthday present as it happens. I shall write to you again when I have read it.

Everything has seemed so uncertain (I refer to the invasion)[2] that I hesitated to write and suggest a night for my visit. But if things continue to drag on as they are now doing, may I come one day this month?

I didn't want to get caught and be unable to get back home! Think if you had been landed with me for the duration of the war.

Would you ever come here if I gave you enough petrol coupons? You know you like a jaunt, and your book is off your mind now. So consider it.

Your
V.

Berg

1. Virginia's *Roger Fry* was published July 25.

2. The *possibility* of a German invasion of southern England. Virginia's brother Dr. Adrian Stephen had provided her and Leonard with a lethal dose of morphine to be used in the event of an invasion.

6th Aug [1940] *Monk's House, Rodmell, near Lewes, Sussex*

. . . *I've been in such a pelt that I couldn't write before. So now merely suggest, emphatically,* Friday 16th . . . *stay the night and its understood that means all Saturday—no evasions about lunch, or someone waiting at Sissinghurst.*

Great lorries are carrying sandbags down to the river: guns are being emplaced on the Banks. So do come before its all ablaze. . . .

Berg

Sissinghurst Castle,
Kent.
9th August 1940

Look, I can't come on the 16th because I have promised to go to a demonstration of thatching (Women's Land Army) on the 17th, but may I come after the 26th? which seems to be my first clear run. I am short of petrol now, as they have unexpectedly emptied my reserve tank, but will save up coupons for the pleasure of seeing you. Isn't that polite? but more genuinely meant than most polite remarks.

I am liking your book so much.[1] "Good book," as Mr [E. M.] Forster remarks. Clever Potto to write such a good book. What amuses me about it amongst other things, is Potto's sudden straight forward sobriety, with only a whisk of the tail now and then to remind one that it really *is* by Potto. And then it's unmistakable.

I haven't finished it yet. We had a garden-fête in the village; that's why; partly.

Two other things I had to say. One is that I am sending Leonard a present which may amuse him. It costs 4d, so the Woolf pride may allow him to accept it; and his penchant for gadgets will certainly be tickled. If he has come across it already I shall be disappointed.[2] The second thing is that I have a lot of my 'Country Notes'[3] accumulated since Michael Joseph published them in an illustrated book. Would the Press like to reprint these unpublished ones in a cheap, unillustrated little pamphlet this autumn? say

1/- thus catching the Christmas-card sale?[4] I shan't be in the least offended if Monsieur my publisher says no thank you. The cigarette-making outfit is not meant as a bribe.

I will now repeat my urgent invitation that you should come here—only, *damn* it, I am no longer in a position to fill your tank with petrol. I was so petrol-proud last week, and now all my lovely gallons have gone. I knew they might; but hoped for the best. Anyhow I think I could still produce a gallon for you—if only you'd come.

Your loving
V.

Did I ever tell you that I sent my jewels and my Will away to a safer place some time ago,[5] and that the only other treasure I sent was the manuscript of Orlando?

Berg

1. *Roger Fry: A Biography*
2. Leonard, in fact, did possess this gadget, a cigarette-making outfit.
3. Written as weekly articles for the *New Statesman*
4. The first collection had been published in 1939. The Hogarth Press published *Country Notes in Wartime* in autumn 1940.
5. To Harold's brother, Eric Nicolson, in his house on the edge of Dartmoor, Devon

❧ *12th Aug. [1940]* *Monk's House, Rodmell, near Lewes, Sussex*

1. What about Friday 30th?—same condition: Saturday lunch.
2. Leonard must admit that he had *this gadget already; but is none the less grateful:*
3. Country notes idea enthusiastically accepted: good news already sent to John [Lehmann]: who will communicate officially. . . .

Berg

Friday [30 August 1940] *Monk's House, Rodmell, near Lewes, Sussex*

I've just stopped talking to you. It seems so strange. Its perfectly peaceful here—theyre playing bowls—I'd just put flowers in your room. And there you sit with the bombs falling round you.

What can one say—except that I love you and I've got to live through this strange quiet evening thinking of you sitting there alone.

Dearest—let me have a line. . . .

You have given me such happiness. . . .

Berg

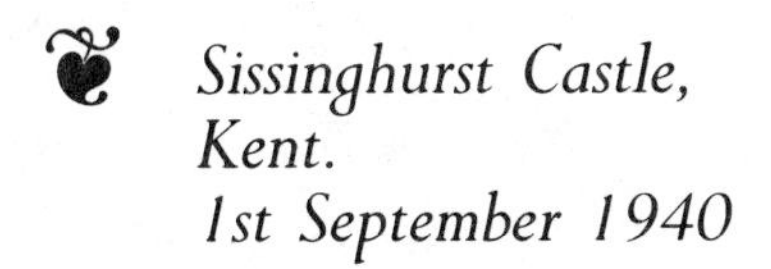
Sissinghurst Castle,
Kent.
1st September 1940

Oh dear, how your letter touched me this morning. I nearly dropped a tear into my poached egg. Your rare expressions of affection have always had the power to move me greatly, and as I suppose one is a bit strung-up (mostly sub-consciously) they now come ping against my heart like a bullet dropping on the roof. I love you too; you know that.

I didn't like to go away last Friday because they had no other ambulance-driver for the village ambulance but me—and fights were going on all day and distant sinister thuds—not so very distant. But I have now secured the services of a lady who could drive the ambulance in my place if necessary. She has a most romantic life-history which you would enjoy—It includes a vine-yard in Corsica which she ran for 5 years until brigands made her life impossible. But that is nothing to her matrimonial tragedies.

Anyhow, it means that I can now get away. So may I telephone one morning and ask if it would be convenient for me to come?

Would you tell Leonard that I sent my Country Notes off to the Press? also my signed copy of our agreement.

Your loving, very and permanently loving

V.

Berg

❧ *4th Oct. [1940]*

Monk's House, Rodmell,
near Lewes, Sussex

"Oh I'm glad"—those were the very words Leonard spoke when I said Vita says she'll come. If you could hear what the Wolves usually say when people say theyre coming—.

So do. Wednesday *we suggest: and the compact is you stay for Thursday luncheon. . . .*

Air raids pretty constant. Two bombs as I ordered dinner, a mile away in the marsh. . . .

Berg

Sissinghurst Castle,
Kent.
Thursday 10th October 1940

How nice it was to be with you—how much I enjoyed my visit. I like being with you more than I can say. You know I love *you*, and you know I like Leonard. There is a difference between love and like. So you are my love and Leonard is my like. I do like Leonard extremely.

Which reminds me: I return the 15/- he lent me, and please tell him again that I am writing to Doubleday. I hope he didn't think I was meaning to behave immorally towards the Hogarth Press.[1] I think he knows I have never done that, at least not intentionally.

Anyhow, I am putting my mistake right at once—tell him.

Darling—thank you for my happy hours with you. You mean more to me than you will ever know.

Your
V.

Berg

1. Vita had arranged with Doubleday, Doran, the American publisher of Vita's *Country Notes in Wartime*, without consulting Leonard, publisher of the book in England.

❧ *29th Nov [1940]* *Monk's House [Rodmell, Sussex]*

I wish I were Queen Victoria: then I could thank you—From the depths of my Broken Widowed *heart.* Never never Never *have we had such a* rapturous astounding glorious*—no, I cant get the hang of the style. All I can say is that when we discovered the butter in the envelope box we had in the household—Louie that is—to look. Thats a whole pound of butter I said. Saying which I broke off a lump and ate it pure. Then in the glory of my heart I gave all our weeks ration—which is about the size of my thumb nail—to Louie—earned undying gratitude; then sat down and ate bread and butter. It would have been desecration to add jam.*

. . . Bombs fell near me: trifles; a plane shot down in the marsh: trifles: floods dammed—no, nothing seems to make a wreath on the pedestal fitting your butter.

Berg

❧ *Boxing day [26 December 1940]* *Monk's House [Rodmell, Sussex]*

If my admiration for you could be increased, it would be by the fact that your divine butter arrived on Christmas morning. Anybody else, I that is, would have sent it any other day. As it was, Leonard and I, economising with a duck this year, had such an orgy of butter eating it was worth ten turkeys. Oh what a gift!

Oh Vita what a Cornucopia of Bounty you are! . . .

Two pounds of fresh butter.

And I never give you a thing—I wonder why that is. Then I have to add about £2,000 from your books, let alone the meaning of 'em.

Have you got a life of Bess of Hardwick; a life of Lady Clifford;—well, if you have, bring them, on loan, when you come. Another Bounty . . . and would you like me to ask Edith [sic] *Jones to lunch? That would save you going, which would be intolerable; and I'd slip out into the garden and leave you. Not that I want to—Lord no. . . .*

Berg

Sissinghurst Castle,
Kent.
2nd January 1941

I thought perhaps you would like this extract from a letter I've just had from Ben. Perhaps you'll like it even better than the butter:

"When people say Virginia is timeless, I agree. No attempt has yet been made to tie a neat label round her neck with the words in Cyril Connolly's hand-writing, 'Elegant 1922 abstractionist; no sense of reality; ivory tower romanticism.' Only the very purest* minds escape his docketting. Forster has escaped it, Huxley has not. Hardy escaped it, Housman did not. Proust escaped it, Barrès did not. For all your bitterness against the new school of literary criticism, you must admit that the giants,—Proust, Gide, Virginia, Forster, Yeats, Joyce,—have always received the respect they deserve."

Yes, I have a life of Lady Anne Clifford but not of Bess Hardwick.[1]

Yes, do ask Enid (NOT EDITH) Jones to luncheon.[2] (Her address is The Elms, Rottingdean.) That would not only save me a mort of trouble, and would save me from leaving you earlier than I want, but would flatter Lady Jones no end. You needn't leave us; we have no secrets. Our friendship is purely Platonic and always has been.

She has a phaeton built in 1880 in which she drives herself about—so could drive over from Rottingdean. The horse she drives in it is an ex-hunter and jumps all the marks in the roads.

You wouldn't write 6 lines about Hilda, would you?[3] for a little book which your friend Irene [Noel] Baker and I are compiling?[4] I know you never liked [*Remainder of letter is missing.*]

*This word may be 'purest' or 'fiercest.' I can't read his writing.

Berg

1. Lady Anne Clifford's diary with an introduction was published by Vita in 1924. Bess of Hardwick was Elizabeth, Countess of Shrewsbury, a famous contemporary of Queen Elizabeth I.
2. She was Enid Bagnold, the novelist and playwright, who lived only a few miles from Rodmell. She had been an intimate friend of Vita's since their youth, less so of Virginia's. She was married to Sir Roderick Jones, chairman of Reuters.
3. Hilda Matheson died on October 30, 1940, aged fifty-two. The memorial booklet about her contained no tribute from Virginia, but was published by the Hogarth Press.
4. Virginia had known her as Irene Noel since they were both young women, and had visited her at her father's estate in Euboea, Greece, in 1906. Irene married Philip Noel-Baker, the British politician who was awarded the Nobel Prize for Peace in 1959.

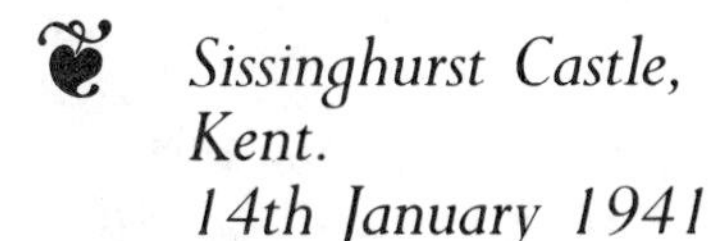

Sissinghurst Castle,
Kent.
14th January 1941

Business first. I've seen an epipsychidion[1] or whatever you call it, but don't know if my slides are suitable. So I send you a slide. It is an extra one that got duplicated by mistake, so don't worry if it gets broken.

Then, why did Irene Noel Baker come to stay? Chiefly because she wanted to see me about Hilda (dear me, I never realised your dislike of poor Hilda was so vigorous—I thought it was just a negative feeling—) and as it's impossible to ask anybody to come here for lunch only nowadays, unless they have a car, which she hasn't, and as I had no intention of going to London on purpose, I had no alternative but to ask her to stay. You must tell me more about knowing her behind the scenes; she was discreet and didn't let on, whatever it may have been. Was it perhaps to do with your brother?[2]

I don't feel that any of the foregoing remarks are useful for keeping friendship in repair—if indeed it needs repair—does it? Personally I had quite lost the drifting feeling. All the same, what can I tell you that will evoke a sense of intimacy? So little has happened to me since the snow came and incarcerated me completely among my ruins. Harold has been away touring England and Scotland,[3] and as I've been without a car since Christmas day (Ben having taken it away and left it out all night so that it got frozen and isn't back yet) the outside world has quite ceased to exist. But before that happened my past arose and looked me in the face in the person of Violet (Trefusis) whom I hadn't seen for about 10 years.[4] We had a queer à la recherche du temps perdu luncheon together on the neutral ground of a country inn. She has lost everything in France, and now the M.S.S. of her book has been burnt in Paternoster Row.[5] Much to my relief she has taken herself off to Somerset, after threatening to take a house near me, but we correspond. She is rather pathetic really,—so forlorn—with her house and all her possessions gone—

Oh how I look forward to the 3rd Tuesday in February

Your
V.

Violet asked me what's known as a leading question about you and me.

Berg

1. Virginia wrote that it was an "Epi-dia-scope." The slides were for Vita's lecture on Persia to the Rodmell Women's Institute on February 18.
2. In reply to Vita's question, Virginia threw no light on what had happened "behind the scenes."
3. Harold was now a Minister in Churchill's government, at the Ministry of Information under Duff Cooper.
4. Violet had fled France after the German invasion, and visited Sissinghurst several times during the war, but there was no renewal of her passionate intimacy with Vita.
5. The district of London near St Paul's, where many British publishers had their offices and warehouses. It was partly obliterated by German bombs.

❧ *19th Jan [1941]* *Monks House, Rodmell*
[Sussex]

I must buy some shaded inks—lavenders, pinks violets—to shade my meaning. I see I gave you many wrong meanings, using only black ink. It was a joke—our drifting apart. It was serious, wishing you'd write. It was not true that I disliked Hilda [Matheson]. I only felt—What? Something opaque, pulverising: my fault, as much as hers. And one pang of wild jealousy seized me, inopportunely, dining at Sibyls. No; no, I must buy my coloured inks. . . .

What did you say when Violet T[refusis] asked you a leading question? I still remember her, like a fox cub, all scent and seduction. . . . Now why did you love her? And did you love Hilda? We must go into all this. I rather think I've a new lover, a doctor, a Wilberforce, a cousin—ah! does that make you twitch! Am I still on the 3rd rung from the top? . . .

Berg

 *Sissinghurst Castle,*
Kent.
27th February 1941

Shame on me, I have never written you a Collins[1] nor sent you the promised fire lighter. But here they both are, arriving together. The fire-lighter is known in America as the Little Wonder, and indeed deserves the name. Whatever you do, don't leave the jam-pot of paraffin in which it should live, near the fire. Sparks may fall into the paraffin if you do. So stand it always to one side of the fireplace and *never* put the Little Wonder back into the jam-pot when it is hot. Otherwise it is apt to flare up, so enthusiastically does it perform its job.

Did Enid [Bagnold] send you her play, "Lottie Dundas"? She sent it to me, and it seems to me a play which would make her fortune, so that Sir [Roderick] Jones' resignation from Reuter's won't matter in the family fortunes.

I was interrupted here by an officer wanting to climb to the top of my tower. I asked why, being cautious. His reply was truly Elizabethan: "Because we are coming to guard from dawn to dusk. You will have the Home Guard from dusk to dawn."

Your
V.

Berg

1. To thank her for her Rodmell visit on February 17–18

❧ *4th March [1941]* *Monks House [Rodmell, Sussex]*

Oh dearest Creature—now you've topped the whole hill of your benefactions with a firelighter. Po: butter: wool: books: firelighter on top. There you must stop. You cant add anything to fire. You see the poetic fitness of ending there. What a magnificent conception of life you have—O damn the law. Leonard says we cant use your petrol. Another gift. . . .

I suppose you havent any Hay to sell? Octavia Wilberforces cows at Henfield, which give us butter, are starving. So I said I'd ask.

Silence means no.

Berg

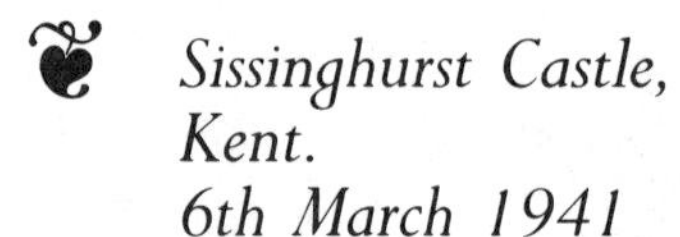

Sissinghurst Castle,
Kent.
6th March 1941

HAY! Good God, hay! Have I not been scrounging all over the Weald of Kent for hay? No hay; scarce milk; and that's why you haven't had any more butter—and that's why all the lawns of Sissinghurst are not going to be mown this year but allowed to grow. Hay! My holy aunt!

Leonard was mistaken for once about the petrol coupon. I wouldn't do anything illegal any more than he would. However, if you can really bear to come by bus I can easily meet you at Hawkhurst. I'd take you to Ellen Terry [Smallhythe] in the afternoon, and restore you to Hawkhurst later. All you have to do is to let me know. Any day except March 19th and 20th. On the 19th I have a committee and on the 20th—guess what? a local Women's Institute.

Love
V.

Berg

❧ *Saturday [22 March 1941]* *[Monk's House, Rodmell, Sussex]*

Look at this letter [lost]*, sent to the New Statesman, addressed to 'Miss Virginia Woolf'.—What a queer thought transference! No, I'm not you. No, I dont keep budgerigars.*

Louie's survive: and she feeds them on scraps—I suppose they're lower class, humble, birds. If we come over [to Sissinghurst], may I bring her a pair if any survive? Do they die all in an instant? When shall we come? Lord knows—

Berg

Postscript

These were the last words Virginia would write to Vita. Six days later, on March 28, Virginia drowned herself in the River Ouse. On March 31, Vita wrote to Harold: "I've just had the most awful shock: Virginia has killed herself. It is not in the papers, but I got letters from Leonard and also from Vanessa telling me. . . . He says she had not been well for the last few weeks and was terrified of going mad again. . . . I simply can't take it in. That lovely mind, that lovely spirit. And she seemed so well when I last saw her. . . ." Many years later, again in a letter to Harold, Vita wrote: ". . . I still think that I might have saved her if only I had been there and had known the state of mind she was getting into." Vita was probably right.

INDEX